Internet Economics

Internet Economics

Edited by
Lee W. McKnight and Joseph P. Bailey

The MIT Press
Cambridge, Massachusetts
London, England

ZA3203 .I57 1998

Internet economics

First paperback edition, 1998

©1997 Massachusetts Institute of Technology

This book was set in Baskerville by Wellington Graphics and printed and bound in the United States of America.

Library of Congress Cataloging-in-Publication Data

Internet economics / edited by Lee W. McKnight and Joseph P. Bailey.
    p. cm.
Papers presented at MIT workshop on Internet economics. March 1995.
Includes bibliographical references and index.
ISBN 0-262-13336-9 (hb), ISBN 0-262-63191-1 (pb)
    1. Internet (Computer network)—Economic aspects—Congresses. 2. Internet (Computer network)—Prices—Congresses. 3. Internet (Computer network)—Government policy—Congresses. 4. Information superhighway—Economic aspects—Congresses. 5. Wide area networks industry. I. McKnight, Lee W. II. Bailey, Joseph P.
ZA3203.I57   1997
384.3′.3—dc21   96-39442
                                                                              CIP

"To our families"

Contents

Contents

Internet Economics and Policy

Preface

,

The economics of the Internet and its social, political, organizational, and technical impact have been the subject of growing speculation on the eve of the next millennium. Substantial progress has been made through research on the business and engineering practices of the Internet to increase understanding in each of these areas. The issues of Internet economics, however, have proven especially difficult to grapple with. To contribute to the dialogue across disciplines on how economics might contribute to the self-sustaining growth of the Internet, a Workshop on Internet Economics was held March 9 and 10, 1995, at the Massachusetts Institute of Technology with the support of the National Science Foundation. That workshop was a watershed event, and laid the foundation for this book. It was clear by that time that research on economics and the Internet was taking place within different communities with very little overlap and interaction between them. Perhaps one of the biggest barriers that existed was language—researchers often misinterpreted the writings of authors from other fields. With support from the National Science Foundation[1], the Defense Advanced Research Projects Agency[2], and our organizing committee[3], and encouragement from

1. Grant number NCR-9631983.

2. Contract number N00174-93-C-0036.

3. Members of the workshop's organizing committee included Dave Clark, Deborah Estrin, Jeff MacKie-Mason, and Hal Varian.

the Federal Networking Council, we decided it was time for academics from different fields, business people, special interest groups, and government officials to put aside their differences and work together on the fundamental economic challenges for the sustainable growth of the Internet.

The workshop succeeded, many of the participants informed us, in enabling participants to gain a deeper appreciation of the nature of the Internet and the economic challenges confronting it. We intended from the beginning to share the results of the workshop with policymakers, academics, businesses, and the concerned public as expeditiously as possible. The workshop itself was broadcast live over the Internet's MBONE, and repeated later. Summary workshop notes were distributed widely over the Internet within a month of the meeting. And Lee McKnight presented to the Federal Networking Council Advisory Committee in April and October 1995, reporting on the state of the nascent field of Internet economics. We received positive feedback from participants and other interested observers that the workshop and the material presented there had succeeded in heightening understanding, clarifying unresolved issues, and identifying areas for further work for the emerging field of Internet economics.

Recognizing the growing importance of Internet economics, the Sloan Foundation[4] encouraged us to pursue electronic and print publication of refined versions of the work presented at the workshop. Through a solicitation of the workshop participants and other leading scholars in the field, we collected a number of submissions for a potential book, many of which, following further revision, are included in this volume. MIT Press and University of Michigan Press agreed to informally collaborate in the multiple-media publication process. Both published an edited volume of the papers (MIT Press in book form after further work in 1997, and University of Michigan Press as a special issue of the on-line *Journal of Electronic Publishing* in May 1996, which can be found at http://www.press.umich.edu/jep). Our hope is that this collection may become a cornerstone of this budding field.

4. Grant number B1995-17.

The Workshop on Internet Economics was held two years ago, but many of the issues first discussed at that meeting are still relevant today. This is largely due to the difficult questions that members of the growing Internet community continue to ask. How can infrastructure providers recover their costs? What incentives will help infrastructure providers to provision their network in alignment with the wishes of the customers? How do new technologies and applications change the nature of the use and value of the Internet? What role does price have in influencing the use, growth, and development of the Internet? Which organizations gain a competitive advantage through various technology or pricing strategies? Considering the dynamism of the Internet, these questions are impossible to answer definitively. However, we believe that the ideas and concepts presented in this volume by some of the leading thinkers in the field bring us several steps closer to ensuring the self-sustaining growth of the Internet.

Through this book, it is our intention to expand the audience of readers and participants in discussions of these difficult questions concerning Internet economics. We asked the contributors to revise their chapters to a style that would be understood by the diversity of people who have expressed interest in this project. We did not ask them to abandon their ability to make contributions to the academic literature that are technical or theoretical in some instances. Rather, we asked them to address serious topics in a manner that would be readable by all. This does not mean that we expect every reader to be able to derive the mathematical equations that are featured in some of the chapters, but we do hope that readers of this volume will understand the premises and significance of the equations and proposed approaches to Internet economics that are explained in its chapters.

The first chapter, the introduction, provides an overview of the topics addressed in the book, and how the issues addressed relate from section to section and from chapter to chapter. As with most edited books, this volume does not have to be read sequentially. Admittedly, the chapters could have been placed in different orders and combinations as certain issues are addressed repeatedly from various authors' perspectives. We grouped the material differently in the on-line collection a year earlier. We hope the new order of chapters and their further revision for the book will be more helpful for readers while retaining the spirit of cross-disciplinary dialogue and debate of the workshop.

We welcome your comments on this book, thank all of who have contributed to this work, and are pleased to have had a chance to contribute to the growing and exciting field of Internet economics!

Lee W. McKnight   mcknight@rpcp.mit.edu
Joseph P. Bailey   bailey@rpcp.mit.edu
Cambridge, Massachusetts

November 1996

Acknowledgments

We would like to thank the numerous authors whose chapters are included in this book for their valuable contribution to the growing debate on Internet economics. The views expressed in their chapters reflect their own perspectives, and not those of their organizations or sponsors.

A grant from the Sloan Foundation, and the support of Doron Weber and Raphael Kasper, made this book possible. We are grateful for their generous support.

The Internet Economics Workshop, held in Cambridge, Massachusetts, at the Massachusetts Institute of Technology on March 9 and 10, 1995,[1] and supported by National Science Foundation grant NCR-9509244, was the catalyst for this book. The organizing committee of David Clark, Deborah Estrin, Jeffrey MacKie-Mason, and Hal Varian made the workshop a success. Workshop notes by MIT students Sharon Gillett, David Gingold, Brett Leida, Doug Melcher, Joseph Reagle, jae Roh, Russell Rothstein, and Grady Seale served as an important aid for the authors to reflect on their own and others' views of Internet economics.

MIT Press encouraged us and patiently taught us the subtleties of editing. In particular, Deborah Cantor-Adams, Terry Ehling, Julie Grimaldi, Ann Sochi, and Terry Vaughn were extremely helpful.

---

1. Please consult the Internet Economics Workshop home page (http://rpcp.mit.edu/ Workshops/cfp.html) for workshop notes and other workshop information. The workshop notes are also available as part of a special issue on Internet economics from the University of Michigan Press's *Journal of Electronic Publishing* (http://www.press.umich.edu/jep).

Colin Day, Michelle Miller, and Eve Trager of *The Journal of Electronic Publishing* of the University of Michigan Press shaped an earlier version of this book into an on-line journal, which was also supported by the grant from the Sloan Foundation.

The substance of our work benefited from many knowledgeable and generous people who contributed to our thinking about Internet economics. The Federal Networking Council and its Advisory Committee gave substantial time and feedback at an early stage of the research. Petros Kavassalis helped with the introduction, and Joseph Reagle provided input on the section on Internet commerce. Dr. James T. McKnight and Dr. Glenna B. McKnight provided helpful feedback on the book prospectus. John Nicholson also provided helpful advice on the book's organization.

Gillian Cable-Murphy, Julia Malik, and Elizabeth Yoon provided superb administrative support from the workshop proposal to final publication, support which was critical to the book's timely completion. Jack Ruina, Agnes Chow, and Dan Roos of the MIT Center for Technology, Policy, and Industrial Development provided a supportive research environment for this work. Exceptional copyediting by Mary Albon, desktop publishing by Wellington Graphics, indexing by Richardson and Associates, and help from Peter Nicholson on the cover artwork, is gratefully acknowledged. Our research was supported in part through MIT Research Program on Communications Policy contracts from the Defense Advanced Research Projects Agency, contract number N00174-93-C-0036, National Science Foundation grant NCR-9307548, and NASA fellowship NGT-51407.

The love of our families has provided the most constant support and encouragement for our work. To our wives, Elaine McKnight and Wendy Bailey, our parents, and our siblings we are thankful. And special thanks go to Phillip and William McKnight for the opportunity cost incurred while their daddy was working on the book.

Lee W. McKnight and Joseph P. Bailey
Cambridge, Massachusetts
December 1996

Introduction to Internet Economics

An Introduction to Internet Economics

Lee W. McKnight and Joseph P. Bailey

Introduction

Internet economics is the study of the market for Internet services. This chapter is an introduction to the methods, issues, and alternative approaches addressed by studies of Internet economics. The converging digital technologies of television, publishing, telephony, and computers are diffusing the innovations of the Internet throughout the global economy, and are increasing the importance of understanding Internet economics. Digital video, audio, and distributed, interactive multimedia communication services are growing in popularity and potentially will affect virtually all sectors of society in all nations, while increasing demand for Internet bandwidth. As of yet, however, there has been no convergence or consensus on the economics or future policy framework of the Internet.

Prior work has been done on the policy development of the Internet, and, of course, on the Internet's technical development (e.g., Hart, Reed, and Bar 1992; Clark 1988; Cerf and Kahn 1974). This volume focuses on integrated research on Internet engineering and economics. In this chapter we describe the structure of the book, which includes architectural models and analyses of Internet usage as well as alternative pricing policies. We also identify areas for further research.

Many issues of Internet economics are not new. Accounting and pricing have long been concerns, first for operators, regulators, and users of telecommunications networks, and later for designers and operators of computer networks.[1] For example, in 1974, Leonard Kleinrock wrote about future issues of computer communications (Kleinrock 1974). While he focused on the technical problems of scalability and heterogeneity in networks, he also identified many of the central challenges for Internet economics: "[H]ow does one introduce an equitable charging and accounting scheme in such a mixed network system? In fact, the general question of accounting, privacy, security and resource control and allocation are really unsolved questions which require a sophisticated set of tools." Work to date on the development of the Internet has been largely technical, focusing on the design of tools and mechanisms. Most of the authors of chapters in this book would agree that new research and a deeper understanding of these economic and policy issues are required to support continued growth of the Internet. The call for new research directions has been echoed by Shenker et al. (1996).

Research on Internet economics attempts to improve our understanding of the Internet as an economic system. The lack of accepted metrics for economic analysis of the Internet is increasingly problematic as the Internet grows in scale, scope, and significance to the global economy. This introduction brings together interdisciplinary research on the Internet—a network of networks employing common standards to achieve technical statistical sharing, economic positive network externalities, and the policy objective of interoperability.

Two commonly held misconceptions about the Internet involve its economics. The first is that the Internet's development was paid for by the United States government, when in fact by 1994 the National Science Foundation paid for less than 10% of the Internet "cloud,"[2]

1. For decades, accounting and pricing for telecommunications networks and services were based on the principles of "Ramsey pricing" (Ramsey 1927). For much longer, accounting and pricing have been critical functions of businesses in market economies (Stickney, Weil, and Davidson 1991). Neither Ramsey pricing—reflecting the willingness of different users (e.g., businesses or residential users) to pay in a monopoly market—nor traditional accounting methods apply neatly to the Internet, composed as it is of heterogeneous networks as well as diverse user communities and applications.

2. The term "cloud" refers to the network of networks (owned and operated by multiple partners) which provides data transport through use of Transmission Control Protocol/

and far less than that percentage of the cost of Internet infrastructure and software development. For users, the cost of Local Area Networks, computers, and local telephone lines far exceeds the costs which can be ascribed exclusively to Internet connectivity. By 1996, the level of U.S. federal government support of the Internet, beyond ensuring access for the U.S. research and education communities, was dwarfed by the enormous worldwide commercial investment in the Internet.

The second misconception is that the Internet is free. For users accessing the Internet from a company, public agency, or educational institution, Internet access may seem to be free—just as the electricity and heat available at one's place of work may appear to be free. The end-user may not experience directly the costs incurred for any of these services—but of course they are not free! Paradoxically, however, the economic use of the Internet may at times incur no costs. Jeffrey MacKie-Mason and Hal Varian detail the frequently asked questions concerning the economics of the Internet and the economics or the infrastructure in their chapter of this book. In previous work, they show that the marginal cost for some Internet traffic may be zero due to statistical sharing, although other costs, such as congestion costs, may be significant (MacKie-Mason and Varian 1995).

As an investor and large user of the Internet, the U.S. government, like other governments, is concerned with the self-sustaining economic growth of the Internet. The mission agencies, such as the National Aeronautics and Space Administration (NASA) and the Department of Energy, operate their own wide area Internet Protocol (IP) networks, which interconnect with the Internet. The Office of Management and Budget (OMB) in Circular A-130, "Management of Federal Information Resources," provides guidance on federal agency investment in and use of the Internet (OMB 1994). This

---

Internet Protocol (TCP/IP). Because the actual network topology is complicated, the "cloud" represents a part of the Internet where data goes in and out of the "cloud" but users do not need to understand what happens inside the "cloud." The field of Internet Economics has among its goals the development of a more precise understanding of what happens within the "cloud," why it exists, and what are its critical properties.

circular suggests how federal agencies should coordinate their efforts so that they may provide Internet services cost-effectively.

Economically, the Internet exhibits positive network externalities.[3] Technically, it benefits from statistical sharing of network resources.[4] It also achieves the policy objective of interoperability.[5] Developing more refined models of pricing the Internet that preserve the low transaction costs enabled by statistical sharing, positive network externalities, and interoperability is the common goal of the chapters presented here. Areas of disagreement are evident, particularly on the costs and benefits of alternative approaches to overcoming congestion through usage-sensitive pricing. Nonetheless, we believe that the chapters in this volume contain the seeds of a new Internet technical, economic, and policy architecture.

The issue is not only how to develop effective Internet pricing mechanisms, but how to do so without losing the benefits of interoperability and positive network externalities currently gained through the Internet's reliance on statistical sharing. Achieving economic efficiency without inciting users and network providers to abandon the Internet's technical approach of statistical sharing, and hence without abandoning the Internet as such, is the challenge that businesses, policymakers, and users must now face. Indeed, it is difficult to conduct research across disciplines on Internet economics. The communities that study, design, and use the Internet have many

3. A network externality is the benefit gained by incumbent users of a group when an additional user joins the group. The group can be thought of as a "network" of users, hence the term network externality. When the economic benefit of an additional user positive, it is a positive network externality.

4. Statistical sharing is the ability of networks to allocate bandwidth to users based upon the users' needs. The network does not allocate a fixed bandwidth for all users, so that the bursty nature of the traffic can be accommodated. As the bursty traffic gets aggregated by all users, better performance can be realized. For example, when user A is idle, more bandwidth can be given to user B, who may be making a large file transfer.

5. Lee McKnight suggested at the MIT Internet Economics Workshop that the growth of the Internet could best be understood as a result of the combined effect of the economic benefits of the Internet's positive network externalities, the Internet's technical efficiency gained by its statistical sharing, and the policy benefits of the Internet's interoperability. The question addressed by this book is how to retain these mutually reinforcing economic, technical, and policy attributes of the Internet while developing new approaches to Internet economics and Internet commerce.

ideas on Internet economics, and are beginning to consider how to develop a framework combining the merits of the various proposed solutions. But better understanding of both the engineering and economics of the Internet is needed for this cross-disciplinary (and cross-interest group) dialogue to bear fruit.[6]

Structure of the Book

In this first chapter, we provide an overview of the issues addressed in the book. Each chapter conveys the most recent and, at times, contradictory, thoughts of leading scholars on Internet economics. Models and frameworks for Internet technical, economic, and policy analysis are presented in these chapters.

The first section, "The Economics of the Internet," reviews the basic economic qualities of the Internet from different perspectives. This section also introduces and places in historical context the debate over flat-rate and usage-sensitive pricing. The second section, "Interconnection and Multicast Economics," explores how Internet Service Providers share costs of interconnecting their networks and providing multicast service. While interconnection arrangements for Internet traffic are rapidly evolving, these chapters focus on the underlying economic issues involved in developing commercial patterns of network interconnection. The third section, "Usage-Sensitive Pricing," presents a number of models for pricing Internet services on the basis of actual usage. All of these chapters explore how the use of various pricing mechanisms might provide an enhanced quality of service over the best effort service typically provided to users of the Internet. The fourth section, "Internet Commerce," addresses the economics of Internet services provided at a layer above the infrastructure layer discussed in the third section. Some of the requirements for users and service providers to

6. By publishing an earlier version of this book as a special issue of the *Journal of Electronic Publishing* on the World Wide Web (McKnight and Bailey 1996), we were able to disseminate the ideas and approaches suggested by the authors and solicit feedback prior to distributing the collected works in hard copy. We hope this period for further reflection on and refinement of the ideas and the text has improved the quality of this book, and served to stimulate cross-disciplinary dialogue. But that is for the authors and the readers to judge.

have confidence in the Internet as a marketplace—such as insurance, security, and payments—are described. The last section, "Internet Economics and Policy," brings the infrastructure, commerce, and pricing questions into the broader context of public policy. The authors of these chapters argue for the continued provision of Internet public goods, even as commercial development of the Internet continues. Each section will now be discussed in greater detail.

The Economics of the Internet

The four chapters which follow this introduction provide an overview of Internet economics. The chapter by Jeffrey MacKie-Mason and Hal Varian, "Economic FAQs About the Internet," introduces and answers many questions about the economics of the Internet. It is organized as a FAQ—an Internet acronym for frequently asked questions—so it can easily be scanned for answers to some of the most fundamental questions underpinning the field of Internet economics. The process of writing and distributing FAQs is an integral part of the Internet community. FAQs on many topics are on servers scattered around the Internet. MacKie-Mason and Varian's FAQs are very influential in the domain of Internet economics: for many technologists and economists, they have served as an introduction to the field. The feedback the authors have received from readers have helped them to revise and improve their work, and we are pleased to include their latest version in this book. The central issue for MacKie-Mason and Varian is that, just as the laws of physics cannot be suspended, so too the laws of supply and demand—that is, of economics—cannot be suspended in the Internet. In colloquial terms, there is no such thing as a free lunch. Rather, the challenge for economists is to determine how to apply the tools of economic analysis across a network of networks, and how to use those economic tools to improve the performance of the Internet. MacKie-Mason and Varian suggest a number of ways in which the economic performance of the Internet can be enhanced.

The remaining chapters in the first section address broad issues of Internet economics from three different perspectives: architectural, empirical, and historical. Taking the architectural approach in "The Economics of Layered Networks," Gong and Shrinagesh offer an economic assessment of the effect of layering networks—one of the most powerful technological forces behind achieving interoperability in the Internet. Their chapter analyzes the effects of a competitive market on prices for digital services. While later chapters in the book explore the consumer-network provider relationship, Gong and Srinagesh's chapter analyzes the market for network services in a competitive environment. The methodology they use is economic (game theory), but the chapter is written so the most novice economist can understand it. It focuses on the question of competition for a commodity service (digital network provision) if suppliers compete solely on price.

Nevil Brownlee uses an empirical case study in his chapter on Internet pricing in practice to show how a usage-sensitive pricing policy works in real networks. He explains the development of usage-sensitive pricing for Internet services in New Zealand and demonstrates the feasibility of usage-sensitive pricing for the Internet, which adds credibility to subsequent chapters that suggest sophisticated variants on the approach successfully applied in New Zealand. New Zealand has taken advantage of a benefit of the Internet's structure, which allows for innovation—including pricing models— to occur independently of conditions on other Internet networks. New Zealand implemented a pricing scheme in which users are charged for every bit they send and receive via their trans-Pacific gateway. However, the benefit of innovation in this distributed fashion may also be a drawback, since it is difficult to implement a ubiquitous settlement process for the entire Internet. We hope that readers will keep the New Zealand experience in mind when considering other proposals for implementing usage-sensitive pricing models. However, one should also understand the factors, such as New Zealand's geographic isolation and the expensive trans-Pacific network link, that may limit the applicability of the New Zealand approach to Internet pricing.

The final chapter in the first section concerns flat-rate pricing, and approaches Internet economics from the historical perspective. Loretta Anania and Richard Jay Solomon, the chapter's authors, examine the development of B-ISDN (Broadband-Integrated Services Digital Networks) services in the 1980s. They suggest that the new digital networks would be most beneficial from a user perspective if coupled with a traditional flat-rate pricing model. The chapter is reproduced in this book as it was first published (Anania and Solomon 1988), but with a new introduction that links the position the authors took almost a decade ago with the contemporary debate on Internet pricing models. Their chapter illustrates that while Internet economics may be a new field, issues of pricing for new communication services have existed from the earliest days of telecommunications.[7] As Anania and Solomon point out, the question of how to weigh the apparent benefits for users versus the costs to network providers of employing flat-rate or usage-sensitive pricing models is a recurring theme. Anania and Solomon argue that, in the end, users will demand easily understandable and predictable flat-rate pricing for the Internet, as they have for prior communications networks. Whether user demand is satisfied depends in part not only on the economics but also on the regulatory and industrial structure for Internet service provision, which may vary from country to country, region to region, and market to market.

As Brownlee's chapter points out, however, usage-sensitive pricing for the Internet can work. The challenge addressed in most of the rest of the book is how this can be done in a technically and economically efficient manner. But Anania and Solomon's admonition to remember history—and user preferences—is important to keep in mind as one evaluates proposed alternatives to flat-rate pricing.

Interconnection and Multicast Economics

This section of the book explores the economics of interconnection between Internet networks and the economics of multicast services.

7. While we maintain a clear focus on the Internet in the remainder of the book, the Internet *is* dependent upon other telecommunications infrastructure elements, and it is important to understand the pricing of telecommunications services as well as the role of regulation, Public Telephone and Telegraph organizations (PTTs), and standards bodies such as the International Telecommunication Union (ITU). For an excellent summary of research on telecommunications pricing, see Mitchell and Vogelsang (1991).

Internet Service Providers (ISPs) are in the rapidly growing business of providing network connectivity to users. Until now, the relative homogeneity of users and the Internet culture of cooperation have given firms incentives to interconnect. However, this situation is changing rapidly as ISPs are providing competitive services, appealing to a variety of niche markets, upgrading the capacity of their networks, and providing new services, such as multicast.

The chapters in this section analyze the economic factors that encourage firms to interconnect and share the cost of interconnection. While much of the cost-sharing is based upon point-to-point communication, this section also explores the ability of the Internet to provide multicast services. Unlike a transmission that is sent from one node to another throughout the network, a multicast transmission originates at the source and is replicated at various network nodes to form a tree-and-branch structure. The transmission will then reach many different end-users without a separate transmission required for each user. There is a considerable resource savings with multicast, but also complex questions of equitable cost-sharing.

Perhaps the greatest economic concern for network and service providers with regard to interconnection, and one that requires further exploration, is resale. Economic payments for interconnection can either encourage or discourage resale.[8] For example, with a flat-fee interconnection agreement, it is possible for two firms to aggregate their traffic before the interconnection point and split the fee of the interconnection. Therefore, interconnection points with flat-fee settlements may provide improper incentives for use and may lead to inequitable cost recovery by the interconnected firms. It may be possible, however, to design an economic model which uses usage-sensitive pricing to discourage resale. This may encourage aggregated user behavior to change as well. Nevertheless, if some of the usage-sensitive pricing models (discussed in the next section) are

---

8. Resale is another issue which has long been of concern to both telecommunications firms and governments. For example, until recently, resale of telecommunications circuits was prohibited by international treaty. Resale is now prevalent, and has not had the disastrous effects predicted by early simplistic assessments. In fact, resale can be argued to be a significant positive factor in promoting deregulation and competition and in encouraging efficiency. See Mitchell and Vogelsang (1991).

successfully introduced, the current "sender pays" model, which obviates the need for settlements and is unconcerned with resale, may still be a viable approach.

The first chapter in this section, "Internet Cost Structures and Interconnection Agreements," written by Padmanabhan Srinagesh, discusses interconnection agreements that exist in today's Internet. This chapter characterizes these agreements as the "glue" of the Internet and discusses the economics, technologies, and contracts that define the Internet interconnection agreements. The use of empirical data coupled with an industry analysis makes this an informative and useful introductory chapter.

Joseph Bailey's chapter, "The Economics of Internet Interconnection Agreements," characterizes four different models of Internet interconnection agreements. These models define how networks of different sizes, technologies, and markets interconnect. Bailey uses a methodology from economics, incomplete contract theory, to suggest why some types of interconnection agreements are more prone to opportunism than others.

The final chapter in this section, "Sharing Multicast Costs," discusses the pricing of shared data streams from multicast services. While other pricing models can be applied for point-to-point services, this chapter introduces a different model for a growing Internet application area. Herzog, Shenker, and Estrin present a rigorous mathematical representation of a multicast model which complements their discussion.

Usage-Sensitive Pricing

Internet pricing is a growing area of concern for members of the technical, business, academic, and user communities. With new applications, new users, and new connections, the Internet has become an important medium for communication, information dissemination, and electronic commerce. But the economic policies currently undergirding the Internet may be less extensible. The chapters included in this section of the book present new thinking and research on Internet resource allocation and pricing.

Pricing is still a taboo term for some when put in the same sentence with "the Internet." It is considered to be against the traditional Internet culture to adopt a pricing scheme that requires users to put a "postage stamp" on every letter (in this case, a packet of data) to pay for its delivery. There has also been a lack of understanding and miscommunication over Internet pricing issues. We hope to contribute to clarity in the debate by defining pricing models as being one of three varieties:

1. Flat-rate pricing. Currently, most Internet users pay a fee to connect but are not billed for each bit sent. For example, users may pay for a T1 link regardless of how many bits they receive or send.[9]

2. Usage-sensitive pricing. Users pay a portion of their Internet bill for a connection (this price could be zero, but rarely is) and a possibly varying portion for each bit sent and/or received. The marginal monetary cost of sending or receiving another bit is non-zero during some time period. It is possible, for example, to have usage-sensitive pricing during peak hours and flat-rate during off-peak hours, but we define the overall system as being usage-sensitive.

3. Transaction-based pricing. As with usage-sensitive pricing, the marginal monetary cost of sending and/or receiving another bit is non-zero. However, prices are determined by the characteristics of the transaction and not by the number of bits.

We do not use the term "usage-based" pricing in the remainder of this book because it has too many conflicting definitions. For example, the costs of a T1 and a T3 link are different and based upon the predicted use of the link, so the price could be construed as usage-based.[10] However, others have used the term usage-sensitive pricing synonymously with usage-based pricing.

While most current research on Internet economics analyzes usage-sensitive pricing models, we recognize that flat-rate pricing models have tremendous advantages. Administrative overhead for billing systems can be avoided or minimized with a flat-rate pricing system.

9. A T1 link is a circuit between two points at 1.544 megabits per second. Joseph Bailey first introduced these definitions in his presentation at the MIT Internet Economics Workshop.

10. A T3 link is a communications circuit between two points operating at a data rate of 45 megabits per second.

The percent of the overhead is unknown, but perhaps we can learn from the telephony case where the billing overhead is significant.[11] Flat-rate pricing does not, however, provide an economic congestion control mechanism for bandwidth resource allocation. This is especially important with development of the next generation Internet Protocol. version 6 (IPv6). The delivery of multiple service classes across the Internet provides different qualities of service to different packets. If there are no usage-sensitive fees for the packets receiving better service, all users may prefer better service. This may lead to a demand for bandwidth that exceeds what is available.

The chapters in this section offer a fresh look at usage-sensitive pricing policies from a number of different perspectives. The chapters outline new pricing models, most of them usage-sensitive, for Internet bandwidth. Each chapter uses a different approach.

Traditionally, the Internet technical community has not concerned itself with pricing. Technologists preferred to implement technical solutions to allocate bandwidth. The current Internet Protocol version 4 (IPv4) offers users best effort service and the Transmission Control Protocol (TCP) enables congestion control.[12] The Internet cloud is inherently a statistically shared resource of best effort service. When the shared resources of the Internet become congested, users experience additional latency or delay and TCP reduces its bit rate when sending data over a congested network. Thus it has not been necessary to ration a resource using economics since technology has solved this problem.

The multiple service qualities of IPv6 will require packets to be handled differently in some circumstances. David Clark's chapter, "Internet Cost Allocation and Pricing," proposes such a scheme

11. This purported statistic of 50% was discussed during the MIT Internet Economics Workshop. See Bailey et al. (1996) for the documented discussion.

12. Resource reservation schemes for use in conjunction with usage-sensitive pricing for IPv4 traffic may be developed soon now that IPv4-based resource reservation protocols have been successfully demonstrated. Consult documentation on RSVP (ReSerVation Protocol) for more information about the technical details (Braden et al. 1996; Zhang et al. 1993). The ability of the Internet to provide current best effort quality service, a guaranteed quality of service through RSVP, and many qualities in between is part of a larger research area on integrated services (Braden et al. 1994).

whereby a token bucket system could be used for these multiple services. By "flagging" a packet that requires a better quality of service, it is possible for the network service provider to manage traffic differently and "bill" users for their service on a usage-sensitive basis. Clark suggests that users should pay for their "expected capacity" requirements rather than their actual use, which moves his proposal partially back toward the flat-rate pricing approach that Anania and Solomon champion. One of the benefits of Clark's chapter is that it presents a very compelling idea that is consistent with the protocols of the Internet and its design philosophy. Unlike other chapters that explore technology as exogenous to the problems, this chapter endogenizes the technical parameters and describes them in such a way that even the hard-core economist can understand them. The use of numerical examples gives the reader the right order of magnitude for the delays users experience.

Frank Kelly's chapter, "Charging and Accounting for Bursty Connections," complements the previous chapter by introducing the important concept of effective bandwidth to the pricing debate. Kelly's work also complements other chapters which indicate that the Internet is known by its technical property of statistical sharing by providing a quantitative framework for evaluating the amount of statistical bandwidth a user has—that is, effective bandwidth. There is a natural fit between this work and the task of designing a token bucket with optimal pricing which flags packets "in" or "out" of the user profile, as discussed by Clark. Kelly's work may help users design the token rate and bucket depth based upon their effective bandwidth requirements and the price of such a service.

Users are ultimately the ones who feel the effects of congestion and will determine which pricing policies are acceptable by their purchase and use decisions. Even with flat-rate pricing, users who do not wish to experience delays choose to use the network when it is less congested. Thus we can think of the Internet and congestion control as a user feedback mechanism. However, with flat-rate pricing, the users' only choice is to change their behavior by either sending/receiving or not sending/receiving data, or by switching to a possibly overprovisioned network provider. The implementation of usage-sensitive pricing will increase the number of indicators users can give to their network provider and, furthermore, increase the complexity (and presumably the efficiency) of the feedback process. The next two chapters in this book map the effects of user responses as a function of feedback from network congestion.

The chapter by MacKie-Mason, Murphy, and Murphy, "Responsive Pricing in the Internet," takes a broader view of feedback response and tries to explain how feedback to the user changes the aggregate user behavior. They bring together user considerations to design a "fair" Internet service, identify economics as the proper mechanism to give incentives for "fair" use, and explore both the positive and negative aspects of responsive pricing. There are some synergies between this and other chapters to enhance and expand the appropriateness of usage-sensitive pricing for the Internet. For example, responsive pricing requires truthful feedback from the network to change user behavior. Network providers may have the incentive to alter this feedback by lying or by artificially congesting their network to increase price. This "incentive compatibility problem" (the fact that the user's incentive to get good performance and the network provider's incentive to increase profits are not compatible) is addressed in the chapters by Gupta, Stahl, and Whinston, and by Crawford.

The chapter by Danielsen and Weiss, "User Control and IP Allocation," proposes a mechanism to control how much money users spend on their usage-sensitive traffic. While many chapters in *Internet Economics* discuss different usage-sensitive pricing policies, this chapter, as well as the one by MacKie-Mason, Murphy, and Murphy, does a particularly good job at including the user in the discussion of pricing. In particular, it discusses the important concept of controlling costs, which has been an argument against usage- sensitive pricing in the past. For example, the difficulty in budgeting for unknown networking charges and fear of exceeding the expected charges for networking are often pointed to as reasons users may prefer flat-rate pricing.

These two chapters lead the way to further studies concerning user response and feedback in Internet pricing models. Perhaps the clearest feedback will come when some of the new usage-sensitive pricing policies are implemented. Then questions regarding the Danielsen and Weiss mechanism can be answered and the feedback loop modeled by MacKie-Mason, Murphy, and Murphy can be tested.

Economists look at issues of usage-sensitive pricing from a different perspective and with a different set of tools than some of the technical solutions proposed in the previous chapters. Instead of having two qualities of service through a token bucket, as Clark's chapter suggests, why not have qualities of service which correspond to price and demand?[13] Since "bidding models" were first suggested, much work has been done to further the research in this area.[14] We believe that the authors of this volume have succeeded in showing how notions of economic efficiency can be applied through pricing models to the Internet.

The chapter by Gupta, Stahl, and Whinston, "Priority Pricing of Integrated Services Networks," analyzes the effectiveness of usage-sensitive pricing through the use of modeling. It presents very important pieces of the Internet economics puzzle by simulating a usage-sensitive pricing model. While other chapters can only speculate about the benefit of a usage-sensitive pricing mechanism, this one goes a step further, showing the relative benefit of a usage-sensitive pricing scheme over the traditional flat-rate scheme.

The chapter by Wang, Sirbu, and Peha, "Optimal Pricing for Integrated Services Networks," addresses the issue of pricing for Asynchronous Transfer Mode (ATM) networks. While the Internet Protocol is not the same as ATM, ATM technologies are expected to be widely deployed and IP can be layered above ATM. This chapter presents an innovative approach to pricing the Internet because it considers the possibility of pricing the Internet at a layer other than the IP layer and uses a protocol designed for multiple classes of service (unlike IPv4) which has direct significance on the introduction of integrated services and RSVP.

---

13. In fact, Clark's proposal could accommodate a more complex billing system, but requires only two qualities of service embedded in the core Internet Protocol, IPv4. Clark (1995) extends the discussion of qualities of service and pricing.

14. MacKie-Mason and Varian (1995) have a good description of a second-price auction bidding model. Vickrey (1961) was the first to propose the second-price auction.

Internet Commerce

Pricing questions extend beyond the market for Internet bandwidth and into discussions of the market for information, or content. While research on Internet commerce, including payment, insurance, licensing, as well as information security mechanisms, has developed relatively separately from the work of the previous sections on pricing bandwidth, we believe there will be more similarities than differences among these areas in the future. For example, billing and settlement processes developed for information goods likely will use the same infrastructure used to bill for Internet bandwidth. While the work of integrating billing and resource allocation may occur at some future point in time, the framework for Internet commerce and information privacy and security is being developed today.

The true economic benefits of the Internet will probably only appear when electronic commerce is as pervasive on the Internet as in other marketplaces. The foundations that are now being laid, as evident in the chapters in this section, should bring us closer to realizing a future of still greater network externalities, lower transaction costs, and innovative networked services. There is a need for further research on characterizing network externalities and transaction cost benefits of Internet services in light of the developments of technologies for electronic commerce and information security.

David Crawford's chapter, "Internet Services: A Market for Bandwidth or Communication?" explains why networks other than the Internet price on characteristics that are more similar to pricing communication than bandwidth. For example, pricing for electric power is based upon power characteristics, not the transmission grid characteristics. Crawford further explains that a network provider that gets revenues by charging for different qualities of service and tries to maximize profit may under-provision or artificially congest its network to increase the usage-sensitive price.

The chapter on Internet payment services by Neuman and Medvinsky presents examples of components of an electronic commerce system on the Internet using different mechanisms for payment. This chapter reviews two different payment systems which are emerging on the Internet—NetCash and NetCheque—and enable lower-cost electronic commerce transactions. The understanding and jux-taposition of these two systems allow the chapter to compare across attributes like those outlined in the section on usage-sensitive pricing.

The chapter by Lai, Medvinsky, and Neuman, "Endorsements, Licensing, and Insurance for Distributed Services," presents exam-ples of licensing and reimbursements in nonelectronic markets and creates analogous models for electronic markets. One of the com-mon points of emphasis throughout the chapters in this book is the notion of heterogeneity and incentive compatibilities that result from multiple organizations interoperating but also competing. This chapter explores items necessary for electronic commerce to be conducted on the Internet without necessarily trusting the organiza-tions involved in the transaction. It identifies key Internet commerce issues at a layer above the internetworking (Internet Protocol) or transport (Transmission Control Protocol) layer. Like the chapter by Neuman and Medvinsky, this chapter addresses the Internet com-merce problem from a security perspective by discussing methods for establishing trust between the supplier and provider of a good.

The chapter by McKnight et al., "Internet Commerce and Infor-mation Security," integrates the public policy issues of electronic commerce development on the Internet with the technological and economic issues. While identifying the different disciplines that af-fect this development and arguing for informed federal policymak-ers, this chapter discusses specific instances of technology, policy, and business that will affect Internet commerce development. The chapter's hypothesis is that Internet commerce and information security are tightly coupled and should be examined together. To support this hypothesis, the authors provide an overview of how electronic commerce and information security have developed re-cently. The main thrust of the chapter is that security becomes an enabler for electronic markets. Current U.S. federal policy and global Internet business practices still fall far short of the goal of providing a coordinated and secure infrastructure for Internet commerce.

Internet Economics and Policy

When firms do not cooperate and social welfare is threatened, governments may intervene. Regulation, or even criminal prosecution for violation of antitrust or restraint of trade laws, may occur if a service provider, for example, excludes some firms that want service. The role of public policy in Internet economics is addressed in the last section of this book.

Public policy affecting the Internet has focused on three distinct areas: regulation of the communications infrastructure (including rules on privacy, security, fraud, and false advertising); funding for Internet networks; and public investment in science and technology for digital computing and communications systems. One example of the effects of public policy on the Internet is the high leased line rates mandated by government ministries in the past; this has been identified as a cause of the slow growth of the Internet in countries such as Japan into the early 1990s. The future development of Internet economics also will be affected by government actions. The two chapters in this section discuss some of these roles of government, and argue for the continued provision of Internet public goods.[15]

The chapter by Hallgren and McAdams, "The Economic Efficiency of Internet Public Goods," explores the economic benefits of supporting public goods for further development of the Internet. The authors explain that the market may not provide the right incentives for private development of tools to help the Internet grow, and argue that a consortium model may be the only way to support Internet public goods. Certainly, the federal government of the U.S. has taken lead roles previously with the development of Internet public goods such as ARPANET and the NSFNET. This chapter

15. Other issues, such as the nature and importance of Internet culture, were discussed at the workshop but are not addressed in most of the chapters collected here. See Bailey et al. (1996) for further information on how the subject of the Internet culture kept popping up during discussions of Internet economics. Privacy, child protection, pornography, and censorship issues which are receiving significant public and government attention—but have not yet been the subject of replicative empirical research—are also beyond the scope of this book. A recent treatment of some of these public policy issues appears in Kahin and Keller (1995).

shows how publicly funded goods may be necessary even with the privatization of the Internet. This conclusion reinforces that of the previous chapter by supporting a public policy consistent with Internet commerce.

The final chapter by Mitrabarun Sarkar, "Internet Pricing: A Regulatory Imperative," focuses on market failures of the Internet and makes a case for regulation. Regulation of the Internet may come in many forms, ranging from common carriage rules regulating the sale of circuits to content regulation. Arguably, the Internet is already regulated, since many of the telecommunications circuits that make up the Internet are regulated—in the U.S., for example, at rates set at the state or federal level. The chapter suggests why an important alternative to developing a pure free-market system—introducing regulation—may be needed especially in light of recent pricing proposals by Bohn et al. (1994) and MacKie-Mason and Varian (1995).

Conclusion

This collection of work on Internet economics introduces models of Internet pricing intended to preserve the low transaction costs enabled by statistical sharing, positive network externalities, and interoperability. There is as yet little consensus on the merits of the proposed Internet pricing models. We hope this book motivates the authors and others to take the next step beyond building models to implementing, evaluating, and comparing proposed approaches to Internet economics. The effects of user behavior on performance of alternative models of the economics of the Internet may then be assessed.

Each of the chapters in this book represents some of the best work yet done in areas of research and development which are still in their infancy. While this publication is a step toward advancing the field of Internet economics, much more work is needed for the level of understanding required to determine business strategies or public policies. Although advanced information and communication technologies make the Internet work, economic and policy issues must now be addressed to sustain the growth and expand the scope of the Internet.[16]

Finally, we should note that much more work needs to be done under the rubric of usage-sensitive pricing. While the models do help, implementation and empirical data would advance our collective understanding of Internet economics tremendously.

Of particular interest is how users will react to new pricing policies. Ultimately it will be users, or the market if one prefers, who will decide which Internet pricing approaches are accepted.

Principles of Internet economics will be developed as economists, engineers, and others collaborate on further research. We believe there are at least five areas of opportunity in which new solutions to Iproblems may be explored:

1. New empirical work. This is especially needed vis-a-vis user behavior. Combinations of flat-rate bandwidth pricing with usage-sensitive or transaction-based pricing offer a promising area for further research and commercial interest.

2. Congestion control protocols, pricing policies, and user feedback. These should be tested in concert with one another. Likewise, integrated approaches to Internet economics problems should be explored further.

3. Pricing as a congestion control method or as part of an interconnection settlements process. This should be tested in concert with enhancements to the TCP/IP protocol suite, such as RSVP and IPv6.

4. Increased data collection and analysis across Internet Service Providers. This will provide an understanding about the growth of the Internet and provide a rich data set to develop economic models and increase our understanding of the subtle interaction between Internet engineering, economics, policy, and cultural practices. However, the increasingly competitive nature of Internet Service Providers may make this information less available.

5. Further research on the development of technologies and policies for Internet commerce and information security and privacy

16. Continued work on these issues is planned as part of the Internet Telephony Interoperability Consortium, begun in 1996 at MIT to explore, among other things, efficient resource allocation issues for the Internet. See http://itel.mit.edu for more information.

protection. This is needed to support services for the Internet marketplace. Preliminary evidence suggests that the further technological advance of the Internet will be hampered by lack of adequate attention to how these issues should interrelate with national security and other policy concerns of governments.

The Internet has become a powerful innovation engine for the emerging Global Information Infrastructure. To encourage further research, advance the public policy debate, facilitate business decision-making, and support technological advance, we offer this collection of some of the best current thinking on Internet economics. We hope this book helps the reader understand the issues involved and leads to stronger business performance while safeguarding the Internet culture.

References

Anania, L. and R. J. Solomon. 1988. Flat—The minimalist B-ISDN rate. Telecommunications Policy Research Conference, Solomons Island, MD.

Bailey, J., S. Gillett, D. Gingold, B. Leida, D. Melcher, J. Reagle, J. Roh, R. Rothstein, and G. Seale. 1996. Internet economics workshop notes. In Special Issue on Internet Economics, McKnight and Bailey, eds., *Journal of Electronic Publishing*, available at http://www.press.umich.edu/jep.

Bohn, R., H.-W. Braun, K. Claffy, and S. Wolff. 1994. Mitigating the coming Internet crunch: Multiple service levels via Precedence. Applied Network Research Technical Report, San Diego Supercomputer Center.

Braden, R., D. Clark, S. Shenker. 1994. Integrated services in the Internet architecture: An overview. Internet Engineering Task Force, Request for Comments 1633, Available at http://ds.internic.net/rfc/rfc 1633.txt.

Braden, R., L. Zhang, S. Berson, S. Herzog, S. Jamin. 1996. Resource ReSerVation Protocol (RSVP)—Version 1 functional specification. Internet Draft, Internet Engineering Task Force (November 5). Available at ftp://ietf.org/internet-drafts/draft-ietf-rsvp-spec-14.txt.

Clark, David D. 1988. The design philosophy of the DARPA Internet protocols. *Computer Communication Review* 18 (4): 106–114.

Clark, D. D. 1995. Adding service discrimination to the Internet. Telecommunications Policy Research Conference, Solomons Island, MD.

Cerf, V., and R. Kahn. 1974. A protocol for packet network intercommunication. *IEEE Transactions on Communications* 22 (5): 637–648.

Hart, J. A., R. R. Reed, and F. Bar. 1992. The building of the Internet: Implications for the future of broadband networks. *Telecommunications Policy* (November): 666–689.

Kahin, B., and J. Keller, eds. 1995. *Public access to the Internet.* Cambridge, MA: MIT Press.

Kleinrock, L. 1974. Research areas in computer communication. *Computer Communication Review* 4 (3): (July).

MacKie-Mason, J., and H. Varian. 1995. Pricing the Internet. In *Public access to the Internet,* B. Kahin and J. Keller, eds. Cambridge, MA: MIT Press.

McKnight, L., and J. Bailey, eds. 1996. Special Issue on Internet Economics, *Journal of Electronic Publishing* (April), http://www.press.umich.edu/jep.

Mitchell, B. M., and I. Vogelsang. 1991. *Telecommunications pricing: Theory and practice.* New York: Cambridge University Press.

OMB. 1994. Management of federal information resources. Executive Office of the President, Office of Management and Budget, Circular A-130 (July 15).

Ramsey, F. P. 1927. A contribution to the theory of taxation. *The Economic Journal:* 47–61.

Shenker, S., D. Clark, D. Estrin, and S. Herzog. 1996. Pricing in computer networks: Reshaping the research agenda. *Telecommunications Policy* 20 (3): 183–201.

Stickney, C. P., R. L. Weil, and S. Davidson. 1991. *Financial accounting: An introduction to concepts, methods, and uses.* San Diego: Harcourt Brace Jovanovich.

Vickrey, W. 1961. Counterspeculation, auctions, and competitive sealed tenders. *Journal of Finance* 16 (March): 8–37.

Zhang, L., S. Deering, D. Estrin, S. Shenker, and D. Zappala. 1993. RSVP: A new resource ReSerVation Protocol. *IEEE Network* 7 (5) (September): 8–19.

The Economics of the Internet

Economic FAQs About the Internet

Jeffrey K. MacKie-Mason and Hal R. Varian

Introduction

This is a set of frequently asked questions (and answers) about the economic, institutional, and technological structure of the Internet. We describe the history and current state of the Internet, discuss some of the pressing economic and regulatory problems, and speculate about future developments.

What is a FAQ?

FAQ stands for frequently asked questions. There are dozens of FAQ documents on diverse topics available on the Internet, ranging from physics to scuba diving to how to contact the White House. They are produced and maintained by volunteers. This FAQ answers questions about the economics of the Internet (and toward the end offers some opinions and forecasts).

Where can the current version of this FAQ be found?

An earlier version of this FAQ was published in the Summer 1994 issue of the *Journal of Economic Perspectives*.[1] The Internet is changing

---

1. We are grateful to the American Economics Association for permission to reprint substantial portions of that material.

at an astonishing rate, so we have used this opportunity to revise and update the information in that earlier document. Future updates can be found on the Web servers at the School of Public Policy at the University of Michigan (Telecom Information Directory) or the School of Information Management and Systems at the University of California at Berkeley (The Information Economy).

Background

What is the Internet?

The Internet is a worldwide network of computer networks that use a common communications protocol, TCP/IP (Transmission Control Protocol/Internet Protocol). TCP/IP provides a common language for interoperation between networks that use a variety of local protocols (Ethernet, Netware, AppleTalk, DECnet and others).

Where did it come from?

In the late 1960s, the Advanced Research Projects Administration (ARPA), a division of the U.S. Defense Department, developed the ARPAnet to link together universities and high-tech defense contractors. The TCP/IP technology was developed to provide a standard protocol for ARPAnet communications. In the mid-1980s, the National Science Foundation (NSF) created the NSFNET in order to provide connectivity to its supercomputer centers, and to provide other general services. The NSFNET adopted the TCP/IP protocol and provided a high-speed backbone for the developing Internet.

What do people do on the Internet?

Probably the most frequent use is electronic mail (email), followed by file transfer (moving data from one computer to another) and remote login (logging into a computer that is running somewhere else on the Internet). In terms of traffic volume, as of December

1994 about 32% of total traffic was file transfer, 16% was World Wide Web (WWW), 11% was netnews, 6% was e-mail, 4% was gopher, and the rest was for other uses (Merit Statistics). People can search databases (including the catalogs of the Library of Congress and scores of university research libraries), download data and software, and ask (or answer) questions in discussion groups on numerous topics (including economics research).

How big is the Internet?

From 1985 to December 1994, the Internet grew from about 200 networks to well over 45,000 and from 1,000 hosts (end-user computers) to over four million. About one million of these hosts are at educational sites, 1.3 million are commercial sites, and about 385,000 are government/military sites, all in the United States. Most of the other 1.3 million hosts are elsewhere in the world (Network Wizards). NSFNET traffic grew from 85 million packets in January 1988 to 86 billion packets in November 1994. (Packets are variable in length, with a bimodal distribution. The mean is about 200 bytes on average, and a byte corresponds to one ASCII character.) This is more than a 600-fold increase in only six years. The traffic on the network is currently increasing at a rate of 6% a month. (NSFNET statistics are available at Merit's Network Information Center.[2])

John Quarterman estimates that as of October 1994 there were about eight million people directly connected to the Internet, and about six million more people who could access the Internet "indirectly" through online services. The numbers in the latter category are likely substantially larger today. Of course, the total number of people who have access to the Internet via email is much larger—it may even approach the 20–30 million figures bandied about in the mass media.

---

2. Beginning in the early 1990s, the statistics do not reflect the size of the total U.S. network because alternative backbones began appearing. It is generally believed that the NSFNET accounted for at least 75% of U.S. backbone traffic until around September 1994, after which its share rapidly fell as the NSFNET was gradually phased out. Shutdown occurred on April 30, 1995.

Organization

Who runs the Internet?

The short answer is, no one. The Internet is a loose amalgamation of computer networks run by many different organizations in more than 70 countries. Most of the technological decisions are made by small committees of volunteers who set standards for interoperability.

What is the structure of the Internet?

The U.S. portion of the Internet is best thought of as having three levels. At the bottom are Local Area Networks (LANs); for example, campus networks. Usually the local networks are connected to a regional or mid-level network. The mid-level networks connect to one or more backbones. A backbone is an overarching network to which multiple regional networks connect, and which generally does not serve directly any local networks or end-users. The U.S. backbones connect to other backbone networks around the world. There are, however, numerous exceptions to this structure.

A few years ago, the primary U.S. backbone was the NSFNET. On April 30, 1995, the NSFNET ceased operation. Now traffic in the United States is carried on several privately operated backbones. The new "privatized Internet" in the United States is becoming less hierarchical and more interconnected. The separation between the backbone and regional network layers of the current structure are blurring as more regionals are connected directly to each other through network access points (NAPs), and traffic passes through a chain of regionals without any backbone transport.

What are the backbone networks?

In January 1994, there were four public fiber-optic backbones in the United States: NSFNET, Alternet, PSInet, and SprintLink. The NSFNET was funded by the NSF; it evolved directly out of ARPANET, the original TCP/IP network. The other backbones were private, for-profit enterprises.

By summer 1995 there were at least 14 national and superregional high-speed TPC/IP networks in the United States. As interconnection proliferates, this distinction becomes less important. A map of the major interconnection points and the numerous networks that use them is available at CERFnet.

MCI, which helped operate the original NSFNET, is probably the largest carrier of Internet traffic today; it claims to carry 40% of all Internet traffic. However, this is a highly competitive market; Sprint, Alternet, and PSInet are also signing up many customers.

What was the NSFNET?

The NSFNET was the first backbone for the U.S. portion of the Internet. It was originally conceived as a means by which researchers could submit jobs to supercomputers located at various universities around the United States. Subsequently it was realized that the excess capacity on this backbone could be used to exchange data among universities that had nothing to do with supercomputing. The NSF paid about $11.5 million annually for the NSFNET operation for several years, but eventually decided that the technology was mature enough that it could be more effectively provided by the private market.

What happened to the NSFNET?

The NSFNET backbone was shut down on April 30, 1995, as its NSF funding ended. The NSF is continuing to fund some regional nets, but this funding is steadily decreasing to zero over five years. Instead, the NSF is funding Network Access Points (NAPs) near Chicago, San Francisco, and New York. The NAPs are interconnection points for backbone providers. See Fazio (1995) for an article describing the transition in detail; current information is available at the Merit Web site for information on the transition (Merit Architecture). The NSF is also funding a routing arbiter service to provide fair and efficient routing among the various backbones and regional networks.

The NSF is also funding the vBNS (very-high speed Backbone Network Service) to connect five of its supercomputer sites at

155 megabits per second. Its emphasis will be on developing capabilities for high-definition remote visualization and video transmission.

How much did NSFNET cost?

It is difficult to say how much the Internet as a whole costs, since it consists of thousands of different networks, many of which are privately owned. However, it is possible to estimate the cost of the NSFNET backbone since it was publicly supported. In 1993, the NSF paid Merit about $11.5 million per year to run the backbone. Approximately 80% of this was spent on lease payments for the fiber-optic lines and routers. About 7% of the budget was spent on the Network Operations Center, which monitored traffic flows and troubleshot problems.

To give some sense of the scale of this subsidy, add to it the approximately $7 million per year that the NSF paid to subsidize various regional networks, for a total of about $20 million. Based on estimates that there were approximately 20 million Internet users (most of whom were connected to the NSFNET in one way or another), the NSF subsidy amounted to about $1 per user per year. Of course, this was significantly less than the total cost of the Internet; indeed, it does not even include all of the public funds, which came from state governments, state-supported universities, and other national governments as well. No one really knows how much all this adds up to, although there are some research projects under way to try to estimate the total U.S. expenditures on the Internet. It has been estimated—read "guessed"—that the NSF subsidy of $20 million per year was less than 10% of the total expenditure by U.S. public agencies on the Internet.

Who provides access outside of the United States?

There are now a large number of backbone and mid-level networks in other countries. Most West European countries, for example, have national networks that are attached to EBone, the European backbone. The infrastructure is still immature, and quite inefficient in some places. For instance, the connections between countries often are slow or of low quality, so it was common to see traffic between two countries routed through the NSFNET in the United States (Braun and Claffy 1993).

Technology

Is the Internet different from telephone networks?

Yes and no. Most backbone and regional network traffic moves over leased phone lines, so at a low level the technology is the same. However, there is a fundamental distinction between how the lines are used by the Internet and the phone companies. The Internet provides connectionless packet-switched service whereas telephone service is circuit-switched. (We define these terms below.) The difference may sound arcane, but it has vastly important implications for pricing and the efficient use of network resources.

What is circuit switching?

Telephone networks use circuit switching: an end-to-end circuit must be set up before the call can begin. A fixed share of network resources is reserved for the call, and no other call can use those resources until the original connection is closed. This means that a long silence between two teenagers uses the same resources as an active negotiation between two fast-talking lawyers. One advantage of circuit switching is that it enables performance guarantees such as guaranteed maximum delay, which is essential for real-time applications like voice conversations. It is also much easier to do detailed accounting for circuit-switched network usage.

How is packet-switching technology different from circuit-switching technology?

The Internet uses packet-switching technology. The term "packet" refers to the fact that the data stream from a computer is broken up into packets of about 200 bytes (on average), which are then sent out onto the network.[3] Each packet contains a "header" with information necessary for routing the packet from origination to destination. Thus each packet in a data stream is independent.

The main advantage of packet switching is that it permits statistical multiplexing, or statistical sharing, on the communications lines. That is, the packets from many different sources can share a line, allowing for very efficient use of the fixed capacity. With current technology, packets are generally accepted onto the network on a first-come, first-served basis. If the network becomes overloaded, packets are delayed or discarded ("dropped").

How are packets routed to their destination?

The Internet protocol is connectionless.[4] This means that there is no end-to-end setup for a session; each packet is independently routed to its destination. When a packet is ready, the host computer sends it on to another computer, known as a router. The router examines the destination address in the header and passes the packet along to another router chosen by a route-finding algorithm. A packet may go through 30 or more routers in its travels from one host computer to another. Because routes are dynamically updated, it is possible for different packets from a single session to take different routes to the destination.

Along the way packets may be broken up into smaller packets, or reassembled into bigger ones. When the packets reach their final destination, they are reassembled at the host computer. The instructions for this reassembly are part of the TCP/IP protocol suite.

Some packet-switching networks are connection-oriented (notably, X.25 networks, such as Tymnet, and frame-relay networks). In such a network a connection is set up before transmission begins, just as in a circuit-switched network. A fixed route is defined, and information necessary to match packets to their session and defined route is stored in memory tables in the routers. Thus connectionless

---

3. Recall that a byte is equivalent to one ASCII character.

4. TCP is a connection-oriented protocol that is overlaid on the Internet Protocol by most, but not all, applications.

networks economize on router memory and connection setup time, whereas connection-oriented networks economize on routing calculations (which have to be repeated for every packet in a connectionless network).

What is the physical technology of the Internet?

Most of the network hardware that comprises the Internet consists of communications lines and switches or routers. In the regional and backbone networks, the lines are mostly leased telephone trunk lines, which are increasingly fiber-optic. Routers are computers; indeed, the routers used on the NSFNET were modified commercial IBM RS6000 workstations, although custom-designed routers by other companies such as Cisco, Wellfleet, 3-Com and DEC probably have the majority share of the market.

What does "speed" mean?

"Faster" networks do not move electrons or photons faster than the speed of light; a single bit travels at essentially the same speed in all networks. Rather, "faster" refers to sending more bits of information simultaneously in a single data stream (usually over a single communications line), thus delivering bits faster. Phone modem users are familiar with recent speed increases from 300 bits per second to 2,400, 9,600 and now 19,200 bits per second. Leased-line network speeds have advanced from 56 kilobits per second to 1.5 megabits per second (known as T-1 lines) in the late 1980s, and then to 45 megabits per second (T-3) in the early 1990s. Lines of 155 megabits per second are now available, though not yet widely used. The U.S. Congress had called for a gigabit-per-second backbone by 1996. This goal has been nearly achieved in testbeds, though it now looks like it will be at least a couple of more years before we see gigabit speeds in the public backbone.

Current T-3 45 Mbps lines can move data at a speed of 1,400 pages of text per second; a 20-volume encyclopedia can be sent coast to coast in half a minute. However, it is important to remember that this is the speed on the wide area network—the "access roads" via the regional networks still primarily use the much slower T-1 connections.[5]

Why do data networks use packet switching?

Economics largely explains the preference for packet switching over circuit switching in the Internet and other public networks. Circuit networks use lots of lines in order to economize on switching and routing. That is, once a call is set up, a line is dedicated to its use regardless of its rate of data flow, and no further routing calculations are needed. This network design makes sense when lines are cheap relative to switches.

The costs of both communications lines and computers have been declining exponentially for decades. However, since about 1970, switches (computers) have become relatively cheaper than lines. At that point packet switching became economical: lines are shared by multiple connections at the cost of many more routing calculations by the switches. This preference for using many relatively cheap routers to manage few expensive lines is evident in the topology of the backbone networks. For example, in the NSFNET any packet coming on to the backbone had to pass through two routers at its entry point and again at its exit point. A packet entering at Cleveland and exiting at New York traversed four routers but only one leased T-3 communications line.

What are ATM and cell-switching technologies?

The international telephone community has committed to a future network design that combines elements of both circuit and packet switching to enable the provision of integrated services. The International Telecommunication Union (ITU, an international organization for telecommunications), has adopted a cell-switching technology called Asynchronous Transfer Mode (ATM) for future high-speed networks. Cell switching closely resembles packet switch-

---

5. As with almost everything in this FAQ, the details are constantly changing. As of the final editing of this version (May 1996), some of the Internet backbone links are running at 155 megabits per second.

ing in that it breaks a data stream into packets which are then placed on lines that are shared by several streams. One major difference is that cells have a fixed size whereas packets can have different sizes. This makes it possible in principle to offer bounded delay guarantees (since a cell will not get stuck for a surprisingly long time behind an unusually large packet).

An ATM network also resembles a circuit-switched network in that it provides connection-oriented service. Each connection has a set-up phase during which a "virtual circuit" is created. The fact that the circuit is virtual, not physical, provides two major advantages. First, it is not necessary to reserve network resources for a given connection; the economic efficiencies of statistical multiplexing can be realized. Second, once a virtual circuit path is established, switching time is minimized, which allows for much higher network throughput. Initial ATM networks are already being operated at 155 megabits per second, while the non-ATM Internet backbones operate at no more than 45 megabits per second. The path to 1,000 megabit (one gigabit) networks seems much clearer for ATM than for traditional packet switching.

What changes are likely in network technology?

At present there are many overlapping information networks (e.g., telephone, telegraph, data, cable TV), and new networks are emerging rapidly (paging, personal communications services, etc.). Each of the current information networks was engineered to provide a particular type of service and the added value provided by each different type was sufficient to overcome the fixed costs of building overlapping physical networks.

However, given the high fixed costs of providing a network, the economic incentive to develop an "integrated services" network is strong. Furthermore, now that all information can be easily digitized, separate networks for separate types of traffic are no longer necessary. Convergence toward a unified, integrated services network is a basic feature in most visions of the much publicized "information superhighway" (e.g., National Academy of Sciences 1994). The migration to integrated services networks will have important implications for market structure and competition.

When will the "information superhighway" arrive?

The federal High Performance Computing Act of 1991 aimed for a gigabit-per-second national backbone by 1995. Five federally funded testbed networks are currently demonstrating various gigabit approaches. To get a feel for how fast a gigabit per second is, note that most small colleges or universities today have 56 Kbps Internet connections. At 56 kilobits per second it takes about five hours to transmit one gigabit!

Efforts to develop integrated services networks also have exploded. Several cable companies have already started offering Internet connections to their customers.[6] AT&T, MCI, and all of the "Baby Bell" operating companies are involved in mergers and joint ventures with cable TV and other specialized network providers to deliver new integrated services such as video-on-demand. ATM-based networks, although initially developed for phone systems, ironically have been first implemented for data networks within corporations and by some regional and backbone providers.

How is Internet access priced?

What types of pricing schemes are used?

Until recently, nearly all users faced the same pricing structure for Internet usage. A fixed-bandwidth connection was charged an annual fee, which allowed for unlimited usage up to the physical maximum flow rate (bandwidth). We call this "connection pricing." Most connection fees were paid by organizations (universities, government agencies, etc.) and the users paid nothing themselves.

Simple connection pricing still dominates the market, but a number of variants have emerged. The most notable is "committed information rate" pricing. In this scheme, an organization is charged a two-part fee. One fee is based on the bandwidth of the connection,

6. Because most cable networks are one-way, many of these initial efforts use an "asymmetric" network connector that brings the input in through the TV cable at 10 megabits per second, but sends the output out through a regular phone line at about 14.4 kilobits per second. This scheme may be popular since most users tend to download more information than they upload.

which is the maximum feasible flow rate; the second fee is based on the maximum guaranteed flow to the customer. The network provider installs sufficient capacity to simultaneously transport the committed rate for all of its customers, and installs flow regulators on each connection. When some customers operate below that rate, the excess network capacity is available on a first-come, first-served basis for the other customers. This type of pricing is more common in private networks than on the Internet because a TCP/IP flow rate can be guaranteed only network by network, greatly limiting its value unless a large number of the 20,000 Internet networks coordinate on offering this type of guarantee.

Networks that offer committed information pricing generally have enough capacity to meet the entire guaranteed bandwidth. This is a bit like a bank holding 100% reserves in case all depositors want to withdraw on the same day. However, full provisioning is necessary with existing TCP/IP network technology since there is no commonly used way to prioritize packets, and because the statistical fluctuations in traffic are huge.

For most usage, the marginal packet placed on the Internet is priced at zero. At the outer fringes there are a few exceptions. For example, several private networks (such as Compuserve) provide e-mail connections to the Internet. Several of these charge per message above a low threshold. The public networks in Chile (Baeza-Yates et al. 1993) and New Zealand (Brownlee 1994, 1996) charge their customers by the packet for all international traffic. An economic study of the New Zealand system can be found in Carter and Guthrie (1994).

What other types of pricing have been considered?

Standard economic theory suggests that prices should be matched to costs. There are three main elements of network costs: the cost of connecting to the net, the cost of providing additional network capacity, and the social cost of congestion. Once capacity is in place, direct usage cost is negligible, and by itself is almost not worth charging for given the accounting and billing costs (see MacKie-Mason and Varian 1995b).

Charging for connections is conceptually straightforward: a connection requires a line, a router, and some labor effort. The line and the router are reversible investments and thus are reasonably charged for on an annual lease basis (though many organizations buy their own routers). Indeed, this is essentially the current scheme for Internet connection fees.

Charging for incremental capacity requires usage information. Ideally, we need a measure of the organization's demand during the expected peak period of usage over some period to determine its share of the incremental capacity requirement. In practice, it might seem that a reasonable approximation would be to charge a premium price for usage during predetermined peak periods (a positive price if the base usage price is zero), as is routinely done for electricity. However, casual evidence suggests that peak demand periods are much less predictable than for other utility services. One reason is that it is very easy to use the computer to schedule some activities for off-peak hours, leading to a shifting peaks problem.[7] In addition, so much traffic traverses long distances around the globe that time zone differences are important. Network statistics reveal very irregular time-of-day usage patterns (MacKie-Mason and Varian 1995a).

How can the Internet deal with increasing congestion?

If you have read this far in the chapter, you should have a good basic understanding of the current state of the Internet—we hope that most of the questions you have had about how the Internet works have been answered. Starting here we will move from FAQs and facts toward conjectures, firmly expressed opinions (FEOs), and partially baked ideas (PBIs). We first discuss congestion problems.

Nearly all usage of the Internet backbones is unpriced at the margin. Organizations pay a fixed fee in exchange for unlimited access up to the maximum throughput of their particular connection. This is a classic problem of the commons. The externality exists

---

7. The single largest current use of network capacity is file transfer, much of which is distribution of files from central archives to distributed local archives. The timing for a large fraction of file transfer is likely to be flexible. Just as most fax machines allow faxes to be transmitted at off-peak times, large data files could easily be transferred at off-peak times—if users had appropriate incentives to adopt such practices.

because a packet-switched network is a shared-media technology: each extra packet that Sue User sends imposes a cost on all other users because the resources Sue is using are not available to them. This cost can come in form of delay or lost (dropped) packets.

Without an incentive to economize on usage, congestion can become quite serious. Indeed, the problem is more serious for data networks than for many other congestible resources because of the tremendously wide range of usage rates. On a highway, for example, at a given moment a single user is more or less limited to putting either one or zero cars on the road. On a data network, however, a single user at a modern workstation can send a few bytes of e-mail or put a load of hundreds of megabits per second on the network. Today any undergraduate with a new Macintosh is able to plug in a digital video camera and transmit live videos to another campus or home to Mom, demanding as much as one megabit per second. Since the maximum throughput on current backbones is only 45 megabits per second, it is clear that even a few users with relatively inexpensive equipment could bring the network to its knees.

Congestion problems are not just hypothetical. For example, congestion was quite severe in 1987 when the NSFNET backbone was running at much slower transmission speeds (56 kilobits per second) (Bohn et al. 1993). Users running interactive remote terminal sessions were experiencing unacceptable delays. As a temporary fix, the NSFNET programmed the routers to give terminal sessions (using the telnet program) higher priority than file transfers (using the File Transfer Protocol [FTP] program).

More recently, many services on the Internet have experienced severe congestion problems. Large FTP archives, Web servers at the National Center for Supercomputer Applications, the original Archie site at McGill University, and many services have had serious problems with overuse. See Markoff (1993) for more detailed descriptions.

Congestion on the trans-Atlantic link, which has been only 6 megabits per second, has been quite severe, causing researchers who require substantial bandwidth to schedule their work during the wee hours. Since the advent of WWW and CU-SeeMe video-conferencing, there has also been seriously disruptive congestion in Europe.

Indeed, for a period beginning in 1995, EUnet (the main European Internet backbone) forbade the use of CU-SeeMe without advance permission.

If everyone just stuck to ASCII, e-mail congestion would not likely become a problem for many years, if ever. However, the demand for multimedia services is growing dramatically. Although the supply of bandwidth is increasing dramatically, so is the demand. If congestion remains unpriced, it is likely that there will be increasingly damaging episodes when the demand for bandwidth exceeds the supply in the foreseeable future.

What non-price mechanisms can be used for congestion control?

Although administratively assigning different priorities to different types of traffic is appealing, it is impractical as a long-run solution to congestion costs because of the usual inefficiencies of rationing. However, there is an even more severe technological problem: it is impossible to enforce. From the network's perspective, bits are bits and there is no certain way to distinguish between different types of uses. By convention, most standard programs use a unique identifier that is included in the TCP header (called the port number); this is what NSFNET used for its priority scheme in 1987. However, it is a trivial matter to put a different port number into the packet headers: for example, to assign the telnet number to ftp packets to defeat the 1987 priority scheme. To avoid this problem, NSFNET kept its prioritization mechanism secret, but that is hardly a long-run solution.

What other mechanisms can be used to control congestion? The most obvious approach for economists is to charge some sort of congestion price. However, to date, there has been almost no serious consideration of congestion pricing for backbone services, and even tentative proposals for usage pricing have been met with strong opposition. We will discuss pricing below but first we examine some non-price mechanisms that have been proposed.

Many proposals rely on voluntary efforts to control congestion. Numerous participants in congestion discussions suggest that peer pressure and user ethics will be sufficient to control congestion costs. For example, recently a single user started broadcasting a 350–450 Kbps audio-video test pattern to hosts around the world, blocking the network's ability to handle a scheduled audio broadcast from a Finnish university. A leading network engineer sent a strongly worded e-mail message to the user's site administrator, and the offending workstation was disconnected from the network. However, this example also illustrates the problem with relying on peer pressure: the inefficient use was not terminated until after it had caused serious disruption. Moreover, it apparently was caused by a novice user who did not understand the impact of what he had done; as network access becomes ubiquitous there will be an ever-increasing number of unsophisticated users who have access to applications that can cause severe congestion if not properly used. And of course, peer pressure may be quite ineffective against malicious users who want to intentionally cause network congestion.

One recent proposal for voluntary control is closely related to the 1987 method used by the NSFNET (Bohn et al. 1993). This proposal would require users to indicate the priority they want each of their sessions to receive, and for routers to be programmed to maintain multiple queues for each priority class. Obviously, the success of this scheme would depend on users' willingness to assign lower priorities to some of their traffic. In any case, as long as it is possible for just one or a few abusive users to create crippling congestion, voluntary priority schemes that are not robust enough to withstand forgetfulness, ignorance, or malice may be largely ineffective.

In fact, a number of voluntary mechanisms are in place today. They are somewhat helpful in part because most users are unaware of them, or because they require some programming expertise to defeat. For example, most implementations of the TCP protocols use a "slow start" algorithm which controls the rate of transmission based on the current state of delay in the network. Nothing prevents users from modifying their TCP implementation to send full throttle if they do not want to behave "nicely."

A completely different approach to reducing congestion is purely technological: overprovisioning. Overprovisioning means maintaining sufficient network capacity to support the peak demands without noticeable service degradation.[8] This has been the most important mechanism used to date on the Internet. However, overprovisioning

8. The effects of network congestion are usually negligible until usage is very close to capacity.

is costly, and with both very-high-bandwidth applications and near-universal access fast approaching, it may become too costly. In simple terms, will capacity demand grow faster than the decline in capacity cost?

Given the explosive growth in demand and the long lead time needed to introduce new network protocols, the Internet may face serious problems very soon if productivity increases do not keep up. Therefore, we believe it is time to seriously examine incentive-compatible allocation mechanisms, such as various forms of congestion pricing.

Can bandwidth be reserved?

The current Internet offers a single service quality: "best efforts packet service." Packets are transported first-come, first-served with no guarantee of success. Some packets may experience severe delays, while others may be dropped and never arrive.

However, different kinds of data place different demands on network services. E-mail and file transfer require 100% accuracy, but can easily tolerate delay. Real-time voice broadcasts require much higher bandwidth than file transfers, and can only tolerate minor delays, but they can tolerate significant distortion. Real-time video broadcasts have very low tolerance for delay and distortion.

Voice telephony networks handle the quality-of-service problem by assigning each call a physical circuit with fixed resources sufficient to guarantee a minimal quality of service. One limitation of this scheme is that the amount of resources devoted to each call is hardwired into the engineering of the network. As we have discussed, the Internet takes the approach of sharing all of its resources all of the time, which accommodates the wildly varying bandwidth requirements of different applications, and which gains from averaging over the wildly varying bandwidth requirements during a session with most applications. A hybrid approach to offering different resources, along with guarantees, to different uses would be to allow flexible, dynamic resource reservation. That is, allow a user (or her software agent) to declare how much bandwidth, what maximal delay and what type of delay variation she requires for a given session, and allocate those resources to her. An experimental implementation of such a scheme is given in the RSVP protocol (Zhang et al. 1993).

How can users be induced to choose the right level of service?

Because of different resource requirements, network efficiency can be increased if the different types of traffic are treated differently—giving a delay guarantee to, say, a real-time video session but not to routine email or file transfer. But in order to do this, the user must truthfully indicate what type of traffic he or she is sending. If real-time video bit streams get the highest quality service, why not claim that all of your bit streams are real-time video?

Cocchi et al. (1992) point out that it is useful to look at network pricing as a mechanism design problem. The user can indicate the "type" of his transmission, and the workstation in turn reports this type to the network. In order to ensure truthful revelation of preferences, the reporting and billing mechanism must be incentive compatible. The field of mechanism design has been criticized for ignoring the bounded rationality of human subjects. However, in this context, the workstation is doing most of the computation, so that quite complex mechanisms may be feasible.

Why should pricing be taken seriously for congestion control?

Let us turn this question on its head: Why should data network usage be free even to universities, when telephone and postal usage is not?[9] The question is, does society benefit more from priced or unpriced network resources?

As we have argued, other approaches to controlling congestion are either flawed or have undesirable side effects. Pricing

---

9. Many university employees routinely use email rather than the phone to communicate with friends and family at other Internet-connected sites. Likewise, a service is now being offered to transmit faxes between cities over the Internet for free, then paying only the local phone call charges to deliver them to the intended fax machine. And during early 1995, several versions of Internet voice telephone software were released, allowing people to hold two-way conversations—using large amounts of bandwidth—but paying nothing to offset the service quality degradation they were imposing on other users.

approaches have the overwhelming advantage that they permit users, acting individually (or as organizations if the pricing is only applied at the organizational level), to express the value that they place on obtaining network services. Thus, pricing directly provides the information needed to allocate scarce resources during times of congestion to those users who value them most. There is no need to assign arbitrary priorities, or to force high-value users to suffer from being stuck in a first-come, first-served line behind low-value users. The chapter by MacKie-Mason et al. in this volume and MacKie-Mason and Varian (1995c) discuss the advantages of pricing for congestion in greater detail.

How might prices be used to control congestion?

We have elsewhere described a scheme for efficient pricing of the congestion costs (MacKie-Mason and Varian 1995b, 1995a). The basic problem is that when the network is near capacity, a user's incremental packet imposes costs on other users in the form of delay or dropped packets. Our scheme for internalizing this cost is to impose a congestion price on usage that is determined by a real-time Vickrey (1961) auction. Following the terminology of Vernon Smith and Charles Plott, we call this a "smart market."

The basic idea is simple. Much of the time the network is uncongested, and the price for usage should be zero. When the network is congested, packets are queued and delayed. The current queuing scheme is first in, first out. We propose instead that packets should be prioritized based on the value that the user puts on getting the packet through quickly. To do this, each user assigns her packets a bid measuring her willingness to pay for immediate servicing. At congested routers, packets are prioritized based on bids. In order to make the scheme incentive-compatible, users are not charged the price they bid, but rather are charged the bid of the lowest priority packet that is admitted to the network. It is well known that this mechanism provides the right incentives for truthful revelation.

This scheme has a number of nice features. In particular, not only do those with the highest cost of delay get served first, but the prices also send the right signals for capacity expansion in a competitive market for network services. If all of the congestion revenues are reinvested in new capacity, then capacity will be expanded to the point where its marginal value is equal to its marginal cost.[10]

What are some problems with a smart market?

Prices in a real-world smart market cannot be updated continuously. The efficient price is determined by comparing a list of user bids to the available capacity and determining the cutoff price. In fact, packets arrive not all at once but over time, and thus it would be necessary to clear the market periodically based on a time-slice of bids. The efficiency of this scheme, then, depends on how costly it is to clear the market frequently and on how persistent the periods of congestion are. If congestion is exceedingly transient, then by the time the market price is updated the state of congestion may have changed.[11]

A number of network specialists have suggested that many customers—particularly not-for-profit agencies and schools—will object because they do not know in advance how much network utilization will cost them. We believe that this argument is partially a red herring since the user's bid always controls the maximum that network usage costs. Indeed, since we expect that for most traffic the congestion price will be zero, it should be possible for most users to avoid ever paying a usage charge by simply setting all packet bids to zero.[12] When the network is congested enough to have a positive congestion price, these users will pay the cost in units of delay rather than cash, as they do today.

10. See Gupta et al. (1994, 1996) for a related study of priority pricing to manage Internet congestion.

11. MacKie-Mason, Murphy, and Murphy (1996) and Murphy and Murphy (1994) describe an alternative congestion pricing scheme that would set prices based on a current measure of congestion in a gateway, then communicate these to the user. The user would then decide how much traffic to send during the current pricing interval. This mechanism is easier to implement, but at least in principle it does not match the efficiency of the smart market.

12. Since most users are willing to tolerate some delay for email, file transfer, and so forth, most traffic should be able to go through with acceptable delays at a zero congestion price, but time-critical traffic will typically pay a positive price.

We also expect that in a competitive market for network services, fluctuating congestion prices would usually be a "wholesale" phenomenon, and that intermediaries would repackage the services and offer them at a guaranteed price to end-users. Essentially this would create a futures market for network services.

There are also auction-theoretic problems that have to be solved. Our proposal specifies a single network entry point with auctioned access. In practice, networks have multiple gateways, each subject to differing states of congestion. Should a smart market be located in a single, central hub, with current prices continuously transmitted to the many gateways? Or should a set of simultaneous auctions operate at each gateway? How much coordination should there be between the separate auctions? All of these questions need not only theoretical models, but also empirical work to determine the optimal rate of market-clearing and inter-auction information sharing, given the costs and delays of real-time communication.

Another serious problem for almost any usage pricing scheme is how to correctly determine whether sender or receiver should be billed. With telephone calls it is clear that in most cases the originator of a call should pay. However, in a packet network, both "sides" originate their own packets, and in a connectionless network there is no mechanism for identifying party B's packets that were solicited as responses to a session initiated by party A. Consider a simple example: A major use of the Internet is for file retrieval from public archives. If the originator of each packet were charged for that packet's congestion cost, then the providers of free public goods (the file archives) would pay nearly all of the congestion charges incurred by a user's file request.[13] Either the public archive provider would need a billing mechanism to charge requesters for the (ex post) congestion charges, or the network would need to be engineered so that it could bill the correct party. In principle this problem can be solved by schemes like telephone 800 and 900 numbers

13. Public file servers in Chile and New Zealand already face this problem: any packets they send in response to requests from foreign hosts are charged by the network. Network administrators in New Zealand are concerned that this blind charging scheme is stifling the production of information public goods. For now, those public archives that do exist have a sign-on notice pleading with international users to be considerate of the costs they are imposing on the archive providers.

and collect calls, but the added complexity in a packetized network may make these schemes too costly.

How large would congestion prices be?

Consider the average cost of the NSFNET backbone in 1993: about $1 million per month, for about 60 billion packets per month. This implies a cost per packet (on average about 200 bytes) of about 1/600 of a cent. If there are 20 million users of the NSFNET backbone (10 per host computer), then full cost recovery of the NSFNET subsidy would imply an average monthly bill of about eight cents per person. If we accept the estimate that the total cost of the U.S. portion of the Internet is about ten times the NSFNET subsidy, we come up with 50 cents per person per month for full cost recovery. The revenue from congestion fees would presumably be significantly less than this amount.

The average cost of the Internet is so small today because the technology is so efficient: the packet-switching technology allows for very cost-effective use of existing lines and switches. If everyone only sent ASCII email, there would probably never be congestion problems on the Internet. However, new applications are creating huge demands for additional bandwidth. A video email message could easily use ten thousand more bits than a plain text ASCII email with the "same" information content, and providing this amount of incremental bandwidth could be quite expensive. Well-designed congestion prices would not charge everyone the average cost of this incremental bandwidth, but instead charge those users whose demands create the congestion and need for additional capacity.

What are the problems associated with Internet accounting?

One of the first necessary steps for implementing usage-based pricing (either for congestion control or multiple service class allocation) is to measure and account for usage. Accounting poses some serious problems. For one thing, packet service is inherently ill-suited to detailed usage accounting because every packet is independent. As an example, a one-minute phone call in a circuit-switched network requires one accounting entry in the usage database. But in a packet network that one-minute phone call would require around 2,500 average-sized packets; complete accounting for every packet would then require about 2,500 entries in the database. On the NSFNET alone, nearly 60 billion packets are being delivered each month. Maintaining detailed accounting by the packet similar to phone company accounting may be too expensive.

Another accounting problem concerns the granularity of the records. Presumably accounting detail is most useful when it traces traffic to the user. Certainly if the purpose of accounting is to charge prices as incentives, those incentives will be most effective if they affect the person actually making the usage decisions. But the network is at best capable of reliably identifying the originating host computer (just as phone networks only identify the phone number that placed a call, not the caller). Another layer of expensive and complex authorization and accounting software will be required on the host computer in order to track which user accounts are responsible for which packets.[14] Imagine, for instance, trying to account for student e-mail usage at a large public computer cluster.

One interesting approach has been tested and reported by Edell et al. (1995). They found that most traffic could be treated as connection-oriented by tracking the setup and tear-down of TCP sessions. On that basis, they were able to collect real-time usage accounting data on two T-1 lines leaving the UC Berkeley campus, and to introduce a pilot billing server. Another tool is NetTraMet, which has been used in New Zealand for several years to do network accounting (Brownlee 1996).

Accounting is more practical and less costly the higher the level of aggregation. For example, the NSFNET collected some information on usage by each of the subnetworks that connect to its backbone (although these data are based on a sample, not an exhaustive accounting for every packet). Whether accounting at lower levels of aggregation is worthwhile is a different question that depends sig-

---

14. Statistical sampling could lower costs substantially, but its acceptability depends on the level at which usage is measured—e.g., user or organization—and on the statistical distribution of demand. For example, strong serial correlation can cause problems.

nificantly on cost-saving innovations in internetwork accounting methods.

What are some of the economic problems for commerce on the Internet?

Imagine walking into a bookstore, looking up a book, finding it on the shelves, browsing through its neighbors on the shelf, and finally paying for it with a credit card at the counter. None of this required an explicit set of prenegotiated contracts or complicated protocols. The value of the Internet will be much greater if this kind of "spontaneous commerce" becomes commonplace. For this to become a reality, it will be necessary to design Internet search and discovery tools, browsing tools, and payment mechanisms. Research on all these topics is under way.

However, the Internet environment also offers new challenges. One big one is security: What protocols can ensure that your credit card number or, for that matter, the details of your purchase, remain private and secure?

How does electronic currency work?

What is the problem with electronic currency? After all, debit and automatic teller machine cards are in common use over networks. Credit cards are widely used over the telephone network. It turns out that there are several difficult problems to be solved, though the problems vary with the type of currency under discussion. For example, bank debit cards and automatic teller machine cards work because they have reliable authentication procedures based on both a physical device and knowledge of a private code. Digital currency over the network is more problematic because it is not possible to install physical devices and protect them from tampering on every workstation. Credit cards used over the phone network are relatively secure because phone tapping is difficult and costly, and there is no central database connected to the network that contains all of the voice-provided credit card numbers. When a credit card number is transmitted over the Internet in the clear, however, "sniffing" it is relatively easy and inexpensive, and following its path may lead to a massive database of valid card numbers.

A variety of schemes are being developed. See Economics and the Internet and the Telecom Information Resources Directory Web pages for comprehensive catalogs of different systems and research papers on this topic. Many of these systems use forms of public key cryptography to encrypt payment records. This is relatively straightforward for, say, credit card numbers, but becomes substantially more difficult if you want to ensure anonymity. See Chaum (1992) for a description of one such electronic cash system.

Why are so many different types of electronic currency being developed?

There are many different types of currency in ordinary, non-network use: cash, personal checks, cashier's checks, money orders, credit cards, debit cards, bearer bonds, and so forth. Each of these has different characteristics along a number of dimensions: anonymity, security, acceptability, transaction costs, divisibility, hardware independence, off-line operation, etc. Likewise, for a rich variety of commercial transactions to develop on the Internet, it will be necessary to have a variety of currency types in use.

How will electronic currency affect the money supply, taxes, illicit activity?

There is already a casino on the Internet, as well as some pornography. It is claimed that various hate groups have used electronic mail and bulletin boards for correspondence. Private electronic cash transactions on public networks are likely to facilitate tax evasion and illegal transactions (such as narcotics). No one knows how the introduction of electronic cash will affect macroeconomic variables.

How should information services be priced?

Our focus thus far has been on the technology, costs, and pricing of network transport. However, most of the value of the network is not in the transport, but in the value of the information being transported. For the full potential of the Internet to be realized it will be necessary to develop methods to charge for the value of information services available on the network.

There are vast troves of high-quality information (and probably equally large troves of dreck) currently available on the Internet, all available as free goods. Historically, there has been a strong base of volunteerism to collect and maintain data, software and other information archives. However, as usage explodes, volunteer providers are learning that they need revenues to cover their costs. And, of course, careful researchers may be skeptical about the quality of any information provided for free.

Charging for information resources is quite a difficult problem. A service like Compuserve charges customers by establishing a billing account. This requires that users obtain a password, and that the information provider implement a sophisticated accounting and billing infrastructure. However, one of the advantages of the Internet is that it is so decentralized: information sources are located on thousands of different computers. It would simply be too costly for every information provider to set up an independent billing system and give out separate passwords to each of its registered users. Users could end up with dozens of different authentication mechanisms for different services. Information discovery and retrieval would suffer from delays in setting up accounts as well.

A deeper problem for pricing information services is that our traditional pricing schemes are not appropriate. Most pricing is based on the measurement of replications: we pay for each copy of a book, each piece of furniture, and so forth. This usually works because the high cost of replication generally prevents us from avoiding payment. If we buy a table, we generally have to go to the manufacturer to buy one for ourselves; we cannot simply copy yours. With information goods the pricing-by-replication scheme breaks down. This has been a major problem for the software industry: once the sunk costs of software development are invested, replication costs essentially zero. The same is especially true for any form of information that can be transmitted over the network. Imagine, for example, that copy shops begin to make course packs available electronically. What is to stop a young entrepreneur from buying one copy and selling it at a lower price to everyone else in the class? This is a much greater problem even than that which publishers face from unauthorized photocopying since the cost of replication is essentially zero.

There is a small literature on the economics of copying that examines some of these issues. However, the same network connections that exacerbate the problems of pricing "information goods" may also help to solve some of these problems. For example, Cox (1992) describes the idea of "superdistribution" of "information objects" in which accessing a piece of information automatically sends a payment to the provider via the network. However, there are several problems remaining to be solved before such schemes can become widely used.

Regulation and Public Policy

What does the Internet mean for telecommunications regulation?

The growth of data networks like the Internet are an increasingly important motivation for regulatory reform of telecommunications. A primary principle of the current regulatory structure, for example, is that local phone service is a natural monopoly, and thus must be regulated. However, local phone companies face ever-increasing competition from data network services. For example, the fastest-growing component of telephone demand has been for fax transmission, but fax technology is better suited to packet-switching networks than to voice networks, and faxes are increasingly transmitted over the Internet. As integrated services networks emerge, they will provide an alternative to voice calls and video-conferencing as well. This "bypass" is already occurring on the advanced private networks that many corporations, such as General Electric, are building.

As a result, the trend seems to be toward removing barriers to cross-ownership of local phone and cable TV companies. The regional Bell operating companies have filed a motion to remove the remaining restrictions of the Modified Final Judgment that created them (with the 1984 breakup of AT&T). The White House, Congress, and the Federal Communications Commission are all developing new models of regulation, with a strong bias toward deregulation (for example, see the Telecom Act of 1996).

Internet transport itself is currently unregulated. This is consistent with the principle that common carriers are natural monopolies and must be regulated, but the services provided over those common carriers are not. However, this principle has never been consistently applied to phone companies: the services provided over the phone lines are also regulated. Many public interest groups are now arguing for similar regulatory requirements for the Internet.

One issue is universal access, the assurance of basic service for all citizens at a very low price. But what is basic service? Is it merely a data line, or a multimedia integrated services connection? And in an increasingly competitive market for communications services, where should the money to subsidize universal access be raised? High-value uses for which monopoly providers traditionally charged premium prices are increasingly subject to competition and bypass.

A related question is whether the government should provide some data network services as public goods. Some initiatives are already under way. For instance, the Clinton administration has required that all published government documents be available in electronic form. Another current debate concerns the appropriate access subsidy for primary and secondary teachers and students.

What are some of the competing visions for the National Information Infrastructure (NII)?

There are probably as many visions of the NII as there are nodes on the Internet. But the two broad models are the Internet model ("many to any") and the cable TV model ("broadcast to couch potatoes"). A well-written discussion of the Internet model is available in National Academy of Sciences (1994). One critical issue is the amount of bandwidth provided from the home. The Internet model sees bandwidth as being more or less symmetric; the cable TV model sees a much more limited outbound bandwidth: essentially enough for home shopping. As one wit has said about interactive TV networks, "how much bandwidth do you need to send 'I want it' to the Home Shopping Network?"

What will be the market structure of the information highway?

If different components of local phone and cable TV networks are deregulated, what degree of competition is likely? Similar questions arise for data networks. For example, a number of observers believe that by ceding backbone transport to commercial providers, the federal government has endorsed above-cost pricing by a small oligopoly of providers. Looking ahead, equilibrium market structures for the emerging integrated services networks may be quite different from those for the current specialized networks.

One interesting question is the interaction between pricing schemes and market structure. If competing backbones continue to offer only connection pricing, would an entrepreneur be able to skim off high-value users by charging usage prices but offering more efficient congestion control? Alternatively, would a flat-rate connection price provider be able to undercut usage-price providers, by capturing a large share of low-value "baseload" customers who prefer to pay for congestion with delay rather than cash? The interaction between pricing and market structure may have important policy implications because certain types of pricing may rely on compatibilities between competing networks that will enable efficient accounting and billing. Thus, compatibility or interoperability regulations similar to the interconnect rules imposed on regional Bell operating companies may be needed.

How will the choice of service architecture affect the network services available?

The architecture of a network can have important implications for the nature of goods available. For instance, the Internet provides access to an incredibly diverse array of information sources, from personal home pages to fully searchable and professionally managed archives. We believe that the salient feature that drives the diversity of the Internet is that the network provides only bit transportation services; it is up to the end hosts to construct higher-level applications on top of this raw transport service. This architecture has the great advantage that it need not be modified as new applications arise because applications are implemented entirely at the end hosts and no centralized authority needs to approve such implementations. We call such an architecture application-blind.

There are also a wide variety of services available via 900 numbers on the phone network. In this case the network is application-aware (voice telephony circuits) but content-blind. In comparison, the offerings of cable television, which is content-aware, are rather limited in scope. To what extent do these differences reflect the effect of architecture on the provision of content? MacKie-Mason, Shenker, and Varian (1996) explore this question, focusing on opportunities for price discrimination, service provider liability, the costs of implementing an aware architecture, and the effects of clutter from the availability of too many applications or too much content.

What are other important economic problems for the future Internet?

How will network distribution and electronic publishing affect intellectual property rights?

One immediate challenge for information service provision over public networks is the definition and protection of intellectual property rights. Existing intellectual property law is far from adequate to handle digital materials. The standard motivation for copyright is that it will encourage the creation and distribution of new works. But if copies of digital works can be produced at zero cost and distributed with perfect fidelity, what will this do to the incentive to produce originals? Several writers have suggested that a new conception of the value of intellectual property, and a new focus on the locus of the value-added, will be necessary. See, for example, Barlow (1994) and Dyson (1995).

What problems will the Internet face in the next two years?

We think that the major network service challenge in the next two years will be to find ways to support interconnection. The technical

problems are relatively straightforward; it's the accounting and economic problems that are tricky. We think it inevitable that a system
of settlements will emerge.

What are settlements? When you place a call to Paris, you transit
at least three telecommunications networks: your local provider, a
long-distance company, and France Telecom. These companies keep
track of calls and make payments to each other based on how much
traffic flows in each direction through their networks. There is a
similar system in place for post offices.

Some economists have suggested that such a settlement policy will
likely arise for the Internet. Since one carrier imposes costs on
another by sending it incremental traffic, it seems appropriate that
some monetary payments accompany this traffic. Others argue that
traffic flows are sufficiently symmetric that a "no settlements" policy
is workable, especially given the nearly zero incremental cost of
transport (as long as capacity is sufficient). Indeed, to date, interconnected Internet networks have not used settlements.

Nonetheless, resource usage is not always symmetric, and it appears that the opportunities to free ride on capacity investments by
other network providers are increasing. For example, suppose a new
Internet provider hosts a number of World Wide Web servers near
a NAP, and then purchases a very short connection to the NAP. Web
traffic flows are very asymmetric: a handful of bytes come in from
users making requests, and megabytes are sent back out in response.
Thus, for the low cost of leasing a short-distance connection to a
NAP, a provider could place a huge load onto other networks to
distribute to their users, while this provider does not have to deliver
much incoming traffic.[15] Other networks provide substantial transit
between two other networks, and thus do not receive a direct share
of the end-user payment for either end.

The new NAPs (funded by the NSF) allow for the possibility that
interconnected networks will want to implement settlements. The

---

15. If this example does not seem compelling because the costs are borne by the networks
whose users are generating the demand for the large Web traffic flows, then imagine that
the free-riding provider instead services junk email servers that send out vast quantities
of unsolicited email. Other users do not want to reach these servers, so this network does
not have to provide capacity to handle incoming traffic.

conditions of use for the NAPs explicitly permit settlements, but they must be negotiated independently by the interconnecting networks; as of this writing, it appears that none have yet done so. Moreover, the necessary technical, accounting, and economic infrastructure is not in place.

What economic problems will the Internet face in the next three to five years?

New protocols such as Real-Time Protocol (RTP), Reservation Protocol (RSVP), Internet Protocol version 6 (IPv6) and ATM will become more widespread in this timeframe. Such protocols will be better able to deal with integrated services and congestion management. This should allow for new applications such as video-based conferencing and collaboration tools to become widely used. Also, we expect to see some progress made on standardizing new tools for information discovery, search, and collaboration.

What economic problems will the Internet face in the next five to ten years?

Once flexible protocols and killer applications are available, users will likely demand considerably more bandwidth. For example, all-optical networks could spring up in high-density areas (Gilder 1992). But along with this increase in demand for bandwidth will come a recognition of the commodity nature of network transport. The industry will have to find some way to recover fixed costs. One approach is common carriage and regulation, but we hope that less regulated and more competitive solutions can be found.

Further Reading

We have written several papers that provide further details on Internet technology, costs, and pricing problems (see, e.g., MacKie-Mason and Varian 1995b, 1995a, 1995c, and 1995d). We maintain two large, comprehensive WWW servers containing links to related information. A comprehensive catalog of electronic materials concerning the economics of the Internet can be found at the

"Economics and the Internet" site (Varian 1994). A comprehensive directory of information available on the Internet concerning tele-communications more broadly is available at the Telecom Information Resources Directory site.

References

Baeza-Yates, Ricardo, José M. Piquer, and Patricio V. Poblete. 1993. The Chilean Internet connection, or, I never promised you a rose garden. In proceedings of INET '93.

Barlow, John Perry. 1994. The economy of ideas. *Wired* 2(3). Available from URL: http://ippsweb.ipps.lsa.umich.edu/ipps744/docs/economy-ideas.html.

Bohn, Roger, Hans-Werner Braun, Kimberly Claffy, and Stephen Wolff. 1993. Mitigat-ing the coming Internet crunch: Multiple service levels via precedence. Technical report, University of California at San Diego Supercomputer Center and NSF. Avail-able from URL: ftp://ftp.sdsc.edu/pub/sdsc/anr/papers/precedence.ps.Z.

Braun, Hans-Werner, and Kimberly Claffy. 1993. Network analysis in support of Internet policy requirements. In proceedings of INET '93. Available from URL: ftp://www.sdsc.edu/pub/sdsc/anr/papers/inet93.policy.ps.Z.

Brownlee, Nevil. 1994. New Zealand experiences with network traffic charging. *Con-neXions* 8(12). Available from URL: http://www.auckland.ac.nz/net/Account-ing/nze.html.

————. 1996. New Zealand's experiences with network traffic charging. In *Internet economics*, ed. Lee McKnight and Joseph Bailey. Cambridge, Mass.: MIT Press.

Carter, Michael, and Graeme Guthrie. 1994. Pricing Internet: The New Zealand experience. Technical report, University of Canterbury, Christchurch, New Zealand. Available at URL: ftp://gopher.econ.lsa.umich.edu/pub/Archive/nz-internet-pric-ing.ps.Z.

CERFnet. Network Service Provider Interconnections and Exchange Points. Avail-able at URL: http://www.cerf.net/cerfnet/about/interconnects.html.

Chaum, David. 1992. Achieving electronic privacy. *Scientific American* 8:96–101. Avail-able at URL: A http://www.digicash.com/publish/sciam.html.

Cocchi, Ron, Deborah Estrin, Scott Shenker, and Lixia Zhang. 1992. Pricing in computer networks: Motivation, formulation, and example. Technical report, Uni-versity of Southern California, October 1992. Available from URL: ftp://ftp.parc.xerox.com/pub/net-research/pricing2.ps.Z.

Cox, Brad. 1992. What if there is a silver bullet and the competition gets it first? *Journal of Object-oriented Programming* 10(6). Available from URL: http://reposi-tory.gmu.edu/bcox/Cox/CoxWhatIfSilverBullet.html.

61
Economic FAQs About the Internet

Dyson, Esther. 1995. Intellectual property on the net. *Wired* 3(7). Available from URL: http://www.eff.org/pub/Publications/Esther_Dyson/ip_on_the_net.html.

Edell, Richard J., Nick McKeown, and Praveen P. Varaiya. 1995. Billing users and pricing for tcp. *IEEE Journal on Selected Areas in Communications* 9. Available from URL: http://www-path.eecs.berkeley.edu/ edell/papers/Billing/article.ps.

Fazio, Dennis. 1995. Hang on to your packets: The information superhighway heads to valley fair. Technical report, Minnesota Regional Network. Available at URL: http://www.mr.net/announcements/valleyfair.html.

Gilder, George. 1992. The coming of the fibersphere. *Forbes ASAP* 10(12): 111–124. Available from URL: http://www.seas.upenn.edu/ gaj1/fiber.html.

Gupta, Alok, Dale O. Stahl, and Andrew B. Whinston. 1994. Managing the Internet as an economic system. Technical report, University of Texas at Austin, July 1994. Available from URL: http://cism.bus.utexas.edu/ravi/pricing.ps.Z.

———. 1996. A priority pricing approach to manage multi-service class networks in real time. In *Internet economics,* ed. Lee McKnight and Joseph Bailey. Cambridge, Mass.: MIT Press.

MacKie-Mason, Jeffrey K., and Hal Varian. 1995a. Pricing the Internet. In Public Access to the Internet, ed. Brian Kahin and James Keller. Englewood Cliffs, N.J.: Prentice-Hall. Available from URL: ftp://gopher.econ.lsa.umich.edu/pub/Papers/Pricing_the_Internet.ps.Z.

———. 1995b. Some economics of the Internet. In Networks, infrastructure and the new task for regulation, ed. Werner Sichel. Ann Arbor, Mich.: University of Michigan Press. Available from URL: ftp://gopher.econ.lsa.umich.edu/pub/Papers/Economics_of_Internet.ps.Z.

———. 1995c. Pricing congestible network resources. *IEEE Journal of Selected Areas in Communications* (September). Available at URL: http://www.spp.umich.edu/ipps/papers/info-nets/useFAQs/useFAQs.html.

———. 1995d. Some FAQs about usage-based pricing. *Computer Networks and ISDN Systems* 28. Available from URL: http://www.spp.umich.edu/ipps/papers/info-nets/useFAQs/useFAQs.html. Also in proceedings of WWW '94, Chicago, Illinois; and proceedings of the Association of Research Librarians 1994.

MacKie-Mason, Jeffrey K., John Murphy, and Liam Murphy. 1996. The role of responsive pricing on the Internet. In *Internet economics,* ed. Lee McKnight and Joseph Bailey. Cambridge, Mass.: MIT Press. Available from URL: http://www.spp.umich.edu/spp/papers/jmm/respons.pdf.

MacKie-Mason, Jeffrey K., Scott Shenker, and Hal Varian. 1996. Network architecture and content provision: an economic analysis. *Telecommunications Policy.* 1996. Available from URL: http://www.spp.umich.edu/spp/papers/jmm/clutter.pdf.

Markoff, John. 1993. Traffic jams already on the information highway. *New York Times,* November 3: A1.

(Merit Architecture) Merit Network, Inc. Overview of the new networking architecture. Available at URL: http://www.merit.edu/nsf.architecture/.index.html.

(Merit Statistics) Merit Network, Inc. NSFNET statistics. Available at URL: http://www.merit.edu/nsfnet/statistics/.

Murphy, John, and Liam Murphy. 1994. Bandwidth allocation by pricing in ATM networks. In proceedings of IFIP Broadband Communications '94, Paris, France, March 1994. Available from URL: ftp://gopher.econ.lsa.umich.edu/pub/Archive/Murphy_Bandwidth_Pricing.ps.Z.

National Academy of Sciences. 1994. Realizing the information future. Washington, D.C.: National Academy Press. Available from URL: http://xerxes.nas.edu:70/0h/nap/online/rtif/.

Network Wizards. Internet domain survey. Available from URL: http://www.nw.com/zone/WWW/top.html.

Telecommunications Act of 1996. Public Law No. 104-104, Section X, 110 Stat 56. http://thomas.loc.gov/cgi-bin/query/z?c104:s.652.enr:.

Telecom Information Resources Directory, a World Wide Web server. Jeffrey K. Mackie-Mason. Located at URL: http://www.spp.umich.edu/telecom-info.html.

Varian, Hal. 1994. Economics and the Internet, a World Wide Web server. Available from URL: http://www.sims.berkeley.edu/resources/infoecon.

Vickrey, W. 1961. Counterspeculation, auctions, and competitive sealed tenders. *Journal of Finance*. vol. 16, pp. 8–37.

Zhang, L., S. Deering, D. Estrin, S. Shenker, and D. Zappala. 1993. RSVP: A resource ReSerVation protocol. *IEEE Network Magazine*. Available from URL: ftp://ftp.parc.xerox.com/pub/net-research/rsvp.ps.Z.

The Economics of Layered Networks

Jiong Gong and Padmanabhan Srinagesh

Introduction

The creation of a National Information Infrastructure (NII) will require large investments in network facilities and services, computing hardware and software, information appliances, training, and other technologies. The investment required to provide all business and households with broadband access to the NII is estimated to be in the hundreds of billions of dollars; large investments in the other components of the NII will also be required. In *The National Information Infrastructure: Agenda for Action,* the Clinton administration states: "The private sector will lead the deployment of the NII."

What network architecture and economic framework should guide the private sector's investment and deployment decisions? Is the Open Data Network (ODN) described by the NRENAISSANCE Committee[1] an appropriate economic framework for the communications infrastructure that will support NII applications? A key component of the ODN is the unbundled bearer service, defined as "an abstract bit-level transport service" available at different qualities of service appropriate for the range of NII applications. The committee states that "[t]he bearer services are not part of the ODN unless they can be priced separately from the higher level services . . ." (p. 52).

---

1. *Realizing the Information Future: The Internet and Beyond.* NRENAISSANCE Committee, National Research Council (Washington, D.C.: National Academy Press, 1994).

The rationale for this requirement is that it "is in the interest of free entry at various levels" (p. 52).

What effect will the unbundled bearer service proposed by the NRENAISSANCE Committee have on the investment incentives of network providers in the private sector? Will carriers that invest in long-lived assets be given a fair opportunity to recover their costs? This chapter provides a preliminary discussion of the economics of an unbundled bearer service.

Convergence and Emerging Competition

Technological advances are rapidly blurring traditional industry boundaries and fostering competition between firms that did not previously compete with one another. For example, cable television providers in the United Kingdom (some of which are now partly owned by U.S. telecommunications firms) have been allowed to offer telephone service to their subscribers since 1981, and now serve more than 500,000 homes.[2] Numerous telephone companies in the United States are currently testing the delivery of video services to households over their networks. In addition, new firms have recently entered markets that were not subject to major inroads in the past. Competitive Access Providers (CAPs) have begun to serve business customers in the central business districts of many large cities in competition with Local Exchange Carriers (LECs), and Direct Broadcast Satellite (DBS) services have begun to compete with cable providers. In sum, new entrants are using new technologies to compete with incumbents, and incumbents in previously separate industries are beginning to compete with one another.

Theoretical Approaches to the Economics of Pricing under Differing Market Structures

In a pure monopoly, a variety of price structures may be consistent with cost recovery, and the firm (or regulators) may be able to select price structures that promote political or social goals such as univer-

2. "Cable TV Moves into Telecom Markets," *Business Communications Review* (November 1994): 43–48.

sal service or unbundling of raw transport. In a competitive market, this flexibility may not exist. Under perfect competition (which assumes no barriers to entry and many small firms), the price per unit will be equal to the marginal cost per unit (where costs are defined to include the opportunity costs of all resources, including capital, that are used in production). There is no pricing flexibility. When neither of these pure market forms exist, economic theory does not provide any general conclusions regarding equilibrium price structures or industry boundaries. While substantial progress has been made in developing game theory and its application to oligopoly (Fudenberg and Tirole 1992), no completely general results on pricing are available. This is particularly true in the dynamic context where interdependencies between current and future decisions are explicitly considered.

Some theoretical work in this area is summarized in Shapiro (1988). An important result in game theory asserts that no general rules can be developed. The best-known result about repeated games is the well-known "folk theorem." This theorem asserts that if the game is repeated infinitely often and players are sufficiently patient, then "virtually anything" is an "equilibrium outcome."[3] In the absence of general results, specific features of the industry may provide a useful starting point for economic analysis.

The economic analysis of competition among Internet Service Providers is further complicated by the presence of externalities and excess capacity. Call externalities arise because every communication involves at least two parties, the originator(s) and the receiver(s). Benefits (possibly negative) are obtained by all participants in a call, but usually only one of the participants is billed for the call. A decision by one person to call another can generate an uncompensated benefit for the called party, creating a call externality. Network externalities arise because the private benefit to any one individual of joining a network, as measured by the value he places on communicating with others, is less than the social benefits of his joining the network, which would include the benefits to all other subscribers of communicating with him. Again, the subscription decision creates benefits that are not compensated through the market mechanism.

3. See Fudenberg and Tirole (1988).

Mitchell and Vogelsang (1991) argue that the prices chosen by competitive markets are not economically efficient (in the sense of maximizing aggregate consumer and producer benefits) when externalities are present.

Economides and Himmelberg (1994) also argue that "[i]ndustries with network externalities exhibit positive critical mass—i.e., networks of small sizes are not observed at any price." The consequent need to build large networks, together with the high cost of network construction (estimated by some to be $13,000–$18,000 per mile for cable systems),[4] implies a need for large investments in long-lived facilities. The major cost of constructing fiber-optic links is in the trenching and labor cost of installation. The cost of the fiber is a relatively small proportion of the total cost of construction and installation. It is therefore common practice to install "excess" fiber. According to the Federal Communications Commission (FCC),[5] between 40 and 50% of the fiber installed by the typical interexchange carrier is "dark"; the lasers and electronics required for transmission are not in place. The comparable number for the major local operating companies is between 50 and 80%. The presence of excess capacity in one important input is a further complicating factor affecting equilibrium prices and industry structure.

To summarize: A full economic model of the networking infrastructure that supports the NII would need to account for at least the following features:

• oligopolistic competition among a few large companies that invest in the underlying physical communications infrastructure;

• network and call externalities at the virtual network level; and

• large sunk costs and excess capacity in underlying transmission links.

An analysis of the optimal industry structure is well beyond the scope of this chapter; it is a promising area for future research. This chapter focuses on the implications of two of these issues—oligopo-

4. Larry J. Yokell, "Cable TV Moves into Telecom Markets," *Business Communication Review* (November 1994): 43–48.

5. *Fiber Deployment Update* (May 1994).

listic competition and sunk cost with excess capacity—for industry structure and the unbundled bearer service. The Internet is used as a case study to illustrate trends, and provides a factual background for future analyses. This chapter provides a description of the current Internet industry structure, current Internet approaches to bundling/unbundling and reselling, some recent examples of the difficulties raised by resale in other communications markets, and the increasing use of long-term contracts between customers and their service providers. It also details the implications for the unbundled bearer service.

Layered Networks

The Internet is a virtual network that is built on top of facilities and services provided by telecommunications carriers. Internet Service Providers (ISPs) previously located routers at their network nodes, and interconnected these nodes (redundantly) with point-to-point private lines leased from telecommunications companies. More recently, ISPs have been moving from a private-line infrastructure to fast-packet services such as Frame Relay, Switched Multimegabit Data Service (SMDS) and Asynchronous Mode Transfer (ATM) service. For example, providers with national backbones in 1995 had the following architecture:

• PSI runs its Internet Protocol (IP) services over its Frame Relay network, which is run over its ATM network, which in turn is run over point-to-point circuits leased from five carriers;

• AlterNet runs part of its IP network over an ATM backbone leased from MFS and Wiltel;

• ANS's backbone consists of 45 Mbps links leased from MCI;

• SprintLink's backbone consists of its own 45 Mbps facilities; and

• CERFnet, a regional network based in San Diego, uses SMDS service obtained from Pacific Bell to connect its backbone nodes together.[6]

---

6. Fuller descriptions of these networks can be obtained from their Web pages. The URLs are: http://www.psi.com; http://www.alter.net; http://www.sprint.com; and http://www.cerf.net.

These examples reveal a variety of technical approaches to the provision of IP transport. They also show different degrees of vertical integration, with Sprint the most integrated and AlterNet the least integrated ISP in the group listed above. The variety of organizational forms in use raises the following question: Can ISPs with varying degrees of integration coexist in an industry equilibrium, or are there definite cost advantages that will lead to only one kind of firm surviving in equilibrium? The answer to this question hinges on the relative cost structures of integrated and unintegrated firms. The costs of integrated firms depend on the costs of producing the underlying transport fabric on which IP transport rides. The cost structures of unintegrated firms are determined in large part by the prices they pay for transport services (such as ATM and DS3 services) obtained from telecommunications carriers. These prices in turn are determined by market forces. More generally, the layered structure of data communications services leads to a recursive relationship in which the cost structure of services provided in any layer is determined by prices charged by providers one layer below. In this layered structure, a logical starting point for analysis is the lowest layer: the point-to-point links on which a variety of fast-packet services ride.

Competition at the Bottom Layer

For illustrative purposes, consider a common set of services underlying the Internet today. At the very bottom of the hierarchy, physical resources are used to construct the links and switches or multiplexers that create point-to-point channels. In the emerging digital environment, Time Division Multiplexing (TDM) in the digital telephone system creates the channels out of very long-lived inputs (including fiber-optic cables). The sunk costs are substantial.

Large network service providers in the United States like AT&T, MCI, Sprint, and Wiltel serve all major city-pairs with national fiber-optic networks. Each of these providers has invested in the fiber and electronics required to deliver point-to-point channel services, and, as was stated earlier, each has substantial excess capacity. The cost structure of providing channels includes: high sunk costs of construction, the costs of lasers and electronics needed to light the fiber, costs of switching, high costs of customer acquisition (marketing and sales), costs associated with turning service on and off (provisioning, credit checks, setting up a billing account, etc.), costs of maintaining and monitoring the network to assure that customer expectations for service are met, costs of terminating customers, and general administrative costs. The incremental cost (or short-run marginal cost) of carrying traffic is zero, as long as there is excess capacity.

If all owners of national fiber-optic facilities produced an undifferentiated product (point-to-point channels) and competed solely on price, economic theory predicts that they would soon go out of business: "With equally efficient firms, constant marginal costs, and homogeneous products, the only Nash equilibrium in prices, i.e., Bertrand equilibrium, is for each firm to price at marginal cost."[7] If this theory is correct[8] and firms compete on the basis of price, a firm could recover the one-time costs of service activation and deactivation through a nonrecurring service charge, and recover ongoing customer support costs by billing for assistance, but they would not be able to recover their sunk costs. Industry leaders seem to be aware of this possibility. Recently, John Malone, CEO of TCI, stated: ". . . we'll end up with a much lower marginal cost structure and that will allow us to underprice our competitors."[9]

The history of leased line prices in recent years does reveal a strong downward trend in prices. According to *Business Week*,[10] private line prices fell by 80% between 1989 and 1994, and this is consistent with Bertrand competition. During the same period there was also a dramatic increase in the use of term and volume discounts. AT&T now offers customers a standard month-to-month

7. See Shapiro (1988).

8. An example of an alternative theoretical approach is Sharkey and Sibley (1993). Other circumstances that may prevent Bertrand competition from happening are bundling technical and nontechnical elements to differentiate service, including different pricing strategies like usage sensitive pricing (Clark 1995; Gupta et al. 1995; and Brownlee 1995); the affect of marketing in creating band recognition; and different quality of services and customer support.

9. "Brave Talk from the Foxhole," *Business Week* (April 10, 1995): 60.

10. "Dangerous Living in Telecom's Top Tier," (September 12, 1994): 90.

tariff for 1.544 Mbps service and charges a nonrecurring fee, a fixed monthly fee, and a monthly rate per mile. Customers who are willing to sign a five-year contract and commit to spending $1 million per month are offered a discount of 57% off the standard month-to-month rates. Smaller discounts apply to customers who choose shorter terms and lower commitment volumes: a one-year-term commitment to spend $2,000 per month obtains a discount of 18%.[11] The overall trend toward lower prices masks a more complex reality. "There are two types of tariffs: 'front of the book' rates, which are paid by smaller and uninformed large customers, and 'back of the book' rates, which are offered to the customers who are ready to defect to another carrier and to customers who know enough to ask for them. The 'front of the book' rates continue their relentless 5 to 7 percent annual increases."[12] In 1994, AT&T filed over 1,200 special contracts, and MCI filed over 400.[13]

There are some theoretical approaches that address the issues discussed above. Williamson's (1988) discussion of nonstandard commercial contracting as a means of sharing risk between the producer and consumers is relevant to the term commitments described above. In addition to risk reduction, long-term contracts reduce customer churn, which often ranges from 20 to 50% per year in competitive telecommunications markets.[14] As service activation and termination costs can be high, reduction of churn can be an effective cost-saving measure.

There appears to be an empirical trend toward term/volume commitments that encourage consumers of private line services to establish an exclusive, long-term relationship with a single carrier. There is little published information on long-distance fast-packet prices. According to Toth (1995), none of the long-distance carriers or enhanced service providers (e.g., CompuServe) tariff their Frame

11. Tariffs change rapidly in the increasingly competitive environment, and current tariffs may differ from those reported in this chapter.

12. Hills (1995).

13. Ibid.

14. See FCC Docket 93-197, Report and Order, 1.12.95, p. 8 for statistics on AT&T's churn in the business market.

Relay offerings. Some intraLATA (intra-Local Access Transport Area) tariffs filed by Local Exchange Carriers do offer term and volume (per PVC Permanent Virtual Circuit) discounts, and the economic forces that give rise to term/volume commitments for private lines have probably resulted in term/volume commitments for long-distance fast-packet services as well.

Competition among Internet Service Providers

The effect of term/volume commitments on private lines and fast-packet services affects the cost structures of ISPs that do not own their own transport infrastructure. It may be expected that large ISPs that lease their transport infrastructures will sign multiyear contracts, possibly on an exclusive basis, with a single carrier. These providers will then have sunk costs since they will have minimum payments due for a fixed period to their carriers. Competition at this level will then be similar to competition at the lower level, and we may expect to see term/volume contracts emerge in the Internet. A quick survey of Internet sites shows this to be the case. For example, in January 1995, AlterNet offered customers with a T1 connection a 10% discount if they committed to a two-year term. Global Connect, an ISP in Virginia, offers customers an annual rate that is ten times the monthly rate, amounting to a 17% discount for a one-year commitment. There are many other examples of this sort.

The Internet is beginning to resemble the private-line market in one other aspect: prices are increasingly being viewed as proprietary. ISPs that used to post prices on their File Transfer Protocol (FTP) or Web server now ask potential customers to call for quotes. Presumably, prices are determined after negotiation. This development mirrors the practice of long-distance carriers to use special contracts that are not offered on an open basis at the "front of the book," but are hidden at the back.

Economics of Resale

Kellogg, Thorne, and Huber (1992) describe the history of the FCC's decision on resale and shared use. Noam (1994) analyzes the impact of competition between common carriers and contract carriers (such as systems integrators and resellers), and concludes that common carriage cannot survive the competitive struggle. Recent events lend some credence to this view. According to one recent study, "resold long distance services will constitute an increasing portion of the total switched services revenue in coming years, growing at a compound annual growth rate of 31% from 1993 to 1995. . . . The number is expected to rise to $11.6 billion, or 19.2% of the estimated total switched services market in 1995."[15] The growth of resale of cellular services suggests that there are equally attractive resale opportunities in this market.[16] In the Internet, some ISPs charge resellers a higher price than they charge their own customers.[17] Other ISPs, such as Sprinkling, make no distinction between resellers and end-users. Facilities-based carriers have had a rocky relationship with resellers, and both carriers and resellers have often resorted to the courts.[18]

The pricing model that is emerging appears to resemble rental arrangements in the real estate market. In the New York area, low-quality hotel rooms are available for about $20 per hour. Far better hotel rooms are available for $200 per day (which is a large discount off 24 times $20). Roomy apartments are available for monthly rentals at much less than 30 days times $200 per day. And $6,000 per month can be used to buy luxury apartments with a 30-year mortgage. Term commitments are rewarded in the real estate market, where sunk costs and excess capacity are (currently) quite common. The telecommunications industry appears to be moving in the same direction. Contracts are not limited to five-year terms; MFS and SNET recently signed a 20-year contract under which MFS will lease fiber from SNET,[19] and Bell Atlantic has a 25-year contract with the

15. *Telecommunications Alert* 13, No. 2 (February 1995): 6.

16. "Restless in Seattle," *Forbes* (March 27, 1995): 72.

17. For example, Alternet's policy in January 1995 was: "Because wholesale customers use more of our backbone facilities and because they also place greater demand on our staff, we charge more for our wholesale services."

18. For example, see "Oregon Jury Decides against AT&T in Reseller Case," *Telecommunications Reports* (July 4, 1994): 34; and "AT&T Sues Reseller for Unauthorized Trademark Use," *Telecommunications Reports* (November 7, 1994): 26.

19. *Telco Business Report* (February 14, 1994): 4.

Pentagon.[20] The term structure of contracts is an important area for empirical and theoretical research.

Implications for Unbundled Bearer Services

Unbundled bearer services have much in common with common carriage: both approaches facilitate greater competition at higher layers (in content, with common carriage, and in enhanced services of all types with the bearer service). The dilemma facing policymakers is that, if Noam (1994) is right, competition in an undifferentiated commodity at the lower level may not be feasible. In his words: "The long term result might be a gradual disinvestment in networks, the re-establishment of monopoly, or price cartels and oligopolistic pricing."[21] Thus policies promoting competition in the provision of unbundled bearer services among owners of physical networks may ultimately fail. In the Internet, for example, some service providers charge resellers a higher price than they charge end-users. The market may be moving toward contract carriage based on term/ volume commitments and increasing efforts at differentiation, and away from the ideal of an unbundled bearer service. Should unbundled bearer services be aligned with this trend by being defined as a spectrum of term/volume contracts? The competitive mode that is emerging is quite complex, and the effects of unbundling in this environment are hard to predict.

Even if unbundled bearer services become a market reality as envisioned by policymakers, some sort of regulatory mechanism may need to be instituted so that investments in physical facilities may be encouraged and recouped. Bertrand competition with marginal cost less than average cost entails the making of unbundled bearer services into a natural monopoly. Therefore the question becomes how can competition and regulation be appropriately balanced. If a competitive bearer services market is unlikely to develop, does it always justify government regulation perhaps at an even higher social cost?

20. Ray Smith, CEO of Bell Atlantic, in an interview in *Wired Magazine* (February 1995): 113.

21. Noam (1994): 447.

Sarkar (1995) provides an extensive exposition on this important policy issue.

Conclusions

This chapter does not suggest specific architectures or policies for the emerging NII. It identifies some difficult economic problems that may need to be addressed. These are the familiar ones related to resale and interconnection, with the added complication of competition among multiple owners of geographically coextensive physical networks. This chapter has provided references to recent developments in telecommunications markets, and identified strands in the economics literature that are relevant to the central issues raised by the bearer service.

There is an urgent need for a clearer economic analysis of these issues, and it is critical that the analysis pay close attention to the realities of competition and evolving competitive strategy. Three specific areas appear particularly promising:

• empirical analysis of evolving price structures that quantifies the movement from pricing by the minute (the original Message Toll Service) to pricing by the decade (contract tariffs);

• game theory models of competition in long-term contracts with sunk costs; and

• experimental approaches to network economics (Plott, Sugiyama, and Elbaz 1994).

References

Brownlee, N. 1996. New Zealand's experience with network traffic charging. In *Internet economics*, ed. Lee McKnight and Joseph Bailey. Cambridge, Mass.: MIT Press.

Clark, D. 1996. A model of cost allocation and pricing in the Internet. In *Internet economics*, ed. Lee McKnight and Joseph Bailey. Cambridge, Mass.: MIT Press.

Economides, N., and C. Himmelberg. 1994. Critical mass and network size. Working paper, New York University.

Fudenberg, D., and J. Tirole. 1988. Noncooperative game theory. In *Handbook of industrial organization*, ed. R. Schmalensee and R. Willig. Amsterdam: North Holland.

Fudenberg, D., and J. Tirole. 1992. *Game theory.* Cambridge, Mass.: MIT Press.

Gupta, A., D. Stahl, and A. Whinston. 1996. A priority pricing approach to manage multi-service class networks in real-time. In *Internet economics,* ed. Lee McKnight and Joseph Bailey, Cambridge, Mass.: MIT Press.

Hills, M.T. 1995. Carrier pricing increases continue. *Business Communications Review* (February): 32.

Kellog, M., J. Thorne, and P. Huber. 1992. *Federal telecommunications law.* Boston: Little, Brown and Company.

Mitchell, B., and I. Vogelsang. 1991. *Telecommunications pricing: Theory and practice.* Cambridge: Cambridge University Press.

Noam, E. 1994. Beyond liberalization II. The impending doom of common carriage. *Telecommunications Policy:* 435–452.

Plott, C., A. Sugiyama, and G. Elbaz. 1994. Economics of scale, natural monopoly, and imperfect competition in an experimental market. *Southern Economic Journal* (October): 261–287.

Sarkar, M. 1995. An assessment of pricing mechanisms for the Internet. In *Internet economics,* ed. Lee McKnight and Joseph Bailey. Cambridge, Mass.: MIT Press.

Shapiro, C. 1988. Theories of oligopoly behavior. In *Handbook of industrial organization,* ed. R. Schmalensee and R. Willig. Amsterdam: North Holland.

Sharkey, W., and D. Sibley. 1993. A Bertrand model of pricing and entry. *Economic Letters* 41: 199–206.

Williamson, O.E. 1988 Transaction cost economics. In *Handbook of industrial organization,* ed. R. Schmalensee and R. Willig. Amsterdam: North Holland.

Internet Pricing in Practice

Nevil Brownlee

Introduction

The New Zealand experience with Internet pricing has implications
for the viability of usage sensitive pricing models for the Internet.
This chapter first provides some background information on the
development of the Internet in New Zealand, and then describes
how the Tuia and Kawaihiko networks, two of New Zealand's
Internet backbones, are managed. Cost sharing through usage sensitive pricing is shown to be effective for managing Internet growth
in New Zealand.

New Zealand's Internet Gateway

New Zealand's link to the Internet began as a joint development
project with NASA and formed part of the Pacific Communications
program, PACCOM. The gateway itself was known as the PACCOM
gateway, but was later renamed NZGate. NZGate was managed by
Waikato University on behalf of Tuia, an incorporated society whose
mission is to further the networking interests of the Research and
Education community within New Zealand. Tuia is a Maori word
meaning bound together.

NZGate began in April 1989 with a 9,600 bps analog cable link to
Hawaii. Connectivity inside New Zealand was provided by PACNET
(Telecom's public X.25 service) and Colored Book software at each

of the universities. PACNET access speeds were typically 9,600 bits per second.

One slightly unusual aspect of NZGate was that although NASA provided generous support for the costs at the U.S. end of the link, no subsidy was provided by the New Zealand government, which meant that all the link costs had to be recovered by charging the users. To get the project established, six of the universities agreed to pay one-sixth each of the start-up and operating costs.

Shortly after this the universities agreed that volume charging (a usage-sensitive pricing method) would be a better approach to sharing the costs. The underlying goals were:

• measure traffic in both directions through NZGate for each participating site and charge for it by volume; i.e., for the number of megabytes moved in and out each month;

• charge enough to cover actual costs, plus a percentage for development; and

• use the resulting development funds to buy more capacity as demand grew.

These goals led to an effective charging scheme for shared use of the single common link, but it was rather simple-minded. To make it useable the universities had to address several other matters, the first of which was predictability. Universities wanted to know well in advance how much they would have to pay for the NZGate service so that they could budget for it.

To provide predictability Kawaihiko adopted the notion of committed traffic volume per month. The charging scale had large steps, and the price per megabyte decreased as the volume increased. Each university made an initial choice of its committed volume, and thus its monthly charge. The actual traffic was monitored month by month and reported back to all the university sites. If a site's traffic moved into a different charging step for more than one month, that site's committed volume was changed to the actual rate. This allowed a site to have a single unusual month, and it gave at least a month's warning of a change in the charge. It was simple to administer, since the committed volumes were changed automatically by the NZGate management.

Internet Pricing in Practice

Another potential problem was that of paying for unsolicited in-coming electronic mail. As an example, a user at Auckland had a colleague in the United States who emailed him a 200-kilobyte file. The remote system kept on aborting after sending about 150 kilo-bytes, and did this every half hour over a three-day weekend. By the time Auckland's network manager realized what was happening many tens of megabytes had been received, which the site had to pay for. Kawaihiko doesn't have a good answer to this—after all, Kawai-hiko has no control over systems outside New Zealand—but in more than five years of operation it has not happened often enough to be worth worrying about.

Volume charging for NZGate began in late 1990 using metering software developed at Waikato University, running on a 286-based IBM PC. The metering has been progressively improved since then, and now runs on a Sun SPARCstation. The charging scheme has since been refined, with discounts to encourage off-peak use. A summary of the charge rates is given as an appendix to this chapter.

Traffic volumes have risen steadily, and the link capacity has been increased as follows:

Providers of intercontinental data circuits provide them as half circuits, i.e., each end is separately billed. In NZGate's early stages PACCOM paid for the U.S. half circuit and NZGate paid for the New Zealand one. For some time now, however, NZGate has paid the charges for both ends. The New Zealand access circuit is provided by Telecom New Zealand; over the years NZGate has used various intercontinental telecommunications providers.

Table 1
Timetable of NZGate Link Specifications

Date	Data Rate	Mode
April 1989	9,600 bps	analog cable to Hawaii
November 1990	14.4 Kbps	analog cable to Hawaii
September 1992	64 Kbps	satellite link to NASA Ames
February 1992	128 Kbps	satellite link to NASA Ames
March 1994	256 Kbps	digital cable to NASA Ames
July 1994	512 Kbps	digital cable to NASA Ames
November 1994	768 Kbps	digital cable to NASA Ames
June 1995	1.5 Mbps	Frame Relay to NASA Ames
November 1995	2.5 Mbps	Frame Relay to NASA Ames

Most of the above growth can be attributed to a steadily increasing user population, but there were also several events which caused sudden increases in traffic. The first of these was the setting up of the Kawaihiko network in April 1991, linking together all seven of the New Zealand universities. Kawaihiko is a Maori word, derived from *kawai* (a branching structure, like tree roots) and *hiko* (electricity). It began with Cisco routers at each university, linked by 9,600 bps leased lines which were later upgraded to 48 kilobits per second. It was an Internet Protocol (IP) network (at last), which made it possible to use TCP/IP services such as FTP and greatly simplified access to UseNet News.

Another event was the establishment of the Tuia network, which provided links between Kawaihiko, DSIRnet, and MAFnet on an informal basis. This provided Internet access to all of New Zealand's government-funded research establishments, thus increasing the number of sites using NZGate.

A third event occurred in July 1992, when the Department of Scientific and Industrial Research (DSIR) and Ministry of Agriculture and Fisheries (MAF) were restructured by the government and split into 11 crown research institutes (CRIs). The Tuia Society was created, and a new network using a Frame Relay backbone was set up to link the universities, CRIs, the National Library, and the Ministry of Research, Science and Technology (MoRST). The Frame Relay backbone provided significantly higher link capacities, which in turn boosted the total NZGate traffic.

During the formative phase of Tuia's shared use of the NZGate service, charging by volume provided a cost-sharing mechanism which was visibly fair for each of the participating sites. The notion of committed volumes smoothed out short-term usage transients, and thereby helped the budgeting process at each site.

The Internet grew rapidly in New Zealand during 1995, with a growing number of Internet Service Providers (ISPs) serving an ever-increasing number of users. NZGate continued to provide New Zealand's main international gateway, and coped well with the ever-increasing traffic volumes.

From its beginnings in 1990, NZGate had been run as a not-for-profit operation. This worked well in the early years, when an international Internet service would not have been commercially viable. During 1995, it became apparent that this was no longer the case, and that the New Zealand Internet community would be better served by having several competing suppliers of international connectivity. To achieve this, Waikato University began implementing NZIX, an Internet Exchange for all ISPs serving New Zealand. (More information about NZIX is available from http://www.waikato.ac.nz/nzix.)

NZGate operation was scaled down from January 1996, allowing NZIX to provide a neutral interconnection point for many ISPs, offering both international and New Zealand connectivity. A competitive market for Internet service is well established, with ISPs offering a variety of different charging models to meet the needs of their users. The notion of paying for Internet service continues to be well accepted by New Zealand Internet users.

The steady growth in transport volumes demonstrates the success of the NZGate service and its charging scheme. This as in stark contrast with the Chilean experience of charging (see Baeza-Yates, Piquer and Poblete 1993).

Management of the Tuia Network

Before 1992 there were three research and education networks in New Zealand: DSIRnet (a leased-line network linking DSIR sites), MAFnet (a private X.25 network linking MAF sites) and Kawaihiko (a TCP/IP network linking the universities). These three national networks were interlinked so as to provide a single TCP/IP network known as Tuia. This network had no formal management structure, relying instead on occasional coordinating meetings of the three participants, but it nonetheless provided reliable, effective communication between the sites, and (via NZGate at Waikato University) access to the Internet.

When the Tuia network backbone was set up in 1992 it linked 13 sites: five universities, six crown research institutes, the National Library of New Zealand and New Zealand's Ministry of Research, Science and Technology. The locations of the TuiaNet backbone sites are shown in Figure 1; the universities are labeled in italics and the CRIs in plain text.

Figure 1
TuiaNet Sites

Tuia is an incorporated society, providing its members (the CRIs, universities, etc.) with a legal entity and a formal structure within which to set up and run a single backbone network, known as TuiaNet. Rather than set up a new management structure for TuiaNet, its members decided to continue with the old groupings of the sites, which became management groups within Tuia. Thus Kawaihiko is the Tuia management group which coordinates inter-university networking, while Industrial Research Limited (IRL) and AgResearch coordinate groups of CRIs which correspond to the old DSIR and MAF. The remaining sites (National Library and MoRST) could have joined one of the three groups but chose not to, which effectively makes them single-member groups.

TuiaNet uses a Frame Relay backbone provided by Netway Communications, a subsidiary of Telecom New Zealand. Netway's monthly charges for each site have two components, an access cost (determined by the line speed, 64 to 768 kilobits per second) and a set of Committed Information Rate (CIR) costs (reflecting the maximum continuous data rate for virtual circuits to other sites). CIR charges were set at a flat rate of NZ $8.75 per Kbps when TuiaNet began using Frame Relay; they have reduced slightly in the last year. Netway's monthly bills are paid by each of the management groups, and each group then recovers these costs from its own users as its management requires.

For sites which are entirely within a management group (e.g., the University of Auckland), the site pays its share of the costs to the group (as explained for Kawaihiko below).

Where a site provides services for more than one management group (e.g., Massey University provides backbone access for IRL and AgResearch), simple settlements have been reached. These usually have each group paying a fixed share of the access charge, and paying CIR costs to other sites within the group. A special case of this occurs when virtual circuits run between management groups, e.g., between Waikato (Kawaihiko) and Gracefield (IRL). Tuia has found that the traffic between members of a group is much greater than their traffic to other groups, so groups needing virtual circuits to other groups are happy to pay for the CIR at both ends.

The settlements are therefore capacity-based in the sense that the amount each group pays is determined purely by the traffic capacity they agree to. They make no attempt to charge by volume or for different network services; these possibilities are explored in the next section.

The simple arrangements for cost sharing within Tuia have worked well. Having the management groups reduces the number of parties involved in settlements to a manageable number, allowing them to reach agreement quickly on the simple settlements. It seems unlikely that a flatter management structure, such as a single group which would then negotiate settlements between every pair of sites, would have been as effective.

Kawaihiko

Late in 1990, the universities began planning the Kawaihiko network to link all the universities with their own IP network. Each site had a Cisco router, and the sites were interconnected with Digital Data Service (DDS) links. The topology was a central triangle joining Waikato, Victoria, and Canterbury, with the others connected to it (see Figure 2).

The network was installed and running in April 1990, providing greatly improved communications between the universities. Its on-going costs were Telecom's monthly access and transmission charges for the links. Following the success of volume charging for NZGate, the universities resolved to implement volume charging to recover Kawaihiko's ongoing costs. It was not, however, possible to measure traffic volumes at that time, so instead they agreed—as an interim measure—to share the costs in fixed proportions, which were one-thirteenth for Lincoln and two-thirteenths for the other six sites.

This simple arrangement continued for about two years, during which time most of the links were upgraded to 48 kilobits per second. Waikato continued to measure traffic volumes through NZGate

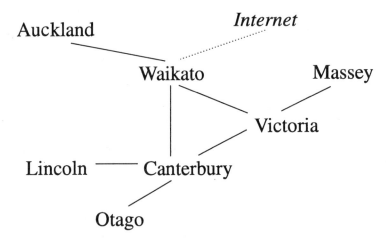

Figure 2
Kawaihiko Topology

for each site. So as to provide metering of traffic between the Kawaihiko sites (rather than just the traffic on each of the Kawaihiko links), work was begun at Auckland in 1992 on implementing the Internet accounting model (RFC 1272).

The Kawaihiko network was reengineered in July 1992, when the universities and crown research institutes implemented TuiaNet using Frame Relay as the dominant transport technology, but continuing to use DDS links where Frame Relay would have been too expensive. The effect of all this for Kawaihiko was to make it more obviously part of a larger network, with some of the Kawaihiko sites providing connectivity for some of the CRIs. Obviously a more elaborate cost-sharing scheme was called for.

A site requesting a Frame Relay connection must decide on its required access rate, and the Committed Information Rate it wants to all the other sites. The access rate should be greater than the sum of the CIRs, and there are good reasons to have it much larger. One of these is that access speed determines the maximum burst rate, another is that it can be expensive to change access rates (especially if it involves changing the underlying technology, for example from DDS to fractional E1).

Since the access rate had to be determined by each site separately, the universities agreed that each site would pay its own access cost. Access costs for sites providing common access for CRIs were divided using a set of percentages agreed locally at each site. Initially it was necessary to have a fully connected network, with at least two kilobits per second of CIR between every pair of sites. The universities therefore agreed to share the costs using the one-thirteenth formula until they were able to measure the traffic volumes between sites.

The overall effect of these changes was that the Kawaihiko network was treated as being made up of links with access costs paid by individual sites, and transport costs shared between all sites—regardless of the type of link. Effectively, the universities have tried to visualize their transport network as comprising local (and locally funded) elements plus a single shared element the costs of which were shared on the basis of traffic volumes, just as was done for the single international link element (NZGate).

Since 1992, work on the Internet accounting project has continued, resulting in the public-domain release late in 1993 of an accounting meter, NeTraMet, and its manager/collector program, NeMaC. (NeTraMet is available via anonymous FTP from ftp. auckland.ac.nz, directory pub/iawg/NeTraMet.)

There were three further releases of NeTraMet in 1994, prompting considerable interest from other sites looking for a way of metering network traffic. Kawaihiko sites have now deployed NeTraMet meters on their gateway networks, and these allow the Kawaihiko management to produce matrices showing traffic volumes between the sites, subdivided into a number of traffic types. If volume charging continues to be appropriate for all or part of the cost sharing, these meters will provide the raw data for it. They will, in any case, provide data for other purposes, such as verifying that traffic flows do not exceed their agreed levels in the long term.

Initial work with the NeTraMet meters classified traffic by site into local traffic, traffic to and from other Kawaihiko sites (or networks connected to them), and traffic with the rest of the world. Traffic types of particular interest so far include Simple Mail Transfer Protocol (SMTP), Network News Transfer Protocol (NNTP), Telnet, File Transfer Protocol (FTP), gopher, World Wide Web (WWW) and Domain Name System (DNS).

Cost Sharing within Kawaihiko

A charging scheme based on fixed shares worked well initially, but as Kawaihiko traffic volumes grew and new services developed, the need for a better algorithm became steadily more apparent. Charges based on amounts of data actually moved were helpful throughout Kawaihiko's start-up phase, during which institutions struggled to obtain funding for even a minimum level of service. This was essentially a cost-minimization regime for the participating sites, and most appropriate for queued transfers whose transit time was not important. Not surprisingly, these were dominant until quite recently.

One of the requirements of a charging algorithm is that it should handle higher-layer services well. Some of these, such as Domain Name Service (DNS), and Network Time Protocol (NTP), are an essential part of the TCP/IP infrastructure. They must therefore be shared as common good elements of the network. Network News is somewhat similar in that all sites want access to it, and it is essential to minimize the number of times any news item is replicated. Overall it seems better to charge separately for transport (including common good services) and other value-added services. Service providers can be charged for their transport costs, and then recover them from their end users.

As an example of this, consider a site wishing to offer a World Wide Web (WWW) cache as a chargeable service. Transport costs for traffic to and from the cache could be measured and paid for by the cache provider, who would set charges for the service so as to cover the transport charges both within New Zealand (to the customers) and to NZGate (source of the cached Web pages).

Another requirement is the emerging need to provide higher-bandwidth pipes within Kawaihiko which are site-specific; e.g., pairs of sites such as Waikato and Victoria would like 128 kbps capacity between them for experiments with packet video. These dedicated capacities should clearly be paid for by the sites requiring them, and not be a shared cost for all of Kawaihiko. Charging directly for capacity provides predictable costs for sites and allows for special link needs. Specified capacities appear to be the most effective way to provide for the continued growth of Kawaihiko, and are the basis of the new charging algorithm described below.

Each site nominates the required capacities for its links to every other site. From the lists of link capacities we produce a full matrix—not necessarily symmetric—of actual link capacities (CIRs or line speeds) which will be sufficient to meet the stated requirements. In most cases these will be the CIRs needed to meet current traffic levels plus any anticipated needs for the next year or so.

Each site pays its own access costs, whether they are connected via Frame Relay or DDS lines. Sites continue to make their own arrangements with distal (i.e., locally connected) sites. For these aspects, cost recovery simply continues our existing practice.

Transport costs are paid by the sites. For each link or virtual circuit the costs are shared between the two sites involved. This cost sharing may be equal, which amounts to having each site paying all its CIR costs directly. Or it may be unequal, for example, if an Auckland distal site wants 128 kilobits per second of CIR to Waikato, Auckland could pay access and 128 kbps CIR costs for both ends of the virtual circuit, then recover these from the distal site.

Conclusion

Over the last five years New Zealand has had a very effective Internet gateway, the speed of which has steadily increased to meet users' traffic demands. Because NZGate charged users by volume for their traffic, users always perceived that their payments were closely related to the benefits they derived. This perception was enhanced by NZGate's ability to develop the New Zealand Internet gateway so as to handle the increasing traffic volumes.

The early stages of the Internet in New Zealand seem to have benefited significantly from it being a very homogeneous user community. At that time it was not difficult for the community to work together for a common goal, which was well served by usage-sensitive pricing. Since then, Kawaihiko has explored other forms of pricing, tailored to meet particular needs. The current regime—competitive service providers peering at NZIX—seems to work well, and certainly allows providers to offer a variety of pricing options to their users.

The overheads of charging are significant. Operation and development of the NZGate traffic monitoring and usage-billing software occupy about one half-time person. Development of NeTraMet is an ongoing research activity, which takes about one-fifth of my time. The management of Kawaihiko takes one person about half a day each week. The benefits provided by charging are, however, well worth their cost to the Kawaihiko members.

Within New Zealand we have used fixed-share algorithms to recover costs, which has worked well within our simple management structures. Kawaihiko, the universities management group, has invested a great deal of effort in developing traffic accounting and cost-sharing methods, and implementing a specified capacity algorithm for sharing their traffic costs. The Kawaihiko members believe that this will more accurately reflect our users' expectations, allowing Kawaihiko to handle the newer, more bandwidth-intensive services the users demand.

Acknowledgments

The author records his appreciation to the New Zealand Vice Chancellors' Committee for their support of networking within the New Zealand universities, to NASA for their enthusiastic support of our international Internet gateway in its early stages, and to the network support staff at all the New Zealand sites, especially to John Houlker (j.houlker@@waikato.ac.nz). It was John who made our first contact with NASA and PACCOM, implemented the gateway, and has managed it so effectively ever since.

References

Baeza-Yates, R., J.M. Piquer, and P.V. Poblete. 1993. The Chilean Internet connection, or, I never promised you a rose garden. In proceedings of INET '93.

Carter, M. and Guthrie, G. 1995. Pricing Internet; The New Zealand experience. Department of Economics, University of Canterbury, Christchurch, New Zealand.

Mills, C., G. Hirsch, and G. Ruth. 1991. Internet accounting: background. RFC 1272. Internet Request for Comment, http://www.ietfiorg.

Appendix: NZGate Charging Rates

The NZGate International Internet charging rates as of April 8, 1994, are given below. Uncommitted rate $6.00 per megabyte and committed rates are shown in the following table:

Commitment (megabytes/month)	NZ$/megabyte	Fee (NZ$)
100	4.00	400
200	3.80	760
300	3.70	1,110
400	3.60	1,440
500	3.50	1,750
600	3.40	2,040
700	3.30	2,310
800	3.20	2,560
900	3.10	2,790
1000	3.00	3,000
1,000–1,250	2.90	3,625
1,250–1,500	2.80	4,200
1,500–2,000	2.60	5,200
2,000–2,500	2.50	6,250
2,500–3,000	2.50	7,500
3,000–3,500	2.50	8,750
3,500–4,000	2.50	10,000
4,000–4,500	2.40	10,800
4,500–5,000	2.40	12,500
5,000–5,500	2.40	13,200
5,500–6,000	2.30	13,800
6,000–6,500	2.30	15,000
6,500–7,000	2.30	16,000

Committed rate buffer period: If the committed rate is exceeded for a single month, the charge step remains unchanged (and similarly if it is not reached for a single month).

Low-priority discounts: Low-priority traffic (currently FTP and MAIL) is discounted by 30%. Normal priority traffic is discounted by 15%. The full rate is charged for high-priority traffic (currently TELNET and FTP commands). These are applied before the committed rate is determined.

Off-peak discount: An off-peak discount of 80% applies to all traffic between 8:00 pm and 9:00 am. This is applied after the committed rate is determined.

An earlier version of this chapter appeared in **ConneXions** 8 No. 12, (December 1994). *ConneXions—The Interoperability Report* is published monthly by Interop Company, a division of SOFTBANK Expos; 303 Vintage Part Drive, Suite 201; Foster City, CA 94404-1138, USA; Phone: (1-415) 578-6900; FAX: (1-415) 525-0194; Toll-free (in USA): 1-800-INTEROP; Email: connexions@@interop.com. Free sample issue and list of back issues available upon request.

Flat—The Minimalist Price

Loretta Anania and Richard Jay Solomon

In the real world, pricing has little to do with cost, since entrepreneurs will charge whatever price they can get away with (Mulgan 1988). Pricing decisions by management typically precede cost-benefit analysis, leaving the theoretical study of pricing mechanisms to regulatory economists, auditors, and academics.

In 1986, well before the pricing dilemma for digital networks became an issue with the commercialization of the Internet, we studied the parameters constraining historical network pricing models in order to forecast the implications for future broadband networks. The original version of that "flat rate" paper (Anania and Solomon 1988) is included in this chapter to add a historical dimension to the study of Internet economics.

Several chapters in this book illustrate why new features and new networks require new economics and enhanced ways of charging. Our chapter argues that since pricing decisions have little to do with cost and more to do with nontechnical imperatives such as competition and public policy, looking back to history and politics may help to understand the future of communication systems.

In 1987, the future was foreseen to be composed of Broadband Integrated Services Digital Networks (B-ISDN), based on a rudimentary form of Asynchronous Transfer Mode (ATM) protocols. While the history and technology of the Internet's Transmission Control Protocol/Internet Protocol (TCP/IP) differ from that of ATM, and only narrowband ISDN is visible to present-day consumers as an option in the marketplace, the charging dilemma then and now is identical: how to price distributed processing?

Two key features of the Internet and B-ISDN are heterogeneity and distributed control. There is very little business experience with pricing networks with these advanced features. Business models will have to be invented for this purpose.

Heterogeneous networks are advanced communications systems inherently capable of supporting multiservice environments. Equally important with advanced networks, resources and control are not concentrated within a central-office-based architecture.

The distributed, time-sharing phenomena of the late 1960s had some of the same features; however, the pricing dilemma for re-source access was not evident at that time to either regulators or network operators. Regulators were more concerned at that time with keeping the regulated telephone business out of the unregu-lated computing business. But before the legal and tariff questions could be resolved, time-sharing was rapidly replaced by new tech-niques—techniques which led to today's Internet. Unfortunately (or fortunately, depending on whether you are a user or a provider), the Internet's predecessor—the ARPANET—never had to confront the pricing issue either. To the ARPANET's military sponsors and archi-tects, only cost mattered, not price. So, for time-sharing, as well as its progeny, packet networks such as the Internet, the pricing di-lemma has never been resolved.

Distributed, multiservice resource access characterizes the pre-sent-day Internet. Just as with time-sharing and packet networks, soon regulators may no longer be able to distinguish between the merging telephone network and the Internet.

The legal problem with pricing processing rapidly gets complex and unnecessarily obscure. We take a historical approach to telecom-munications pricing to illustrate the processes by which market choices were made in the past. We proposed a decade ago a flat rate for access to an ATM network for a number of reasons that we will review in Internet terms in this chapter.

The 1988 paper presciently predicted the basic problem now fac-ing the Internet, albeit in technical terms more relevant to the B-ISDN technology of the day. We believe that the fact that the

B-ISDN architecture differed from Internet's TCP/IP has no bearing on our observation that cost allocation and pricing for either B-ISDN or TCP/IP networks cannot follow the same model as that of a relatively simple double-star telephone network. The competitive environment, complex mix of services, order-of-magnitude range of carriage speeds, and the blurring of administrative boundaries, exacerbates the dilemma for pricing interconnection. Interconnecting distributed computers is all the Internet really does—hence the name, "Internet."[1]

Based upon our monthly "Open Networks" column published during 1986–1987 in *Telecommunications Magazine* (Solomon and Anania 1987b), and on doctoral thesis work at MIT (Anania 1990), the paper suggested a simple, flat rate for access to increasingly complicated interconnected networks. It was presented at the annual Telecommunications Policy Research Conference on October 31, 1988. A strong debate ensued about whether it is best to price access on a flat rate, or to count bits to limit congestion. Today there is a growing literature on broadband pricing, with the pricing solutions getting more intricate than the networked interconnection itself. One can always price users out of a market. Price discrimination may eliminate congestion, but reducing demand does not solve the access or interconnection dilemma, you just have fewer customers.

We used a historical approach which demonstrates that Internet pricing issues are not new and can be understood within the larger context of telecommunications. Since the Internet is an "aggressive" overlay on other telecom infrastructure elements, it is important to understand the role of regulation, of the carriers, and the user's own infrastructure, which often comprises the bulk of the investment for Internet access. The congestion problems of today are more likely due to insufficient investment on the local end of the network rather than to the backbone architecture. Applying a flat rate for access to the Internet will have no adverse effect on the users' own investment profile.

Ten years ago, ISDN and B-ISDN were the fashionable, up-and-coming acronyms. Today, the Internet is all the rage, and the

---

1. Vint Cerf, personal communication.

functional equivalent to B-ISDN. Unlike B-ISDN, which never got off the ground, there are millions of real Internet users worldwide and (so far) few Internet regulators or auditors, but plenty of Internet economists, lawyers, technologists, social scientists, and entrepreneurs. Although we could not have predicted it then, in jurisdictions where ISDN is priced right—usually at a low, if not flat, rate—the demand for Internet access has resurrected ISDN and has created new demands for broadband, whatever form that may take in the future. Surprisingly, the network engineering models which we used in the 1988 paper (see below) are still relevant to today's unresolved public policy problem: how to price access and interconnection.

Our main points in the 1988 paper were the following:

(1) A large percentage of the world's telecom traffic has always been carried on flat-rate circuits. We illustrated this with examples from the history of both digital telegraphy and analog telephony.

Early this century, when American Telephone and Telegraph bought out its chief telegraph competitor, Western Union, the largest share of U.S. intercity telecom traffic was carried via private circuits dedicated to railway usage, both telephone and telegraph.[2] Today's global multinationals and largest users are no longer railroads, however, telecommunications traffic is still predominantly carried on private leased lines.[3]

We predicted that B-ISDN, using Asynchronous Transfer Mode, would not change this historical, flat-rate pattern except to accelerate the customer shift away from costlier usage-sensitive circuits. So far, this has proved true for Internet traffic.[4] B-ISDN as a telephone

---

2. For long-distance telephony in the United States, more than half of the circuits and most of the traffic were on private, mostly railroad lines, operated by AT&T up until the 1930s, as described in Neuman et al. (1997) and Rhoads (1924).

3. "Study of 100 Largest Multi-nationals: Do More with Less," *Communications Week International,* June 26, 1995.

4. Anthony Rutkowski, Executive Director, The Internet Society, Letter to the Editor, *Communications Week International,* October 11, 1993: "Internet usage is exploding because . . . commercial providers are offering mass market connectivity at low *flat rates;* . . . a 'Sender keeps all' accounting practice where customers and providers purchase *flat-rate* bandwidth at all levels of the providing chain; . . . [and] inherent very low cost of the technologies employed. . . ."

administration-controlled, public-switched broadband service with usage-sensitive pricing has never gotten off the ground (Finnie 1992).

(2) Regulators, auditors, and academic economists often fail to realize an important distinction between telecom usage and flat-rate access mechanisms. This misunderstanding persists due to distortions in data collection that emphasize counting traffic volume and access lines on public-switched networks while ignoring the utility and unique characteristics of private traffic, and different architectures of private corporate, government, and other networks.

(3) The lines of demarcation between private and public network access, and between process and network control, would become blurred with multimedia applications. We correctly forecast that this would happen for all-digital networks, and that packet and circuit-switched technologies might merge. With impending voice services on the Internet, this merger has now become a clear threat, or promise, for the near future. The Internet's very name implies nomenclature obfuscation. Without service specificity, yesterday's tariffs and today's regulations have become unenforceable.

(4) It is impossible to simply count bits and come to any conclusion about the relationship between tariff structure and value. Forecasters fail to recognize that compression is important and often inherent in data processing. For example, fax transmissions, which have accounted for the largest share of "telephone" traffic and access line growth in the past few years, are today subsumed under voice. Yet, the fax revenue stream will likely vanish as compressed, bit-mapped images shift to Internet-like packet networks. And as for value, the same number of bytes may define either a billion dollars or one cent, since on data networks representation is done with exponents, not words.

(5) A flat rate is more convenient for customers. The key Internet advantage is not to maximize cash return on investment in plant, but to maximize the free flow of information. Since the money will be made on content, it is in the interest of the content provider to keep carriage simple and cheap. Therefore,

(6) User control of the network will continue to increase with direct access to control software such as TCP, Signaling System No. 7 for telephony, private virtual network overlays on the public network, deregulation, and competition. The converse, Advanced Intelligent Network packages, have been slow to gain market share. It is interesting to note that we predicted the advent of "rate arbitrage on an international scale," which international call-back schemes have fulfilled, an unexpected consequence of permitting user control of network software on Intelligent Networks.

(7) Regulators will have difficulty updating their rule-making since, as we stated, "there is no way to have a service-specific tariff for a virtual, software-defined, accessed, and controlled network," especially if the customer can obtain cheaper service by having their digital devices call other devices on a transparent, end-to-end, self-routing packet network. This may explain why national regulators are moving from regulating access pricing to greener pastures, such as privacy, pornography, and encryption.

(8) We stated that "cost-based pricing models guarantee neither sufficient access nor sufficient capital for the future" public networks. For the last 10 years, most capital expenditure has been for private, not public-switched telecommunications, including customer-premises equipment such as PCs, Local Area Networks (LANs), routers, etc.

(9) We noted that "rapid technological change in telecom . . . appears to reduce marginal costs even more than average costs." Surprisingly, at least to many in the conventional carrier business, the Internet's marginal cost of sending an additional bit is, indeed, zero, or sometimes paradoxically, less than zero (due to processing anomalies). So, our conclusion to this forecast still holds: "if marginal costs are below average costs, and price is set to marginal cost, total revenues will still be less than total costs," admittedly a frightening scenario for some carriers.

(10) The telephone system has undergone a fundamental transformation from tree-and-branch, fixed-channel topography to a logical, virtual network by incorporating computer control (Custom Local-Area Signaling Services (CLASS), System Seven (SS7), etc.). Instead

of making it easier to engage in usage-sensitive pricing, this has facilitated different levels of network access (Anania and Solomon 1988). The paradigm shift has less to do with welfare economics and pricing of carriage, and more to do with completely restructuring networks.

(11) Future network planning should radically address the problems and paradoxes of the future, not be a straight-line projection of the past (Anania 1990, 1992).

This is why, a decade later, our conclusion remains the same: A flat-rate tariff for access to a flexible, open, and general-purpose network is the best choice for all players when the future is unknown and risky, and the only certainty is change.

Flat—The Minimalist B-ISDN Rate[5]

Abstract: This paper examines how the allocation of costs in the telephone distribution plant might change with the introduction of new infrastructure models—fiber optics technology and Broadband ISDN control mechanisms. We suggest that as variable costs approach zero with a B-ISDN network, a flat rate for access only may be the only practical pricing method. Pricing per bit, usage, or by differential services can only encourage the sophisticated user to manipulate future software reconfigurable systems for various types of arbitrage.

Former infrastructure models for both analog telephony and digital telegraphy established policies that maximized access while raising sufficient capital for future infrastructure improvements. With the decline of common-carrier regulation, and increased competition from alternative technologies, the system is being driven toward cost-based pricing and short-term planning. However, with oncoming computer-driven ISDN, fiber-based B-ISDN, and massive capital plant recapitalization, cost-based pricing price models guarantee neither sufficient access nor sufficient capital for the future.

5. (originally presented at the Telecommunications Policy Conference, Oct. 31, 1988, Airlie House, Va.)

The Problem

When computers are introduced into the telephone system the network does not just change from analog to digital, with faster switching times. It becomes more like a computer: dynamic, user
programmable, and less predictable. We have seen this before, in a
different context. With the addition of time-sharing software and
telecommunication channels to stand-alone computers, the computer changed from a batch-processing, centralized environment, to
a distributed, more accessible networked system. We should expect
changes just as radical when the dial-up network itself becomes a
mythical computer. Whether this network will be truly open depends
upon the success of nonproprietary standardization efforts.

The implementation of an Open Network Architecture (ONA)
regime[6] and Integrated Services Digital Network (ISDN) technology
implies a reallocation of resources among public and private networks. This new telecommunication system is sufficiently different
from the past that the transition to a digital infrastructure may
neither be smooth nor equitable. Ultimately an end-to-end digital
architecture will emerge, with virtual, logical connections defining
communications channels.

As telephone networks become complex computer networks, user
control—not carrier control—*increases*. With the user taking control
of routing, bandwidth allocation, and administration, there will be
unexpected applications of the public network, including rate arbitrage on an international scale!

The allocation of fixed costs in the local distribution network has
increased in response to technological innovation, new capital and
depreciation requirements, and changing regulatory regimes. The
policy question is: who pays for the costs of modernization, and how
is it to be implemented? Infrastructural choices must be made, and
some of the economic models that were found to work well in the
past, but are unsuitable now, may paradoxically soon work again.

6. FCC Computer Inquiry III (ONA), June 1986. (see Neuman et al. [1997]). The European Community's equivalent is the 'Open Network Provision.' See COM(88) 240, EC,
Brussels, and [European] Council Recommendation 86/659/EEC, 22 Dec. 1986.

Former infrastructure models for both analog telephony and digital telephony worked out policies that maximized access while raising sufficient capital for future plant. With the demise of the old common-carrier legislation, and increased competition from alternative technologies and newly built distribution plants, the current system is being driven toward cost-based pricing and short-term planning. With oncoming ISDN and fiber-based B-ISDN commitments requiring massive plant recapitalization, cost-based pricing models guarantee neither sufficient access nor sufficient capital for the future.

No one can predict where the ISDN demand and supply curves will meet. Given the uncertain market forecasts, and huge investment in new plants, the carrier's strategy is to maximize both scale (user access) and scope (service flexibility). This plan offers them but a mixed blessing. Not being able to precisely predict how a network will be used is an argument for building a general-purpose network, which is what an *integrated* digital network should be. But integration does not fit into a regulatory scheme where the network tariffs are specific to the services.

There is no way to have a service-specific tariff for a virtual, software-defined, accessed, and controlled network. And, as networks interconnect, there is no way to separate the sender from the receiver, and the ownership of the "value-adding" portion. In the past you could locate your "tax" on a physical part of the information plant. For example, the earliest tax on information was a license charge per page for each impression made by the printing press. In telephony, the equivalent is a metered charge based on the theory that each person's voice throughput is equivalent. Profit maximization may fit the goals of a private monopoly, but hardly exhaust those of a public service operation.

Public service obligations require that during the transition, digital/virtual and analog/specific networks must coexist and interconnect.[7] If ISDN pricing is not competitive, potential subscribers remain on the older systems. If charges are "just right" to attract ISDN customers, we have a paradox: the faster and more

---

7. FCC Computer Inquiry III (ONA), June 1986. (see Neuman et al. [1997]).

programmable the network becomes, the more the subscribers compete with the carrier for the added value portion of the service. In other words, the older voice and low-speed data revenue streams "vanish" into the interstices of the faster digital network. If the charges are fair for the older systems, ISDN never has a chance to attract traffic. You cannot have a general-purpose network with service-specific charges.

Furthermore, the dynamic allocation of network resources will become increasingly difficult to meter and expensive to track by the carrier (or regulator). With integrated digital networks, the flat-rate, or pay-in-advance subscription solution, may be the best method of pricing.

Models

To see how tariffing will change, it is useful to compare elements from the old and new models of telecommunications infrastructure. Whether rational or not, it is common to find that the regulation of new technologies is patterned after some older one which it appears to resemble, at least at first (Pool 1983). The old system of analog telephony was patterned on a 19th century rail transport model. Luckily the telephone analogy was to intercity rather than a 19th century local transit. That (streetcar) model in most cities was no piece of cake: multiple companies with multiple fares, and no interconnections, either locally or intercity.

This telephone wire/rail model was worked out architecturally (trunk and branch/loop), politically (essentially one carrier and one service, except at major nodes), and for tariffing purposes (distance and time-sensitive variable costs for interregional links). It is of interest that the Federal Communications Act of 1934 was carried over almost word for word from the Interstate Commerce Act of 1887, replacing transport language with the relevant communications language, and merely adding the 1927 Federal Radio Act wordage for spectrum management!

Under the common-carrier model, telephony in the United States evolved to meet the following policy objectives: universal subscription, end-to-end plant capitalization, customer price stability, and

Table 1.
U.S. Common-Carrier Model of Telephony

- **State-mandated universal service,** but with business and residences splitting the cost of the fixed plant according to a Ramsey pricing scheme—differential pricing for essentially the same service. Business paid value of service, while residential prices reflected ability to pay (even if below cost).
- **Capital was raised by the 'dominant' carrier** for the entire, end-to-end system.
- **Cost-engineering function averaged for the network as a whole,** but the network was artificially separated into State and Federal domains, which reflected the fact that calls were predominantly local.
- **Rates were based on plant investment.** With most calls being local, unlimited flat rates for local service stabilized revenue projections.
- **No creamskimming.** To prevent erosion of the rate base, no resale, and no private attachments were permitted.

final responsibility for telecommunications infrastructure from security to research and development. The policy implications are illustrated in Table 1.

Though telecommunications traffic patterns and applications have changed over the decades in the United States, especially with post-World War II suburbanization and the further growth of decentralized management and production,[8] this fundamentally *railroad* transport model was, until recently, rarely challenged. Beginning in the 1960s, the telephone network underwent a fundamental transformation by incorporating digital connections and signal processing. Adoption of digital computer technology was essential for modernization and economic efficiency.

The current network is computer-controlled (Stored Program Control [SPC], in other words, a digital stored-program computer), provides different levels of network access, and connects sophisticated customer-owned equipment including other networks. As new

---

8. The United States has been more decentralized than most industrialized nations ever since the latter decades of the 19th century—a socioeconomic national preference aided (or abetted) by the rapid spread of first steam and then electric interurban railways into the countryside (the latter the functional forerunners of the U.S. highway system built in the 1920s); this transport revolution took place simultaneously with the growth and penetration of the telephone. This decentralized infrastructure may help explain the tolerance for the U.S. decentralized and fragmented common carrier regulatory system. Only prewar Germany approached the U.S. level of industrial decentralization; but communications in Germany, like its railways, has always remained centralized under the national government.

services other than "plain old telephones" abound—at least in name and in advertising vaporware—the available rate structures vary tremendously. They range all the way from lifeline flat rates to complex Centrex packages. As a system, today's "telephone" network is very different from the original wireline-cum-transport model.

The assumptions of the old integrated national network included: fixed overhead, fixed bandwidth, physical analog connections, and a hierarchical network architecture. The new public and private networks that are being built are increasingly fiber-based and digitally switched. The new technology brings with it a new set of assumptions, including variable bandwidth allocations with logical, instead of physical connections and a nonhierarchical network architecture with distributed processing nodes and terminals, all under shared carrier/customer control.

On the old network it was possible, originally, to separate embedded local plant from interoffice and interregional plant. That physical distinction became more artificial as more integrated equipment evolved. Still, the economics of regulation and the corporate structures of the telephone companies encouraged this artificial separation for local/long-distance, and across state boundaries, even where it was not in the public interest and probably not even in the companies' economic interest. In the future, as single-mode fiber makes possible even greater efficiencies from resource sharing and intense use of all-digital networks, such separations just for accounting purposes will be almost impossible to justify rationally.

Infrastructure

Changes in technology and social policy are already causing stress to pre-established costing and regulatory pricing practices. Bypass, resale, and access charges to the network exemplify this readjustment. Radical, sudden shifts in regulation, customer demands for network control, and the competitive push for new plant investment may even threaten the major carriers' viability. (See Table 2.)

The most efficient network designs for future highspeed, broadband, integrated digital communications should not resemble the telephone plant of the past—either in architecture or functionality.

Table 2.
Network Trends

Technology
- **Virtual end-to-end connectivity**
  user-to-machine,
  machine-to-machine, and
  user-to-user communication
- **Faster and faster computer processors**
  intelligent customer premises equipment and "smart" receivers
  merged "packet" and virtual circuit switching
  variable bit rate (Asynchronous Transfer Mode)
- **Shared process and network control**
  between carrier and subscriber
  line of demarcation blurred

Policy Implications
- **Increased international competition for service offerings**
- **Mandatory interconnection of public/private networks**

Results
- **Flexible choices among technologies, carriers, rates, and services**
- **Variable pricing and tariff arbitrage**
- **Decline of network integrity and national sovereignty**

If current trends continue, network usage will be different, more dynamic, and less predictable. To maximize overall system efficiency, customers will demand direct access to network resources, including operations, administration, and maintenance. Efficient computer interworking requires transparent standards. Hence it will become increasingly difficult to pinpoint whether the customer or carrier is conducting a digital transaction. At any node, the "customer" may be another network or even a competing carrier. This has already begun: in economic terms, 'equal access' has merged carriage with the commodity being carried.

To maximize the profitability and use of the existing plant, the carrier—whoever actually owns the link or switch—will have strong incentives to expand into new areas of business, often in competition with their own customers or other users. To maintain universal access, while at the same time expanding network provision, requires innovative rate making and novel depreciation schemes. So far, public inertia, regulatory lag, and defaulting to yesterday's tariff formulae have artificially constrained current technological reality, making the economic transition even more painful than it need be.

Pricing Your Processing

Voice telephony was intended for everyone, at a cost that local residents and businesses could afford and subscribe to, paying one month in advance for their lifetime. Truly differentiated voice services under the original telephony model—as contrasted to differentiated pricing—were too difficult and too expensive to provide. Before computers, billing for any disaggregated customer base was not feasible.

Then came time-shared data processing—a special, new, and potentially 'enhanced' revenue generator. The general subscriber (and regulator) neither understood (nor was prepared to pay for) access to the universal "computer utility."[9]

As it happened, computing has been unregulated, and telecommunications heavily regulated. Now that the two businesses have been integrated from a technical viewpoint, regulatory attempts— Computer I, II, and III[10]—have tried (and failed) to resolve the inherent anomalies of telephones that compute and computers that communicate by physically separating infrastructural elements. It barely worked for transport, but with invisible electronic memory machines, it is simply impractical.

All digital telephone switches are general-purpose computers and therefore data processors. With the network doing de facto processing, pricing becomes much more difficult than with mere transport, as in the original telephone model (based on an analogy to physical transport).

9. Loretta Anania, "Network Planning in the Information Society," Chapter 1 of unpublished Ph.D. dissertation, MIT, 1988. While so far data constitutes 6% of the traffic, it has recently grown at a rate of 30% per year. The "plain old telephone system" has grown only about 10% per year (1988 figures).

10. Computer I: 17 FCC 2d 587 (1969) and Docket No. 16979 (FCC 66-1004) passim.; Computer II: 77 FCC 2d 384 (1980) and Docket No. 20828 (FCC-76-745, July 29, 1976); and Computer III (Open Network Architecture): Docket No. 85-229 (104 FCC2d 958, May 1986)

Deregulation is easier to pull off than effective "re-regulation"! The *Computer Inquiries* were for the regulatory convenience of keeping data processing and telecommunications separate, at least as far as the businesses' accounting and revenue base were concerned. But it has created even more economic and political distortions: Neither regulators nor carriers have devised an acceptable plan for pricing a shared *process* connection between computer peripherals and the distributed database network.

Pricing For Capital Formation

According to classical pricing theory, in the simplest case where a single entity provides an indistinguishable basic service, price is driven to equal marginal cost. If prices are lower than marginal cost, customers tend to buy more of the service. Though volume increases, if price does not cover the cost of incremental plant, a firm (or service provider) loses money on every sale (Anania and Solomon 1987a, 1987d; Pool, Sirbu, and Solomon 1981). Yet, local regulators like marginal-cost pricing because it tends to maximize social goals such as universal telephone service.

Pure marginal-cost pricing for an expanding utility produces a deficit which can be made up in several ways, as listed in Table 3 below.

In the short term, the first and last options are the least unpalatable, and a rich assortment of such schemes exists in many nations today. Telephone and telegraph services may have begun as natural

Table 3.
How Deficits Are Covered

· **through cross-subsidies** (capitalization from within the system); or
· **by levying special assessments on users** to pay for modernization (taxation); or (catastrophically) when all else fails,
· **by permitting an obsolescent entity to go bankrupt** and then nationalizing it at bargain values; alternatively, if it is a bankrupt state entity,
· **denationalizing** at bargain values (a political measure); or
· **some other form of corporate reorganization** (e.g. "voodoo" refinancing).

monopolies, but regulation, the threat of anti-trust, and increased competition, each in its own way, have prevented large monopoly rents. Cross-subsidy, according to classical economics, would be inefficient, except perhaps as direct cash flows to the indigent user. In practice, of course, capital formation for expansion without sufficient profits would have been even more difficult without initial or subsequent cross-subsidies. Indeed, nationalized firms have had difficulty raising capital, until some financial reorganization convinced the investors (taxpayers) to contribute more funds.

How could a new network service be extended to all of us willing to pay at least marginal costs if we hypothesize that telecommunications would have indistinguishable service characteristics? The answer, in terms of regulatory checks and balances, is in Table 1. Except for the customer premises equipment (CPE) and resale provisions at the bottom (these are very important and will be discussed in the arbitrage section below), some common-carrier package may return with future B-ISDN systems.

How fast are we getting there? Not too fast. So far, demand for data processing by businesses has grown at three times the rate of the demand for residential POTS (plain old telephone service). The internationalization of the market for telecommunications and information services increases business demand for network digitization and the capacity to provide faster connections, end-to-end connectivity, and especially greater access to network resources. Customer-provided computer-based terminals and private switches for easy connection to an all-digital network shift a significant portion of what would have been carrier costs to the user.

Prospective deficits can also be filled by disaggregating services—finding some with increasing costs to be priced above marginal cost for different market segments: Private Branch Exchanges (PBXs) and key sets for businesses; POTS for residences. Monopoly privileges help enforce such disaggregation.

One basic factor in marginal-cost pricing is that telecommunications, so far, has been a declining cost industry—where marginal costs drop as production is expanded. Rapid technological change in telecommunications, even without expansion, appears to reduce marginal costs even more than average costs. If marginal costs are below average costs, and price is set to marginal cost, total revenues will still be less than total costs.

Nevertheless, despite declining marginal costs due to technological advances, the telecommunications link traditionally had not decreased in price as fast as advances in electronics had lowered computing costs and increased computer processing speeds. But a significant change is in the offing: with photonic switches and high-speed fiber connections, telecommunications throughput may finally overtake most computer bus (input/output) speeds. For the first time, *network resources may be faster than what the terminal equipment can support.*

This is what historians call a paradigm—or model—shift. Not only could this reverse the historical trends of computing and communications costs, *but demand profiles will be greatly different than those of today.* For example, new demands for fiber-based telecommunications may come from (fiber-based) very highspeed, Local Area Network users. So the demand for seamless ISDN standards—and improved access to dial-up public network resources—may initially come from today's private network enthusiasts. This is something very difficult to put into predictive, linear demand models.

Altered demand profiles, no matter how potentially profitable, are a mixed blessing for carriers that have been gearing up for a different market. Despite rosy quarterly returns, a rapidly expanding and changing computer-communications plant should flag a warning that there may not be enough money for tomorrow.[11] Capital recovery for modernization may become a more critical telecommunications issue than whether basic or enhanced services should be offered, or what color and label cheaper phones should have.

Arbitrage

Integrated digitization of the network will not permit temporary cross-subsidization and price discrimination among customers who have the know-how and resources to bypass. The resources may be

11. See Anania and Solomon (1987d) for an explanation of the puzzling phenomena that telecommunications are both expanding and undercapitalized. See also Solomon (1986).

economic, technological, or political. Because control of the bit-stream is shared between the carrier and the customer (and the customer may be another network), the regulatory distinction between user and carrier becomes as blurred as the separation between services. With greater user control, the subscriber can balance use of the network resources versus greater investment in CPE. Reconfiguration of "fungible" networks will be easier on ISDN systems because of their inherent fast connection times and digital access.

When further evolution toward implementation of B-ISDN, variable-rate, networks proceeds, network control may become the most important commodity being bought and sold in the telecommunications market.

Under these circumstances, how is it possible to justify different network pricing for data versus voice when these are physically indistinguishable bits on a fast link? Continuing to charge differential prices only leads to inefficient use and network arbitrage.

Arbitrage occurs when there is a discrepancy between price and cost, yielding an opportunity for a third party to profit by reselling. In some circumstances this is not quite legal, but there may be some way around it. Arbitrage is a market concept that has not been previously applied to telecommunications; but with deregulation and virtual, end-to-end digital networks, as we will attempt to demonstrate, arbitrage is increasingly viable as long as carriers maintain a significant separation between actual costs and charges to the customer.

The new technology of integrated digital systems could result in a distinct paradox when it comes to tomorrow's carrier revenue. Though it may appear on the surface that putting all telecom services onto one network enhances the concept of natural monopoly (and monopoly rents for captive users), the integration of these services into just one form of carriage—an invisible, and nondistinguishable, digital bitstream—has created economic pressures for cost-based pricing.

How can this revenue paradox exist? ISDN promoters claim that the technology will permit the abolition of private lines and other forms of competition to carrier monopoly. The answer lies in simple economic common sense: you cannot charge an educated customer more for one service when you are offering a cheaper substitute (albeit under a different name), at least not in the long run.

Some carriers currently view ISDN as a way of offering value-added data processing services—protocol conversion and information manipulation. They see this as a new way of establishing new multipart (Ramsey) tariffs based on differential value of service. Where business uses dominate, service kinks like call forwarding are priced at higher than the marginal and average costs of their digital software. Where traffic-sensitive rates apply, average costs should then replace marginally priced flat rates for private lines and local calling.

But there is a flaw: the new technology brings more than tariff and price changes, it brings incentives for *usage* change. With ISDN, or any all-digital switched network, subscribers have the option of only paying for pure bit transmission and providing for most enhancements with their own resources, wherever arbitrage makes it worthwhile.

The customer may be given some opportunity to whipsaw the carrier (for a change). There is little in enhanced services that a carrier can offer that a sophisticated user cannot get from well-programmed customer premise equipment. Computer-based CPE technology, therefore, will drive carrier pricing close to marginal costs. With broadband interfaces (following open architecture principles) part of the frame overhead *must* be customer accessible. If carriers were to restrict use by monitoring content and terminal type, this would likely drive the largest users to build their own networks offering flexible, dynamic, frame-structured wideband services.

Distributing Bypass

A basic ISDN principle is that an ISDN voice call between two points will not cost any more than a voice call over the conventional public switched telephone network (PSTN) between the same two points. Attempts to charge more for a data call than a voice call on a integrated digital network will be impossible to enforce since the bitstream will be indistinguishable by the carrier or regulator.

Equal charging will make it possible to seize a 64 kbps digital line at the bargain-basement voice rates. If the carrier needs to know, you

Anania and Solomon

can tell them (digitally, of course) that you are "talking" to your customers, but really your firm will subdivide the circuit into two, four, six or more voice/data circuits, using sophisticated voice and data compression equipment already on the shelf. The carrier will be charging for only one voice circuit and you can hang onto it all day, creating a virtual, multicircuit, tie-line.

The rate elements that were used to price services on the local loop will no longer suffice. Rate elements based on (1) call frequency, (2) duration, (3) distance, and (4) time of day assume that the costs of switching and trunking plant (interoffice and tandem) are variable. Features and functions like call-forwarding, speed-dialing, and call-waiting added a new variable element based on SPC memory and processing increments. But ISDN and B-ISDN technologies are not straight-line extrapolations of today's Stored Program Control circuit switching, especially in the packet mode (for voice and data).

Memory tables are inherent in any case for Data-Channel and common-channel ISDN signaling. Adding features is more a matter of toggling bit positions in already existing memory space. Memory space enhancement, therefore, becomes virtual and depends on signaling under user control, especially when disparate terminals must negotiate before a "call" actually begins.[12] In B-ISDN, as we already mentioned, user signaling is even more powerful, including routing and temporal feedback information for possible operations, administration, and maintenance purposes.

Broadband Service

Yesterday's discount dealers have been preparing for Picturephone and tomorrow's customers have been buying into a cheaper-than-

12. See CCITT "Red Book" (1984), Q.723 (SS7 Formats and Codes); I.311 sect. 9.2 (ISDN Numbering Plan, subaddressing); and controversy on user-to-user signaling using the subaddress field, and data transfer via "switch-through" before call charging begins in CCITT Study Group XVIII Document R-4-E, "Report of sub-group on numbering and addressing," July 1985, sect. 7.6; CCITT Working Party III/6 on "Charging and Accounting for the ISDN and common channel signaling network," TD Nos. 609-E, 616-E, and 619-E through 625-E, June 1986, Kobe, Japan; and updates in SG XVIII Rep. R49 (A–C), Seoul, February 1988 ("Network Aspects"), esp. sect. I.333, "Terminal Identification in ISDN," pp. 17*ff.*

voice-telephony electronic mail service. Occasionally technology push and demand pull are synchronized.

Who needs Broadband ISDN? Predicting future demand for services that do not exist borders on witchcraft anyway. The curious thing about B-ISDN is that we may be paying for it in any case. The fiber is being installed for the trunk and local distribution plant today. How—and whether—the digital bitstream on these fibers is switched, and what strategy may be pursued to reach the end-user, are a matter of current debate. Nevertheless, broadband capability is part of the natural evolution of the telephone network; only the details remain to be worked out.

But broadband does not mean bandwidth-wasteful services, it only means broadband-capable speeds. End-to-end, highspeed digital communication may generate totally different demand profiles. In the network of the future, most of today's favorite services may not require continuous channel occupancy. For example, movies can be encoded to be sent over medium-bandwidth lines in compressed time (not in real time on the network). Packetized voice needs hardly any bandwidth at all.[13]

Virtual networking entails network transparency for optical broadband interfaces (Solomon 1988). B-ISDN is an order of magnitude more powerful, with a potentially steeper decline in transmission and switching marginal costs. Single-mode fiber can be upgraded almost without limit by adding more interface electronics; it is not necessary to string new links. This fact, along with the possibility of altogether new architectures for superfast switching, has led to proposals for B-ISDN to leapfrog narrowband ISDN technology.[14]

Broadband "fast-packet" networks do not imply that services will demand continuous holding times, as in a circuit-based model (like

13. In the bit-metered, digital world, female voices can be compressed more than male, English more than German, and other inequities may emerge, especially with digital applications of Time Assigned Speech Interpolation (D-TASI) algorithms.

14. For a more complete description of the issues in B-ISDN and a technical bibliography, see Solomon (1987); this paper contains a detailed technical bibliography. The October 1987 issue of *IEEE Selected Issues in Telecommunications* is devoted to broadband switching concepts. A tutorial is in Minzer (1987). See also Finnie (1992) and Anania (1990). For future evolution, see CCITT SG XI, Ad-hoc Group on New Questions, "Proposed Study Questions for the Next Study Period," TD 154 and TD142, Geneva, 16–27 May 1988.

today's telephone network). Most services tend to be intermittent, and fit well in the technologies proposed for switching fiber-optic networks. Television, as well as telephony, can be asynchronously transmitted. This is a very important technological concept which underpins B-ISDN pricing schemes. Despite data that indicates that high-definition television (HDTV) requires hundreds of megabits per second, this does not mean HDTV needs that bandwidth continuously![15]

The development of "fast-packet" switching, and especially single-mode fiber, makes B-ISDN an altogether different beast than Narrowband ISDN (N-ISDN). N-ISDN is a end-to-end digital solution offering a basic rate of 144 kilobits per second, channeled into two 'B' (64 Kbps) and one 'D' (16 Kbps) streams (conventionally, 2B+D), the D channel ostensibly for signaling.[16] A primary rate of 1.5 or 2 megabits/second is also specified. These rates were originally intended for existing twisted copper-pair plant, though the primary rate uses mostly coaxial cable or fiber today (or four-wire copper). Moreover, it may be that much of the copper plant has to be rebuilt because the old wires are not conditioned to carry the 2B+D digital rate below acceptable levels of electromagnetic interference.[17] Should this be the case, rebuilding with fiber may be the more economical expedient for the long run; Broadband ISDN may therefore leapfrog N-ISDN in many areas.

B-ISDN standards apply sophisticated relational database software across a highspeed digital link for both transmission and routing. Hence B-ISDN subsumes the narrowband 2B+D rate. Switching un-

15. Sophisticated motion detection algorithms permit video information to be transmitted only when sections of an image change. Raw information can be sent in "compressed time" that is *faster* than it would be ultimately viewed to recreate a full movie. See Anania and Solomon (1987c). For a discussion of the current state of video encoding see Lippman (1988).

16. The D channel is perfectly capable of transmitting a customer payload since the 16 Kbps rate is overkill for signaling—even during call setup and teardown. Note that in the primary rate, 64 Kbps is reserved for the D channel. (N.B.: Since this was written, telephone companies have offered customers ISDN at 128 kilobits per second for 2B, but not the full 2B+D bandwidth. Other schemes, such as HDSL and ADSL, may supersede basic and primary rate offerings on twisted copper.)

17. Swiss PTT, "EMC and COMSEC problems on ISDN basic access installations (rec. I.430)," CCITT SG XVII, D.1740/XVIII, Geneva, 6–17 June 1988.

der this scheme gains enormous power, but can be under the control of the subscriber, instead of just the carrier. The packets and signaling system are combined so as to be essentially self-routing.

The key to network design is the use of enormous bandwidths for overhead made possible with fiber. Current International Telegraph and Telephone Consultative Committee (CCITT) standards call for an H_4 rate at about 150 megabits per second.[18] The "payload" is 90 times larger than the primary rates, or 1,000 times the basic rate for a local loop. Indeed, overhead alone is about ten times larger than the entire payload capacity of primary circuits.

The new interface arrangement is in the form of a matrix, replete with pointer cells. It is these pointers which allocate the system resources. This matrix, called a "frame" can accommodate various headers, and subheaders in an "envelope," so that these very high-speed packets or envelopes of frames can be self-routing (independent of nodal "hierarchies"). Variable rates could be transmitted under an Asynchronous Transfer Mode.[19]

Envelopes permitting variable bandwidths give users powerful network control options without reducing the carriers' management and operations control. The new software-controlled options could be designed to permit carriers and customers to share control of a "virtual" network, without mandatory co-location. (*This* is what the FCC's Open Network Architecture proceedings should be all about.)

18. N.B.: We use the original notations and terminology for B-ISDN, even though there have been some changes.

19. Some of the following references and related discussion may be out of date, but we offer them to keep the paper in its original historical perspective. See CCITT, Study Group XVIII, "Report of the Working Party XVIII/7 (Transmission Aspects of Digital Networks)" COM XVIII-R 44 (A, B, & C), August 1987 (Hamburg Report); and the CCITT "Red Book," I-series recommendations (1984) for more detailed information on ISDN specifications. Current material on B-ISDN proposals and standards is in Minzer (1987) and in CCITT reports from SG XVIII, R55 (A, B, & C), Seoul, February 1988 ("Broadband Task Group"). These are being codified for the 1988 Blue Book; drafts are available in the CCITT reports from the July 1988 SG XVIII meeting in Geneva. Also see note 6 *infra*. Early on, there was a controversy over whether to use synchronous packet transfers (sometimes called SONET) for B-ISDN, or asynchronous transfers. The latter was to be optimized for optical fibers. Eventually both concepts merged, with synchronous carried by ATM, and, indeed, ATM working on copper as well as fiber circuits. Today, a similar debate is occurring between the use of IP or ATM, but we expect the two transfer modes to merge, as SONET merged into ATM.

Anania and Solomon

The H_4 channel would accommodate two digitized, compressed, but continuous high-definition TV signals, or 4,500 uncompressed, simultaneous telephone calls. But, as we noted, sending such data in real time is an insufficient use of ATM framing. The beauty of the frame matrix structure is its elegance in handling multiple services and bandwidths in very short time intervals (125 microseconds per frame), facilitating video in *delayed* time, or data in *compressed* time, or packetized voice. Again, we emphasize that B-ISDN does not necessarily mean wideband, continuous occupancy of a channel.

These drastic ratio differences between Narrowband ISDN (and analog telephony) and Broadband ISDN are bound to affect tariffing theories and increase the range of user-defined services. Moreover, as long as carriers have to put in single-mode fiber for the distribution network, and are willing to adopt B-ISDN frame interfaces, it makes little difference in cost whether the packets are running at 151 megabits per second or one gigabit per second!

The Universal Flat Rate

Figure 1[20] suggests that the true variable costs will approximate a step function based on incremental costs for bandwidth, dependent on the laser access to the fiber (i.e., the remote electronics). Access to the network via the "local loop" would be based on the maximum instantaneous bandwidth a subscriber required. This might be the simplest, most effective way to tariff broadband transactions. (In addition to access, a charge could be levied for degrees of non-blocking or priority service.) While the average user of POTS may not need to access all of the Library of Congress on line via B-ISDN, video-on-demand could well justify a flat rate for fiber access to the home. And it is likely that even Narrowband ISDN will find that access is a more productive policy for capital expansion than policing bit-per-second usage.

Until 1980, 80–90% of the costs of the Bell System plant were joint for local, short-haul and long-haul services (Oettinger et al. 1981).

---

20. A fixed hierarchy had not been agreed at the time the original paper was written, so these steps in the figure were suggestions.

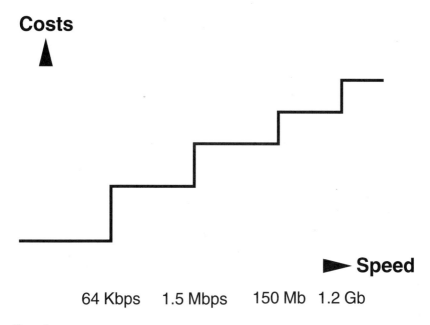

Figure 1
Relative Costs vs Speed For Future B-ISDN Plant

On a distributed computer network like the ARPANET, or even BITNET (where ownership of each link is somewhat mysterious!), the users mainly pay for access; usage costs vary depending on their CPE architecture. Like these relatively slow-speed, customer/carrier shared-packet nets, future transparent "fast-packet" networks, based on SONET (synchronous) frame transfers (working their way at gigabit speeds through a mesh instead of a hierarchical network) will find variable switching costs too small to measure or detect.[21] ATM architectures make pricing the *whole* of the network relevant to any local tariff scheme. Local will be inseparable from medium-, if not long-distance, in B-ISDN. Artificial costing separations, as in today's state/federal network, will only encourage bypass.

As the separation of basic service elements increases in complexity with end-to-end digitization, the only feasible solution from the

21. See footnote 14.

aggregate user perspective becomes a universal flat rate for access. A flat rate is even more attractive under B-ISDN, because with the vast inherent capacity of optical fiber, fixed costs of the distribution plant overwhelm any variable costs. With a flat-rate solution, the sum of customer access costs then would be equal to the total revenue requirement for each carrier. This might even solve the arbitrage problem and the carrier revenue paradox as well.

Conclusion

Three systems or network models were reviewed here: (1) "carrier-based" telephone, telegraph and railroad; (2) transitional service-dedicated analog/digital; and (3) integrated, fiber-based, all-digital and switched broadband. During the current transition period (a hybrid mix of analog/digital systems of nonuniversal character), the combined public and private global networks exhibit a "duplicative functionality." This situation permits clever users to manipulate these systems to their own advantage, thereby bypassing the common-carrier pricing rationale.

In a distributed data processing environment—which is what ISDN is all about—the old revenue requirement game may no longer work. Conventional economics is leading to some bizarre rates and service offerings. The underlying digital process subverts the previous rules, because computer network architecture does not respect artificial physical boundaries which previously regulated access and interconnection.

New tariff policies will ultimately be worked out for ISDN access. When old plant has to be amortized at the same time the new system is capitalized, a painful reallocation of resources and privilege may be necessary in order to avoid future revenue losses.

An Integrated Service Digital Network brings systemic change as multiple *and fungible* services and resources can be reallocated in real time. If transparent networking capabilities are realized (this would require full adherence to international standardization efforts for interoperability between different vendors' CPE and public ISDNs), carriers will lose the ability to differentiate between services. Cross-subsidization policies will then be difficult to continue.

References

Anania, Loretta. 1990. The politics of integration: Network planning in the information society. Ph.D. dissertation, Massachusetts Institute of Technology.

———. 1992. The protean complex: Are open networks common markets? In *The economics of information networks*, ed., Cristian Antonelli. Amsterdam: North-Holland.

Anania, L., and R. Solomon. 1988. User arbitrage and ISDN. *Intermedia* (London) (January).

Finnie, Graham. 1992. The rise and fall of B-ISDN. *Communications Week International* (June 22): 18–19.

Lippman, Andrew. 1988. Video technology: High-definition television. In *National Computer Graphics Association '88 conference proceedings* 2: tutorials.

Minzer, Steven. 1987. Preliminary special report on broadband ISDN access. Bellcore SR-TSY-000857, Issue 1 (December).

Mulgan, Geoff. 1988. Cost and prices: Whatever you can get away with . . . . Paper presented at the International Telecommunications Society meeting, Cambridge, Mass.

Neuman, W. Russell, Lee McKnight, and Richard Jay Solomon. 1997. *The Gordian knot: Political gridlock on the information highway.* Cambridge, Mass.: MIT Press.

Oettinger, A., et al. 1981. Players stakes and politics . . . . Harvard Program on Information Resources Policy, Harvard University.

Pool, Ithiel. 1983. *Technologies of freedom.* Cambridge, Mass.: Harvard University Press.

Pool, I., M. Sirbu, and R. Solomon. 1981. Tariff policy and capital formation in telecommunications. *Evoluzione delle Telecommunicazioni Negli Anni 80.* Rome.

Rhoads. C. S. 1924. *Telegraphy and telephony with railroad applications.* New York: Simmons-Boardman.

Solomon, R. J. 1986. Changing the nature of telecommunications networks. *Intermedia* (May).

———. 1987. Open network architectures and broadband ISDN: The joker in the regulatory deck. In *ICCC-ISDN '87: Evolving in ISDN in North America.*

———. 1988. Vanishing intellectual boundaries: Virtual networking and the loss of sovereignty and control. *Annals of the American Academy of Political and Social Science* 495 (January).

Solomon, R. and L. Anania. 1987a. Integrated digital systems a threat to carrier revenue requirements? *Telecommunications Magazine* (February).

Solomon, R. and L. Anania. 1987b. Paradoxes and puzzles of digital networks, Parts 1 and 2. *Telecommunications Magazine* (January, February).

Solomon, R. and L. Anania. 1987c. The ghost in the machine: A natural monopoly in broadband timesharing? *Telecommunications Magazine* (October).

Solomon, R. and L. Anania. 1987d. Capital formation and broadband planning: Can we get there from here? *Telecommunications Magazine* (November).

Interconnection and Multicast Economics

Internet Cost Structures and Interconnection Agreements

Padmanabhan Srinagesh

Introduction

This chapter is concerned with the relationship between the costs of Internet Service Providers (ISPs) and optimal interconnection arrangements. In the absence of interconnection arrangements, end-users may need to subscribe to multiple networks in order to reach their communities of interest. Interconnection arrangements are important because they enable seamless interconnectivity among all end-users without requiring multiple subscribership. The chapter begins with an introduction to the Internet, which is followed by a description of the costs of Internet Service Providers, including the costs of various support activities. It then develops an economic history of interconnection agreements on the Internet. The chapter goes on to describe the layered structure transport services that constitute the infrastructure on which the Internet is built, and how costs of service provision can influence the choice of an architecture for interconnection. It ends by offering some conclusions on ISP costs and their relationship to interconnection arrangements.

What is the Internet?

The Internet is a network of networks connecting a large and rapidly growing commuity of users spread across the globe. Individuals use the Internet to exchange electronic mail, to obtain and make available information on file servers, and to log on to computers at remote locations. In August 1996, there were 12.8 million host computers on the Internet. This number has been increasing by 72% every year. A 1995 Nielsen poll estimates that there are 28.8 million Internet users. The revenue generated by Internet Service Providers is not known with certainty.

The Internet is a loose federation of networks, each of which is autonomous. There is no central point of control and no overarching regulatory framework. More detailed descriptions of the Internet's history and organizational structure can be found in numerous sources, including Comer (1991) and MacKie-Mason and Varian (1994).

Internet Services and their Costs

Internet Service Providers offer their customers a bundle of services that typically includes hardware and software, customer support, Internet Protocol (IP) transport, information content and provision, and access to individuals and information sources on the Internet.

The service mix varies across providers and over time. Customers usually obtain an access link from their location to the ISP's nearest node. While many ISPs will arrange for this connection and pass the cost on to the customer, the access link is not usually considered a service offered by the ISP. Access through an 800 number or other options in which the called party pays for the telephone call (such as Feature Group B access) are the major exceptions.

Access to the Internet is a minor miracle that is often taken for granted. There are dozens of commercial ISPs offering a variety of service options. At the low end are dial-up accounts with limited electronic mail capability suitable for some individuals. At the high end is 45 Mbps connectivity that is suitable for institutions with sophisticated campus Local Area Networks (LANs), such as large universities. At the level of basic email connectivity, all customers can reach, and be reached by, the same set of people and machines. In this sense, the Internet is like the Public Switched Telephone Network (PSTN), though a key difference between the Internet and the PSTN is that broad connectivity on the Internet resulted without explicit regulations or government mandates on interconnection. A major purpose of this chapter is to describe the economic environment that resulted in this connectivity, and to analyze how fundamental changes in the economic environment will impact the connectivity of the Internet in the future.

As a prelude to this analysis, we describe the cost structure of Internet service provision. Two caveats are in order. First, we focus on the incremental costs of Internet service provision, with occasional references, where relevant, to examples of Internet costs that are directly borne by end-users. The Internet has been built incrementally on a very expensive infrastructure which includes the facilities of the telephone companies, the computing environment of end-users (including department LANs and systems administration) and the campus LANs around which the original regional networks were built. ISPs pay for a part of this infrastructure through their purchase of leased lines and, in some cases, payments to universities for rent and local administration. For the most part, the joint costs of the infrastructure are picked up directly by end-users and are not included in the prices charged by ISPs. Second, in the absence of results generated by a more methodical approach, we rely on anecdotal evidence. Below we list the major categories of cost and describe which elements of cost are sunk, fixed, or variable. The analysis is a useful first step toward understanding Internet competition and interconnection arrangements.

Costs of Hardware and Software

Customers have a choice between dial-up and leased-line access to the Internet. Dial-up access is of two types: shell accounts and Serial Line Internet Protocol (SLIP) or Point to Point Protocol (PPP) accounts. With a shell account, a customer uses his computer, a modem and communications software to log on to a terminal server provided by the ISP. The terminal server is connected to the Internet, and the customer can use the Internet services that the ISP has enabled for his shell account. As most potential purchasers of shell accounts already own a computer and a modem, the incremental hardware and software costs on the user's end are negligible.

An ISP offering dial-up service must purchase a terminal server, a modem pool, and several dial-up lines to the telephone network. For example, in March 1993, the World (an ISP selling shell accounts in

Boston) reported using a Solbourne SPARCserver as its host computer. At that time, the host computer was reported to have 256 MB of memory and 7 GB of disk space. The World had sixty five incoming lines serving approximately 5,000 customers. By August 1994, the number of subscribers had doubled to over 10,000. The World's SPARCserver was reported to have 384 Megabyte of memory and 16 gigabyte of disk space. In 1994, the World did not report the number of incoming lines, but there are reliable estimates that this number has doubled.

The costs of supporting shell accounts are partly fixed and partly variable. When the number of customers and the amount of usage increase, increases in computer memory, disk space, and the number of incoming lines may be necessary. The link from the ISP to the Internet (typically through one of the major backbone providers such as AlterNet, PSI, or the NSFNET) may also need to be upgraded. Investments in the elements of Internet infrastructure described above are typically not sold in small increments. For example, private lines are commonly available at sizes of 56 kilobits per second, 1.5 megabits per second and 45 megabits per second. While fractional speeds are sometimes offered, customers are faced with a limited, discrete set of options, and do not always have the freedom to upgrade capacity in small increments.

SLIP and PPP accounts require software in the customer's host computer to packetize data according to the IP protocol suite, and format the packet for transmission over a telephone line. A suitable modem is required. The hardware and software costs of SLIP connectivity are comparable to similar costs for shell accounts. However, SLIP software has been difficult to configure in the past, and has often been priced above dial-up shell accounts. At the ISP end, costs are incurred in purchasing dial-up routers and in-bound telephone lines. No terminal server is required. Additional customers and additional use will eventually result in additional costs for ports on the router and upgrades in the link from the router to the rest of the network.

Leased-line customers typically have multiple users who are already connected to an enterprise network consisting of one or more LANs. Internet connectivity for these customers often requires the purchase of a router and Channel Service Unit/Data Service Unit (CSU/DSU). AlterNet's prices for equipment suitable for a 56 kbps and T1 connections are about $2,500 and $5,700, respectively. At the ISP end, additional hardware costs may include the purchase of matching CSU/DSU and a port on a router, or an additional router if existing routers are loaded fully. Hardware costs increase in a step-wise manner with the number of customers. Upgrades of the ISP's internal links may also be necessary. Prices for leased-line service vary considerably among providers.

The hardware and software costs described above are part of the costs of obtaining Internet service, as is the cost of the users' computers, and the LAN infrastructure in which large customers have invested. This is an important feature of Internet economics: substantial elements of cost are borne by the user and not by the ISP. Consequently, user costs are considerably higher than the charges set by the ISP. The incremental costs of Internet connectivity are small in comparison to the larger investments that potential customers have already made.

Costs of Customer Support

ISPs incur support costs when a customer is acquired, on an ongoing basis during the business relationship, and when the business relationship is terminated. Service establishment may require a credit check, consultation with the customer on the appropriate choice of service options, set up of a billing record that accurately reflects the customer's selected options, facilities assignment, configuration of the ISP's network to recognize the new customer, analysis of the network infrastructure for possible upgrades to support the added load, and other activities necessary to maintain service at the level expected by customers. In addition, some initial debugging may be required to ensure that the hardware and software at both ends of the connection interoperate. Ongoing customer support is required during the business relationship. Large corporate customers may upgrade their LAN hardware and/or software, and this may require reassignment of IP addresses and reconfiguration of their Internet link. Individual dial-up customers may upgrade their operating system software or install new Internet search tools, and they may require help with configuration. ISPs must also undertake network management and maintenance activities to assure an acceptable quality of service. Costs at service termination include a final settling of accounts, and reconfiguring routers and domain name servers to ensure that the records accurately reflect the termination of the relationship. While all customers require some support, the level and cost of supporting customers varies widely across individual customers.[1]

BARRNet's service description in January 1993 (obtained via anonymous File Transfer Protocol [FTP]) provides some information on the nature and cost of service activation. When it was founded in 1986, BARRNet did not view customer support as a component of its service mix:

BARRNet was conceived and implemented as a network of networks. It connects "sites" or "campuses" rather than individual computers. Our assumption has been generally that our member sites operate their own networks, and support their own users. BARRNet is then more a provider of "wholesale" network service than "retail service". . . .

This view had changed substantially by 1993, when BARRNet offered a wide range of support services. For example, by 1993, T1 connectivity was offered in two options: full service and port-only. Full service had a nonrecurring fee of $17,000. With this option, BARRNet owned, operated, and maintained the hardware at the customer's end, provided spares, and upgraded the software as necessary. The port-only option required the customer to provide the router at its location and to assume responsibility for configuration, management, and maintenance on its end. The nonrecurring fee for port-only service was $13,000 (24% less than for full service). It can thus be inferred that the cost of configuring, managing, and maintaining a router added up to approximately $4,000 over the expected lifetime of the contract.

BARRNet offered other elements of customer support as unbundled options. The Basic Internet Connectivity Package, priced at

1. A technical description of support activities can be found in D.C. Lynch and M.T. Rose (1993), chapter 14.

Internet Cost Structures and Interconnection Agreements

$1,500, included assistance in acquiring an Internet number and domain name, specification of a hardware platform for domain name service and email, configuration of the platform, and training for one person in the maintenance of the platform. The Deluxe Internet Connectivity Package, priced at $3,000, offered the following additional services: specification of equipment to secure internal networks, configuration of packet filters, configuration of secure mail servers on the internal network, and configuration of a Network News server. Additional consulting services, such as specification of technical platforms, remote monitoring of internal links, and training, were available at $125 per hour.

In 1996, BARRNet's equipment and installation fee for a full service T1 customer was $13,750, and a two-year, prepaid contract for service was $22,800. For high-speed connections (T1 and 56 kbps), the nonrecurring charge for equipment and service activation exceeded the ongoing charge for a year's service. For low-speed service, the installation fee was about half the annual service fee. BARRNet's service activation fee varied from $13,750 for full service T1 to $1,300 for 14.4 kbps leased-line or dial-up SLIP or PPP access. Port-only T1 service cost $2,000 less at installation than full service. While the additional charge for the full service option had fallen by 50% between 1992 and 1994, the hourly charge for consulting services had risen to $175 per hour, an increase of $50 per hour. This suggests that the costs of standard support tasks have fallen, while the cost of customized advice has risen sharply.

AlterNet provides another data point. It charges a nonrecurring fee of $5,000 for T1 service; the fee does not include necessary hardware and software, but does include help in configuring the customer's router. While these charges vary across ISPs, similar patterns emerge: the charge associated with account activation is a very significant component of a customer's cost. To the extent that there is active competition among ISPs, the structure of prices reveals, at least in part, the structure of ISP costs; also, customer support appears to be significant. In sum, there appears to be considerable expense and effort involved in connecting a new customer to the Internet, and considerable variation in cost across support services and customer types.

IP Transport

In this section, we discuss a relevant aspect of IP transport: the method by which an IP packet is transported from one location to another. Within a campus LAN (local area network), the entire IP packet (data plus header) is treated as a data unit by the LAN, encapsulated in a LAN packet and transported in accordance with the LAN's protocols. An important consequence is that LAN protocols will determine access to the LAN. From an economic point of view, the significance is that the IP header cannot be used to allocate a potentially scarce resource (access to the LAN) without accommodation by the underlying LAN protocol. The identification of bottlenecks and the design of resource allocation mechanisms in a layered architecture is complex and beyond the scope of this chapter.

On wide area networks built on private lines competition for the scarce resource takes on a different form. A router receives packets from various interfaces, consults its routing table, and forwards each packet on the appropriate outward link. When the incoming rate exceeds the outgoing rate, packets can be temporarily queued. The IP header has a Type of Service (TOS) field that can, in principle, be used to manage queues in routers, but this function has not been implemented widely. Bohn et al. (1993) describe an episode during the mid-1980s when router queues were managed to offer priority to some delay-sensitive uses of the network. They propose that the TOS field be implemented and used to manage access to congested links. When IP runs over private lines (or any time-division multiplexed service) the Internet protocol can be used to implement smart markets (MacKie-Mason and Varian 1995) or other congestion management schemes without any change in protocols at lower layers in the stack.

Wide area networks that use so-called "cloud technologies" (also called fast-packet services) such as Frame Relay (FR), Switched Multimegabit Data Service (SMDS) and Asynchronous Transfer Mode (ATM) raise a different set of economic issues. Fast-packet services statistically multiplex packets over time slots carried on underlying physical facilities. The fast-packet technology treats the IP packet as a Protocol Data Unit, just as LANs do. As was the case with LAN technologies, the IP header, by itself, cannot deal adequately with resource allocation issues. Below, we briefly describe the role of IP transport in the provision of Internet services.

Costs of Transporting IP Packets over Private Lines In the late 1980s, most ISPs had internal backbones consisting of routers connected redundantly to one another by private lines ranging in speed from 56 kilobits per second to 1.5 megabits per second. Most lines were leased from telephone companies. There were a few exceptions. NEARNET, in Boston, had its own wireless Ethernet (10 Mbps) backbone connecting five nodes, and BARRNet had its own wireless link between the University of California at San Francisco and Berkeley. Statistical multiplexing of IP packets on the underlying leased lines led to significant cost savings. The cost of transporting IP packets was determined by leased-line tariffs, the costs of the routing hardware and software at the nodes, and the ongoing costs of monitoring the network and remedying supply disruptions in a timely manner. These costs were fairly substantial. MacKie-Mason and Varian (1993) estimate that the costs of leased lines and routers amounted to 80% of total NSFNET costs. The cost of the Network Operations Center (NOC) amounted to another 7%. With high transport costs, the ability to use bandwidth efficiently through statistical multiplexing is a major benefit. However, it should be noted that the NSFNET service provided by ANS (a nonprofit joint venture of IBM, MCI, and the state of Michigan) was part of a research experiment in high-speed networking funded by the National Science Foundation. Almost all NSFNET customers were large regional networks, not end-users, and ANS's cost structure differed significantly from that of other ISPs. An estimate based on an analysis of several mid-levels suggests that IP transport accounts for 25 to 40% of a typical ISP's total costs. While efficient use of bandwidth was inportant to these ISPs, it should be noted that bandwidth was often a small portion of total costs. The efficient use of other resources that could substitute for bandwidth (network administration and maintenance) may imply that a certain amount of overengineering (excess capacity in bandwidth) may be optimal.

For many ISPs, transport costs are suk over the business planning horizon. A brief digression on leased-line tariffs may be useful, both for an understanding of IP transport costs and because the evolution of leased-line prices may foretell similar developments on the Internet. Currently, most long haul transmission links are provided over optical fiber. The major cost of constructing fiber-optic links is in the trenching and labor cost of installation. The cost of the fiber is a relatively small proportion of the total cost of construction and installation. It is therefore common practice to install "excess" fiber. According to the Federal Communication Commission's Fiber Deployment Update (May 1994), between 40 and 50% of the fiber installed by the typical interexchange carriers is "dark"; i.e., the lasers and electronics required for transmission are not in place. The comparable number for the Major Local Operating Companies (MLOC) is between 50 and 80%. Private lines are provided out of surplus (lit and unlit) capacity available in the networks constructed by telephone companies. The incremental cost of providing private-line service is determined by the costs of lighting up fiber if necessary (lasers plus electronics at the ends), the costs of customer acquisition (sales effort and service order activation), and ongoing costs of maintaining a customer account. Private-line tariffs must recover these incremental costs and contribute to the very substantial sunk costs of the underlying facilities. Furthermore, these tariffs are set in a very competitive environment. The effect of this competition has been to drive down the price of leased capacity. According to *Business Week*, private-line prices have fallen by 80% since 1989 ("Dangerous Living in Telecom's Top Tier," September 12, 1994, p. 90).

The cost structure described above, together with competitive forces, has resulted in two increasingly common features of the price structure: volume discounts and term commitments. The standard interLATA (inter-Local Access Transport Area) private-line tariff consists of a nonrecurring charge, and a monthly charge based on the airline mileage between the two locations to be connected. Customers can select optional features at an extra charge. The standard charges vary with the bandwidth of the private line, but there are no usage-sensitive charges. Private-line tariffs offer discounts based on volume and term commitments. AT&T's Accunet 1.5 (T1) tariff offers a discount of 57% to customers whose monthly bill for a specified bundle of services, including T1 lines, exceeds $1 million at standard rates, and who commit to maintaining that level of expenditure for five years. The volume discount may reflect the fact that large customers are more desirable: it may be less costly selling to one customer with a $1 million bill than to 1,000 customers, each of whom has a $1,000 bill. The term commitment may be the telephone company's response to the long-run cost structure of building physical networks and the high cost of churn: as there are fixed costs of service activation and termination, companies seek to provide their customers with incentives to be loyal.

In a competitive environment with excess capacity, there is a tension between the large sunk costs of physical networks and very low incremental costs of usage. On the one hand, the need to recover sunk costs suggests using price structures with high up-front charges and low (or zero) usage rates. On the other hand, with significant excess capacity present, short-run profits can be increased by selling at any price above incremental cost. Economic theory would suggest that the pricing outcome in this situation might be unstable, unless regulatory forces or other influences inhibiting competition were present.

The consequence of the leased-line tariff structure described above for the cost of IP transport is straightforward. Given a high nonrecurring service order charge, ISPs with leased-line backbones have an incentive to size their needs over a three-to-five-year period, and commit to a level of purchase determined by projected demand. In a rapidly growing Internet, this can result in substantial excess capacity among ISPs in the short run. The incremental cost of carrying IP packets will be close to zero. (If private lines charged for usage, this would not be true). However, the sunk costs of IP transport can be substantial. An examination of ISP network maps in mid-1993 suggested that none of the national providers had backbones large enough to qualify for AT&T's largest discount. However, many ISPs were large enough to qualify for smaller, but nevertheless substantial, discounts, on three-to-five-year contracts. Competition among these ISPs may be subject to the economic tension present in the private-line market. Indeed, the use of volume discounts and term commitments is emerging in the ISP market. ISPs typically charge their T1 customers twice the rate they charge their 56 Kbps customers, even though the T1 customers have 24 times the bandwidth. Term commitments can be seen in BARRNet's price structure: 56 Kbps customers are offered a 17% discount over monthly rates if they take a two-year, prepaid contract.

There are at least three types of ISPs whose cost structures do not fit the model described above. One type is represented by Sprint, which offers a national IP service, SprintLink. As Sprint owns a large national fiber-optic network with substantial excess capacity (45% dark in 1992), it faces a lower incremental cost for transport provision than other ISPs which lease lines. However, Sprint has far higher sunk costs. The second type of ISP is represented by small mid-levels or regional networks. These ISPs obtain access to the global Internet by connecting to a larger ISP. Very often this larger ISP is ANS, which historically provided interregional connectivity to the regional networks sponsored by the National Science Foundation. The third type of ISP is the small reseller, which appears to have grown rapidly in the last year or so. To the larger ISP, the reseller often appears to be a customer with 56 kilobits per second or T1 access. The mid-level or reseller has a very small (perhaps non-existent) backbone: customers are responsible for the connections to the reseller's node (and there may be just one node), and the reseller purchases the connections to the larger ISP (and there may be just one connection). The small ISP/reseller has relatively small sunk costs and little excess capacity. Small providers working out of their basements may require an initial investment of approximately $30,000 for electronic gear and about $1,000 per month for telephone connections. For these providers, incremental costs for transport are relatively high as significant volume discounts are not applicable on the links to their customers and to the larger ISP.

Not surprisingly, the range of prices charged by service providers varies widely. In a competitive environment where the costs structures of different providers are radically different, where average costs are very different from incremental costs, and where there is substantial excess capacity in one key input (raw bandwidth), the equilibrium outcome is not obvious. The prices for shell and SLIP accounts vary dramatically among providers, and serve to make the point. AlterNet, which leases an extensive international backbone, charges $20 per month for 25 hours of access, and $2 per hour for direct dial to an AlterNet Point of Presence (POP). The one-time fee is $25. At the other extreme, Scruz-Net, a small network in Santa

Cruz, offers single-host SLIP/PPP connectivity at 28.8 kilobits per second for $25 per month, with an allowance of 100 free hours and only a $12.50 one-time setup fee. JVNCnet, a commercial provider with a backbone spanning many states, offers SLIP access at $35 per month for 20 hours and $2.50 for each additional hour, and a $29 one-time setup fee. Whether these large price variations are accompanied by significant variations in quality is not known.

In sum, the cost structure of IP transport provision varies considerably among ISPs. The four broad classes of ISPs include providers who own a physical network, national backbones based on leased facilities, small regional networks, and resellers. Sunk costs of transport are highest for the first type and lowest for the last. Variable costs (according to number of customers and usage) are lowest for the first type and highest for the last. Prices across providers vary greatly.

The Impact of Fast-packet Technologies on IP Transport Cost The introduction of new fast-packet services such as Frame Relay, SMDS, and ATM may have a significant impact on an ISP's cost structure and its role as a provider of low-cost transport. Fast-packet services (also referred to as cloud technologies) statistically multiplex variable-size packets or fixed-size cells onto time slots carried on an underlying physical facility. IP packets ride on top of this statistically multiplexed service. As is true of LANs, a fast-packet service will treat an IP packet (header plus data) as a data unit, add its own header, and transport it over the underlying network in accordance with its own rules. Currently, NEARnet and PSI run IP over Frame Relay; CERFnet runs IP over SMDS; and AlterNet runs IP over Ethernet over ATM. The additional statistical multiplexing gains of IP transport over those obtained by the underlying "cloud" service will be less than the gains obtained when ISPs use private lines. The extent to which an ISP can offer additional multiplexing gains will be determined in part by the proportion of the traffic over the physical link that is generated by the ISP; the higher this proportion, the greater the potential gain generated by the ISP.

Early tariffs for fast-packet services had monthly rates that varied with bandwidth. There were no charges for usage or for distance. One example is a Frame Relay tariff filed by US West in September

1992. This tariff offers a small discount (about 10%) to customers who commit to a five-year contract. MCI's SMDS price structure (announced in August 1994) is considerably different. There are usage and distance charges, but the usage charges are capped at relatively low levels (*Business Wire,* August 16, 1994). For large users (with an access speed of 34 megabits per second), MCI's SMDS price can vary from $13,000 to $20,000 per port per month, depending on the customer's usage.

Both tariffs discussed above show a movement away from the deep term discounts that characterize private-line charges. ISPs that lease fast-packet services from others will have a weak incentive to sign long-term contracts for their backbones. A smaller proportion of their transport costs will be sunk. In addition, connectivity among multiple ISPs can be established at significantly lower costs than was possible with private lines. Once an ISP pays a flat rate to connect to a fast-packet cloud, the incremental costs of virtual connections to multiple ISPs are very small. With MCI's SMDS service, for example, there are no additional costs involved in communicating with multiple SMDS customers (though an ISP will have to pay for each port it connects to on the SMDS cloud). Small ISPs with a few nodes can reach out to anyone else on the national SMDS cloud without investing in a national backbone consisting of multiple private lines. With Frame Relay and ATM service, there are incremental costs of reaching additional sites on the cloud, as Permanent Virtual Circuits (PVCs) must be configured and managed. However, these costs are relatively small (as little as $1.19 per month in US West's tariff for Frame Relay).

Even if IP transport provides minimal multiplexing gains when it is run over a cloud technology, IP service will perform important functions. These include uniform global addressing (Frame Relay, for example, has reusable addresses with only local significance) and wide connectivity, protocol conversion across varying LAN, MAN (metropolitan area network), and WAN (wide area network) technologies, and an important "bearer service" role that helps insulate embedded investments from ongoing technical change in network hardware. Most of these functions can be performed at the edge of the network, and IP may migrate to the network border over time.

This may accelerate the evolution of some ISPs into systems integrators, or "market-makers," in the terminology of Mandelbaum and Mandelbaum (1991).

The Impact of Multimedia Traffic on IP Transport Costs The share of transport in ISP costs is likely to change as new multimedia applications grow in popularity. Voice, video, data, and images differ in the requirements they place on the network, and raise difficulties for the use of IP transport in its current form.

Efficient coding schemes vary greatly for the different media; an excellent discussion of coding schemes can be found in Lucky (1991). Voice can now be digitized and compressed by a factor of 16 to 1 on commercially available chips, such as Qualcomm's Q4400 vocoder, which claims to achieve near-toll voice quality at less than 10 kilobits per second. Video compression using the MPEG (Motion Pictures Experts Group) standard allows for VCR picture quality at a bandwidth of 1.5 megabits per second. Video applications over the Internet (MBone and CU-SeeMe) use a different compression scheme. The MBone uses the JPEG (Join Pictures Experts Group) standard to digitize each frame and transmits data using User Datagram Protocol (UDP) and IP tunneling. These techniques offer low picture quality at 100 to 300 kilobits per second (two to ten frames per second). Transmission of data files requires no specific bandwidth; there is a trade-off between bandwidth and delay. For many current applications (email, file transfer, and even fax) 9.6 kilobits per second is adequate, and store-and-forward techniques are acceptable. High-quality image transfer (such as that needed in medical applications) requires considerably more bandwidth; schemes using lossy JPEG allow for the transfer at 56 kilobits per second in reasonable time.

If bandwidth were essentially infinite, variations in bandwidth use would not be a problem for mechanisms like IP that treat all packets equally. However, most ISPs pay for added bandwidth, and must treat it as a scarce resource. A simple computation highlights the problem. At 300 kilobits per second for a video session on the Internet, it takes only 150 simultaneous sessions to congest a link on the NSFNET, the Internet's major backbone, with the highest-speed links. The congestion created by video use is pernicious; it destroys some valuable mechanisms that are part of the Internet's discipline and efficiency. Transmission Control Protocol (TCP) is used by host computers to provide a reliable byte stream to the applications that are run by an end-user. TCP selects a window size, which determines the number of packets it can send to the other side before stopping for an acknowledgment. Large window sizes allow for faster throughput. With the implementation of the slow start mechanism, TCP monitors round-trip times, and if it detects congestion, reduces the window size, and contributes to better system behavior. Video sessions use User Datagram Protocol. Unlike TCP, UDP does not reduce its transmission rate during periods of congestion. Other users running data applications over TCP pay disproportionately in delay when video sessions congest any link. If congestion should become severe, TCP users may have an incentive to stop using the slow start mechanism.

ISPs recognize that there is a problem with high bandwidth users and uses. In the absence of pricing solutions that can be implemented with the IP header structure, they have resorted to blunt instruments. For example, anonymous FTP sessions on NEARnet's server begin with a welcome message announcing that only paying subscribers may access the Internet Talk Radio files. In view of the fact that some of these files are greater than 30 megabytes, the prohibition appears to be motivated by a desire to preserve bandwidth. If the Internet supported a more sophisticated billing mechanism, or if the cloud technology underlying IP service supported multiple quality of service types, blanket prohibitions such as this might not be necessary. Current work on IPng (Internet Protocol—next generation) and real-time protocols may solve the bandwidth allocation problem at some point in the future. In the meantime, IP remains a very cost-efficient transport mechanism for applications (like email and image transfer) that are not affected by delay.

Summary of Transport Costs The costs of providing IP transport represent a substantial fraction (25–40%) of an ISP's cost. This proportion will fall as less costly fast-packet services are more widely deployed. However, the increase in the use of multimedia applications may result in a proportionally greater increase in the need for bandwidth. The tension between satisfying customers with bandwidth-intensive needs and satisfying customers with low-bandwidth applications cannot be efficiently resolved with current technology. MacKie-Mason and Varian (1992) have suggested a "smart market" mechanism that allows bandwidth to be efficiently priced. An attractive feature of their pricing scheme is that it generates the correct signals for investing in new capacity. More work needs to be done in this area, taking into account the more complex layered structure that is now emerging in the Internet. In addition, the issue of bundling transport, support, and information content needs to be addressed by new pricing approaches.

Information Content and Provision

There is usually a fixed cost associated with the production formatting, and organization of information suitable for database applications and a low cost of duplication (Perritt 1991). Some examples suggest that the revenue generated by information provision will greatly exceed the revenue generated by the underlying transport. Audiotex services (900 and 976 numbers) usually set per-minute charges that are many multiples of standard toll charges. Further supporting evidence can be found in the price list published by Dialog. The connect-time charge for transport has traditionally been in the range of $3 to $12 per hour, depending on the network used to access Dialog. Once the user has logged on, the charge for database access ranges from $15 to $300 per hour. Peter Huber (1987) reports that on-line services spend only 8 to 10% of their expenses on local and long-distance transport. Approximately 40 to 45% of their expenses are spent in acquiring information content, and approximately 45% is spent on sales, marketing, and administration.

For much of its life, the Internet has offered "free" information. This reflects the Internet's roots in the academic community, which encourages the free dissemination of scholarly research. In addition, various government agencies have begun to use the Internet as a means of making public information available in electronic form. For example, the FCC posts its daily digest on an FTP server.

Archives of Usenet groups and the ongoing contributions to news-groups provide another source of free information. The use of Web servers to establish company "presence" on the Internet represents yet another source of "free" information; the supplier of the information pays to display advertisements in a nonintrusive way.

There is, however, a rapid increase in the number of subscription-based information services on the Internet. All the major information services (Dialog, Orbit, etc.) offer telnet access to subscribers. Dialog provides an itemized bill that separately lists charges for transport and database access. Such services appears to be taking root in the university community too. The ORION system at the University of California at Los Angeles charges for access and usage, with a minimum charge of $25 per month (CERFnet News, January 1991). The clari.* hierarchy in Usenet is available only to paying customers, who are charged $75 per site plus $1 per user at the site.

It appears likely that the Internet will see a variety of free and commercial information services develop. While information services are accustomed to paying for all transport charges incurred by their clients and billing them for network use, providers of free information may resist this arrangement for the recovery of transport cost since they have no paying clients to bill. Currently, free Internet service satisfies the academic community's needs. However, if budgetary pressures on academia should increase, universities may decide to charge for the use of information they produce, and the needs of this community may align with those of the on-line industry.

There is a considerable research effort under way on a variety of security, privacy, and billing mechanisms that will support commercial information provision over the Internet. The experience of the on-line industry suggests that the commercial potential of information content and provision will be significantly greater than the cost of the underlying transport, and the needs of information providers may have a significant influence on payment mechanisms for transport.

The Bottom Line on Costs The Internet was originally developed to meet a specific goal: the interconnection of academic sites for the purpose of open scholarly research and education. In meeting this goal, the Internet was not just successful, it was too successful. The rapid growth of the Internet into sectors of the economy that it was never designed to serve (such as banks and on-line information services) has revealed some gaps in capability that were not important to early users, but are very important to new users. These include higher levels of customer service, greater reliability, assured security and privacy, and billing mechanisms. In response to these changing market needs, the nature of Internet service and the cost structures of service provision are being transformed. At the same time, the spread of fast-packet services is reducing the Internet's value as a provider of cheap transport. As competitors continue to emphasize service quality as a differentiating factor, the share of transport in total cost will fall, and the share of existing and new support services and sales expenses will rise. As Noll (1994) has pointed out, AT&T's expenses on sales and advertising for voice services grew rapidly in absolute and relative terms after equal access was implemented and competition grew more intense.

Economics of Interconnection

This section develops a brief economic history of interconnection agreements on the Internet, with a view to understanding future developments.

The Early Years: 1986–1991

A logical starting point for a discussion of Internet interconnection agreements is the first NSFNET backbone, which was constructed in 1986. The NSFNET was the top tier of a growing network of networks organized as a three-layer hierarchy. The second tier in the hierarchy was made up of mid-level networks, each consisting of ten to 30 universities. Many mid-levels were formed with funding from the National Science Foundation. Each mid-level attached to a nearby NSFNET node. The bottom layer consisted of campus LANs, which attached to a mid-level network.

The Internet's hierarchical structure, crowned by a single backbone, resulted from early decisions by Internet architects. In discussing their work, Comer (1991) states: "They came to think of the ARPANET as a dependable wide-area backbone around which the Internet could be built. The influence of a single, central wide area backbone is still painfully obvious in some of the Internet protocols . . . and has prevented the Internet from accommodating additional backbone networks gracefully" (pp. 33–34).

Early routing protocols, such as the Gateway-to-Gateway Protocol (GGP) and the Exterior Gateway Protocol (EGP), bear out Comer's observation. Internet routers typically use hop-by-hop destination routing. The router reads the destination address in the packet header, looks up its routing table, and forwards the packet on the next hop. Routing protocols specify the rules by which routers obtain and update their routing tables. Exterior or border gateways that connect a network to the rest of the Internet use only the network portion (the first eight to 24 bits of the 32-bit IP address) of the destination address for routing purposes.

GGP partitioned Internet gateways into two groups: core gateways controlled by the Internet Network Operations Center and noncore gateways controlled by others. The core gateways contained full routes. All other gateways were permitted to maintain partial routes to destinations that they were directly connected to, and to point a default route up the hierarchy toward a core gateway. This arrangement simplified routing at the core and noncore gateways, and reduced the amount of information that routers had to exchange over the network. The set of core gateways and the links connecting them together formed the backbone at the top of the hierarchy. It is worth noting that a major justification for a single backbone was simplicity in routing, and this was unrelated to economies of scale in transport. GGP does not easily accommodate multiple backbones connected to one another at multiple points.

We provide a brief example (based on Comer's discussion) that highlights a technical problem and a pricing puzzle that arise when multiple backbones are multiply interconnected. Suppose two coast-to-coast backbones are interconnected on the East and West Coasts. Suppose Host 1 located on the East Coast on Network 1 wishes to send a packet to Host 2 located on the East Coast on Network 2. It would make sense for the packet to go through the East Coast interconnect point. Suppose Host 1 wishes to send a packet to Host 3 on Network 2 on the West Coast. If Network 1 has a better (less congested) backbone, it might make sense for Network 1 to transport the traffic across the continent, and deliver it to Network 2 at the West Coast interconnect. Routing will depend on the host address, not just on the network portion of the address. Routing schemes that require this level of detail are not scalable: the size of routing tables would increase too rapidly with the growth of the Internet.

Apart from such technical problems, there is an economic problem. For transcontinental communication between users on different backbones, which backbone should carry the traffic? In the absence of settlements. it is not clear that either network has any incentive to volunteer for the job. As long as backbones are not congested, the issue of transport will not be a weighty one. But in a world of rapidly growing traffic, when frequent upgrades are needed, there are good reasons for an ISP to advocate routing arrangements that use another ISP's backbone instead of its own. This is not merely a theoretical possibility. A relatively large proportion of traffic between sites in Mexico transits the United States over the NSFNET.

Of course, all ISPs cannot pursue the strategy of shifting traffic onto others' backbones successfully. An alternative is for some form of settlements among interconnected networks. The most important criteria for an efficient settlements mechanism are that it should not impose high administrative costs, that it should provide the correct incentives for routing, and that the net flow of funds should allow all suppliers to recover their costs. As the Internet goes through periods of substantial excess capacity, followed by periods of congestion and capacity expansion, different settlement mechanisms will be required. The smart market mechanism described by MacKie-Mason and Varian (1993) can adapt well to these changing circumstances. More work may be needed to accommodate routing protocols to the smart market mechanism.

The alternative to competing peer backbones is a single backbone. The drawback to this alternative is that there will be no competition for the provision of a key service: routing and long-haul transport.

While economists have developed sophisticated regulatory schemes to deal with the lack of competition, the practical difficulties in implementing these schemes can be enormous. The early architecture of the NSFNET apparently avoided these issues by selecting a simple routing scheme and the architecture it implied. As the net was not commercial, there was little danger of monopoly pricing, and much to be gained by centralizing the routing function.

The next-generation routing protocol, EGP, addressed several weaknesses of GGP by introducing the notion of an autonomous system. (Interested readers are referred to the discussion of EGP in Chapter 14 of Comer [1991].) Despite its advances, EGP shared the key drawback of GGP. As Comer points out: "EGP is inadequate for optimal routing in an architecture that has multiple backbones interconnected at multiple points. For example, the NSFNET and DDN backbone interconnection . . . cannot use EGP alone to exchange routing information if routes are to be optimal. Instead, managers manually divide the set of NSFNET networks and advertise some of them to one exterior gateway and others to a different gateway" (p. 238).

The Interconnection, 1991–1994

From the very beginning the business plans of key ISPs appeared to be inconsistent with one another. ANS provided a bundle of services that included full routing and long-haul transport. The new backbones had constructed national networks of their own, and had no need to purchase transport or routing from ANS. However, they did need to offer their customers full access to all Internet sites. As most of these sites were connected to ANS, an interconnection agreement with ANS would have met their customers' needs. The commercial ISPs argued that such connectivity (without routing and transport) should be settlement-free. The rationale advanced by the commercial providers was as follows. When a customer of one ISP communicates with a customer of another ISP, both customers benefit. Each customer pays his or her ISP for the use of its network. Both ISPs are paid by their customers, and there should be no further need for the ISPs to settle. Proponents of this view recognized that their argument did not apply to transit traffic. But when there are only two networks involved, there is no transit traffic, and no settlements are required. It was this philosophy, together with the inability of the new entrants to obtain interconnection agreements with ANS on terms acceptable to them, that led to the formation of the Commercial Internet Exchange (CIX) in August 1991. The three founding members were CERFnet, PSI, and AlterNet. The CIX members agreed to exchange traffic without regard to type (commercial or R&E (research and education) and without settlements. The CIX router was installed in Santa Clara and managed by PSI; other founding members leased private lines from their networks to the CIX router.

Initially, ANS did not join the CIX. It formed a for-profit subsidiary, ANS CO+RE, and proposed a gateway agreement that would lead to full connectivity. At its core, the gateway agreement entailed three steps. First, determine separate attachment fees for commercial and R&E customers. Second, use statistical samples of each attached network's traffic to estimate the proportion of R&E traffic. Third, charge each attached network a weighted combination of the commercial and R&E attachment fees, with weights obtained from the sample. A portion of the revenue generated by gateway agreements was to be put in a pool that would be used to upgrade the NSFNET infrastructure.

The proposals from ANS and the CIX members had little in common. Nevertheless, after some negotiation it was agreed that ANS and the CIX members would interconnect without settlements. ANS did not pay the CIX membership fee, and CIX members did not pay ANS for NSFNET services.

In October 1993, the CIX, apparently without warning, blocked ANS traffic from transiting the CIX router. At this point, ANS (through its subsidiary CO+RE) joined the CIX and full connectivity was restored. In the ten months following this episode, CIX membership rose from about 20 to about 70 ISPs.

The right of resellers of IP service to transit the CIX router has been, and continues to be, debated. The CIX membership agreement has contained, for at least two years, some rules suggesting that assured connectivity was limited to the "direct" customers of member

ISPs. The term was not defined in the agreement. As of November 1994, resellers of IP services had their packets blocked at the CIX router if they did not join the CIX and pay the $7,500 annual membership fee. The cost of resale has gone up. AlterNet requires resellers to purchase a special wholesale connection that costs about three times as much as a retail connection. In addition, AlterNet requires resellers to use a complex addressing scheme and routing protocol, Border Gateway Protocol 4 (BGP4), rather than the simpler PPP protocol used by end-users. PSI does not sell wholesale connections. Sprint apparently treated resellers just like its other customers, but CIX rules, together with the ability of the CIX to filter routes, may affect Sprint's policy on resale. The growth of resellers and the change in the way established ISPs treat them is an interesting and unsettled phenomenon.

In order to simplify the exposition, only the roles of the NSFNET and the CIX in Internet connectivity have been discussed so far. There are several additional arrangements that are important for assuring connectivity. The more complex arrangements described below were made possible by developments in routers and routing protocols. Routers can now accommodate large routing tables, reducing the need for default routes. The current routing protocol of choice, BGP4, has automated the maintenance of routing tables and is flexible enough to accommodate routing policy based on configuration information. BGP4 also permits the use of more flexible addressing and aggregation of routes. Routing technology is not an absolute constraint on the development of a multiply connected multiple backbone architecture.

The Metropolitan Area Ethernet-East   The Metropolitan Area Ethernet-East (MAE-East) started as an experimental interconnect arrangement developed by AlterNet, PSI, and SprintLink. MAE-East differs from the CIX in two important ways. First, MAE-East is a distributed Ethernet service (provided by Metropolitan Fiber Systems) spanning a wide geographic area. An attraction of a cloud service like MAE-East is its cost, compared to that of a physical connection to a single router. Second, there are no multilateral agreements in place at MAE-East. ISPs need to work out a set of bilateral agreements that meet their needs for connectivity. Currently, none of the bilateral agreements are in written form. It has been unofficially reported that there are no settlements at MAE-East. Every provider accepts all traffic from and delivers all traffic to any ISP with which a bilateral agreement exists. The transactions costs of multiple bilateral negotiations can be high.

The CIX placed a router on Pacific Bell's SMDS cloud. The CIX will retain its multilateral connection agreement, which reduces the transactions cost of establishing connectivity. These developments suggest that there is broad agreement on the benefits of using cloud technologies as interconnection mechanisms. But the large ISPs have not yet settled on a common business agreement for interconnection. The simultaneous existence of two very different interconnection models (multilateral and bilateral) naturally raises the question of how many types of interconnection agreements can be expected in equilibrium. If a standard agreement emerges, will it look like the CIX agreement (multilateral), the MAE-East agreement (bilateral), or something else?

Analysis of Interconnection Agreements

Consider first an architecture based on the CIX model: multiple backbones interconnected at a single point (a), exchanging traffic among the direct customers of all members without settlements. Members pay a fixed membership fee. Assume that ISP networks are based on leased lines and not on fast-packet services. Advantages of this architecture are as follows:

• Membership in the XIX is necessary and sufficient for connectivity to the Internet.

• Members whose routers cannot carry the full complement of routes can keep local routes and point a default to the XIX.

• Competition among backbone providers is feasible (supported by the routing technology).

Some disadvantages of this architecture:

• If too many networks use the XIX as the only interconnect point, the XIX router could experience congestion and provide poor service.

• End-users who are geographically close to one another, far away from the XIX, and on different networks will experience needless delay as their packets make the round-trip journey to the XIX.

• Small regional providers that join the XIX will have the same reach as large ISPs that have invested in national backbones. However, small regional networks will have smaller sunk costs, and will be able to offer lower prices than the national providers. Cost recovery may become a significant issue for the larger providers. However, if the national backbones cannot recover costs and go out of business, the small regionals lose the connectivity that their customers want.

• Given their cost structures, large ISPs with national backbones will set prices that are not proportional to bandwidth. Small resellers can arbitrage the difference profitably for customers who do not require much support since they do not have large sunk costs to recover. There will be little incentive for anyone to invest in a national backbone (facilities-based or leased).

The first two disadvantages can be avoided by setting up multiple points of interconnection between ISPs with national backbones. This will reduce the load on the XIX router, and reduce latency. The third difficulty can be removed by restricting membership to ISPs with national backbones, or requiring small regional ISPs that join the XIX to pay settlements to the larger ISPs. Both these possibilities are hinted at in the CIX's membership agreement. Arbitrage by resellers can be handled by prohibiting resale, or by raising the price to resellers. Large ISPs have already taken this step. The current situation may be stable.

The network topology of an ISP using fast-packet services may be quite complex. An ISP's customers may be scattered all over the globe, and different cloud technologies may be in use at the various customer locations. The ISP can use the Internet protocol to integrate its network over these disparate clouds. The ISP will provide customer support, some network management and possibly information content. The ISP will not provide the multiplexing function that reduces the cost of underlying transport; this function will be performed by the firms producing the underlying clouds. In this environment, the original CIX philosophy may be an attractive model for interconnection, and the distinction between large ISPs with national backbones and small regionals disappears. Every provider purchases access to the designated underlying clouds, and shares the costs of the underlying transport by paying the price charged by the supplier of the cloud. The costs of interconnection become symmetric. As some (large) ISPs do not have sunk costs that other (small) ISPs can take advantage of, the incentives to interconnect will not be hampered by gamesmanship.

As transport charges faced by ISPs fall, the prices they charge their customers will not be proportional to their access speed, and resellers may continue to find the Internet a profitable business. The treatment of resellers in this environment is difficult to predict. The economic forces governing resale in the Internet are not very different from those at work in the market for interLATA voice traffic. (An excellent discussion of resale in the long-distance market can be found in Briere [1990], Chapter 16.) The rapid growth of resellers in both the voice market and the Internet may raise difficult issues regarding the stability of competition.

Architectures for Interconnection

A fundamental question that is not often asked is: Why should networks interconnect? This question does not have an obvious answer when the networks in question are virtual and not physical networks, and when "network interconnection" is used to refer to a business relationship between network service providers. At a purely physical level, it is true that a continuous path is needed between the equipment used by the communicating parties. However, three examples presented below suggest that full connectivity among users does not require all intervening networks to establish business relationships with one another. The optimal degree of interconnection is part of a larger architectural decision.

Consider first the case of an end-user who wishes to purchase a private line to connect two points, one on the West Coast and one on the East Coast. One option currently available to the customer is to lease (from the New York Local Exchange Carrier) a private line to an Interexchange Carrier's (IXC) Point of Presence (POP), lease

from the IXC a private line from the New York POP to the California
POP, and lease a private line from the California Local Exchange
Carrier linking the California POP to the customer's location on the
West Coast. The end-user pays a separate charge to each of the three
networks for their segments of the private line. While the three
networks must agree on technical matters (timing and format of the
signal), there need be no explicit business arrangements linking the
network service providers that provide the private lines. Interconnection on the physical level does not require the network providers
to maintain explicit business relationships. The customer may
choose to designate one of the three networks to be its agent, and
this would result in business agreements among the three networks;
but such a designation is not required. The choice between the two
arrangements would seem to hinge on transactions costs (who bills
whom, who reports and coordinates repairs of outages, etc.).

For the second example, consider a community of electronic mail
users who belong to networks that are not connected to one another.
Suppose this community wants to establish a bulletin board or news-
group-like service to which its members can post, and on which they
can read each other's contributions. One solution would be for the
networks to interconnect and arrange for the transfer of e-mail.
Another possibility would be for one of the users in the set (or even
a third party) to establish email accounts with all the networks to
which the community is connected, and to operate a mail relay that
passes email transparently across networks. Which of these options
is the lower-cost solution? It is not clear that there are economies of
scale in the customer support required for small operations of this
sort. If all e-mail prices were based only on usage, with no monthly
fees, then there would appear to be no cost differences between the
two alternatives. Indeed, with pure usage-sensitive pricing, each
member of the list could join all the networks at no additional cost.
If email prices consisted of flat monthly fees, with no usage charge,
then the solution based on a mail relay might be more expensive.
This solution would require that at least one user belong to all
networks, and that user would face higher email charges than if the
networks were interconnected. This might (or might not) be offset
by lower costs for customized support. In this example, the connec-

tivity of the email networks is not necessary to support full email connectivity among users, and other alternatives could conceivably be more efficient than full network interconnection. The support costs associated with different arrangements are one important determinant of efficient interconnection arrangements.

Finally, consider a hypothetical situation in which ISPs enter into bilateral interconnection agreements that result in a fragmented Internet. Suppose that there are two sets of ISPs, each of which is fully interconnected, but there are no interconnection agreements between the two sets. If all ISPs sit on a fully interconnected SMDS cloud, end-users can be fully connected to one another by joining one ISP in each set. With a cloud technology like SMDS, a customer who joins two ISPs does not have to purchase two private lines or access ports, and there will be no additional costs associated with the need to reach two ISP nodes rather than one. If ISP costs are based on usage, and not on pipe size, the end-user may see no additional costs to joining a fragmented Internet.

However, if (as is true today) many SMDS and Frame Relay clouds are not interconnected, ISPs straddling these clouds can provide full interconnectivity among users. Thus a customer in Boston who is connected to NEARnet over a Frame Relay link can communicate seamlessly with a customer in San Diego who is connected to Cerfnet over an SMDS cloud.

The relative costs of the various interconnection modes discussed above appear to depend on a variety of prices, support and transaction costs and not on the costs of raw bandwidth alone. The earlier discussion of Internet costs suggested that support activities are becoming a larger component of overall costs. Owners of physical networks who provide a full range of services to end-users may spend very little on the underlying physical facilities. According to Pitsch (1993), transmission costs account for only 3% of AT&T's annual expenses. The modeling of support and other service-related costs appears to be important not just because they constitute a significant component of services for which end-users pay, but also because they have an important bearing on interconnection arrangements.

The economics of interconnection agreements is complex when there are multiple layers of virtual networks, built one over the other.

Any layer in this chain has its costs determined by the prices charged by the virtual network below it, and its prices in turn determine the cost structure of the layer above.

What is the economic rationale for pricing in this layered structure? For illustrative purposes, consider a common set of services underlying the Internet today. At the very bottom of the hierarchy, real resources are used to construct the links and switches that constitute the first virtual network. In the emerging digital environment, Time Division Multiplexing (TDM) in the digital telephone system creates the most evanescent of outputs (SONET (Synchronous Optical Network) time slots lasting 125 milliseconds) out of very long-lived investments (including conduits and fiber-optic cables). The pricing of these time slots determines the cost structure of the first layer of virtual networks (currently, ATM services) created on top of the TDM fabric. When multiple providers with sunk costs attempt to sell a very perishable good (time slots), unit costs will not be constant, but will decline with volume. Perfect competition will not be viable. If there is considerable excess capacity, no equilibrium may exist, and some providers may exit the market. If providers at this level do reach an oligopolistic equilibrium, will their price structure involve volume discounts and term commitments? If they do (as is the case with private-line tariffs), then providers of ATM services (the next layer in the hierarchy) may be faced with relatively large sunk costs and their unit costs will not be constant. Again, perfect competition will not be viable. If providers at this level do reach an oligopolistic equilibrium, will their price structure involve volume discounts and term commitments? If so, the next level of service (SMDS and Frame Relay) will not be characterized by constant unit costs, and a perfectly competitive equilibrium will not be possible. The same questions of the existence of equilibrium and the use of volume discounts and term commitments arise, and will keep arising as we move upstream.

The fundamental economic problem arises from the large sunk costs required to build physical networks, and the technological reality that optical fiber has so much capacity that it is prudent for a network to lay large amounts of excess capacity during construction. A possible conclusion is that there are economies of scale, and the industry should be treated as a natural monopoly. It is too late for this solution. There are four large nationwide fiber-optic networks (and some smaller ones) and 95% of all households are passed by both telephone and cable TV wires. In addition, alternative access providers have built fiber rings in every major business district, and most business customers in these areas have a choice of alternative service providers for voice and data communications. How might competition evolve in these circumstances? Peter Huber (1993) has suggested one interpretation of the apparent stability of some prices and market shares in the long-distance market. He concludes that competition is apparent and not real. A regulatory umbrella prevents instability. Eli Noam (1994) discusses the stability of open interconnection (more specifically, common carriage) in these circumstances, and concludes that nondiscriminatory contracts cannot survive in a competitive environment similar to the one described above. The success of resellers of Internet access, and the strong reaction to them by incumbents with national backbones, are consistent with Noam's view.

The Internet is one component of a very complex environment, and it shares costs with other services (such as long-distance calling) that run on the same underlying transmission links. Of more immediate interest is the relationship of the Internet to some new services (SONET, ATM, SMDS, and Frame Relay) over which IP can be run. There are clearly many alternative interconnection arrangements in this layered structure that can result in full connectivity among end-users. What is the socially optimal set of interconnection arrangements? Is full interconnectivity of virtual networks at each layer of the hierarchy necessary for optimality? If not, what is the minimal acceptable set of arrangements? How will this be impacted by vertical integration and vertical partnerships? Will an unregulated market provide this level of interconnectivity at acceptable cost? If not, what forms of regulation are optimal? Is the bearer service proposal of the Open Data Network (in the Computer Science and Telecommunications Board's *Realizing the Information Future: The Internet and Beyond*) an optimal form of regulation? Clearly, economic theory can contribute to the analysis of this problem, but the work has barely begun.

Conclusion

The market for Internet services is highly competitive, and cost structures are driving pricing decisions. As transport costs fall and firms seek to differentiate their services, support costs will tend to rise as a fraction of total ISP cost. Support costs are not proportional to the bandwidth used by customers, and so prices will not be proportional to bandwidth. Small resellers may be able to arbitrage across the tariffs offered by large ISPs, and leverage off their own lack of sunk costs. Possible responses to arbitrage include a flat prohibition on resale, and special wholesale prices. Both these strategies are currently in use in the Internet. Nevertheless, ISP resellers represent the fastest-growing segment of the ISP market (Maloff 1994).

It is not clear whether the current price structures and interconnection arrangements represent an industry equilibrium. The wide variation in prices for essentially comparable services, the growth of resale, and the current dissatisfaction with the CIX (as expressed on the mailing list compriv) are symptomatic of an evolving market where prices have not lined up neatly with costs. Part of the problem stems from the sunk costs of creating physical networks, and the resulting trend toward long-term contracts for services that resemble transmission links (i.e., private lines). This pricing strategy results in relatively large sunk costs for ISPs that create a national backbone using private lines. Competition among firms with sunk costs can be problematic, especially when there is excess capacity. At the physical level of fiber-optic links, there is a good deal of excess capacity; as owners of this fiber enter the market as ISPs the distinction between high average embedded costs and low (or zero) short-run incremental costs may lead to repeated and unstable price cuts. Owners of physical networks may decide to avoid potentially ruinous price competition by integrating vertically and differentiating their service. Customer support, information content, and reliability are three elements of product differentiation that are in common use in the Internet. The announcement by the CIX that it will filter resellers' traffic suggests that another differentiating factor may be assured connectivity: CIX members can guarantee greater connectivity than

153

Internet Cost Structures and Interconnection Agreements

a reseller who may be blocked at the CIX router. This may be a cause for future concern if Internet connectivity comes to be viewed as another means of differentiating an ISP's service.

An important problem that remains to be solved is the determination of economically efficient interconnection agreements. This chapter argues that a careful economic analysis of this problem needs to focus on the layered structure of services and the support activities that are required to transform raw bandwidth into communications services that customers will pay for.

References

Bohn, Roger, Hans-Werner Braun, Kimberly C. Claffy, and Steve Wolff. 1994. Mitigating the coming Internet crunch: Multiple service levels via precedence, Applied Network Research Technical Report, GA-A21530, University of California, San Diego.

Briere, Daniel D. 1990. *Long distance service: A buyer's guide*. Boston: Artech House.

Comer, Douglas. 1991. *Internetworking with TCP/IP*, Volume 1. Englewood Cliffs, N.J.: Prentice Hall.

Huber, Peter W. 1987. The Geodesic Network. 1987 Report on competition in the telephone industry. Washington, DC: US Government Printing Office.

Huber, Peter. 1993. Telephones, competition and the candice-coated monopoly. *Regulation*, No. 2.

Lucky, R.W. 1989. *Silicon dreams: Information, man and machine*. New York: St. Martin's Press.

Lynch, Daniel C., and Marshall T. Rose. 1993. *Internet system handbook*. Reading, Mass.: Addison Wesley.

MacKie-Mason, Jeffrey K., and H.R. Varian. 1994. Economic FAQs About the Internet. *Journal of Economic Perspectives* (Summer): 75–96.

MacKie-Mason, J.K., and H.R. Varian. 1995. Pricing the Internet. In *Public access to the Internet*, ed. Brian Kahin and James Keller. Cambridge, Mass.: MIT Press.

MacKie-Mason, Jeffrey K., and H.R. Varian. 1993. Some economics of the Internet. Working Paper, Department of Economics, University of Michigan.

Maloff, Joel. 1994. 1993–1994 Internet service provider marketplace analysis.

Mandelbaum, Richard, and Paulette Mandelbaum. 1992. The strategic future of the mid-level networks. In *Building information infrastructure*, ed. Brian Kahin. New York: McGraw Hill.

Noam, Eli. 1994. Beyond liberalization II: The impending doom of common carriage. *Telecommunications Policy* 18(6): 435–452.

Noll, A. Michael. 1994. A study of long distance rates: Divestiture revisited. *Telecommunications Policy* 18(5): 335–362.

Perritt, H.H. 1992. Market structures for electronic publishing and electronic contracting on a national research and education network: Defining added value. In *Building Information Infrastructure*, ed. Brian Kahin. New York: McGraw-Hill.

Pitsch, Peter. 1993. Earth to Huber. *Regulation*, No. 3.

Acknowledgments

I would like to thank Jeff MacKie-Mason, Stewart Personick, Thomas Spacek, and Hal Varian for comments on an earlier version. Thanks also to Eric Sit for compiling Internet growth and price data. All remaining errors are mine alone.

The Economics of Internet Interconnection Agreements

Joseph P. Bailey

Introduction

Internet growth is occurring in three dimensions: the amount of traffic, the number of users, and the number of applications. This expansion can be explained from the standpoint of technological development, public policy, or economics. While each one of these elements could be argued to be the main engine of Internet growth, it is more likely that each is playing a complementary, and necessary, role. Developments in networking and computer technology allow faster and lower-cost components to drive the system. Developments in software lead to new applications that make the infrastructure more useful. Meanwhile, the cost of these components fall on a cost curve similar to that depicted by Moore's Law,[1] which predicts that the ratio of computing performance to cost doubles every 18 months. U.S. government support of the Internet through agencies such as the National Science Foundation (NSF), NASA, and the Department of Energy helped create the critical mass of users that stimulated the commercial Internet explosion of the 1990s.[2] Finally,

1. While there is no "academic" citation for Moore's Law, it is a widely cited theory that computing performance-to-price ratio doubles every 18 months. Moore was working at Intel when he noticed this diffusion, which continues to hold for the most recent lines of computer memory and microprocessors.

2. Following the critical decades-long early support by the Defense Advanced Research Projects Agency, which supported the initial technical development and diffusion of the Internet to reach universities and industry labs.

traditional Internet policies supporting openness and innovation with respect to standards and interconnection agreements have aided the growth of the Internet as well.

These mutually reinforcing developments provide the backdrop for analysis of the interconnection agreements that have created the Internet's "network of networks." Until 1995, the National Science Foundation's operation of the NSFNET as the "backbone" of the Internet made interconnection relatively clear—you had to connect to a service provider who connected you to the NSFNET. With the movement from the NSFNET to the many Wide Area Networks which collectively compose the Internet backbone, people have become more concerned with connecting to the Internet's network of networks—also known as the Internet cloud. A cloud is a perfect analogy for the wide area networking capabilities of the Internet since there is no fixed form and no undergirding structure which keeps it in place. While backbone providers may enter interconnection agreements at different Network Access Points (NAPs), they are not *required* to. Table 1 shows the Network Access Points that connect some of the major backbone providers as of September 1996, and Figure 1 shows the locations of these Network Access Points.

Table 1.
Network Access Points Supported by Backbone Providers[3]

Internet Backbone Provider	Ameri-tech	CIX	DIX	MAE-East	MAE-West	Pacific Bell	Sprint NAP
Apex Global Information Services	√	√		√	√	√	√
Advanced Network Services, Inc.		√		√	√	√	√
BBN Planet		√	√	√	√		√
DIGEX, Inc.		√	√	√	√		√
MCI	√	√		√	√	√	√
NetCom On-Line Communications Services, Inc.	√	√		√	√	√	√
PSInet			√		√	√	
Sprint	√	√		√	√	√	√
UUNET Technologies		√		√	√	√	√

3. *Network World* (1996): 107.

The Economics of Internet Interconnection Agreements

Figure 1.
Locations of Network Access Points Listed in Table 1

With the fragmentation of the Internet's Wide Area Network service market, interconnection between one Internet network and another becomes possible through many configurations. Each of the interconnection models have different technical, policy, and economic costs and benefits.

This chapter explores four interconnection agreement models from economic, technical, and policy perspectives. It defines these models and assesses the economic scalability of the systems to support continued Internet growth. The chapter concludes that continued Internet growth may only be sustainable with some types of interconnection agreements. This conclusion stems from analysis of the incentives for Internet interconnection agreements, interconnection architectures, and policies for pricing and resale. While there are some interconnection agreements that are not sustainable, there is no one interconnection agreement necessary for continued Internet growth.

Incentives for Interconnection

Perhaps the dominant economic force driving firms to desire interconnection is positive network externalities. A network externality is
the cost or benefit that the user of a network derives from an
additional person using the same network. A network externality is
positive if the additional person is a benefit to users, and negative if
the additional user is a cost. Economic analyses of network externalities have been done (e.g., Katz and Shapiro 1985; Farrell and Saloner 1985), but empirical studies of evidence to support these
analyses are less common. The Internet is an excellent example of
a network in which positive network externalities drive the economics.

The Internet's network externalities are best seen when considering the application level. For example, electronic mail over an infrastructure is only as useful as the number of people it can reach.
Having only one person on a network is not very useful, since that
lone individual cannot send electronic mail to anyone. One should
also consider that some applications may create negative network
externalities under certain conditions. Since Internet resources are
shared among the users of the Internet, an additional user can be a
source of network congestion. If a network resource such as an
Internet server or bandwidth were only available to one person, the
user would incur a congestion cost resulting from another person
connecting to the infrastructure. Positive network externalities, however, in the aggregate dominate the economics of the Internet and
are a motivating factor for networks to interconnect. By interconnecting, users can reach more people and information resources,
and more people and information resources can reach them.
Through interconnection, users can achieve interoperability of their
applications. Interoperability has been defined as

the ability of two or more systems (such as devices, databases, networks, or
technologies) to interact in concert with one another, in accordance with a
prescribed method, to achieve a predictable result; the ability of diverse
systems made by different vendors to communicate with each other so that
users do not have to make major adjustments to account for differences in

products or services; and compatibility among systems at specified levels of interaction, including physical compatibility.[4]

Interoperability accepts heterogeneity of technologies while allowing users to work together to meet some subjective criteria (as the definition suggests). The difficulty of interoperability with respect to interconnection agreements follows from this definition. Since interoperability is defined at the application layer and networks are interconnected at the Internet Protocol (IP) layer, different interconnection architectures may affect interoperability differently.[5]

The implication of interoperability for interconnection agreements is that the agreements may be application driven. Therefore, when designing network protocols, engineers must consider the interoperability implications at the application layer. By taking an application view of interoperability, economists may be able to study the costs and benefits of the Internet by using their traditional tools for studying applications and their effect on economic measures such as productivity. The difficulty in designing interconnection agreements, and in analyzing the economics of such agreements, is that applications on the Internet are dynamic—new applications are constantly being developed, changing traffic patterns and user preferences.

As the Internet matures into an infrastructure with dominant market players, older interconnection agreements may no longer be consistent with a competitive business strategy. For example, if the number of users level off, a business may try to lure customers away from other Internet Service Providers (ISPs) rather than trying to attract non-users. This company, company A, may choose not to interconnect with another service provider, company B, in order to entice customers to switch from company B to A by offering the benefits of content that is unique to A's network. This is not very different from the pattern of development and behavior of the telegraph and telephone networks in the United States in the 19th

4. Computer Systems Policy Project (1994): 2.

5. Assessment of the technical and economic implications of this distinction is beyond the scope of this chapter. Interoperability is defined here only in order to differentiate it from interconnection.

century.[6] Regulation requiring companies to interconnect might then be necessary for the Internet service provision market. Although the analogy between the telephone and the Internet is not entirely appropriate, it would be erroneous to think that the U.S. government would never consider regulating interconnection agreements for Internet service provision. One compelling reason for government intervention is to promote the "common carrier" status of interconnection.[7] If interconnection points became the basis for unfair competition in the Internet industry, common carrier status might help promote more equitable interconnection agreements.

Interconnection Architectures

Interconnection of networks that exchange Internet Protocol traffic is the glue that holds together the Internet as a network of networks. However, interconnection occurs between many different types of networks at many different locations by many different firms (i.e., companies and users). The transmission of an email message or a Web transmission between two computers can span numerous networks and will therefore take advantage of many interconnection agreements. The details of the interconnection agreement do not have to be known by those people who use it. Rather, it is up to the connecting network providers to decide how they wish to interconnect with other networks. Users may in aggregate find these arrangements resulting in satisfactory or unsatisfactory performance.

Four basic models of Internet interconnection agreements—peer-to-peer bilateral, hierarchical bilateral, third-party administrator, and cooperative agreements—presently exist in the Internet, and it is very likely that they will all exist in the future. The interesting thing about the models is that they can coexist and allow for interoperability without one model dominating. This allows different networks and firms with different technologies and customers to select the model that best suits them. Each interconnection model is described in detail below.

6. See Brock (1981) for details.

7. A common carrier must not discriminate between users with identical service requests and they must publish their prices.

Peer-to-Peer Bilateral

A peer-to-peer bilateral model for an interconnection agreement may be adopted by two Internet networks owned by different firms if they are of approximately the same size, experience, technology, and customer base. Interconnecting the two networks with a two-party contract governing their agreement is likely to be preferred by both parties to simplify administration and operation. An example of this model is an interconnection of Internet networks by two Network Service Providers (NSPs) or Internet Service Providers which both have a national reach and are of similar size. Even though these providers are competing in the same market for the same customers, they must provide interconnection between their networks so that their customers will realize the benefits of positive network externalities.

The network externalities are symmetric in the peer-to-peer bilateral agreement, since both networks have approximately the same customer base. Although the users are the ones who actually derive the network externality benefit, the value of a network (and thus the price that can be set for connecting to the network) is proportional to the network externalities that it has. Consider an ISP that is deciding whether to enter into a peer-to-peer bilateral agreement with a company of equal size or one that is half its size. If the ISP connects to the one of equal size, it is doubling the number of users it can directly connect to through this interconnection point. If the ISP connects to the one of half its size, then it is only increasing the number of possible direct connections by 50%. Both connections may connect the ISP with the Internet "cloud,"[8] but connection with the network that is half its size will make more of the connections *indirect*. Direct connections are more desirable than indirect connections, since traffic must traverse fewer links and must pass through

8. The Internet cloud is the network of networks that comprises the Internet. It is drawn as a cloud as opposed to a specific diagram because no one actually knows what exactly is inside the cloud! The interconnection points and technology within the cloud are extremely dynamic and have distributed control; this is why it is impossible for anyone to know what is inside. Traffic is injected at one point of the cloud and exits out a different point of the cloud, depending on the technology, interconnection points, and congestion at the time of transmission.

fewer intermediaries. Therefore, the increase in indirect connections makes the indirect traffic susceptible to the reliability of the intermediary network. However, it may still make sense for the ISP to connect to the smaller network in a hierarchical bilateral agreement, which is discussed below.

The elements that make two firms peers, as opposed to having a more customer-provider relationship, are very important: size, experience, technology, and customer base. The customer base and its implications are apparent in the discussion of network externalities above. The size of a network is very important, since one network may have a national reach while another may have only a regional reach. All else being equal, an interconnection agreement with a network with a larger reach is better, since it can help transport packets a farther distance and thus decrease how many intermediary networks are necessary to reach other Internet locations. Experience is also very important, since the parties entering the interconnection agreement must be able to trust each other to successfully transport the data that is exchanged between them. If the interconnecting parties have asymmetric experience, the party with greater experience (or knowledge) may act as a mentor or teacher to the less experienced party. A similar argument can be made for technology. If there is a large difference in the level of technological development, the network with greater developed technology will benefit less from the interconnection.[9] This effect is magnified by the introduction of new services, such as integrated services.

Hierarchical Bilateral

Similar to a peer-to-peer bilateral agreement, the hierarchical bilateral agreement is governed by a two-party contract. However, it

---

9. An example of this is the interconnection of two countries with the United States. Even though these counties may be adjacent and have similar technology, they both will benefit much more by connecting to a network with greater technology (such as those networks in the United States) than with each other. The effect this has is that countries that are very close route traffic through the United States and experience longer delay paths and cause more congestion in the U.S. portion of the Internet. For example, Australia and New Zealand had to traverse the U.S. backbone in the early 1990s to exchange traffic.

interconnects firms of a discernible difference in size, experience, technology, customer base—and market power. This bilateral agreement is considered separately from the peer-to-peer case because the economics and technology of the interconnection are much different. Both differences usually lead to a customer-provider relationship and not a peer-to-peer relationship. Examples of this interconnection model include an Internet Access Provider or a corporate network connecting to an ISP, or a relatively small International ISP connecting to a U.S. backbone provider.

The technology leader, usually the firm with the larger network, is the one that has less to benefit from the interconnection agreement than the technology follower. The leader may have more experience or network links with greater capacity. The network externality benefits are greater for customers of the smaller network provider. The experience of the technological leader can be of great benefit to the firm with the smaller network, but the experience and knowledge benefits do not flow in the opposite direction. Because of these reasons, we find that the firm with a smaller network takes the role of the customer and pays a larger amount of the costs of interconnection.

The hierarchical bilateral model of interconnection is the most pervasive in today's Internet. Customers connect to Internet Access Providers. Internet Access Providers and corporate networks connect to Internet Service Providers. Most international Internet Service Providers are dwarfed in size, and therefore have far less market power than the U.S.-based backbone providers. All of these interconnection agreements follow the hierarchical model, since they aggregate users and interconnect them with networks which have superior technology and larger network externalities.

Third-Party Administrator

The third-party administrator model is followed when an interconnection point consists of more than two networks exchanging packets and the administration of the interconnection is operated by a firm not operating a network. Examples of this include the Commercial Internet eXchange (CIX), the Network Access Points established by the National Science Foundation, and MAE-East (pronounced "may east"). The role of the third party is to route traffic between the interconnected networks and be a trusted party to facilitate communication and promote nondiscrimination. Because of these roles, a third-party administrator often acts as a common carrier— offering consistent prices to all customers and not refusing interconnection by any party. The objective of the third-party administrator is to cover the operating expenses of the interconnecting points and profit from the endeavor.

The network externalities for the third-party administrator have the characteristic of positive feedback. If the number of people connecting to the third-party administrator's interconnection point is zero, the first network to connect receives zero benefit. As the number of networks that connect to the interconnection point increases, the network externalities also increase. Therefore, it is difficult for a third-party administrator to establish an interconnection point, but once it achieves a critical mass of firms, it can provide a very real benefit to new networks. A wise strategy for these third-party administrators would be to ensure a critical mass before establishing an interconnection point.

The third-party administrator must establish trust, which results partially from a technological edge. Since the third-party administrator does not compete with the networks it interconnects, it can be in a better position to share information with one of its customers without having to share this information with all of its customers. This establishes the administrator in a position of trust. The administrator ability to impart some kind of experience or knowledge to their customers also helps to establish trust. A third-party administrator that knows less than its customers is unlikely to provide adequate service.

Cooperative Agreement

Similar to the third-party agreement, the cooperative agreement has more than two parties sharing an interconnection point, however, the operation of the interconnection point is run by a committee of the interconnecting firms. This interconnection model was the sole example of interconnection when the Internet solely comprised government-supported networks. The Federal Internet eXchanges (FIXen) were created to interconnect government agency networks that had a shared purpose and incentive to promote research and education. While it is unclear whether this model would work in the commercial sector, it is worth mentioning it since the FIXen still exist and are still successful. Unlike the third-party administrator, the cooperative agreement is run by committee and does not need to make a profit—only cost-sharing is necessary.

The cooperative agreement is more desirable than many bilateral agreements, since there are fewer coordination costs and greater economies of scale. This is especially true being that there is an incentive alignment between the parties involved which makes them willing to cooperate and have very incomplete contracts (discussed further below); also, to use their trust in each other to facilitate coordination. In addition, the cost of n bilateral agreements is not only more expensive to coordinate, but may cost more in terms of hardware and leased lines than a single interconnection point of n networks. This gives the cooperative agreement an economies-of-scale benefit that is the same as the economies of scale exhibited by the third-party administrator.

Since information is not a competitive advantage for the cooperative firms, experience and information are shared among all parties involved. Instead of information being absorbed by the administrator, all parties can benefit from committee participation and shared learning.

Resale and Usage-Sensitive Pricing

Internet interconnection agreements are most prone to opportunism when a firm is able to resell its interconnection service. For example, firms A and B may want to interconnect at a node but they do not want to each pay the interconnection fee. As a result, they may decide to aggregate their traffic before it reaches the node. Firm A might also decide to resell the interconnection service to firm B at a price less than the interconnection agreement. Resale issues affect all four models discussed in the previous section. We will explore two mechanisms to manage resale: pricing and policing.

Pricing issues provide incentives or disincentives for resale. For example, a per-bit charge may be assessed for the traffic exchanged at an interconnection node. This is a usage-sensitive pricing scheme, which is different than the flat-rate pricing usually embraced by Internet users.[10] Flat-rate pricing schemes may also deter resale if the flat-rate prices are consistent with the bit rate of the interconnection link. For example, if interconnecting firms are charged a flat rate of a dollar per megabit per second, firms A and B may still aggregate their data, but they will experience latency costs unless they increase the bandwidth of the link, which will in turn cost more.

Policing is another option to enforce a policy of not allowing resale at the interconnection node without using pricing as an incentive. This is similar to the model used by the Commercial Internet eXchange, which charged users a flat fee as long as they did not resell their service. This policy is enforceable by users specifying the allowable Internet Protocol (IP) addresses which can send and receive information over a link. If an IP address outside of the allowable range tries to use this interconnection point, it will be blocked. Policing is very difficult and some users may be able to fool such a blocking mechanism by encapsulating an IP packet inside a legal IP address. Another cost with policing, which also holds for pricing, is the increased administrative costs.

The overhead associated with policing or pricing may increase the cost of interconnection. For example, Bailey et al. (1995) report that the billing overhead for phone calls may account for approximately 50% of a bill. The cost of the additional hardware and operations support for policing may be expensive as well. Both of these costs are realized when firms act opportunistically, which is the case with the third-party administrator model. The bilateral and cooperative agreement models involve a higher degree of trust and a consistency in goals which may result in a policy that does not require the cost of enforcement.

10. Bailey and McKnight (1995) discuss many reasons why the Internet has accepted flat-rate pricing and not usage-sensitive pricing, save in a few cases. The paper also details differences in terminology between flat-rate, usage-based, and usage-sensitive, and argues that usage-based pricing is a poorly defined term that should not be used in this context. Usage-sensitive pricing exists when the marginal monetary cost for sending a bit is non-zero.

Conclusion

Large Internet Service Providers are more concerned about their network reliability and interconnection agreements than providing local services, since their users derive more interoperability benefit from interconnection. Therefore, it would be in their best interest to establish interconnection agreements with firms they trust not to act opportunistically. The coordination cost of this would increase if the ISPs tried to enter into cooperative agreements. Furthermore, the third-party administrator model would involve high vulnerability costs associated with the administrator acting incompetently or opportunistically.

Smaller networks with shared goals may best be served through cooperative agreements. Since the coordination costs are higher than in the bilateral agreement model, a shared vision, such as that of the U.S. government agencies which operate Internet networks, reduces the coordination costs. Furthermore, the shared vision will lead to agreements based on trust among the interconnected firms that creates a policy that prevents resale without having to implement usage-sensitive pricing or policing.

The role of third-party administrators will probably not diminish as the Internet grows. However, the ability of firms to resell this service, coupled with the ability of the administrator to act opportunistically, do not ensure that this will continue to be a good model. In favor of the third-party administrator is the argument that coordination costs will be lower when firms can coordinate through a hierarchy.

Finally, many of the arguments made here could be supported by analysis of network traffic. Support for repositories of comparative Internet interconnection data could help academics and businesses understand the pricing issues and formulate new contracts for interconnection. The Internet can meet the growing demand of users, applications, and traffic through interoperable and scalable interconnection agreements.

References

Bailey, J. P., S. Gillett, D. Gingold, B. Leida, D. Melcher, J. Reagle, j. Roh, R. Rothstein, and G. Seale. 1995. Internet economics workshop: Workshop notes. MIT Research Program on Communications Policy, Massachusetts Institute of Technology.

Bailey, J. P. and L. W. McKnight. 1995. Internet economics: What happens when constituencies collide. Paper presented at INET '95, Honolulu.

Brock, G. W. 1981. The telecommunications industry: The dynamics of market structure. Cambridge, Mass.: Harvard University Press.

CSPP. 1994. Perspectives on the National Information Infrastructure: Ensuring interoperability. Computer Systems Policy Project paper.

Farrell, J., and G. Saloner. 1985. Standardization, compatibility, and innovation. *Rand Journal of Economics* 16 (Spring).

Katz, M. L., and C. Shapiro. 1985. Network externalities, competition, and compatibility. *American Economic Review* 75.

Network World. 1996. Internet backbone provider infrastructure comparison. (September 16):107.

Acknowledgments

The author wishes to thank Lee McKnight, Erik Brynjolfsson, David Clark, Scott Marcus, and the participants in the Internet Economics Workshop for their contributions. The author is solely responsible for any remaining errors. Funding for this work has been provided in part by DARPA contract #N00174-93-C-0036, and NASA grant #NGT-51407. Workshop funding was provided by NSF grant #NCR-9509244.

Sharing Multicast Costs

Shai Herzog, Scott Shenker, and Deborah Estrin

Introduction

Because of the history of government subsidy in the United States and other countries, and the relatively cooperative Internet user population, the data networking research community has paid little attention to the issue of cost allocation. In the United States, however, we are now approaching an almost completely commercial (i.e., unsubsidized) Internet environment. Issues of cost recovery and profit incentives, for better or worse, become much more relevant.[1] In turn, cost allocation is becoming a very important issue in this environment.

By cost allocation we mean the assignment to various users of some measure of the cost of the network resources they are consuming. As we discuss in the next section, these costs are not necessarily monetary in nature; instead these costs could be measures of congestion or usage. Moreover, these costs are not necessarily extracted directly from users. There is an important distinction between cost allocation and pricing, and in this chapter we consider only the

---

1. In addition, as argued in Cocchi et al. (1993), Clark et al. (1992), and Shenker (1995), when data networks offer multiple qualities of service (QOS), a situation which is fast approaching on the horizon, one must consider user incentives to ensure that these QOS features are used appropriately. Appropriate use leads to the efficient use of network resources, where efficiency is defined in Cocchi et al. (1993) and Shenker (1995). These incentive issues are also relevant to controlling usage even in a single QOS environment (see MacKie-Mason and Varian [1995a, 1995b]).

former. However, the allocated costs computed in this chapter can provide useful input to pricing policies. Thus we see cost allocation as being an important component of pricing and other more general usage control strategies.

This chapter discusses cost allocation in the context of multicast flows. The question we discuss is this: When a single data flow is shared among many receivers, how does one split the cost of that flow among the receivers?[2] The whole point of multicast is to increase network efficiency by sharing a delivery tree. We ask: How are these savings allocated among the various members of the multicast group?

We wish to assign costs to each member of the group, with the total costs allocated being equal to the total costs incurred. The cost allocated to an individual member will depend on the structure of the distribution tree and on the number of members present. There are many possible ways to allocate costs; we use an axiomatic approach to discriminate among the various possibilities. We first discuss several desirable properties that a cost allocation scheme should have, such as anonymity (essentially, symmetry among group members). Using these properties as a basic set of axioms, we analyze the family of cost allocation functions that are consistent with these axioms. Thus this axiomatic approach allows us to explore the implications of various notions of fairness and equity in cost allocation. Of course, one must not consider only such idealized properties but also how to implement such a cost allocation strategy. We discuss one approach to implementing cost allocation strategies, called the one-pass approach, and analyze the extent to which this approach can be made consistent with the basic axioms.

To focus attention on the basic issues, our investigation is in the context of a very simple network model (we consider generalizations in the sixth section below). There is a single static distribution tree (i.e., routing and group membership do not change) with a single source and multiple receivers. The network provides a single quality of service (QOS) to all members of the multicast group. There are costs associated with each link traversed by the flow. These costs

---

2. Our treatment here only considers a flow with a single source; the generalization to multiple senders is discussed in the sixth section.

could be tied to usage or reservations or both; for the purposes of our model it does not matter. The problem is to fully allocate the cost of the flow among the receivers. We do not discuss issues of security or network dynamics.

This chapter has six sections and an appendix. We start, in the second section, by clarifying some aspects of our approach and briefly discussing related work. We then present the basic model in the third section, and discuss various cost allocation axioms in the fourth. We turn to issues of implementation in the fifth section, where we discuss the ability of our simple one-pass approach to satisfy the axioms presented in the fourth section. We conclude in the sixth section with a discussion of various directions for future work. The appendix details proofs for the theorems mentioned in the body of this chapter.

Basic Approach and Related Work

This chapter addresses the very specific and technical problem of sharing the cost of a multicast flow in the context of a very simple network model. However, we think cost allocation is a generally useful construct which can be used in a wide variety of settings. In particular, these results are not only applicable to a circumstance in which users are directly charged, in monetary terms, for these allocated costs.

For instance, we note that the costs we allocate are not necessarily financial. If users are cooperative, they want to make the right decision about the wise use of network resources. Such decisions can only be made if users are informed about the "cost" their usage imposes on the network. Feedback about these costs is important if we wish to promote the efficient use of network resources. This cost can be in terms of congestion-induced performance degradation imposed on other users, and/or in terms of the actual capital and maintenance cost of the network facilities themselves.[3]

---

3. Calculating the costs for a unicast flow is a difficult problem. How does one quantify congestion costs? How does one relate capital and maintenance costs to the cost assigned to users? We do not address these questions. Instead, we address the issue of how to split up these costs, no matter how they are calculated, among the users.

Moreover, it is crucial to distinguish between cost allocation and pricing. Pricing is the form and amount of payment extracted from the end-user; pricing schemes are often based on many factors besides cost, such as demand elasticity, market structure, and price stability. Cost allocation is how the network assigns, internally to itself, portions of the total cost to various users. There is not necessarily any direct relationship between the allocated cost and the prices charged individual users. In fact, we do not expect that the typical case will be that the allocated costs, if indeed they are monetary, will be turned directly into prices.

However, even though not charged directly, these allocated costs can serve as useful input to some pricing schemes. For instance, network users might buy a monthly quota of network service. The amount that was debited from this quota would be based on the allocated costs. The users would have the benefit of extreme price stability (in terms of what they paid every month), but would also gain from the increased efficiency of multicast.[4]

We are making the fundamental assumption that costs are assigned to the receivers of the multicast group, and not to the sources. There are two reasons for this. First, it is completely trivial to assign a fixed portion of the costs to the source, and this changes almost nothing in our analysis except to complicate notation. Thus, for convenience, we do not explicitly treat this case. Second, multicast membership is typically receiver initiated (see Deering and Cheriton [1990]), so responsibility for data flowing over links rests primarily with the receivers.[5] There are some applications in which a more sophisticated cost-sharing arrangement between sources and senders is needed, but we consider this to be a higher-layer issue and do not address it here.

We now discuss some related work. There is a rapidly growing literature on pricing in computer networks. For a few representative

---

4. We should also point out that even though costs are allocated to individual users, the recovery of those costs might occur at a much higher level of granularity. For instance, the University of Southern California might be responsible for all of the costs allocated to its students and staff.

5. Clearly data cannot flow without the source sending data, but the source has no control over where that data goes once it leaves the source.

examples, see MacKie-Mason and Varian (1995b); Cocchi et al. (1993); Sairamesh et al. (1995); Braun and Claffy (1993); and Shenker (1995). However, this literature does not typically relate the prices charged to any underlying cost of network usage. The emphasis is on the strategic (utility-maximizing) behavior of users, and the profit-maximizing behavior of firms, rather than on the equitable distribution of costs that we consider here.

There is a large economics literature on cost allocation; see Peyton-Young (1985) and references therein for a brief overview. Cost allocation is usually treated as a special case of a cooperative game. A cooperative game is one in which there are N players and there is some value function V that assigns a value to each coalition or subset of players. The question addressed by this literature is how to assign to each player a share such that the sum of the shares equals the value of the complete set (see Roth [1988]; Myerson [1991]). Axiomatic approaches are often—in fact, almost exclusively—used to analyze such cooperative games. The axioms presented in this chapter are very similar to those used in the theory of cooperative games. Megiddo (1978) considered a family of cooperative games which have the same structure as the problem we consider here. There is also a very extensive literature on minimal cost spanning tree games, which differ from what we consider here in that the routing is always chosen to minimize the total cost. See Sharkey (1995) for a lucid overview of these results and for a much broader discussion of network models in economics. In a more recent paper, Henriet and Moulin (1996) considered a network model in which costs are incurred for connecting to a central switch and the pairwise traffic matrix is known; the spirit of the analysis is very similar to ours, but the network model is rather different. While there is a rather active literature on these network cost allocation problems, we are not aware of any treatment of the mechanisms needed to implement such cost allocation schemes; see our discussion below in the fifth section. While the presentation in this chapter is geared toward the networking research community, we have included several footnotes which relate our work to the economics literature.

The Cost Allocation Model

In this section we first present our abstract model, and then illustrate it by discussing several simple examples of cost allocation policies.

Basic Definitions

In this section we present an abstract model of the cost-sharing problem. This model will serve as the basis for our axiomatic analysis of cost allocation. The abstract model defines a formal description of the network technology for multicast transmission over a network. The abstract model also describes the structure of incurred costs of such a multicast transmission. The model we describe below is illustrated in Figure 1 for a simple network scenario.

The network technology model has three components: network topology, group membership, and routing function. Network topology describes the physical connectivity of the network in terms of vertices (nodes) and links. $N = (V, L, T)$ describes a network N, with nodes $v_i \in V$, directed[6] links $(v_i, v_j) \in L$, and a routing function (protocol) T. Let M describe the set of multicast group members; we denote individual members by $m_\alpha \in M$. Members of a multicast group can join and leave dynamically and can attach themselves to any node. Each packet sent to this multicast group by any source, not necessarily a member of the group, will go to all members M of the group; we will use the terms "member" and "receiver" somewhat interchangeably. The mapping of individual members to specific network nodes is described by the location function loc: $M \to V$. The routing function abstraction describes the path taken by packets when a sender transmits to the group. In unicast routing, the routing function $L' = T(N, R, v_i)$ takes a network N along with a source (root) R and a receiver v_i, and defines the set of directed links that establish the path between R and v_i. While we make no particular assumptions about the optimality of this unicast route, we do assume that the set of unicast routes from a single root R to all other nodes forms a

---

6. Notice that links are directed, and therefore $(v_i, v_j) \neq (v_j, v_i)$ for all nontrivial links (i.e., $v_i \neq v_j$).

tree.[7] In this chapter we assume that multicast routing is based on loop-free unicast routing; that is, multicast routing creates a source-rooted distribution tree created from the union of the unicast paths between the root and the set of receivers: $T(N, R, V') = \cup_{v_j \in V'} T(N, R, v_j)$ for all subsets $V' \subseteq V$.

Each link in a distribution tree creates a distinction, relative to itself, between upstream and downstream portions of the tree: the downstream portion contains all the nodes (and members) that incorporate this link in their unicast path from the root. The upstream portion is merely defined as the portion of the tree that is not downstream.

We now turn to the structure of incurred costs. Our abstract model considers the allocation of costs for each data flow individually (i.e., we do not consider the joint allocation of the costs of multiple flows), where data flow refers to a particular source sending to a particular multicast group destination. Such a flow can be explicit (created by resource reservation) or implicit.[8]

For reasons of simplicity, we associate all costs with the links that the packets traverse.[9] These costs could arise from many different aspects of network usage; for instance, there could be costs associated with each packet and/or costs associated with resource reservations (bandwidth, etc.).[10] We lump all of these different costs into a single quantity.[11] Because we assume that the same quality of service

7. This assumption follows if whenever the route from R to node v_i passes through node v_j, the route from r to v_j is a subset of the route from R to v_i. We also assume that routing is only a function of the location of the receiver. Some routing protocols allow receivers to request different quality of routes (QOR), which would violate our assumption.

8. Data packets can be classified implicitly into flows by examining their source/destination addresses and other significant fields in their headers.

9. Although most reservation protocols reserve link resources and not intranode resources, we acknowledge that some intranode resources may be costly (like internal buffers, CPU cycles, etc.). Intranode costs can be attributed to links by attributing the intranode cost associated with processing incoming data to the incoming link and the overhead for outgoing data to the appropriate outgoing links.

10. The issue of how these local costs are computed is outside of the scope of this work. Various cost components are described in the introduction to this book and in greater detail in the chapters by David Crawford and by Jeffrey MacKie-Mason, Liam Murphy, and John Murphy.

11. These costs are in no way related to the link-metrics used by routing algorithms to calculate routes in the network.

is delivered to all receivers, the link costs are independent of which receivers, or how many, are downstream. Later, in the sixth section, we discuss generalizations of the model to incorporate multiple qualities of service. Moreover, we should note that our abstract model is intended to address the problem of cost allocation among a given set of group members with a given network topology; this chapter does not address dynamics, either in membership or in topology.[12]

The set of link costs for a given network $N = (V, L, T)$ is defined as $c: L \to \Re_+$. The cost function of a distribution tree comprised of links L' is merely the sum of all the directed links in L': $cf(L', c) = \Sigma_{(v_i, v_j) \in L'} c(V_i, V_j)$. This function expresses the total cost incurred by a distribution tree. In this chapter, we explore how to allocate this cost among the individual members.

We denote a cost allocation function by $af(N, R, M, loc, c)$; this represents a specific cost allocation strategy. Given a network technology defined by $N = (V, L, T)$, a group membership defined by M and loc, and a cost structure defined by the link costs c, the allocation function af defines the cost that will be individually attributed to members of the multicast group; $af_\alpha(N, R, M, loc, c)$ denotes the allocation to member α.

For any distribution there may be numerous ways of allocating costs to receivers, and our focus in this chapter is on providing a rationale for discriminating among these allocation policies. We restrict ourselves to policies that fully allocate the costs incurred. We require that:

$$\sum_{m_\alpha \in M} af_\alpha(N, R, M, loc, c) = cf(T(N, R, loc(M)), c) \quad \exists\, N, R, M, loc, and\, c$$

We call this equality the balanced budget condition. Moreover, we restrict ourselves to allocating costs, which means that all allocations are nonnegative (i.e., no receiver is paid for using the network):

$$af_\alpha(N, R, M, loc, c) \geq 0 \quad \forall\, \alpha, N, R, M, loc, and\, c$$

12. Of course, our approach is not limited to the completely static case. For example, one can apply our approach to allocating cost for time slices, assuming static behavior within those time slices. The costs associated with transitioning (either membership or topology) are not addressed here.

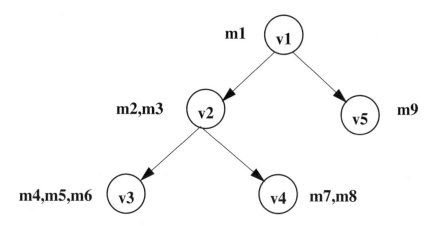

Figure 1
A Simple Example of a Network

Examples

The previous section described our abstract model of cost allocation, and here we present a few examples of allocation strategies. We use the sample problem depicted in Figure 1 to illustrate these example cost allocation strategies.

The simplest approach to allocating costs is to merely divide the total cost equally among all receivers; we call this the Equal Tree Split (ETS) scheme. In the example depicted in Figure 1, all members are allocated the cost $[c(v_1, v_2) + c(v_2, v_3) + c(v_2, v_4) + c(v_1, v_5)]/9$.

The ETS policy does not discriminate between receivers far from the source and those close to the source, and thus does not attempt to hold receivers accountable for the costs their individual membership incurs. However, the cost of a particular link is incurred because there is at least one downstream receiver; therefore, while all downstream receivers can be considered equally responsible for the cost, all other receivers are not responsible at all. This leads to a different approach to allocating costs, one in which the cost of each link is split equally among only the downstream receivers. We call this the Equal Link Split among Downstream members (ELSD) scheme.[13]

---

13. For those familiar with the concept, this is the Shapley Value of this problem.

For instance, in the example above, the cost allocated to ml is zero, since she is not downstream of any links, and the cost allocated to m4 is given by $c(v_1, v_2)/7 + c(v_2, v_3)/3$.

An approach that is midway between the egalitarian approach of ETS and the emphasis on individual accountability of ELSD is to assign the cost of a link equally to all the next-hop links that are part of the distribution tree (with all receivers at that node being treated as part of one other link).[14] This is motivated by the idea that we pass costs on to each downstream next-hop (rather than allocate them to the downstream receivers themselves) and then allocate the costs of those downstream links in a recursive fashion. These costs are recursively forwarded until there are no more downstream nodes and costs are fully allocated. We call this the Equal Next-Hop Split (ENHS) scheme. For the example in Figure 1, the cost allocated to m4 is given by $c(v_1, v_2)/9 + c(v_2, v_3)/3$, and the cost allocated to m2 is $c(v_1, v_2)/6$.

Of course, all of these cost allocation policies should be compared to the unicast costs. The total cost of separate unicast transmissions is higher than the total cost of the multicast transmission, and different allocation policies distribute this surplus differently. Unicast is not a real cost allocation strategy (in the sense of our model) since it allocates to members more than the network costs; however, it does provide a useful point of comparison.[15] The unicast cost of member α is given by $\Sigma_{(v_i, v_j) \in T(N, R, loc, (m_\alpha))}c(v_i, v_j)$. For the example in Figure 1, the unicast cost of m4 is $c(v_1, v_2) + c(v_2, v_3)$.

Axiomatic Analysis

We analyze this abstract model of cost sharing through the use of axioms. We use as axioms some possible properties that desirable cost-sharing formula might have. We then investigate the implications of assuming these properties. What additional properties are implied? What forms of cost-sharing rules are allowed?

14. We give a more precise definition of this scheme in the fifth section below.

15. Note that if the allocated multicast cost is greater or equal to the unicast cost, there may be no incentive to use multicast.

We first identify three basic axioms that describe the process of allocating cost. These axioms describe which aspects of the problem are relevant to the cost-sharing formula. We assume that the basic axioms apply throughout the rest of this section. We discuss the implications of these basic axioms and then present a few examples cost allocation policies which satisfy them. Then we identify a few additional axioms that express different policy objectives of cost sharing, and we explore the implications of each of these axioms when combined with the three basic axioms.

Basic Axioms

The three basic axioms describe aspects of the cost-sharing problem that should be irrelevant to the actual cost-sharing formula. We start by observing that a cost-sharing formula should be invariant under arbitrary relabelling of equivalent members; it should not have an intrinsic and arbitrary asymmetry built into it.[16]

Axiom 1: *Anonymity*[17] *Name labels, by which members are identified, are irrelevant to cost allocation.*

Formal definition:

Given any network N = (V, L, T), root R, link cost function c, member set M, two placement functions loc and loc′ and any two members m_α and $m_\beta \in$ M:

if

$loc(m_\alpha) = loc'(m_\beta)$ and

$loc(m_\beta) = loc'(m_\alpha)$ and

$loc(m_\gamma) = loc'(m_\gamma)$ $\forall\ m_\gamma \in M - m_\alpha - m_\beta$

---

16. This does not mean that there cannot be systematic asymmetries (e.g., charging professors more than students on a campus network), but these asymmetries should be described as a nonequivalency of members (e.g., introducing two classes of members into the formalism).

17. Notice that this axiom implies that two members located at the same node must be allocated the same cost: $loc(m_\alpha) = loc(m_\beta) \Rightarrow af_\alpha(...) = af_\beta(...)$.

then

af_α(N, R, M, loc, c) = af_β(N, R, M, loc', c   and

af_β(N, R, M, loc, c) = af_α(N, R, M, loc', c   and

af_γ(N, R, M, loc, c) = af_γ(N, R, M, loc', c $\forall\; m_\gamma \in M - m_\alpha - m_\beta$

Link costs can come from many sources, such as per-packet costs, per-hour costs, and per-connection costs. They can also come from link transmission costs, buffering costs, congestion costs, etc. (See the introduction to this book and the chapters by Crawford and by MacKie-Mason, Murphy, and Murphy for more detailed discussion of network costs.) In order to avoid the additional complexity and overhead of independently allocating all such costs, it is important that the cost allocation not depend on whether the accounting method allocates these costs separately or jointly. That is, it should not matter if the various components of the link costs are combined into one single cost to be allocated, or if they are separately allocated. This is expressed in the following axiom:

Axiom 2: *Additivity Given any two sets of link costs, the sum of their respective cost allocation functions is equal to the cost allocation function of the sum of the two sets.*

Formal definition:

Given any network N = (V, L, T), root R, member set M, placement function loc, and any two link cost functions c1 and c2:

af(N, R, M, loc, c1 + c2) = af(N, R, M, loc, c1) + af(N, R, M, loc, c2)

The cost allocation formula must depend on the underlying network topology. However, it is preferable for this topological dependency to be restricted to factors related to cost. For instance, if we took a single link and artificially broke it into two links (spreading the cost of the link between the two links), the cost allocation should not change. A more general form of this intention is that the cost allocation should only depend on the set of costs incurred by each subgroup. If two networks incur the same costs for every subgroup of members, then they should allocate the cost in the same way. This condition, that two networks incur the same costs for serving each subgroup of members, is actually quite strong; in particular, every unicast cost must be the same, every cost for a pair of receivers must be the same, and so forth. Any changes in the network that preserve this property might well be considered irrelevant to cost allocation.[18]

Axiom 3: *Equivalency   Consider two networks with the same single group of members; if the cost of serving any subgroup of members is identical in both networks, then the allocated costs must be the same.*

Formal definition:

Given a single set of members M and two different network scenarios N1, R1, loc1, c1 and N2, R2, loc2, c2:

if

$$cf(T(N1, R1, loc1(M')), c1) = cf(T(N2, R2, loc2(M')), c2) \;\; \forall \, M' \subseteq M$$

then

$$af(N1, R1, M, loc1, c1) = af(N2, R2, M, loc2, c2)$$

The Canonical Form of Cost Allocation Formulae

The three basic axioms presented above greatly reduce the scope of allowable cost allocation policies. In this subsection, we show that all cost allocation policies satisfying these three basic axioms can be expressed in a very simple canonical form. We consider functions $F: \{Z_+^2 - (0,0)\} - \mathfrak{R}_+^2$, where we use the symbol Z_+ to denote the nonnegative integers and $\mathfrak{R}_+$ to denote the nonnegative reals.[19] We define the family of functions $\mathfrak{I}$ to be those functions $F: \{Z_+^2 - (0,0)\} - \mathfrak{R}_+^2$ that satisfy the properties[20]: (1) $z_1 F_1(z_1, z_2) + z_2 F_2(z_1, z_2) = 1$; and (2) $F_1(0, z) = F_2(z, 0) = 1$. Note that the set $\mathfrak{I}$ is

18. This axiom implies that the only relevant aspect of the problem is the induced cooperative game; all other aspects of the topology are irrelevant.

19. In case our notation is confusing, the domain of this function is all pairs of nonnegative integers except the pair (0,0).

20. The second condition in the definition of $\mathfrak{I}$ is unrelated to allocations and is merely used to simplify the expression of Theorem 12.

Herzog, Shenker, and Estrin

convex: F, $G \in \Im \Rightarrow (\mu F + (1 - \mu) G) \in \Im$ for all $0 \leq \mu \leq 1$. Also, we know that $F_1(0, z) = F_1(z, 0) = 1/z$ for $z > 0$.[21]

We now use these functions to define cost allocation strategies. Consider a link (v_i, v_j) with a cost $c(v_i, v_j)$ where there are $n_d > 0$ receivers downstream[22] and $n_u \geq 0$ receivers upstream. We use a function $F = (F_u, F_d) \in \Im$ to determine the fraction of the link cost that is allocated to each upstream or downstream receiver. Members are allocated the following costs:

$F_u(n_u, n_d) * c(v_i, v_j)$ for each upstream member, and

$F_d(n_u, n_d) * c(v_i, v_j)$ for each downstream member.

The total cost allocated to a member is the sum, over all links, of its share of each link cost.

Cost allocation strategies that can be expressed in terms of a function $F \in \Im$ are called canonical strategies. Note that the first condition above in the definition of $\Im$ ensures that costs are fully allocated: $n_u F_u(n_u, n_d) + n_d F_d(n_u, n_d) = 1$. It is fairly clear that all canonical strategies satisfy the three basic axioms. More interesting, all cost allocation strategies satisfying the basic axioms are canonical.

Theorem 1: *A cost allocation formula satisfies the basic axioms if and only if it is a canonical strategy.*

Examples of Canonical Cost Allocation Strategies

The set $\Im$ is infinite, and so there are an infinite number of canonical cost allocation strategies. In this subsection we present several examples of functions $F \in \Im$. Two of the functions were already introduced in the third section above. Since we know that $F_d(0, n_d) = 1/nd$ for all $F \in \Im$, we merely describe the functions on the set Z_{++}^2 below (where Z_{++} denotes the positive integers). Since the set $\Im$ is convex, all linear combinations of the examples below are also in $\Im$.

21. For our use in this section we need only have defined F on $Z_+ \times Z_{++}$ (where Z_{++} denotes the positive integers) but we will make use of the family of functions again in the fifth section below where we need the larger domain of $\{Z_+^2 - (0,0)\}$.

22. If there are no receivers downstream, then this link is not part of the distribution tree and we can ignore its costs.

Equal Link Split Downstream (ELSD) The cost is equally split among the downstream receivers and no cost is allocated upstream

$$F_u\ (n_u,\ n_d) = 0$$

$$F_d(n_u,\ n_d) = \frac{1}{n_d}$$

Equal Tree Split (ETS) The total tree cost is equally split among all the receivers

$$F_u(n_u,\ n_d) = F_d(n_u,\ n_d) = \frac{1}{n_u = n_d}$$

Cost is charged to upstream receivers

$$F_u(n_u,\ n_d) = \frac{1}{n_u}$$

$$F_d\ (n_u,\ n_d) = 0$$

Cost is charged relative to the number of receivers upstream/downstream

$$F_u(n_u,\ n_d) = \frac{n_u}{n_u^2 + n_d^2}$$

$$F_d(n_u,\ n_d) = \frac{n_d}{n_u^2 + n_d^2}$$

Additional Axioms

The basic axioms address the issue of what factors can be considered relevant to cost allocation. These axioms have substantial reductive power in that they define a class of canonical cost allocation strategies. However, as the examples above show, one can allocate all costs to upstream nodes, or to downstream nodes, or anywhere in between. Thus this family of canonical cost allocation strategies incorporates a wide variety of distributive notions. We use the term "distributive notion" to mean standards of equity or justice that allow one to discriminate between allocation policies. Our next step is to

184

Herzog, Shenker, and Estrin

examine some additional axioms that express particular distributive notions. These axioms can be used to select a subset of canonical allocation strategies.

Stand-Alone and Related Axioms One such distributive notion is that a member's cost should reflect the benefits of multicast. Just as the total network cost of a multicast flow is less than the sum of the costs of unicast flows to each member, one might require that each individual allocated cost in a multicast flow never be greater than the cost incurred by the appropriate unicast flow. This yields the following axiom:

Axiom 4: *Stand-Alone The unicast cost of a member is an upper limit on her cost allocation.*

Formal definition:

$$af_\alpha(N, R, M, loc, c) \leq cf(T, (N, R, loc(m_\alpha)), c)$$

$$\forall\ N, R, M, loc, c, m_\alpha \in M$$

The stand-alone axiom protects the individual; every individual receiver is guaranteed that joining a group can never cost more than her unicast cost. Assuming that users have the power of choice in their network activities, and assuming that some (even minimal) amount of self-interest guides them, it is hard to imagine why any user would want to join a shared group of receivers if she risks an increase in her allocated costs. Of course, in a cooperative environment, receivers may choose to risk having increased costs if the total cost distributed to the group decreases.

Insisting upon the stand-alone axiom, when combined with the basic axioms, means that there is one and only one applicable cost allocation strategy[23]:

23. This result is closely related to the standard axiomatization of the Shapley Value (see Shapley [1953]; Roth [1988]) in economics. Members attached at the root can be considered dummy members because adding them to a group does not increase the total cost incurred. We can define a dummy member axiom that says that no member located at the root can be allocated a nonzero cost:

Theorem 2: *A cost allocation function satisfies the basic and stand-alone axioms if and only if it is the Equal Link Split Downstream (ELSD) function.*

A stronger form of the stand-alone axiom is the "sharing is good" axiom. This axiom embodies the distributive notion that sharing a multicast tree with more members always benefits everybody.

Axiom 5: Sharing is Good *The cost allocated to a member never increases when another member joins.*

Formal definition:

$$af_\alpha(N, R, M + m_\gamma, loc, c) \leq af_\alpha(N, R, M, loc, c)$$

$$\forall\ N, R, M, loc, c, m_\gamma, \text{ and } m_\alpha \in M$$

The ELSD scheme satisfies the sharing-is-good axiom since the share of costs from each link strictly decreases with the number of downstream members (and is independent of the number of upstream members). Clearly any cost allocation scheme obeying the sharing-is-good axiom also obeys the stand-alone axiom. These two axioms both describe an upper bound on the cost that can be allocated to a particular member. However, we might also be concerned about the problem of free riders, who are members who do not pay their fair share. According to the stand-alone axiom, the most a member should pay is her unicast cost, and the sharing-is-good axiom requires that the allocations decrease as members join. How much can a member benefit without being a free rider? If all members are located at the same node, then they all pay $1/|M|$ of their unicast cost. We suggest that any member paying less than this should be considered a free rider.[24]

$loc(ma) = R \Rightarrow af_\alpha(N, R, M, loc, c) = \forall\ N, R, M, loc, c \text{ and } m_\alpha \in M$

Theorem 2 continues to hold if we replace the stand-alone axiom with the much weaker dummy member axiom. The equivalency axiom means that only the cooperative game matters (i.e., topology is irrelevant aside from the cooperative game it induces). The basic result due to Shapley is that there is one and only one budget balanced cost allocation formula satisfying the additivity, anonymity, and dummy axioms, and this formula is now known as the Shapley Value.

24. This is much like the unanimity bound in economics; see Moulin (1990, 1992).

Herzog, Shenker, and Estrin

Axiom 6: *No Free Rider   The cost allocated to a member is never less than* $1/|M|$ *of her unicast cost.*

Formal definition:

$|M| * af_\alpha(N, R, M, \text{loc}, c) \geq cf(T(N, R, \text{loc},(m_\alpha)), c)$

$\forall$ N, R, M, loc, c, and $m_\alpha \in M$

Eliminating free riders does not pick out a specific allocation scheme, but does narrow the range of possibilities:

Theorem 3: *A cost allocation function satisfying the basic axioms and the no-free-rider axiom must satisfy:*

$F_u(n_u, n_d) \leq F_d(n_u, n_d) \qquad \forall (n_u, n_d) \in Z_{++} \times Z_+.$

Subset Monotonicity   The essential guiding principle behind the equivalency axiom is that cost allocations should depend only on the costs incurred by the various subsets or coalitions of members. Another distributive notion that arises from this principle is that the cost allocated to a particular member should be monotonic with respect to these subset costs. More precisely, if we consider two cost structures c1 and c2 (that is, we consider the network N and the members M fixed and we merely consider two sets of link costs), then, if for every subset M' 173 M the total cost of serving M' is no greater under cost c1 (compared to c2), then one might require that the allocated costs under c1 would not be greater than those under c2. This yields the following axiom:

Axiom 7: *Subset Monotonicity   No cost allocation can increase when subset costs all decrease or stay the same.*

Formal definition:

Consider an arbitrary tree L' = T(N, R, loc(M)) and two link costs c1 and c2:

if

$cf(T(N, R, loc(M')), c1) \geq cf(T(N, R, loc(M')), c2 \quad \forall\ M' \subseteq M$

then

$af_\alpha(N, R, M, loc, c1) \geq af_\alpha(N, R, M, loc, c2 \quad \forall\ m_\alpha \in M$

It turns out that this axiom, when combined with the basic axioms, determines a unique cost allocation strategy; in fact, only two of the three basic axioms are needed for this result.

Theorem 4: *A cost allocation formula satisfies equivalency, anonymity, and subset monotonicity if and only if it is the Equal Tree Split formula.*

Collusion Prevention Another aspect of allocation that is important to consider is collusion. Whenever a cost is shared among clients, it may be possible for several clients to unite and be represented by a single client who then forwards the data on to them. This is analogous to the classic "copy and distribute" security problem. Collusion among some receivers may increase the cost allocated to the other receivers and may decrease the efficiency of sharing the transmission. We would prefer that a cost allocation scheme not encourage collusion among the members. We therefore propose the following axiom:

Axiom 8: *Collusion Prevention The cost allocation scheme does not yield benefits for colluding members.*

Formal definition:

Consider an arbitrary network N = (V, L, T), a root R, a set of link costs c, a set of members M and their location function loc. For each subset $M' \subseteq M$ and $m_\gamma \in M'$:

$$\sum_{m_\alpha \in M'} af_\alpha(N, R, M, loc, c) \leq af_\gamma(N, R, M - M' + m_\gamma, loc, c)$$
$$+ cf(T(N, loc(m_\gamma), loc(M' - m_\gamma)), c)$$

Obviously, collusion prevention is a desirable property for cost allocation formulae. Unfortunately, we can prove that no canonical allocation strategy satisfies this axiom:

Theorem 5: *No cost allocation formula satisfying the basic axioms can satisfy the no-collusion axiom.*

Discussion

We started this section with three basic axioms, which narrowed the space of cost allocation strategies to the canonical ones. Within this class we discussed how various distributive notions pointed toward different choices. Eliminating free riders restricts us to schemes that allocate more to downstream members than to upstream members. Subset monotonicity leads us to the ETS scheme, while the stand-alone axiom suggests the ELSD scheme. Choosing between axioms is purely subjective, but charging a nonzero amount for a member located at the root seems generally inappropriate. The only canonical allocation scheme that always allocates zero to members located at the root is the ELSD scheme, and so perhaps it is the most natural choice.

Our treatment here is completely static. Consider, for a moment, the dynamic policy of allocating to each member the incremental cost of adding them to the distribution tree. The resulting allocations depend on the order in which members joined, which seems rather unfair. It might seem appropriate to then average these incremental costs over all arrival orders. Indeed, this averaging produces the ELSD allocations.[25] However, further research is necessary to expand the models presented here to dynamic policies.

In this section we discussed various cost allocation schemes from an axiomatic perspective. The next section discusses mechanisms for implementing these cost allocation schemes.

Accounting Mechanisms

In this section we use the term "accounting schemes" to denote mechanisms for implementing cost allocation schemes. First, we discuss the general structure of one class of accounting schemes which we call "one-pass" schemes. We then describe two different

25. This is the standard motivation for the Shapley Value.

models of implementation of such schemes which differ in the information provided about downstream members. Each of these models is examined according to the central question raised throughout this section: What forms of cost allocation schemes can this family of accounting mechanisms support?

One-Pass Accounting Schemes

We have made the fundamental assumption that costs are allocated among receivers and not just assigned to the sender. Because the number of receivers can become quite large and widely dispersed geographically,[26] the key concern in designing accounting mechanisms is scalability. It is important that the traffic load imposed by the accounting mechanism on any particular link should not increase (without bound) with the size (in terms of numbers or in geographical dispersion) of the multicast group. Thus scalability concerns rule out any kind of centralized accounting, and so we must turn to a more decentralized approach. In this chapter, we consider only the family of one-pass mechanisms whereby the accounting control messages make a single pass from the source down the multicast tree to all receivers. While this is not the only scalable accounting mechanism one might imagine,[27] it certainly seems among the most natural. In this one-pass method of accounting, nodes allocate costs to members as the accounting message passes through them. The information used to make the allocation decisions comes from two sources. The first source of information is multicast routing (and perhaps the reservation establishment protocol if the costs are related to reservations), which provides information about the downstream links. Traditional multicast routing only provides information about whether or not there exist members downstream of a particular link. We call this Model 1. It is possible,

26. The geographic dispersion is important because it means the amount of information needed to describe the tree topology is also growing.

27. For instance, one could design an accounting method that involved two passes of control messages, one downstream and the other back upstream. Also, one could use an iterative accounting method in which the control messages continued to circulate until an equilibrium had been reached.

Herzog, Shenker, and Estrin

perhaps only because it enables better allocation of costs, that multicast routing could provide the exact number of members downstream of each link. We call this Model 2.[28] If the link costs are tied to reservations, then this information about the number of downstream members making reservations could be provided by the reservation establishment protocol. We will consider both models below. As we shall see, there is an important difference in the functionality that can be achieved in the two models.[29] The second source of information is the accounting message itself. The design of a one-pass accounting mechanism essentially reduces to the question of what information is carried in the accounting message sent downstream. To ensure scalability, this information cannot grow with the size of the multicast group, nor with the number of links traversed. This prevents us from carrying detailed information about each upstream link cost and each member's allocated cost. Instead, we choose to carry only a single piece of information in the accounting message: the unallocated or residual cost passed down from the upstream node. While this is not the most general form of accounting message,[30] it seems a natural and simple choice.

Thus with this form of accounting message, the costs are allocated by the following process. The accounting message arrives at a node on the incoming link from an upstream neighbor, carrying the upstream residual cost; we will call this the input cost to the node, and let $in(v_j)$ denote the input cost arriving at the downstream node v_j. The cost allocation function determines how much of this cost is allocated to each of the local members and how much is passed down to each of the downstream next-hops. We will call the costs that are passed on the residual output from a node, and let $out(v_i, v_j)$ denote the costs that are passed on from node v_i to downstream

28. To do any form of cost allocation we must be able to identify all members at a node, if for no other reason than to give them the feedback about their allocated costs. The question is then which protocol will carry these numbers upstream. It appears to be simple to modify most multicast routing protocols to carry the cumulative membership numbers upstream once the number of local numbers is available.

29. From the point of view of implementation of the accounting schemes themselves, Model 1 and Model 2 are essentially equivalent.

30. One could, for instance, include information of the previous five upstream links.

node v_j. The sum of all residual outputs plus the sum of all locally allocated costs must be equal to input cost as a result of the balanced budget rule.[31] When an accounting message is forwarded to the downstream neighbor, the cost of the link connecting the two nodes is added to the residual costs and this sum is carried in the accounting message as input costs to the next-hop node: thus, $in(v_j) = c(v_i, v_j) + out(v_i, v_j)$ when v_j is a next-hop downstream of v_i. At leaf nodes, all costs are allocated to the local members. At nodes with no local members, all costs are passed down to the downstream next-hops in the accounting message.

One-pass accounting is a distributed accounting scheme. Independent cost allocation decisions are made by each individual node based on the information provided to it by multicast routing (either Model 1 or Model 2) and the accounting message. We assume that no other information about topology or group members can be factored into the allocation decision. For Model 1, since a node can make no meaningful distinctions between downstream links, we require that the residual costs passed on to each next-hop are the same: $out(v_i, v_j) = out(v_i, v_k)$ for all links (v_i, v_j) and (v_i, v_k) in the distribution tree. We further assume, in both Model 1 and Model 2, that all nodes must implement the same allocation rules. In order to achieve a consistent allocation scheme, all nodes, if given the same information, must produce the same allocation.

We will refer to cost allocation schemes that can be implemented with a Model 1 one-pass accounting mechanism as Model 1 allocation schemes, and similarly for Model 2. The basic one-pass structure of cost accounting imposes some significant restrictions on what cost allocation formulae can be supported. In particular, such one-pass accounting schemes can only support cost allocation schemes that satisfy the stand-alone axiom:[32]

---

31. It is straightforward to show that if there is one node with a locally unbalanced budget, then one cannot guarantee that the overall cost budget is balanced.

32. A stronger result holds. No subset $M' \subseteq M$ can be allocated a cost that is greater than their subtree cost: $\{\Sigma subm_\alpha \ll_{M'} af_\alpha(N, R, M, loc, c) \leq cf(T(N, R, loc(M')), c \ \forall \ N, R, M, loc, M' \subseteq M$, and c. This means that all one-pass accounting schemes produce results that are in the core (see Sharkey [1995] for a definition).

Theorem 6: *Given a tree T(N, R, loc(M)), a set of link costs c, and a one-pass accounting mechanism, no member can be allocated a cost greater than her unicast cost.*

We are interested in how many of our original axioms are consistent with our one-pass family of accounting mechanisms. Before we consider Models 1 and 2 separately, we can rule out one axiom that does not apply to either of them:

Theorem 7: *No cost allocation scheme implemented with a one-pass accounting mechanism can satisfy the subset monotonicity axiom.*

We first discuss Model 2 because our treatment of it is closer to our previously developed results. We will then return to Model 1, where we will need to modify our basic set of axioms.

Model 2

As stated above, we are interested in the extent to which these accounting mechanisms can support cost allocation formulae that obey our previous axioms. As we show below, Model 2 can support the basic axioms presented in the fourth section above. In fact, there is only one Model 2 cost allocation formula that obeys the basic axioms:

Theorem 8: *ELSD is the only cost allocation formula that obeys the basic axioms and that can be implemented with a Model 2 one-pass accounting mechanism.*

This follows trivially from Theorems 6 and 2. How is the ELSD formula implemented? Consider some node v_i in the distribution tree; we let $tmem(v_i)$ denote the number of members located in the subtree rooted at v_i and recall that $in(v_i)$ denotes the input costs in the accounting message arriving at v_i.[33] The cost allocated to each

___

33. A node v_i knows the value of $tmem(v_j)$ for all immediate downstream members because this is a basic property of Model 2. The node can calculate $tmem(v_i)$ by adding up all the $tmem(v_j)$ for all immediate downstream members and then adding the number of local members.

local member is $in(v_i)/tmem(v_i)$. For each link (v_i, v_j) in the distribution tree, $out(v_i, v_j) = in(v_i) * tmem(v_j)/tmem(v_i)$ and so $in(v_j) = in(v_i) * tmem(v_j)/tmem(v_i) + c(v_i, v_j)$. Notice that the residual cost passed on to next-hops is proportional to the number of receivers downstream. The cost of the connecting link is passed on fully to the downstream next-hop.

Model 1

We now consider accounting mechanisms in the context of Model 1, where multicast routing only indicates which links have downstream members but not how many members are there.

Reduced Basic Axioms We would like to invoke the basic axioms presented in the fourth section above. Additive and anonymous cost allocation schemes can be supported (as we shall see in examples) by Model 1 accounting schemes. However, we find that the equivalency axiom is not consistent with Model 1.

Theorem 9: *No cost allocation formula that is implemented by a Model 1 one-pass accounting scheme can satisfy the equivalency axiom.*

Thus Model 1 accounting schemes are necessarily dependent on the physical topology, in contrast with the topological independence of the equivalency axiom. For Model 1 we will still require that the *reduced* basic axioms of anonymity and additivity still hold, but must relinquish the equivalency axiom. In the next subsection we develop a canonical form for Model 1 allocation schemes that obey these two axioms. In passing we should mention that these reduced basic axioms lead to the same impossibility result about collusion:

Theorem 10: *No Model 1 cost allocation formula satisfying the reduced basic axioms can satisfy the no collusion axiom.*

The One-Pass Canonical Form Consider any Model 1 allocation scheme that obeys the reduced basic axioms. At leaf nodes, all costs must be allocated equally to local members. At nodes with no local members, all costs much be passed on equally to all downstream links. Thus the only design freedom left is how much of the residual cost to allocate to the local members and how much to pass on to downstream members when both are present. We can express the family of possible design choices with the one-pass canonical form of cost allocation formulae (supporting the Model 1 one-pass accounting scheme).

Each one-pass canonical form is associated with a function $F = (F_l, F_r) \in \mathfrak{S}$ in the following way. Consider a node v_i with an input cost of $in(v_i)$. If there are n_l local receivers and n_r next hop nodes, the allocated costs are:

For a local member on v_i: $F_l(n_l, n_r) * in(v_i)$

For a next hop node v_j: $out(v_i, v_j) = F_r(n_l, n_r) * in(v_i)$

All Model 1 allocation schemes obeying the reduced basic axioms can be expressed in this form:

Theorem 11: *A Model 1 cost allocation formula satisfies the reduced basic axioms if and only if it can be expressed in the one-pass canonical form.*

While the one-pass canonical form appears very similar to the canonical form discussed in the fourth section above, there are important differences. The previously discussed canonical form expressed how the cost of a particular link was allocated to all upstream and downstream members. Here, the canonical form only describes the allocation to local members and to downstream links. To find the resulting allocation to all members, we must recursively iterate this formula down the tree. Thus, it is much harder to understand what allocations will result from a particular one-pass canonical form.

Examples The one-pass canonical form allows for an infinite set of possible allocation strategies. Below we list a few examples. Since we know that $F_l(n_l, 0) = \dfrac{1}{n_l}$ and $F_r(0, n_r) = \dfrac{1}{n_r}$ for all $n_l, n_r > 0$, we merely describe the allocations on the set Z_{++}^2.

1. Local members pay nothing

$F_l(n_l, n_r) = 0$

$F_r(n_l, n_r) = 1/n_r$

2. Local members pay everything

$F_l(n_l, n_r) = 1/n_l$

$F_r(n_l, n_r) = 0$

3. All locals are considered as one next-hop (ENHS):

$$F_l(n_l, n_r) = \frac{1}{n_l * (n_r + 1)}$$

$$F_r(n_l, n_r) = \frac{1}{n_r + 1}$$

4. Local members and next-hops are allocated identical costs:

$F_l(n_l, n_r) = F_r(n_l, n_r) = 1/(n_l + n_r)$

5. Equal split between all the local members and all the next-hops:

$F_l(n_l, n_r) = 1/(2 * n_l)$

$F_r(n_l, n_r) = 1/(2 * n_r)$

6. Majority loses:

if $n_l > n_r$ $F_l(n_l, n_r) = 1/n_l$ and $F_r(n_l, n_r) = 0$

if $n_l < n_r$ $F_r(n_l, n_r) = 1/n_r$ and $F_l(n_l, n_r) = 0$

if $n_l = n_r$ $F_l(n_l, n_r) = F_r(n_l, n_r) = 1/2n_l$

Additional Axioms We already know from Theorem 6 that all the one-pass allocation schemes must satisfy the stand-alone axiom. However, not all such cost allocation schemes obey the sharing-is-good axiom.

Theorem 12: *A Model 1 cost allocation formula satisfies the reduced basic axioms and the sharing-is-good axiom if and only if the functions $F_l(n_l, n_r)$ and $F_r(n_l, n_r)$ are nonincreasing on $\{Z_+^2 - (0,0)\}$.*

Note that, of our examples, only the last one fails this test. Thus all Model 1 allocation schemes obeying this mild restriction ensure that the benefits of multicast are shared among all receivers.

Recall that in Theorem 3 a wide variety of canonical cost allocation policies satisfy the no-free-rider axiom. In particular, the ELSD scheme, which is the only Model 2 allocation policy that obeys the basic axioms, satisfies the no-free-rider axiom. However, no Model 1 allocation policies satisfy the no-free-rider axiom.

Theorem 13: *There is no Model 1 cost allocation formula that satisfies the reduced basic axioms and the no-free-rider axiom.*

As long as our functions F_l, F_r are nonincreasing (so that the sharing-is-good axiom is obeyed), we have little to guide us in our choice of canonical Model 1 allocation schemes. Allocating everything to the local members is unfair, as is passing all costs on to the downstream links. In a very rough intuitive sense, fairness seems to dictate that local members individually are allocated no more than is passed on to the individual links ($F_l(n_l, n_r) \leq F_r(n_l, n_r)$) and the set of local members as a whole are allocated at least as much as is passed on to the individual links ($n_l F_l(n_l, n_r) \geq F_r(n_l, n_r)$). There is wide latitude between these two extremes of treating local members each as a downstream link, and treating the collection of them as a downstream link. How can we choose among the various possibilities that lie within the spectrum $\dfrac{F_r(n_l, n_r)}{n_l} \leq F_l(n_l, n_r) \leq F_r(n_l, n_r)$?

One possibility is to require that the cost allocated to members not depend not on the exact number of members at all other nodes, but only on the set of nodes where there are members. This condition makes little sense for Model 2, because there we had the information about individual nodes downstream. However, Model 1 does not provide this information. Moreover, the contexts in which Model 1 might be deployed may not even have this information at the local level; the costs, rather than being assigned to individuals, might really be assigned to the nodes (subnets) at which members reside. For instance, all costs allocated to members on an ethernet at the University of Southern California (USC) would be assigned to USC rather than to the individual members. This would allow current multicast protocols, which do not keep track of individual members, to be consistent with cost allocation. Given that the number of members at a particular node is not known, the allocation to other members should not depend on it. This requirement means that $F_r(n_l, n_r) = F_r(1, n_r)$ for all $n_l > 0$, and thus narrows the spectrum $$\frac{F_r(n_l, n_r)}{n_l} \leq F_l(n_l, n_r \leq F_r(n_l, n_r)$$ down to the single point $\frac{F_r(n_l, n_r)}{n_l} = F_l(n_l, n_r)$ which is merely the ENHS scheme.

We did not embody the considerations in the previous two paragraphs in axioms because the distributive notions were significantly less general and compelling than our previous axioms. We fully admit that this line of reasoning, which leads to ENHS, is much weaker than our previous results, but we do not see any other general principles at our disposal. This is largely because the allocations that result from Model 1 have unavoidably poor properties (free rider, no equivalency, etc.), and so it is hard to formulate desirable distributive notions that are achievable in this context.

Discussion

In the fourth section we discussed a general axiomatization of allocation policies. The ELSD scheme emerged as the most attractive scheme. We then turned, in this section, to issues of implementation and discussed two different models. Model 2 can implement the ELSD scheme, and in fact this is the only Model 2 scheme consistent with the basic axioms. Therefore, if we adopt Model 2 in our implementations, there seems little question that ELSD would be the most appropriate allocation policy.

However, when we use Model 1 we are faced with a much more confusing situation. We cannot achieve the desired degree of topological independence, nor can we prevent free riders. There are few distributive notions besides the sharing-is-good and stand-alone axioms that we can achieve. We do present an intuitive line of reasoning that suggests that ENHS is the best of this rather sorry lot of allocation policies.

How to choose between these two models? From the perspective of the accounting protocol needed to realize them, the difference in implementation between Models 1 and 2 is very small. The key difference between the two models is in the availability of the exact number of local members; once that number is available, it seems fairly straightforward to provide it upstream either through multicast routing directly or through the reservation establishment protocol, or even through a separate set of accounting control messages.[34] If costs are tied to reservations, then Model 2 is quite practical since the number of local members is already known to receiver-initiated reservation establishment protocols. However, most multicast routing protocols do not determine the number of local members, so if costs are applied more generally, we are faced with the trade-off between the increased implementation difficulty of Model 2 with its correspondingly better allocation policy, and the significantly easier implementation of Model 1, which comes with a seriously flawed allocation policy. An intermediate point is to keep track of the cumulative number of domains with internal members, instead of the number of individual host members. Only border routers would propagate the member-domain counts upstream, eliminating the need for interior-router modifications and thereby sidestepping many of the implementation difficulties.

The discussion in this section has focused exclusively on the one-pass accounting mechanism. There is a wide variety of other approaches available, so why the narrow consideration of this particular family? From a purely mechanistic perspective, the one-pass mechanism has several desirable properties: it is simple, easy to implement, and scalable (in that the state carried in the accounting

34. If the number of local members is available but multicast routing does not propagate these numbers upstream, then one could add such a function directly to the accounting mechanism, which would necessitate a second set of accounting control messages traversing up the distribution tree. This can be viewed as an alternative implementation of Model 2 since, as we observe below, the basic allocation process can be adequately handled with a one-pass mechanism.

message does not grow with the number of members or with the size of the distribution tree). In addition, in the context of Model 2, the one-pass accounting mechanism can implement the ELSD policy, which on purely axiomatic grounds was identified as the most natural allocation policy.[35] The most obvious drawback to the one-pass accounting mechanism is that when it is combined with Model 1 it cannot implement allocation policies that obey the equivalency axiom. While we do think it important to explore other accounting mechanisms, and we plan to do so, we believe that it is essentially impossible to achieve equivalency if allocations must be made without knowledge of the number of downstream members. That is, we believe that the key factor preventing equivalency is the difference between Model 1 and Model 2, not the features of the one-pass mechanism itself.

Future Work

This chapter used a very simple model to illustrate some of the basic issues involved in cost allocation. In this section we briefly discuss several directions in which our model could be made more general.

Multicast Distribution Model

This chapter modeled multicast distributions as source rooted trees, computed from unicast routing. Although this is the most common form of multicast distribution, newer protocols use different models for their distribution. Ballardie, Francis and Crowcroft (1993) advocates Core Based Trees (CBT), or using a shared tree for all sources (core-rooted rather than source-rooted trees). Protocol Independent Multicast (PIM), in its sparse mode, enables mixing source-rooted, shortest path (SP) routes for some groups and shared trees

---

35. We should note that we have also analyzed a two-pass accounting mechanism in which the first pass goes upstream from receivers to senders, and the second pass goes downstream from senders to receivers. In the context of Model 2, this two-pass mechanism is capable of implementing all canonical cost allocation strategies. However, since the ELSD policy seems the most natural policy and does not require the extra complication of the two-pass mechanism, we will not discuss the two-pass mechanism here.

for others (Deering et al. 1994). Our theory only assumes that the route taken from a particular source to a particular receiver is independent of the group membership (i.e., the route will be the same for a specific group member regardless of who else has joined the group). This remains true for both CBT and PIM, and thus our results apply.[36]

Another aspect of routing which can invalidate our theory is the ability to request alternate routes. Typically these alternate routes are not automatically loop-free, so a new alternate route is followed until it hits the tree. This means that the resulting routes will depend on the current membership.

Multiple Sources

Our model considered only a single source. If the costs being allocated are tied to a per-packet metric, then this is sufficient since each packet comes from a single source. Our model is not sufficient, however, if the costs are tied to resource reservations (e.g., bandwidth). The ReSerVation Protocol (RSVP) described in Zhang et al. (1993), uses the idea of reservation styles, and two of these styles, dynamic filter and wildcard filter, allow a single reservation to be shared by several sources. In terms of our theory, this would require the root R to be a set of nodes rather than a single node. This by itself introduces no nontrivial changes to our theory. However, if the costs on a link depended on the particular set of upstream sources (say, for instance, that the bandwidth reserved was the maximal upstream source bandwidth), then our theory needs to be extended.

Multiple Qualities of Service

In this chapter, all members are equivalent (except for location). However, if the network supports multiple qualities of service (e.g., several priority levels or several levels of real-time service) and these different (QOS levels incur different network costs, then the mem-

---

36. Although this assumes that the route used when computing the stand-alone cost is chosen using multicast rather than reverting to a unicast route.

bers are no longer necessarily equivalent. This raises an issue that is in some sense orthogonal to the one considered here. In this chapter we have considered the issue of how to share costs between equivalent users at different locations. Having multiple qualities of service raises the issue of how to share the cost among several members who are in the same place but request different QOS levels.[37] Clearly, for these different QOS requests to be merged onto a single multicast distribution tree, there must be at least a partial set of ordering relations between the qualities of service, and the QOS installed on the link must be greater than or equal to all QOS requests. If the set of qualities of service is completely ordered, then the problem reduces to what has been called in the literature the "airport game" (see Littlechild and Owen [1973]) in which the cost of the link is the cost associated with the highest QOS requested. Here the Shapley Value of this game is easy to compute; it is very much like the ELSD scheme in that every user shares equally the incremental cost of all levels less than or equal to their requested level. This cost allocation formula for this special form of the problem can be axiomatized in a variety of ways (Moulin and Shenker 1994), and appears to be a rather natural choice. If the set of qualities of service is not completely ordered but only partially ordered, then the problem becomes much more complicated.

Multiple qualities of service also present some problems for implementation. If there are a discrete set of QOS levels, then Models 1 and 2 can easily be changed to include information about the presence or exact number of members requesting each level. However, if there is a continuum of QOS levels (e.g., bandwidth), then we must rethink the form of the accounting message.

Other Issues

There are several other areas that we have not yet explored. We did not discuss the issue of dynamics. Clearly in a large multicast group the membership can change rather rapidly, and these changes affect

---

37. Combining the two issues to have different qualities of service at different locations can only be done after one has solved the two problems independently.

the costs allocated to individual members. Is there some principled way to describe and ameliorate these changes? Also, we have not at all considered the issue of incentives. Given some model of strategic behavior, what equilibria result from the various forms of cost allocation methods proposed here?

Acknowledgments

This research was supported in part by the Advanced Research Projects Agency under Ft. Huachuca contract number DABT63-91-C-0001, entitled "Gigabit Network Communications Research." The views and conclusions contained in this chapter are those of the authors and should not be interpreted as representing the official policies, either expressed or implied, of the Advanced Research Projects Agency, the Department of the Army, or the U.S. government. This work was also supported in part by National Science Foundation grant SES-93-20481. An earlier version of this chapter, without the proofs, appeared in SIGCOMM '95.

References

Ballardie, A.J., P.F. Francis, and J. Crowcroft. 1993. Core Based Trees (CBT). *Proceedings of ACM SIGCOMM '93*.

Braun, H.W., and K. Claffy. 1993. A framework for flow-based accounting on the Internet. *Proceedings of SICON '93, IEEE Singapore.*

Clark, D., S. Shenker, and L. Zhang. 1992. Supporting real-time applications in an integrated services packet network: Architecture and mechanism. *Proceedings of ACM SIGCOMM '92.*

Cocchi, R., S. Shenker, D. Estrin, and L. Zhang. 1993. Pricing in computer networks: Motivation, formulation, and example. *IEEE/ACM Transactions on Networking.*

Crawford, D.W. 1996. Pricing network usage: A market for bandwidth or a market for communications? In *Internet Economics*, ed. Lee W. McKnight and Joseph P. Bailey. Cambridge, Mass.: MIT Press.

Deering, S., and D. Cheriton. 1990. Multicast routing in datagram internetworks and extended LANS. *ACM Transactions on Computer Systems* (May): 85–111.

Deering, S., D. Estrin, D. Farinacci, V. Jacobson, C.G. Liu, and L. Wei. 1994. An architecture for wide-area multicast routing. *Proceedings of ACM SIGCOMM '94.*

Henriet, D., and H. Moulin. 1996. Traffic based cost allocation in a network. *Rand Journal of Economics* 27(2): 332–345.

Littlechild, S.C., and G. Owen. 1973. A simple expression for the Shapley Value. *Management Science* 20: 370–372.

MacKie-Mason, J.K., J. Murphy, and L. Murphy. 1995. The role of responsive pricing in the Internet. Technical report, University of Michigan Dublin City and University of Auburn. Available from http://http://www.spp.umich.edu/spp/papers/jmm/responsive-mit96-net.ps.Z.

MacKie-Mason, J.K., and H.R. Varian. 1995a. Pricing congestable network resources. *IEEE Journal on Selected Areas in Communications* 13: 1141–1149. Available from ftp://gopher.econ.lsa.umich.edu/pub/Papers/pricing-congestible.ps.Z.

MacKie-Mason, J.K., and H.R. Varian. 1995b. Pricing the Internet. In *Public access to the Internet*, ed. B. Kahin and J. Keller. Englewood Cliffs, N.J.: Prentice-Hall. Available from http://http://www.spp.umich.edu/spp/papers/jmm/Pricing_the_Internet. ps.Z.

Megiddo, N. 1978. Computational complexity of the game theory approach to cost allocation for a tree. *Mathematics of Operations Research* 3: 189–196.

Moulin, H. 1990. Uniform externalities: Two axioms for fair allocation. *Journal of Public Economy* 43: 305–326.

Moulin, H. 1992. Welfare bound in the cooperative production problem. *Games and Economic Behavior* 4: 373–401.

Moulin, H., and S. Shenker. 1994. Average cost pricing versus serial cost sharing: An axiomatic comparison. *Journal of Economic Theory* 64(1): 178–201.

Myerson, R.B. 1991. *Game theory.* Cambridge, Mass.: Harvard University Press.

Peyton-Young, H., ed. 1985. *Cost allocation: Methods, principles, applications.* Amsterdam and New York: Elseviers Science Publishers, B.V.

Roth, A.E., ed. 1988. *The Shapley value, an essay in honor of Lloyd S. Shapley.* Cambridge: Cambridge University Press.

Sairamesh, J., D.F. Ferguson, and Y. Yemini. 1995. An approach to pricing, optimal allocation and quality of service provisioning in high-speed packet networks. *Proceedings of Infocom '95.*

Shapley, L.S. 1953. A value for n-person games. In *Contributions to the theory of games,* ed. H.W. Kuhn and A.W. Tucker. Annals of Mathematics Studies, vol. 2, no. 28. Princeton: Princeton University Press.

Sharkey, W.W. 1995. Network models in economics. In *Handbook of operations research and management science: Networks,* ed. M.O. Ball et al. Vol. 8.

Shenker, S. 1995. Service models and pricing policies for an integrated services Internet. In *Public access to the Internet,* ed. B. Kahin and J. Keller. Englewood Cliffs, N.J.: Prentice-Hall.

Zhang, L., S. Deering, D. Estrin, S. Shenker, and D. Zappala. 1993. RSVP: A new resource reservation protocol. *IEEE Networks Magazine* (September).

Appendix

Theorem 1: *A cost allocation formula satisfies the basic axioms if and only if it is a canonical strategy.*

It is a straightforward process to verify that any canonical form satisfies the basic axioms. We now show that any cost allocation formula that obeys the basic axioms can be expressed in the canonical form. Consider any cost allocation formula that obeys the basic axioms. We begin with the most general case of a network N = (V, L, T) and a tree L′ = T(N, R, loc(M)). Since the allocation function is additive, we can restrict our attention to cost functions $c_{i,j}$, which have nonzero cost only on the link (v_i, v_j), and have unit cost on that link. More specifically, we know that

$$\sum_{(i, j):(v_i, v_j) \in L} (c_{i,j}(v_i, v_j) * c(v_i, v_j)) = c$$

and so

$$\sum_{(i, j):(v_i, v_j) \in L} (af_\alpha(N, R, M, loc, c_{il}) * c(v_i, v_j)) = af_\alpha(N, R, M, loc, c)$$

$$\forall \, N, R, loc, M, \alpha : m_\alpha \in M.$$

We must now show that the cost allocations that result from cost functions $c_{i,j}$ can be expressed in terms of the canonical form.

Consider the reduced network with the single link (v_i, v_j) and the following loc function:

$$loc'(m_\beta) = \begin{cases} v_j : m_\beta \text{ is downstream } (v_i, v_j) \\ v_i : \text{Otherwise} \end{cases}$$

The subset costs of the reduced network problem are the same as in the original problem, and the equivalency axiom requires that the cost allocations be the same. For example, Figure 2 shows nodes v_1, v_2, v_3 merging to a single node v_2 in the reduced network. The anonymity condition requires that equivalent members be charged the same; in particular, all members at the same node must be allocated the same cost. Thus the allocations in this reduced problem are characterized by two quantities, the allocation to the up-

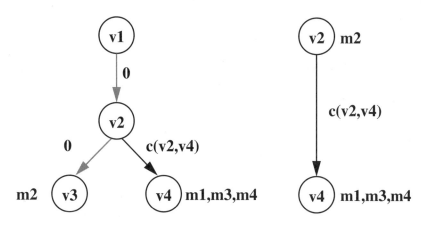

Figure 2
Merging Nodes with No Cost Link: The Equivalency Axiom

stream members and the allocation to the downstream members. These allocations can depend on the number of upstream and downstream members, so they are expressed as functions $F_u(n_u, n_d)$ and $F_d(n_u, n_d)$. These costs must be nonnegative, and the budget balance requirement means that

$n_u F_u(n_u, n_d) + n_d F_d(n_u, n_d) = 1$. This is precisely the canonical form.[38] QED

Theorem 2: *A cost allocation function satisfies the basic and stand-alone axioms if and only if it is the Equal Link Split Downstream (ELSD) function.*

Consider any canonical form F that obeys the stand-alone axiom. The stand-alone axiom implies that $F_u(n_u, n_d) = 0 \; \forall \; n_u > 0$. Combining this with the budget balance condition $n_u F_u(n_u, n_d) + n_d F_d(n_u, n_d) = 1$ yields $F_d(n_u, n_d) = 1/n_d \; \forall \; n_d > 0$, which is the ELSD formula. It is straightforward to verify that the ELSD formula satisfies the stand-alone axiom, so the converse holds as well. QED

38. The conditions $F_u(0, n_d) = 1$ and $F_d(n_u, 0) = 1$ in the definition of $\mathfrak{F}$ are irrelevant to the actual allocations.

Theorem 3: *A cost allocation function satisfying the basic axioms and the no-free-rider axiom must satisfy:*

$$F_u(n_u, n_d) \leq F_d(n_u, n_d) \quad \forall \ (n_u, n_d) \in Z_{++} \times z_+.$$

Consider any canonical form F. The no-free-rider axiom is obeyed if and only if $1/(n_u + n_d) \leq F_d(n_u, n_d)$ whenever $n_d > 0$. However, combining this with the budget balance condition $n_u F_u(n_u, n_d) + n_d F_d(n_u, n_d) = 1$ yields $n_u(F_d(n_u, n_d) - F_u(n_u, n_d)) \geq 0$. Thus whenever $(n_u, n_d) \in Z_{++} \times Z_+$, we must have $F_d(n_u, n_d) \geq F_u(n_u, n_d)$. QED

Theorem 4: *A cost allocation formula satisfies equivalency, anonymity, and subset monotonicity if and only if it is the Equal Tree Split (ETS) formula.*

Clearly the ETS scheme satisfies the anonymity, equivalency, and subset monotonicity axioms. We must now show that any allocation function that obeys the anonymity, equivalency, and subset monotonicity axioms must be the ETS policy. Figure 3 provides an example that follows throughout the proof. Consider any network N = (V, L, T) with a root R, set of members M, location function loc, and cost function c (case A). From this network we build a second network (illustrated in case B) by adding a new link $l' = (R', R)$ with no cost:

$$N' = (V + R', L + l', T')$$

$$L'' = T'(N', R', loc(M)) = L' + l'$$

$$c' = c + \{c'(R', R) = 0\}.$$

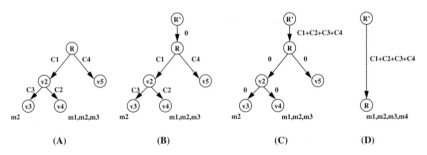

Figure 3
Equal Tree Split Transformations: Cases A, B, C, D

Sharing Multicast Costs

Clearly all of the subset costs are the same under case A and case B, so allocations must not change (due to the equivalency axiom). We now keep the network fixed and consider a new cost function c'' (illustrated as case C), where the cost of the whole tree is on (R', R) while the remaining links have zero costs.

$$c''(R', R) = cf(L', c')$$

$$c''(v_i, v_j) = 0 \quad \forall (v_i, v_j) \in L'$$

Note that no subset costs have decreased, therefore the subset monotonicity condition implies that no individual allocated costs can decrease. Since the total costs have remained the same, the balanced budget implies that total allocated costs must remain unchanged. Under these two constraints, the allocations for this new cost function c'' must be the same as for the old cost function c'. Case D is created by merging all the nodes downstream into R, which, according to the equivalency axiom, does not change the allocated costs. With all the members in one node (R), the anonymity axiom implies that they all share the cost of the link equally, so each member is allocated $c''(R', R)/|M| = cf(L', c)/|M|$. This is the ETS policy. QED

Theorem 5: *No cost allocation formula satisfying the basic axioms can satisfy the no-collusion axiom.*

Consider any canonical form F and assume that is satisfies the no-collusion axiom. Consider a network with a single link, with n_u members at the root and n_d members downstream. Because $5(F_u(5,5) + F_d(5,5)) = 1$, we either have $F_u(5,5) \geq 1/10$ or $F_d(5,5) \geq 1/10$. Since our proof works with either case, let us assume without loss of generality that $F_u(5,5) \geq 1/10$. The no-collusion condition requires that $F_u(n_u - 1, n_d) \geq 2 * F_u(n_u, n_d)$ for any n_u, because otherwise one element would collude with another. Recursing this inequality, we find: $F_u(n_u - k, n_d) \geq 2k * F_u(n_u, n_d)$. Choose $n_u = n_d = 5$ and $k = 4$, and then we find that $F_u(1,5) \geq 2^4 * F_u(5,5) \geq 1.6$. This is a violation of the canonical form, thus a contradiction. QED

Theorem 6: *Given a tree T(N, R, loc(M)), a set of link costs c, and a one-pass mechanism, no member can be allocated a cost greater than her unicast cost.*

From the definition of the one-pass model we know that (1) nodes are budget balanced so their output and allocations are bounded by their input, and (2) $in(v_j) = c(v_i, v_j) + out(v_i, v_j)$ for each v_j downstream to v_i. Thus, $in(v_j) \leq c(v_i, v_j) + in(v_i)$. If we iterate this inequality for each node along the path from R to any node V_k and collapse the inequalities, we get the following result: $in(v_k) \leq cf(T(N, R, V_k), c)$. QED

Theorem 7: *No cost allocation scheme implemented with a one-pass accounting mechanism can satisfy the subset monotonicity axiom.*

Consider an accounting scheme that satisfies the subset monotonicity axiom. Consider the example in Figure 4 of a single tree $T(N, R, loc(M))$ with two different link cost functions: c1, c2. The cost allocations for c1 are straightforward: $af_1(l) = af_2(l) = 10$. Because the total cost of the tree remains the same, while no subset cost decreases, subset monotonicity implies that the cost allocations must be the same for c1 and c2. To achieve this allocation for c2 it must be that $out(v_2, v_3) = 10$. But we must have $out(v_2, v_3) = out(v_2, v_4)$, which violates the local budget balance. This is a contradiction. QED

Theorem 9: *No cost allocation formula that is implemented by a Model 1 one-pass accounting scheme can satisfy the equivalency axiom.*

Consider a Model 1 one-pass accounting scheme that satisfies the equivalency axiom. Consider the following example of a network illustrated in Figure 5, where $c(v_1, v_2) > 0$ and $c(v_2, v_3) = c(v_2, v_4) = 0$. The equivalency axiom implies that the cost allocations to members on v_3 and v_4 should be the same: $af_1(l) = af_2(l) = af_3(l)$. However, the definition of Model 1 implies that $in(v_3) = in(v_4) = \dfrac{c(v_1, v_2)}{2}$. Therefore the cost allocations cannot be the same. This is a contradiction. QED

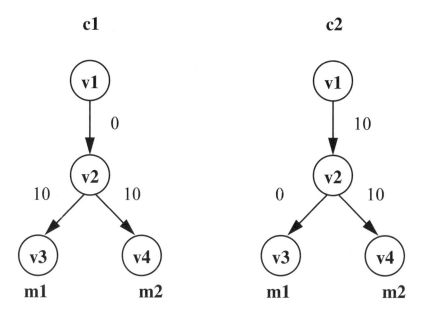

c1   **c2**

Figure 4
Subset Monotonicity vs. One-Pass Model

Theorem 10: *No Model 1 cost allocation formula satisfying the reduced basic axioms can satisfy the no-collusion axiom.*

This proof is identical to the one in Theorem 5 replacing (F_u, F_d) by (F_l, F_r), n_u by n_l and n_d by n_r. QED

Theorem 11: *A Model 1 cost allocation formula satisfies the reduced basic axioms if and only if it can be expressed in the one-pass canonical form.*

It is a straightforward process to verify that any one-pass canonical form satisfies the reduced basic axioms. We now show that any Model 1 cost allocation formula that obeys the basic axioms can be expressed in the one-pass canonical form. Similar to the proof for Theorem 1, we begin with the most general case of a network N = (V, L, T) and a tree L' = T(N, R, loc(M)). Since the allocation function is additive, we can restrict our attention to cost functions $c_{i,j}$, which have nonzero cost only on the link (v_i, v_j) and have unit

Herzog, Shenker, and Estrin

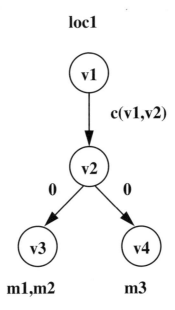

Figure 5
One-Pass Model 1 vs. Equivalency

cost on that link. We must now show that all cost allocations that result from cost functions $c_{i,j}$ can be expressed in terms of the canonical form.

The anonymity axiom implies that all local members are allocated identical costs. The definition of Model 1 requires that the residual costs passed on to all next-hops are the same. Since these allocations can depend on the number of local members and downstream next-hops, they are expressed as functions $F_l(n_l, n_r)$ and $F_r(n_l, n_r)$. These costs must be nonnegative, and the budget balance requirement means that $n_l F_l(n_l, n_r) + n_r F_r(n_l, n_r) = 1$. Using additivity, we can show that the allocations must be proportional to the incoming costs. Therefore:

Local members: $in(v_i) * F_l(n_l, n_r)$

Residual costs to node v_k[39]: $out(v_j, v_k) = in(v_i) * F_r(n_l, n_r)$

39. In the one-pass model, residual costs that are allocated individually to each immediate downstream neighboring node.

In Model 1, the input costs to the next-hop v_k include both residual costs and the cost of the link connecting them:

$\text{in}(v_k) = \text{in}(v_i) * F_r(n_l, n_r) + c(v_i, v_k)$. This is precisely the one-pass canonical form. QED

Theorem 12: *A Model 1 cost allocation formula satisfies the reduced basic axioms and the sharing-is-good axiom if and only if the functions $F_l(n_l, n_r)$ and $F_r(n_l, n_r)$ are nonincreasing on $\{Z_+^2 - (0,0)\}$.*

It is straightforward to show that the sharing-is-good axiom conditions are exactly identical to the nonincreasing formulae conditions. When adding a local member to a node already on the distribution tree, we must have:

$F_l(n_l + 1, n_r) \leq F_l(n_l, n_r) \qquad \forall\ (n_l, n_r) \in Z_{++} \times Z_+$

$F_r(n_l + 1, n_r) \leq F_r(n_l, n_r) \qquad \forall\ (n_l, n_r) \in Z_+ \times Z_{++}$

When adding a member to a node that was not on the distribution tree, at the nearest node on the tree we must have:

$F_l(n_l, n_r + 1) \leq F_l(n_l, n_r) \qquad \forall\ (n_l, n_r) \in Z_{++} \times Z_+$

$F_r(n_l, n_r + 1) \leq F_r(n_l, n_r) \qquad \forall\ (n_l, n_r) \in Z_+ \times Z_{++}$

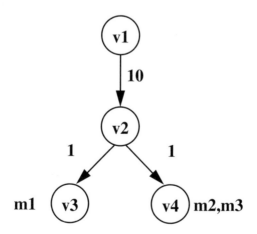

Figure 6
No-Free-Rider Axiom in Model 1

When we combine these equations with the second condition in the definition of $\mathfrak{I}$ we get the nonincreasing condition on all of $\{Z_+^2 - (0,0)\}$. QED

Theorem 13: *There is no Model 1 cost allocation formula that satisfies the reduced basic axioms and the no-free-rider axiom.*

Assume there is a Model 1 cost allocation formula that satisfies the reduced basic axioms and the no-free-rider axiom. In Theorem 11 we have shown that all Model 1 cost allocation formulae obeying the reduced basic axioms can be expressed in the one-pass canonical form. Consider the tree detailed in Figure 6: with no members in v_2, $F_r(0, 2) = 1/2$ for all formulae, resulting in in$(v_4) = 6$. With no next-hops downstream of v_4, $F_l(2, 0) = 1/2$ for all formulae, making the allocation to each member on v_4 exactly 3, which is less than $11/3$ (unicast cost/$|M|$). QED

Usage Sensitive Pricing

Internet Cost Allocation and Pricing

David D. Clark

Introduction

As the Internet makes its transition from a partially subsidized service to a commercial service with all costs recovered by direct charging, there is a pressing need for a model of how pricing and cost recovery should be structured. This model would provide a framework for differentiating among users with different requirements for service, and for rationalization of payments between the different service providers that make up the Internet.

As every economist understands, pricing can be an effective means not only to recover costs, but to allow the user to select among different options for service in a controlled manner. For example, users might like the option of purchasing either more or less capacity on the network during periods of congestion. However, historically the Internet has not relied on pricing to allow the user to select one or another service. Instead, the Internet has implemented one service class, and has used a technical means rather than a pricing means to allocate resources when the network is fully loaded and congestion occurs.

There is debate within the community as to how in the future Internet service should be allocated. One opinion is that we have survived so far. There is rather substantial experience with the current model, and it seems to meet the needs of many users. However, others believe that once commercial Internet service becomes mature, customers will start to have more sophisticated expectations, and will be willing (and will demand) to be able to pay differential rates for different services. Indeed, there is already evidence in the marketplace that there is a real need for service discrimination. The most significant complaint of real users today is that large data transfers take too long, and that there is no way to adjust or correct for this situation. People who would pay more for a better service cannot do so, because the Internet contains no mechanism to enhance their service.

This chapter assumes that there will be a range of services available, and that the user will be able to select among these classes, with pricing set accordingly. Thus, the discussion of pricing is placed in the context of what the offered service actually is. This point may seem obvious, but in fact the service provided by the Internet is rather complex. This chapter will offer some speculation on how service discrimination should be implemented, but there is yet no agreement as to which aspects of the service are seen as valuable to the user. Failure to understand which service features are valued by the user can lead to the implementation of potentially complex control mechanisms that do not meet real user needs. This is a serious error, because while pricing can be changed quickly, the deployment of some mechanism inside the network (involving changes to the packet switches, or routers) can take years to accomplish.

Pricing also serves to recover costs, and this chapter looks at pricing structures that attempt to follow the intrinsic cost structures of the providers. In practice, pricing need not follow cost. However, it is reasonable to look at cost structure in a first attempt to understand pricing, even if providers then deviate from that basis for business and marketing reasons.

This chapter addresses the issue of pricing in a somewhat indirect way. First, it discusses the behavior of the Internet as seen by a user, and offers a hypothesis as to which aspects of the service the users of the Internet actually value. Second, in this context, it considers (and rejects) several possible resource allocation schemes (guaranteed minimum capacity, fair allocation, and priority scheduling), and several pricing schemes (access subscription and simple usage-sensitive), and proposes a new pricing and resource allocation scheme, expected capacity pricing. The effective capacity scheme is used to address both the issues of cost and price to the individual end-user, as well as interprovider connection, the pricing situation usually called settlement. A rational discussion of pricing must consider both perspectives for several reasons, including the central one that the Internet currently has no on-line way to distinguish the two sorts of attachments, which makes it difficult to bill them differently.

The Service of the Internet

The Internet today uses a service model called "best effort." In this service, the network allocates bandwidth among all the instantaneous users as best as it can, and attempts to serve all of them without making any explicit commitment as to rate or any other service quality. Indeed, some of the traffic may be discarded, although this is an undesirable consequence. When congestion occurs, the users are expected to detect this event and slow down, so that they achieve a collective sending rate equal to the capacity of the congested point.

In the current Internet, rate adjustment is implemented in the transport protocol, Transmission Control Protocol (TCP). The general approach is specified as follows. A congestion episode causes a queue of packets to build up. When the queue overflows and one or more packets are lost, this event is taken by the sending TCPs as an indication of congestion, and the senders slow down. Each TCP then gradually increases its sending rate until it again receives an indication of congestion. This cycle of increase and decrease, which discovers and utilizes whatever bandwidth is available, continues as long as there is data to send. TCP, as currently specified and implemented, uses a set of algorithms called "slow start" and "fast retransmit" (Jacobson 1988), which together realize the rate adaptation aspect of the Internet. These algorithms, which have been developed over the last several years, represent a rather sophisticated attempt to implement adaptive rate sources. They seem to work fairly well in practice.[1]

---

1. There has been considerable discussion as to whether it would be worth adding an explicit message to indicate to the source that congestion is occurring, rather than waiting for a packet loss. This point will be addressed briefly later.

It is sometimes assumed that the consequence of congestion is increased delays. People have modeled the marginal cost of sending packets into a congested Internet as the increased delays that those packets encounter. However, this perception is not precisely correct. Because of the rate adaptation, the queue length will increase momentarily, and then drop back as the sources reduce their rates. Thus the impact on the user of using a congested network is not constant increased delays to individual packets, but a reduction in throughput for data transfers. Moreover, observing the delays of individual packets does not give an indication of the throughput being achieved, because that depends not on individual packet delays, but on the current sending rate of the TCP in question.

Observation of real delays across the Internet suggests that wide variation in delay is not, in fact, observed. The minimum round-trip delay across the country, due to speed of light and other factors not related to load, is about .1 seconds. Isolated measurements of delay across the Internet usually yield values in this range, whether the measurements are taken in periods of presumed high or low load. MacKie-Mason and Varian (1993) have measured variation of delay on a number of Internet links, and have observed that in some cases maximum delay does indeed increase under periods of higher loads, but that the average does not usually deviate markedly in most cases.

Assessing the Impact of Congestion

If the delays of individual packets are not much increased by congestion, how then does a user perceive congestion and its impact on performance? For any application, there is a data element of some typical size that characterizes it. This element is sometimes called an Application Data Unit (ADU). For remote login, the element is the single character generated by each keystroke. For a Web browser, the element is a Web page, of perhaps 2 kilobytes average. And for a scientist with large data sets to transfer, the element may be many megabytes. The hypothesis of this chapter is that in each case, the criterion that the user has for evaluating network performance is the total elapsed time to transfer the typical data unit of the current application, rather than the delay for each packet.

For an application with a limited need for bandwidth and a small transfer element size, such as a remote login application, the impact of congestion is minimal. Isolated packets sent through the system will see an erratic increase in delay, but will otherwise not be harmed.[2] For a user moving a large data file, the rate adaptation translates into an overall delay for the transfer that is proportional to the size of the file and the degree of congestion.

There is another dimension to the service quality, beyond the desire for a particular target elapsed time for delivery, which is the degree to which the user is dissatisfied if the target delay is not met. For most services, as the delivery time increases, the user has some corresponding decrease in satisfaction. In some cases, however, the utility of late data drops sharply, so that it is essentially useless if the delivery target is missed. The most common case where this arises is in the delivery of audio and video data streams that are being played back to a person as they are received over the network. If elements of such a data stream do not arrive by the time they must be re-played, they cannot be utilized. Applications with this very sharp loss of utility with excess delay are usually called real-time applications, and the applications in which the user is more tolerant of late data are sometimes called elastic.

Some simple numerical examples will help to get a sense of the impact of congestion on users of the Internet today. Consider the case of a transcontinental 45 Mbps link, and a user trying to transfer an object of three possible sizes. The typical small data transfer across the Internet today, an electronic mail message or a World Wide Web page, is perhaps 2,000 bytes average. An image file will be much larger; 500 kilobytes is a reasonable estimate. And to represent users with very large datasets, presume a typical value of ten megabytes. Table 1 shows the required transfer time assuming two cases: first, that the user gets the entire capacity of the link, and second, that 100 users share the link. The time computed is the transfer time, looking only at the link rate and ignoring all other sources of delay.

2. This statement is not precisely true. For a specific reason having to do with the dynamic behavior of the rate adaptation and the tail-trop first in, first out queue discipline, isolated packets not a part of an ongoing sequence are slightly more likely to be discarded during congestion.

Table 1.
Transfer Times in Seconds for Files over a 45 Mbps Link

	Transfer Size		
Link Share	2KB	500KB	10MB
1	.00035	.088	1.8
.01	.035	8.8	180

Table 2.
Transfer Times Taking into Account .5 Seconds of Fixed Delay

	Transfer Size		
Link Share	2KB	500KB	10MB
1	.5	.59	2.3
.01	.53	9.3	180

The smaller numbers, of course, are not what would be seen in practice. There are a number of effects that impose a lower bound on any transfer. There are perhaps two round trips required to get the transfer started (more if the protocol is poorly designed), and one round trip for the transfer itself, which for a cross-country transfer with .1 second round-trip delay implies a lower bound of .3 seconds. Added to these delays are system software startup costs at each end. If we make the (somewhat conservative) estimate that all these delays impose an overall lower bound of .5 seconds for a transfer, then the corrected delays for a cross-country transfer are as shown in Table 2.

This table shows why users of the Internet today are tolerant of the existing approach to congestion. For small transfers—mail and text Web pages—congestion swings of 100 to 1 are totally hidden to the user by the round-trip delays and system startup latencies. For image transfers, transfer times of ten seconds are mildly bothersome but not intolerable.[3] Only for the case of large dataset transfers is the impact clear. Congestion during the transfer of a 10MB dataset

---

3. For a system with poor software, there may be several seconds of startup time, so that even for the case of image transfer, the impact of congestion may be hidden by fixed overheads. Additionally, most personal computers today will take several seconds to render a 500KB image, so the transfer time is masked by the rendering time.

stretches the overall time from a few seconds to three minutes, which essentially eliminates the interactive nature of the transfer. It is for this reason that parts of the scientific research community have been most vocal for more bandwidth.

One particular point in the above example deserves elaboration: why pick a sharing factor of 100 to represent the congested case? Why not 1,000, or a million? Again, actual numbers help. One can make a rough guess at the sharing factor necessary to yield an inexpensive cross-country service, and assert that we need not look at sharing factors higher than that. Let us make some simple assumptions about a user reading mail or browsing simple Web pages, and estimate that the average reading time is ten seconds. Some pages are discarded after a glance, and some deserve study, but ten seconds seems reasonable for an order of magnitude estimate. So each user goes through an alternating cycle of reading and fetching. If we assume that the bottleneck is the 45 Mbps link, and the user is willing to tolerate no more than the delay computed above (about .5 seconds) for the fetch time, how many total users is the link supporting? A rough answer is 28,000. If we further assume that during a busy period, 10% of the total subscribing users are active, then the user pool would be about 280,000 people. One can do a simple estimate of per-user cost for the Internet backbone shared at this level, and conclude that it is less than six dollars per year.[4] This is roughly consistent with other estimates of actual wide area costs for the existing Internet (MacKie-Mason 1993). It is plausible to claim that the costs associated with this level of sharing are sufficiently low that there is no reason to strive for a higher sharing level.

Enhancing the Internet Service

While the single level of best-effort service offered by the Internet today seems to meet the need of many users, there are real concerns being expressed today. One concern is the impact of mixing users attempting to transfer objects of very different size.

---

4. A very simple network, composed of a single 45 Mbps, 3,000-mile transcontinental link, would cost about $135,000 per month at the tariffed rate of $45 per mile. Dividing this cost by 280,000 users would yield a cost of $.48 per month, or $5.75 a year.

If, on a single network, we were to mix together without any controls 28,000 users browsing the Web (as in the example above) and 280 users (1%) transferring 10 megabyte files, it is not clear that any user would be happy. If the network "just happened" to give all 28,280 users equal shares of the network, the 1% moving bulk data would die of frustration. (In the unrealistic case of static allocation of the bandwidth equally among the pool of users, the 10 megabyte transfer would take about 14 hours.) If the 1% "just happened" to preempt all the bandwidth, the 28,000 Web browsers would be equally frustrated.

The other concern that seems of real significance to users is whether the service provided by the network is in fact stable and predictable. The whole point of the Internet's approach to traffic aggregation is to play the odds statistically, and both the providers and users have a good operational sense of what current performance is. However, if we build a network in which both the customer's expectations for service, and the provider's decisions about provisioning, are based not on explicit bounds on user behavior, but only on observed behavior, and the two are very different, we run the risk that some change in user behavior can change the loads on the network, and render it very quickly overloaded. There is a lot of fear about this, both inside and outside the Internet community.

Other network services such as the phone system base provisioning decisions on observed usage. The phone companies have good models of "intrinsic human phone behavior"; even when phone calls are fixed fee, people do not talk on the phone all day. This sort of observation allows telephone providers some confidence in provisioning based on observed behavior, and offering pricing structures that are not cost related. However, there is a fear that these sorts of assumptions about human behavior will not translate into the computer environment. A computer could easily be programmed to talk all day on the network. Indeed, a similar situation developed with the phone system when modems became popular. The phone system survived, and still offers fixed-price service options to its users, even though some people now make phone calls that last for days. But there is real concern that the Internet, which is subject to applications with much wider intrinsic variation in normal usage, will not remain stable in the future.

Internet Cost Allocation and Pricing

This chapter takes the position that while the Internet does work today, and satisfies most if not all of its customers, there is value in adding mechanism to provide more control over allocation of service to different users. The two most important features to add are a mechanism to control the worst-case user behavior, so that the resulting network service is more predictable, and a mechanism to permit controlled allocation of different sorts of service in times of congestion.[5]

The goal of this chapter is to propose some matching resource allocation and pricing scheme that will accomplish these objectives. A number of approaches have been proposed for control of usage and explicit allocation of resources among users in time of overload. As a starting point, it is useful to look at these, and see how well they meet the criterion for service variation proposed above.

Guaranteed Minimum Capacity Service

This service would provide an assured worst-case rate along any path from source to destination. For example, the Frame Relay service is defined in this way. The subscriber to a Frame Relay network must purchase a Permanent Virtual Circuit (PVC) between each source and destination for which a direct connection is desired. For each PVC, it is possible to specify a Committed Information Rate (CIR), which is the worst-case rate for that PVC. Presumably, the provider must provision the network so that there are sufficient resources to support all the CIRs of all the clients. But capacity not being used can be shifted at each instant to other users, so that the best-case peak rate can exceed the CIR. This makes the service more attractive.

This idea is appealing at first glance, but in fact is not very effective in practice. One issue, of course, is that the user must specify separately the desired CIR along each separate path to any potential recipient. Thus, this approach does not scale well to networks the size of the Internet. This problem might be mitigated by moving

---

5. Other feature enhancements such as security would also be valued. But this discussion focuses on enhancements that have an impact on bandwidth allocation and the quality of the packet delivery service.

from permanent virtual circuits to temporary, or switched, virtual circuits that are established as needed. However, a more basic problem with guaranteed minimum capacity is that it does not actually match the needs of the users based on the usage criterion of this chapter.

The issue is that a simple guaranteed minimum capacity presumes that the traffic offered by the user is a steady flow, while in practice the traffic is extremely variable or bursty. Each object transferred represents a separate short-term load on the network, which the user wants serviced as quickly as possible, not at a steady rate. To provide continuous capacity at the peak rate desired by the user is not feasible. Either the rate would be so low as to be irrelevant, or the necessary provisioning to provide a reasonable worst-case rate would result in a network with vastly increased capacity, and presumably cost.[6]

Consider again the example network consisting of a single 45 Mbps link and supporting 280,000 subscribers. If that network offered a guaranteed minimum capacity, the guarantee must represent the worst-case service, which implies dividing the 45 megabits per second among all the subscribers; this leads to a guaranteed capacity of 160 bits per second. The users of the hypothetical network, who are benefiting from the cost/benefit of the shared service, might not be much comforted by the guarantee of 160 bits per second. This corresponds to delivery of a 2 kilobyte file in 100 seconds, whereas in practice they can usually receive it essentially instantaneously. In fact, from a marketing perspective, they might well be less satisfied to know how much sharing the provider was exploiting.

Since Frame Relay is being widely sold in the market, we are getting real experience with customer reactions. Many customers, to the surprise of the providers, set the CIR to zero. Informal interviews with providers suggest that what customers use in judging the service is the actual performance achieved in practice, not the guaranteed minimum rate.

---

6. Frame Relay also permits bursts of traffic to be sent at rates above the CIR. However, as normally used, this feature is not intended to allow the user to send large application data units into the network at high speed, but to deal with much smaller bursts that arise from the inability to pace precisely the sending of packets.

Fair Allocation Service

Even if the user is willing to accept a service with no assured minimum rate, he may expect a fair allocation among users. If a provider is selling the same service to two users, and giving one a smaller share when they offer equal load, then that user presumably has a complaint. The point of a fair allocation service is to assure the various users that they are being treated in an equitable way relative to each other.

At first glance, it would seem that lacking a guarantee of minimum rate, an assurance of fair access to the capacity would be important in providing a viable commercial service. However, before adding a costly mechanism to the network to insure fairness, we should first consider whether fairness actually helps in meeting subscriber service requirements. In many cases, it does not.

As discussed above, what the user considers in evaluating the service being provided is the total elapsed time to complete the transfer of an object of some typical size, which may be very small or very large. In this context, what does fairness have to do with minimizing total elapsed transfer time? It is obvious that uncontrolled unfairness, in which one user might not get any access to the facility, is not acceptable. But what about "controlled" unfairness? Consider a number of users that happen to arrive at once with equal size objects to transfer, and two possible service techniques. In one, we send one packet of each user in turn; in the other we serve one user to completion, then the next, and so on until all the users are served. In each case, the same number of bytes are sent, so the last byte will be sent at the same instant in both schemes. But in the first case, no user is satisfied until the last round of packets are sent, while in the second case, all the users except the unlucky last one are completed much sooner.

The issue here is whether micro-fairness (at the packet level) leads to best service at the macro level (total elapsed data element transfer time). In the simple (and perhaps atypical) situation described above, total user satisfaction was enhanced by servicing the users to completion in random order, which is certainly not fair at the micro level. In practical situations, micro-fairness has not been shown to be useful in enhancing perceived user service times, and thus not proven an effective mechanism to add to the network.

A more fundamental question is whether fairness is actually the desired service. Consider two users, each transferring a file, with one file being ten times larger than the other. Is giving equal access to the bandwidth most fair? Shifting bandwidth to the user with the larger file may benefit him, but not cause a perceptual degradation to the small user. In this case, what is the proper allocation of resources, either in a theoretical or practical sense? In the practical case of the Internet, one of its features may well be that a user transferring a large file can obtain more than his "fair share" of bandwidth during this transfer. The fairness manifested by this system is not that each user is given an instantaneous equal share, but that each user is equally permitted to send a large file as needed. While this "fairness" may be subject to abuse, in the real world it meets the needs of the users.

A final and critical point about fairness is the question of how we should measure usage to apply a fairness criterion. Consider a specific flow of packets, a sequence of packets that represents one transfer from a source. Each flow, along its path in the network, may encounter congestion, which will trigger a rate adjustment at the source of a flow. In concrete terms, each TCP connection would thus represent a flow.

It would be possible to build a packet switch which assured that each flow passing through it received an equal share. Methods to implement this, such as Weighted Fair Queuing (Demers 1989; Clark 1992), are well known, and very valuable in solving a range of service problems. But this mechanism would only achieve local equality inside one switch. It would not by itself insure overall fairness, because it does not address how many flows each user has, and how they interact. What if one user has one flow, and another has ten? What if those ten flows follow an identical path through the Internet, or go to ten totally disjoint destinations? If they go to different destinations, what does congestion along one path have to do with congestion along another? If one path is uncongested, should a flow along that path penalize the user in sending along a congested flow? And finally, what about multicast flows that radiate out from a source to multiple destinations? Once questions such as these are posed, it becomes clear that until answers are offered, any simple imposition of fairness among competing flows at a single point of congestion has little to do with whether two users are actually receiving balanced service from the network. And, at present, there are not any accepted answers to these questions.

Priority Scheduling

A final scheme that has been proposed for allocation of bandwidth among users is to create service classes of different priorities to serve users with different needs. Such a scheme is proposed in Gupta (1997). The definition of priority is that if packets of different priority arrive at a switch at the same time, the higher-priority packets always depart first. This has the effect of shifting delay from the higher-priority packets to the lower-priority packets under congestion.[7] Slowing down an individual packet does not much change the observed behavior. But the effect of priority queuing is to build up a queue of lower-priority packets, which will cause packets in this class to be preferentially dropped due to queue overflow. While dropped packets will be retransmitted, the rate adaptation of TCP translates these losses into a reduction in sending rate for these flows of packets. Thus, depending on how queues are maintained, a priority scheme can translate into lower achieved throughput for lower-priority classes.

A priority scheme, when combined with a pricing scheme to limit its use, may be a useful building block for explicit service discrimination. The drawback to a priority scheme is that it does not allow a user to express a desire for a particular rate, or link share, or target delay. The higher-priority classes preempt all the available capacity and can drive all lower priorities to no usage. Most proposals suggest that the user will adjust the requested priority until the desired service is obtained. A user adjusting his priority to obtain a desired

7. If there is no congestion, then there is presumably no queue of packets, which means that there is not a set of packets of different priority in the queue to reorder. Thus priority scheduling, like most scheduling algorithms, normally has an effect only during congestion.

service can only adjust his absolute ranking in the service queue, moving ahead or behind other users. This is not a direct way to express a desired network behavior; there is no obvious way to relate a particular priority with a particular achieved service. Thus a priority scheme is a form of price bid, not a specification of service. This is a rather indirect way of obtaining a particular service; it is much more direct to let the user specify the service he desires, and let the network respond.

In fact, service starvation due to priority can easily happen in practice. A well-tuned TCP on a high-performance workstation today can send at a rate exceeding a 45 Mbps DS-3 link. Giving such a workstation access to a high-priority service class could consume the entire capacity of the current Internet backbone for the duration of its transfer. It is not likely that either the service provider or the user (if he is billed for this usage) desired this behavior. But with a priority scheme, there is no way to interact with another user except to be totally ahead of him, totally behind him, or at the same priority with no control over the resulting interaction.

An Alternative: Expected Capacity Allocation

What is needed is a mechanism that directly reflects the user's desire to specify total elapsed transfer time, and at the same time takes into account such issues as the vastly different transfer sizes of different applications, one byte or ten million bytes, and the different target transfer times, which may range from tenths of seconds to minutes or hours.

The Internet does not offer any guarantees of service, but its users do have expectations. Experience using the network provides a pragmatic sense of what the response will be to service requests of various sizes at various times of day. This idea of *expectation*, as opposed to *guarantee*, is an important distinction. One of the successes of the Internet is its ability to exploit the mixing of traffic from a large number of very bursty sources to make very efficient use of the long-distance trunks. To offer hard guarantees is inconsistent with the statistical nature of the arriving traffic, as the discussion of minimum guaranteed capacity illustrated. However, it is reasonable for the user of the network (and the provider as well) to have expectations as to the service that will obtain.

Thus the approach in this chapter is to develop an approach to allocating service among users that attempts to offer a range of expectations, not a range of guarantees. This approach builds on the observed success of the Internet, while extending it to distinguish among users with different needs. We will call such a scheme an expected capacity scheme.

Expected capacity should not be defined in a single rigid way, such as a minimum steady rate. In general, it can be defined in any way that the provider and consumer agree, but the model that will be used in this chapter, based on the discussion above, is to specify a maximum data object size that a user would like to transfer within some specified delay, together with an assumed duty cycle for these transfers. Thus, a useful expected capacity for a Web browser might be a 2KB object with minimal delay every ten seconds. For bulk data transfer, a possible profile would be a 1MB object at 1 megabits per second every five minutes.

Later in the chapter we describe a specific mechanism that can be used to implement expected capacity allocation. But first we relate this approach to allocation to the problem of pricing for services.

Pricing the Internet Service

Pricing serves several purposes. It should recover costs. It should be attractive to users. And, as observed above, it can serve to allow users to select among a choice of services, so that users who wish to use more resources can pay accordingly. This section of the chapter looks at common pricing schemes from these various perspectives in order to lay the groundwork for a new proposal.

To date, there have been two common ways to charge for Internet access. One is the flat fee or subscription. The other, which is not yet common but is being widely considered, is a per-packet or usage-sensitive fee.

As noted above, the most common mode of payment for Internet service today is a flat, or subscription, fee, usually based on the capacity of the access link. The point has been made a number of times (CSTB 1994; Srinagesh 1996; MacKie-Mason 1993) that most of the costs for network providers are sunk costs. Unless there is congestion, the marginal cost of forwarding a packet is essentially zero. So, in the absence of congestion, a fixed charging scheme may well match the intrinsic cost structure. In practice, there are a number of motivations for fixed pricing:

• Predictable fees reduce risk for users, and to some extent for providers as well. Both the provider and the subscriber have a known expectation for payments, which permits planning and budgeting. This makes the price structure more attractive to users.

• Flat fees encourage usage, which (if marginal costs are zero) increases customer satisfaction and does not hurt the provider.

• Flat fees avoid the (possibly considerable) administrative costs of tracking, allocating, and billing for usage.

However, there are problems with simple subscription pricing. First, as discussed above, there are times when the system will become congested, and the network will enter a region where the marginal cost of forwarding a packet is not zero, due to the impact of congestion on other users. So the provider needs some technical and/or pricing mechanism that encourages use when the net is not congested, and pushes back when it is. As discussed above, the TCP rate adjustment algorithms are exactly this sort of technical mechanism, but this chapter presumes that pricing should also play a role here.

Second, there are situations in which it is clear that an access subscription does not capture important aspects of the cost structure. One obvious example is the difference between a single user and a subsidiary provider that aggregates many users and feeds them into the provider in question. Both might ask for the same peak access capacity.[8] In this case, it seems that the source representing the aggregated traffic will present more of a load on the provider, and thus should be expected to pay more.

---

8. This is not an unrealistic assumption. A T1 access link at 1.5 megabits per second might be adequate for the aggregation of a number of small users, but could also be justified for one single user.

To deal with these issues, one proposal has been to regulate usage by the imposition of fees based on the amount of data actually sent. However, there are concerns with pricing sensitive to the total number of packets sent or received.

There is a large worry that pricing based on actual usage will lead to a collapse of the whole revenue model. Usage-sensitive pricing will tend to drive away the large users (who may, for example, build their own network out of fixed-price trunks), leaving only the smaller users, who will (in a usage-sensitive scheme) contribute only small fees. This will require the provider to raise his usage-sensitive fees in an attempt to recover his fixed costs, and this will start a downward spiral of fleeing users and rising prices.

There is now real evidence in the marketplace that some customers, given a choice of fixed or usage-sensitive pricing, will prefer the fixed-fee structure. Thus, whatever the providers may prefer to do, competition may force some forms of fixed-fee pricing in the marketplace.

The fundamental problem with simple usage fees is that they impose usage costs on the user regardless of whether the network is congested or not. When the network is not congested, and the marginal cost of sending is zero, this charging represents a substantial distortion of the situation.

The challenge for a pricing structure, then, is to avoid the problems of usage-sensitive fees, while addressing some of the concerns that are not captured in simple access-based flat fees.

Pricing Expected Capacity

To deal with the sort of issues raised above, another pricing model is needed which captures directly the issue that marginal costs are non-zero only during congestion. Tying pricing to the expected capacity of the user achieves this goal. Expected capacity allocation does not restrict the ability of the user to send when the network is underloaded. Expected capacity only characterizes the behavior that will result when the system is congested. So charging the user for expected capacity is exactly charging the user for the privilege of sending packets when the marginal cost of sending is non-zero.

Expected capacity has a direct relationship to the facility costs of the provider. The provider must provision to carry the expected capacity of his subscribers during normal busy periods, and thus his provisioning costs directly relate to the total of the expected capacity he has sold. Of course, the provider can set prices in any way that he sees fit, but the benefit of using expected capacity as a way of allocating prices is that it relates to actual costs.

Expected capacity is not a measure of actual use; rather it is the expectation that the user has of potential usage. This leads to very simple approaches to implementation since it is not necessary to account for packets and bill users based on the number of packets sent during congestion. Instead, the provider can just provision the network with enough capacity to meet the expectations for which the users have contracted. This has the practical advantage that one need not implement, at each potential point of congestion within the system, accounting tools to track actual usage by each source. Much simpler implementation schemes will suffice, as the example in the next section illustrates.

From the perspective of the user, the resulting price structure can also be very simple. While users with different capacity profiles will see different costs, the costs do not vary with actual usage, and thus meet the needs of many users for fixed or predictable costs. In essence, prices derived from expected capacity are like access subscription prices, except that they relate not to the peak capacity of the access link, but to a more complex expected usage profile for that link. Whatever sort of profile is agreeable to the user and provider can be used. The model here of sending objects of a certain size into the network with some duty cycle is only an example of an expected capacity profile.

A Specific Proposal for an Expected Capacity Service

How might we go about implementing an expected capacity scheme? As an example, here is a specific mechanism. In fact, the proposal in this section is overly simple, and does not address certain issues that will be discussed in later sections. But this discussion will provide a starting point, which will permit further discussion of the relationship between pricing and mechanism.

This mechanism has two parts, traffic flagging, which occurs in a traffic meter at access points where traffic enters the network, and congestion management, which occurs at switches and routers where packet queues may form due to congestion.

At the access point for the user, there will be some contract as to the expected capacity that will be provided. Based on this contract, the traffic meter examines the incoming stream of packets and tags each packet as being either inside (*in*) or outside (*out*) of the profile of the expected capacity. There is no traffic shaping—no queuing or dropping. The only effect is a tag in each packet. To implement a pure expected capacity scheme this tagging always occurs, regardless of whether there is congestion anywhere in the network.

At any point of congestion, the packets that are tagged as being *out* are selected to receive a congestion pushback notification. (In today's routers, this is accomplished by dropping the packet, but an explicit notification might be preferred, as discussed below.) If there is no congestion, of course, there is no discrimination between *in* and *out* packets; all are forwarded uniformly.

The router is not expected to take any other action to separate the *in* and *out* packets. In particular, there are no separate queues, or any packet reordering. *In* packets do not have a higher scheduling priority. Packets, both *in* and *out,* are forwarded with the same service (perhaps first in, first out) unless they are dropped due to congestion.

The consequence of this combination of actions is that a flow of packets that stays within its expected capacity is much less likely to receive a congestion indication than one that tries to go faster. However, Some flows may be going much faster than others under congestion, since they may have negotiated different expected capacities.

As discussed above, it is the nature of adaptive flow control algorithms such as TCP to send at an increasing rate until notified to slow down, and repeat this pattern as long as they have data to send. This is not an error or an unacceptable condition; it is normal. These rate increases discover and use new capacity that may have become available. Thus, the normal behavior for all users will be to exceed their expected capacity from time to time, unless they have so little data to send that they cannot do so. Therefore, under periods of congestion, all senders with significant quantities of data will execute a control algorithm such as the TCP slow start/fast recovery, which will cycle the sending rate. Each TCP will receive a congestion indication when it exceeds its expected capacity and starts to send packets that are flagged as *out*.

The specific expected capacity profile that has been proposed is the sending of an object of some size into the net at high speed at some minimum interval. This sort of profile can be implemented using a scheme called token bucket metering. Imagine that the traffic meter has a bucket of *in* tokens for each user. The tokens are created at a constant rate (the average sending rate of the user) and accumulated, if unused, up to the bucket size, beyond which they are discarded. As each packet arrives from the user, if there are enough tokens in the bucket for all the bytes in the packet, the packet is marked as *in,* and the tokens taken from the bucket. If there are insufficient tokens, the packet is marked as *out.*

Thus, the desired service for a Web browser could be translated into a token rate (a 2KB object every ten seconds is 1,600 bits per second), and a bucket size of 2KB that the user is permitted to inject at a high rate. (The user might like a burst size somewhat larger than his average object size—some small multiple of the 2KB average, but this is a detail ignored here.) If the user exhausts the bucket of tokens by sending an object of this size, the bucket will be replenished at the token rate, which will fill the bucket in ten seconds.

The idea of tagging packets as *in* or *out* is not a new one. For example, researchers at IBM (Bala 1990) proposed tagging as part of a flow control scheme. Frame Relay has the concept of *in/out* packets as does Asynchronous Transfer Mode (ATM) (the Cell Loss Preference, or CLP bit). However, those schemes were proposed in the context of a specific reserved flow or virtual circuit from a source to a destination.[9] In this scheme, there is no implication that the

9. The details of how ATM and Frame Relay work are rather complex. For ATM, there are a number of services defined. For the Available Bit Rate (ABR) service, in which the network gives indication of congestion and the source is expected to adjust, the CLP is not used to mark data cells. The switch is presumed to implement some form of implicit fairness among flows. In the Variable Bit Rate (VBR) service, two variants of the non-real-time subcase use the CLP to allow the user to flag data of lower value in case of congestion. But the VBR schemes do not include rate adjustment at the source; they are based on a

expected capacity for any user is reserved along a particular path. What is contemplated is a much looser coupling between expected capacity profiles and internal provisioning. The traffic meter applies the expected capacity profile to the total collection of packets from the user, independent of where in the network it is going. The resulting packets might then go along one path, might spread out along multiple flows, or might be multicast along a number of links at once. It might be the case that only a small part of the user's packets might be going along a congested path, but even so, if the user is in total exceeding his expected capacity, one of his packets, tagged as *out,* might trigger a congestion pushback signal. This looser definition has benefits to the user. For example, in Frame Relay, the sum of the reserved rates (the Committed Information Rate, or CIR) on all virtual circuits from a source cannot exceed the capacity of that source's access link. If the user has more than a few Frame Relay virtual circuits, this restriction limits the capacity of any one of them. In contrast, this proposal allows the reserved capacity to be used along any path at a given time.

Provisioning for Expected Capacity

For the provider, meeting the customer's expectation is a matter of provisioning. One goal of this scheme, which tags the packets from each user as to whether they are within the expected capacity, is to provide a very clear indication to the provider as to whether the net has sufficient overall capacity. If the provider notices that there are significant periods where a switch is so congested that it is necessary to push back flows that are not tagged as being *out,* then there is not

---

static traffic contract. See ATM Forum (1996) for more details on ATM traffic control; since the ATM standard is evolving, the specification document is the most reliable source of current information. For Frame Relay, the DE bit is used to flag traffic that is outside the service contract, just as in this scheme. However, it is not directly part of the rate adaptation mechanism. That is accomplished by the Forward/Backward Explicit Congestion Notification (FECN/BECN) flags, which are set at the point of congestion. The interaction between the DE flag and the BECN/FECN flags is not well specified. However, in Frame Relay, as in this scheme, a lost packet (controlled by the DE) can trigger a TCP rate adaptation. For an explanation of Frame Relay and its approach to traffic management, see Stallings (1992).

sufficient total capacity. In contrast, if the switch is congested, but some of the packets are flagged as *out*, then the situation is just that some users are exceeding their expected capacity (which is what TCP will always attempt to do), and so pushing back on those users is reasonable, and not an indication of insufficient capacity.

As access links get faster, it will be critical to distinguish between opportunistic utilization of capacity and real user demand. Today, many users attach to the Internet over relatively slow access links (e.g., a dial-up modem or a 128 Kbps Integrated Services Digital Network [ISDN] link); thus the maximum best-case rate from a user is rather insubstantial. But if that same user were attached to a campus net with high-speed internal links and a 45 Mbps access link, one user sending one flow could, if not slowed down, use the entire capacity of a 45 Mbps backbone link. Since that user might be satisfied with an actual transfer rate one or two orders of magnitude slower than that, it is critical that the provider not mistake this opportunistic transfer for an indication of insufficient link capacity.

Designing and Specifying Expected Capacity Profiles

What sorts of expected capacity policies could be implemented using this *in/out* scheme? In essence, the traffic meter can tag packets according to any sort of expected capacity profile at all, subject only to the requirement that there be a reasonable expectation of enough capacity inside the network to carry the resulting flow. For small users, the details of the profile probably do not matter much to the provider; what does matter is the overall capacity required to carry the aggregated traffic, which can be monitored in the aggregate. This leaves the provider great latitude to negotiate profiles (and charges) that meet the needs of the users. For example, a user who wants to send large files, but only very occasionally, could purchase a very small average rate, but a very large token bucket. Frank Kelly's chapter in this book presents an approach to estimating the capacity required to carry a flow with various sorts of burstiness that provides a method of pricing and provisioning for expected capacity profiles.

Internet Cost Allocation and Pricing

A feature of this scheme is that the details of the expected capacity profiles are not specified in some standards document, but can be engineered by the individual service providers in ways that they believe will differentiate their service and better attract customers. In architectures that standardize the form of the service contract, such as the Committed Information Rate of Frame Relay, no single service provider can change the nature of the contract even if that seems to better match its customer's needs. This scheme, by deliberately leaving the specification of the profile unstandardized, should permit greater experimentation in the marketplace to discover what service the users actually prefer.

Multi-provider Internets

The scheme described so far assumed that the source was connected to a homogeneous network: traffic was injected at the source, and the provider tracked the usage along all the links to insure that the network was properly provisioned. But this is too simple a picture. The Internet is composed of regions separately operated by different providers, with packets in general crossing several such regions on the way from source to destination. How does the expected capacity scheme work in this case?

In fact, it generalizes to cooperating groups of providers in a very straightforward way. Consider a link that connects two providers. Across that link in either direction is a flow of packets, some marked *in* and some marked *out*. Presumably the providers have made a contract to carry each other's traffic. The traffic that matters is the traffic marked *in*, since that traffic represents the traffic that each provider agreed to carry under conditions of congestion. So each provider, in determining what its commitment is in carrying the traffic of the other, needs to examine the *in* packets.

This relationship could be implemented in a number of ways. Consider packets flowing from one provider, A, to another provider, B. First, A could purchase from B a certain expected capacity. B would then install a traffic meter at the interface with A. If A offered too many packets marked *in*, B's traffic meter would mark some as *out*. If this happened often, A's customers would notice that even though they were sending within their expected capacity profile, they were receiving congestion notifications, and A should respond by purchasing more capacity from B. (A would not require complaints from its customers to detect that there was insufficient expected capacity on the link; the traffic meter at the boundary could report this directly, of course.) In this way, the commitment between A and B again resembles a provisioning decision.

Another business relationship would be for B to accept all of A's *in* packets, without using a meter to limit the rate, but to charge A according to some formula that relates the fee paid by A to the bandwidth consumption by *in* packets. As noted above, customers may wish to deal with congestion by paying either with delay or with money. This scheme permits both.

Expected capacity is thus proposed both as a means for a user to obtain a defined service from a network, and for two networks to attach to each other. That is, effective capacity can form a rational basis for establishing settlement payments. Each purchases expected capacity from the other; if there is balance, there is no fee, but if there is imbalance, one should pay the other accordingly.

Especially when a user sends packets that cross many provider networks, the question of how the providers are to compensate each other is greatly clarified by this concept. Instead of tracking actual usage of each flow, the providers just compensate each other based on expected capacity, and then carry the packets without usage accounting. There is no requirement to identify individual flows at the interprovider interface. The result is easy to implement, relates to real costs, and scales to cover the case of many interconnected providers.

The Heterogeneous Internet

Imagine that there is a packet path that crosses a number of providers from the source to the destination. In principle, each provider along the way will have purchased enough expected capacity from the next so that the packets flow unimpeded along the path. But what if this is not true? Perhaps the only path to that destination is through a provider network with insufficient expected capacity, and the sender receives congestion notification while sending within the contracted capacity.

Whose fault is this? Does the source have a legitimate complaint that he is not being given the service he paid for? How might this be addressed?

These issues cannot be resolved by demanding that each provider must purchase enough expected capacity from the others. Some providers may simply not have enough real capacity, and will thus represent a necessary point of congestion. And even if all the providers in a path have enough capacity to support the expectation of the sender, the receiver may have a final access link that represents a bottleneck. The users of the Internet must thus understand that even with the additional enhancement of expected capacity service, there is no guarantee that this rate can be achieved to any particular end point. Only if both end points are under the control of cooperating providers, and have sufficient access capacity into the network, can this assurance be expected.

This observation leads to a number of consequences. Most obviously, several providers may join together to insure that users attached to their combined facilities can count on receiving the contracted service. This service assurance will represent an important form of added value in the network, and will allow providers to differentiate themselves from each other. Second, the contract between user and provider about capacity expectation will have to be related in part to which regions of the network the traffic is going to. Certain parts of the network may not have enough physical capacity to offer any expected capacity service, and providers may choose to control the use of expected capacity by pricing expected capacity service based on the destination of the packet. These sorts of enhancements require only changes to the traffic meter at the source, and again give the provider more control over the quality and pricing of the service. The only constraint is the overall limit that along some paths the capacity may simply not be available.

Combining Sender and Receiver Payments

To this point, effective capacity has been described in terms of the sender of the data. The sender purchases capacity from his immediate provider, which purchases it in turn from the next attached providers, and so on all the way to the receiver. Via this arrangement, the sender is permitted to send packets marked as *in* to the receiver. Capacity purchased and used in this manner is called *sender* effective capacity.

In practice, we cannot expect all capacity to be purchased in this way. There are many circumstances in which the receiver of data, rather than the sender, will be the natural party to pay for service. In fact, for much of the current Internet, data is transferred because the receiver values it, and thus a "receiver pays" model might seem more suitable. This assumption may be less universal today; if the World Wide Web is increasingly used for commercial marketing, it may be that the sender of the information (the commercial Web server) is prepared to subsidize the transfer. But in other cases, in which information has been provided on the Internet free as a public service, it seems as if the natural pattern would be a "receiver pays" pattern. In general, both conditions will prevail at different times for the same subscriber.

How can this idea of "receiver pays" be expressed in terms of expected capacity? With *receiver* expected capacity, the receiver would contract with his provider for some capacity to deliver data to the receiver, and that provider would in turn contract with other providers, and so on.

This pair of patterns somewhat resembles the options in telephony, with normal billing to the caller, but collect and 800 billing to the recipient. But technically, the situation is very different. First, of course, the Internet has no concept of a call. Second, the data flows in each direction are conceptually distinct, and can receive different qualities of service. Third, which way the majority of the data flows has nothing to do with which end initiated the communication. In a typical Web interaction, the client site initiates the connection, and most of the data flows toward the client. When transferring mail, the sender of the mail initiates the connection. In a teleconference, whoever speaks originates data.

Abstractly, a mix of sender and receiver capacity makes good sense. The money flows from the sender and from the receiver in some proportion, and the various providers in the network are compensated with these payments for providing the necessary expected capacity. The money will naturally flow to the correct degree; if there is a provider in the middle of the network who is not receiving money, he will demand payment, from either the sender or the receiver, before allocating any expected capacity. And the resulting costs will be reflected back across the chain of payments to the subscribers on the edge of the Internet.

As a practical matter, payments on the Internet today resemble this pattern. Each subscriber pays for the part of the Internet that is "nearby." The payments flow from the "edges" into the "center," and it is normally at the wide area providers where the payments meet. That is, the wide area providers receive payments from each of the attached regional providers, and agree to send and receive packets without discrimination among any of the paying attached providers.

What is needed is a way to meld this simple payment pattern with the more sophisticated idea of expected capacity. And that brings us to a critical technical issue: it is much harder to implement receiver expected capacity than sender capacity because of the structure of the Internet.

Implementing Receiver Expected Capacity

The scheme described above for implementing expected capacity is based on the setting of a flag in each packet as it enters the network. This flag marks each packet as being *in* or *out,* depending on whether the packet is inside the contracted capacity profile. One could attempt to extend this scheme by having the sender meter the traffic relative to the receiver's profile as well, putting two flags in each packet, one reflecting the sender's capacity, and one the receiver's. But this approach has several problems.

The first problem is that the tagging is performed by the traffic meter at the sender's access point. That traffic meter can obviously know about the expected capacity of the nearby sender, but cannot reasonably know in advance which profile each of the many millions of possible receivers has purchased. So for the sender to set the receiver's expected capacity flag, it will be necessary to design some potentially complex protocol by which the receiver informs the sender of what its expected capacity is as the communication begins.

The second problem is that the detailed form of the expected capacity profile is not specified in a standard way. The goal of the scheme was to avoid standardizing the form of the profile, so that each Internet access provider could create profiles that meet the needs of its users. Profiles could take into account the time of day, the total usage over a billing period, the degree of burstiness over various time scales, and so on. How this scheme is implemented is a local matter for the access provider, which implies that there is no simple way for the receiver to express to the sender's traffic meter what the profile is. It might be necessary to send the actual profile as a piece of executable code, which is a very complex and undesirable approach.

The third problem with measuring the receiver expected capacity profile at the source is multicast, in which a single packet goes to many receivers, each of which may have purchased a different expected capacity profile. In fact, in Internet multicast, the sender need not necessarily know who all the receivers are. So even if we were willing to communicate the profile of the receiver to the sender, there would be no practical way to meter the traffic simultaneously against the capacity profile of each receiver.

These issues suggest that receiver expected capacity must be implemented in a way that does not depend on having the sender measure the conformance to the receiver's profile, and set a control flag in the packet accordingly. Instead, there is another approach, which could be viewed as the dual of the sender scheme. By comparison, in the sender scheme described above, the traffic is first flagged by the sender traffic meter to indicate whether it is *in* or *out* of profile, and then passes through potential points of congestion, where it is treated accordingly. In the dual scheme, suited to receiver profiles, the packet first passes through points of potential congestion, where it is flagged to indicate whether congestion actually exists. The traffic is then delivered to the receiver, first passing through the receiver traffic meter. This meter, which has been programmed to know the expected capacity of the receiver, looks at the flow of marked packets, the packets that actually encountered congestion, and determines whether the receiver has purchased enough capacity to receive these packets. If so, they are delivered to the receiver without further action. If not, the receiver is informed that the flow is exceeding its profile, and adjustment is needed. In the case of unicast, this action can be to slow the source, which would also occur if congestion had directly triggered a rate adjustment via the sender scheme. In the case of multicast, the receiver could be forced to remove itself from the multicast receiver group.

Other network specifications contain schemes that are superficially similar to this one. The Frame Relay specification contains the idea of Forward Explicit Congestion Notification (FECN), which informs the receiver that the packet has encountered congestion. However, that scheme has no concept of a capacity profile for the receiver. It is assumed that the congested switch controls the setting of the FECN bit, and if the FECN bit is set in a certain percentage of the packets, the receiver must slow down. This puts control of the allocation at the point of congestion rather than in the receiver. It is much more complex to build a scheme in which all points of congestion know about the usage expectation of all receivers, and the FECN scheme makes no attempt to provide explicit allocations to specific users. Instead, it presumes only some simple local fairness principle.

Combining Sender and Receiver Payment Schemes

Given that we have two forms of the expected capacity scheme, sender and receiver versions, the remaining problem is to determine, at each point of congestion in the network, which profile applies. For part of the network, the receiver paid, and thus the receiver profile should apply. For other parts of the net, the sender profile should apply. But which profile applies in each case? Since it is critical to support payment patterns in which both the sender and the receiver share payment, this limitation must be resolved to make this approach fully applicable.

In general, it is not reasonable to install long-term information in all the packet switches in the network that indicates the region over which each sender and receiver is willing to pay. Instead, it is preferable to allow the packets to carry the information about the region of willingness to pay. Again, the implementation approach cannot be symmetric for the sender and receiver because packets flow from the sender to the receiver. A packet can be marked at the sender to indicate the region over which the sender is willing to pay. But this provides no means to express the region over which the receivers will pay. The dual approach described above, however, can solve this problem.

Once a packet has left the region within which the sender is willing to pay, it proceeds on toward the receiver until it encounters its first point of actual congestion. At this point, a flag is set to indicate that congestion occurred (as discussed above), and the packet is modified to indicate the region in the network where this first congestion event took place. The receiver traffic meter can then take into account this information about the location of the congestion in order to determine whether the receiver is willing to pay for an expected capacity in that region.

A complete scheme, therefore, must combine a sender payment scheme to cover the region within which the sender has purchased an expected capacity, a receiver scheme to cover the expected capacity region of the receivers, and a scheme that allows the boundaries of these various regions to be expressed in an efficient way. See Clark (1996) for a more detailed discussion of how sender and receiver payment schemes can be combined.

Static vs. Dynamic Payment Schemes

The expected capacity scheme has been described to this point as a static payment scheme in which the user enters into a long-term contract for some expectation of usage in times of congestion. It might seem that the static version of the tagging scheme penalizes the user because the user must tag the traffic, and thus uses up potential capacity even if the network is uncongested. Under some circumstances, the user might prefer to hoard these tokens and use them only when they are needed. In terms of user preference, this choice probably depends on the time scale of the burstiness provided by the profile, or (using the token bucket meter as an example) the period over which the bucket is replenished. The examples of burstiness above related to the time scale of individual data unit transfers—seconds to small numbers of minutes. In this circumstance, the user might well be willing to use the tokens in the bucket to tag all his valuable traffic regardless of whether there is actual congestion. Any tokens so "wasted" would be replenished quickly.

However, users and providers might also be interested in usage profiles with longer time scales which could, for example, limit the total number of packets that can be sent per month into a congested network. Consider a user who anticipates a very small total usage per month. Independent of the short-term expected capacity needed by that user (e.g., Web browsing or bulk data transfer), such a user might desire a charging scheme that somehow reflected his very low long-term usage. One way to accomplish this would be for the traffic meter to impose two token buckets on the user at once. One is a short-term bucket expressing the duty cycle of the data transfer, and the other a long-term bucket reflecting the expected usage over some period like a month. In this situation, where the consequences of a "wasted" token might persist for a longer time, it would seem reasonable to assume that the user would prefer to use a token only when actually required.

The sender and receiver schemes, because they have a different structure for dealing with the directional nature of packet flow, support this sort of usage on demand in different ways. For the receiver scheme, this alternative is trivially implemented. By the time the packet reaches the receiver, it is tagged as to whether it actually encountered congestion. So the traffic meter, depending on how it has been configured, can subtract a token from one or another bucket based on the setting of this flag, and thus only consume the capacity of the profile if actual congestion exists.

The sender scheme lacks any automatic way to inform the sender if congestion currently exists down any particular path. To deal with this, two approaches are possible. One is a scheme in which the user is billed (or debited a token) only when the packet encounters congestion inside the network. The user expresses his willingness to pay using some field in the packet, as in the smart market proposal of Mackie-Mason and Varian (1993), and accounting is performed at points of congestion. This accounting is then communicated back to the user, but this information may not be meaningful to the user. The alternative is to inform the user if his stream of packets encounters congestion, and then allow him to tag the packets as he sees fit in that circumstance.

In fact, the sender scheme as described works almost exactly in this way. If a user sends packets marked *out* and they encounter congestion, the user receives either an implicit indication (a discarded packet), or explicit congestion notification. So a valid way to implement expected capacity would be to start a transfer using only *out* packets, and tag them as *in* only after congestion is detected. This might slow the overall transfer time by a few round trips, but would have no other consequence.

This example provides one reason why it would be useful for the traffic meter to be informed when the network is congested. Currently the indication of congestion is a discarded packet. The TCP protocol at the sender detects lost packets using timers to trigger the retransmission of packets and the adjustment of sending rates. This indication could also be used to start the tagging of packets as *in*. But the fact that a packet was discarded somewhere in the network is not visible to the traffic meter, so the traffic meter cannot directly implement schemes that debit or charge the user based on actual congestion. The user must implement part of the scheme by detecting congestion and tagging packets accordingly. If there was an explicit notification of congestion, such as the Internet Source Quench control message (a congestion notification message defined but not currently in use in the Internet), both the source and the traffic meter could observe this event.

The user can send low-priority traffic intermixed with normal-priority traffic by presetting the capacity flag to *out* for the former. The traffic meter should reset the flag from *in* to *out* for traffic that exceeds the profile, but should not promote traffic from *out* to *in*. The consequence of setting all the packets of a flow to *out* would be that, during congestion, the sending rate of that flow would essentially drop to zero, while other flows continued at the expected capacity. And a source, by presetting only some of the packets in a flow to *in*, could limit the busy period rate of that flow to some constrained value.

An alternative service and pricing scheme that could be implemented using the tagging mechanism is payment for actual use under congestion. It is a local matter between user and provider whether the payment model is a long-term fixed-rate contract for a particular expected capacity profile, or a payment by the user each time a tagged packet is sent. Especially if the user's software is sophisticated enough not to use tags unless they are needed, either scheme would seem to work, and thus providers could explore both to determine which better suited different classes of users. The provider would need to provision for this pattern of usage, and would thus need to reflect in the price to the user the burden of allowing usage on demand. But inside the network the operation is unchanged: with adequate provisioning, packets that have been accepted by the provider as *in* are forwarded without triggering congestion notifications.

Conclusions

The Internet provides a service that mixes a large number of instantaneous transfers of objects of highly variable size without any firm controls on the traffic demands each user may make, and with user satisfaction presumptively based on elapsed time for the object transfer. Although the mechanisms in the Internet seem to work today, the most significant service enhancement would be some means to distinguish and separately serve users with very different transfer objectives so that each could be better satisfied, and some means to limit the worst-case behavior of each user so that the resulting overall service was more stable.

There are two general ways to regulate usage of the network during congestion. One is to use technical mechanisms (such as the existing TCP congestion controls) to limit behavior. The other is to use pricing controls to charge the user for variation in behavior. This chapter concludes that in the future it will be desirable to provide additional explicit mechanisms to allow users to specify different service needs, with the presumption that they will be differentially priced. This chapter attempts to define a rational cost allocation and pricing model for the Internet by constructing it in the context of a careful assessment of what the actual service is that the Internet provides to its users.

Key to the success of the Internet is its high degree of traffic aggregation among a large number of users, each of whom has a very low duty cycle. Because of the very high degree of statistical sharing, the Internet makes no commitment about the capacity that any user will actually receive. It does not make separate capacity commitments to each separate user.

Based on this model of the underlying service, the chapter proposes a service enhancement called *expected capacity*, which allows a service provider to identify the amount of capacity that any particular subscriber is to receive under congested conditions. Effective capacity is not constrained to a single service model, such as a minimum fixed bandwidth, but can be any usage profile that the provider and subscriber agree on. The example in this chapter is a profile that lets the user send bursts of a given size, and otherwise limits the user to a lower continuous rate.

This scheme differs from the more common approaches to resource reservation in that it does not make any explicit reservations along a path, but instead takes the much simpler step of aggregating all the traffic that is within the expected capacity profile of all the users, and then views the successful transport of this aggregated traffic as a provisioning problem. This raises the risk that, on occasion, a user will not actually be able to receive exactly the expected capacity, but a failure of this sort, on a probabilistic basis, is the sort of service assurance that the Internet has always given, and that most users find tolerable.

Finally, this chapter claims that expected capacity, is a rational basis for cost allocation. Cost is allocated not on the basis of actual use, but on the basis of the expectation of use, which is much easier to administer, and again reflects the statistical nature of the sharing that the Internet already provides.

The chapter describes two concrete scheme for implementing effective capacity, a sender scheme based on a traffic meter at the source of the packets which flags packets as being *in* or *out,* and a receiver scheme based on tagging the packets to indicate whether they have encountered actual congestion, followed by an accounting at the traffic meter at the receiver. It also describes an approach to the problem of indicating within which region of the network each of the senders and receivers is willing to pay.

Protecting Users from Each Other

The other goal for enhancing current Internet service is to provide a better limit on the impact of worst-case user behavior, so that users are not disrupted by other users sending in an unexpected pattern. In the current Internet, the limit on any one user is the peak speed of the access link for that user. As noted above, the difference between the usage of a normal user and the load generated by a constant transmission at the peak rate of the access link may be very considerable. By contrast, with this expected capacity scheme, the "worst" behavior that a user can launch into the network is to utilize fully the expected capacity profile. Usage beyond that point will be tagged as *out.* It still may be the case that, for many users, their actual usage is less demanding than their profile, and since the providers may provision their networks based on observed loads of *in* packets, there could be excursions beyond average usage that exceed provisioning. But the range between average and worst case is much reduced by this scheme. As a practical matter, since the Internet seems to work fairly well at present without these additional assurances, there is some reason to believe that the expected capacity scheme, even though there is still an opportunity for statistical variation, will be sufficient for providers to make reasonable capacity plans. Note that if a user persists in underusing his profile, it is to his advantage to purchase a smaller profile since this would presumably reduce his fee. Thus there is a natural force that will tend to minimize the difference between normal and worst-case user behavior.

Generality

A principle widely understood and utilized in computer system design is that a given mechanism may be used at different times to implement a wide range of policies. Thus, to build a general system, one should separate mechanism from policy in the design, and avoid, to the extent possible, building knowledge of policy into the core of the system. In particular, a goal for any mechanism that is implemented inside the network is to be as general as possible, since it will take a substantial amount of time to get community consensus on the enhancement, as well as time to implement and deploy it.

The mechanism proposed here, which (in the case of the sender scheme) is the discrimination between packets marked *in* and *out* for congestion pushback at times of overload, has the virtue that it is simple to implement and capable of supporting a wide range of policies for allocation of capacity among users. It allows providers to design widely differing service models and pricing models without having to build these models into all the packet switches and routers of the network. Since experience suggests that we will see very creative pricing strategies to attract users in the future, limiting the knowledge of these to a single point, the traffic meter for the user, is key to allowing providers to differentiate their services with only local impact. What must be implemented globally, by common agreement, is the format of the *in/out* tag in packets, and the semantics that *out* packets receive congestion indications first. Providers use the level of *in* packets to assess their provisioning needs, and otherwise are not concerned with how the expected capacity profile is defined for any particular customer. This design thus pushes most of the complexity to the edge of the network, and builds a very simple control inside the switches.

In fact, this mechanism can implement a wider range of services than just the expected capacity scheme. It can be used to implement essentially any service to which the provider and the subscriber agree, subject to the assumption that the service is implemented by aggregating the traffic from all the users and treating the service assurance as a provisioning problem. Since the Internet works reasonably well today on this basis, an improvement that is based on the same general approach will be sufficient to meet the next generation of needs.

Acknowledgment

This chapter has benefited from criticism and comment from a number of people. A first version of the material was presented at the MIT Workshop on the Economics of the Internet March 9–10, 1995. Many of the participants there provided valuable feedback on the material. I would like to thank Scott Shenker for his comments on an earlier version of this chapter, and to offer special thanks to Marjory Blumenthal, who managed to read two earlier versions and teach me a considerable amount of remedial economics. This research was supported by the Advanced Research Projects Agency of the Department of Defense under contract DABT63–94-C-0072, administered by Ft. Huachuca. This material does not reflect the position or policy of the U.S. government, and no official endorsement should be inferred.

References

ATM Forum Technical Committee. 1996. *Traffic management specification 4.0.*

Bala, K., I. Cidon, and K. Schraby. 1990. Congestion control for high-speed packet switched networks. *Proceedings of Infocom '90.*

Clark, D. 1996. Combining sender and receiver payment schemes in the Internet. Paper presented at Telecommunications Policy Research Conference, Solomon, MD.

Clark, D., S. Shenker, and L. Zhang. 1992. Supporting real-time applications in an integrated services packet network: Architecture and mechanism. In *Proceedings of ACM SigComm '92.*

CSTB. 1994. *Realizing the future: The Internet and beyond.* Computer Science and Telecommunications Board, National Research Council, National Academy Press.

Demers, A., S. Keshav, and S. Shenker. 1989. Analysis and simulation of a fair queueing algorithm. *Journal of Internetworking: Research and Experience,* 1: 3–26; also in *Proceedings of ACM SicComm '89.*

Gupta, A., D. Stahl, and A. Whinston. 1996. Priority pricing of integrated services networks. In *Internet Economics,* ed. Lee McKnight and Joseph Bailey. Cambridge Mass.: MIT Press.

Jacobson, V. 1988. Congestion avoidance and control. *Proceedings of ACM Sigcomm '88.*

Kelly, F. 1996. Charging and accounting for bursty connections. In *Internet Economics,* ed. Lee McKnight and Joseph Bailey. Cambridge, Mass.: MIT Press.

MacKie-Mason, J. and H. Varian. 1993. Pricing the Internet. Paper presented at Public Access to the Internet, John F. Kennedy School of Government, Harvard University. Latest version available via ftp://ftp.econ.lsa.umich.edu/pub/Papers/ Pricing_the_Internet.ps.Z

Srinagesh, P. 1995. Internet cost structure and interconnection agreements. In *Toward a competitive telecommunication industry: Selected papers from the 1994 telecommunications policy research conference,* ed. Gerald Brock. Hillside, N.J.: Lawrence Eribaum.

Stallings, W. 1992. *ISDN and broadband ISDN with frame relay and ATM.* Englewood Cliffs, N.J.: Prentice Hall.

Charging and Accounting for Bursty Connections

Frank P. Kelly

Introduction

The definition of usage in a multi-service network is problematic since the usage of a network resource may not be well assessed by a simple count of the number of bits carried. For example, to provide an acceptable performance to bursty sources with tight delay and loss requirements it may be necessary to keep the average utilization of a link below 10%, while for constant rate sources or sources able to accommodate substantial delays it may be possible to push the average utilization well above 90%.

What is needed is a measure of resource usage which adequately represents the trade-off between sources of different types, taking proper account of their varying characteristics and requirements. In recent years, the notion of an effective bandwidth (Hui 1988; Gibbens and Hunt 1991; Guérin et al. 1991; Kelly 1991) has been developed to provide such a measure. But while it is relatively easy to define quality-of-service requirements, the effective bandwidth of a source also depends sensitively upon the statistical properties of the source, and thus the issue becomes how much of the effort of statistical characterization should fall upon the network and how much upon the user responsible for a source.

Within the telecommunications and computer industries it is possible to discern two extreme approaches to this issue. One approach insists that a user provide the network with a full statistical characterization of its traffic source, which is then policed by the network.

Another approach stresses the difficulty for a user of providing any information on traffic characteristics, and expects the network to cope nevertheless. These descriptions are, of course, caricatures. Note, though, that both approaches recognize the benefits of statistical sharing: they differ in how much characterization effort is required, and how this effort should be distributed over the combined system comprising users *and* network.

The correct balance will necessarily involve trade-offs between the user's uncertainty about traffic characteristics and the network's ability to statistically multiplex connections in an efficient manner. In this chapter we describe a charging mechanism that makes these trade-offs explicit, and show that it encourages the cooperative sharing of information and characterization effort between users and the network. An economist might describe the approach in terms of incentive-compatible tariffs in a stochastic environment. In circumstances where it may be inappropriate for the various charges to be converted into monetary units, the charges may instead be viewed as coordination signals that allow users to assess the impact of their actions on the network. Thus a control engineer might describe the approach in terms of the hierarchical control through Lagrange multipliers of the entire system comprising users and network.

The organization of the chapter is as follows. In the following section we review the concept of an effective bandwidth. In the third section we consider the case of delay-sensitive connections, where statistical sharing is important over short time scales, comparable to or less than round-trip delay times across the network. We assume that such sources are policed, for example by leaky bucket regulators of the sort used to define the peak or sustainable cell rate parameters of an Asynchronous Transfer Mode (ATM) traffic contract (ITU 1995). These policing parameters provide upper bounds on the behavior of sources, but may not characterize sources well: for example, sources may only occasionally need to burst at rates close to the bounds. If charges were based entirely on these bounds, then sources might as well fill the contract specification, and many of the benefits of statistical sharing over short time scales would be endangered. In the third and fourth sections we describe charging and connection acceptance mechanisms based on the traffic produced by a source, as well as any agreed policing parameters, a basis that can encourage statistical sharing. The advantages of statistical sharing are often lauded, but there is little recognition of just how effective it can be: it is quite possible to achieve high levels of statistical sharing *and* loss rates less than one in a billion, provided peak rates are policed and connection acceptance control makes use of both known peak rates and measured traffic volumes. Section five addresses incentive issues.

In the sixth section we consider delay-tolerant traffic. Statistical sharing is somewhat simpler for such traffic since flows may be coordinated over time periods longer than round-trip delay times across the network, and since delay itself is available to convey control information. However, the aims of pricing may be more complex, and may include providing feedback to users on network congestion and the revelation of user valuations (as discussed by MacKie-Mason et al. 1996). We describe a simple scheme based on measurements of time and volume that can again achieve most of what could be expected of any scheme.

In the seventh section we outline a unified pricing model suitable for a wide range of quality-of-service classes, described in terms of static parameters fixed for the duration of a connection and dynamic measurements of time and volume. This charging mechanism is currently undergoing trials as part of the CA\$hMAN project (Songhurst 1996a, 1996b).

Effective Bandwidths

In this section we review the concept of an effective bandwidth, beginning with a simple model of statistical sharing at a transmission, switching, or other scarce resource.

Suppose that J sources share a single resource of capacity C, and let A_j be the load produced by source j. Assume that $A_j, j = 1, 2, \ldots, J$, are independent random variables, with possibly different distributions. Can the resource cope with the superposition of the

J sources? More precisely, can we impose a condition on the distributions of $A_1, A_2, \ldots, A_J$ which ensures that

$$P\left\{\sum_{j=1}^{J} A_j > C\right\} \leq e^{-\gamma} \tag{1.1}$$

for a given value of γ? The answer to this question is, by now, fairly well understood. There are constants s, K (depending on γ and C) such that if

$$\sum_{j=1}^{J} B(A_j) \leq K, \tag{1.2}$$

where

$$B(A_j) = s^{-1} \log E \ e^{sA_j}, \tag{1.3}$$

then condition (1.1) is satisfied. The expression (1.3) is called the effective bandwidth of source j. This result, originally due to Hui (1988), was extended (Kelly 1991) to show that if the resource has a buffer, and if the load produced by source j in successive time periods is a sequence of independent bursts each distributed as Aj, then the probability that the delay at the resource exceeds b time periods will be held below $e^{-\gamma}$ provided inequality (1.2) is satisfied, with B again given by equation (1.3), where K = C and s = $\gamma/(bC)$. It is by now known that for quite general models of sources and resources it is possible to associate an effective bandwidth with each source such that, provided the sum of the effective bandwidths of the sources using a resource is less than a certain level, then the resource can deliver a performance guarantee (see de Veciana and Walrand 1995; Courcoubetis and Weber 1996; and Kelly 1996 for recent results and reviews). Often the relevant definition is of the form

$$B(A_j) = (st)^{-1} \log E \ [e^{sA_j[0,t]} rs] \tag{1.4}$$

for particular choices of s and t, where $A_j[t]$ is the arriving workload from source j over a random interval of length t. There may be several constraints of the form (1.2) corresponding to different physical or logical resources within a network.

For example, suppose a single resource gives strict priority to sources $j \in J_1$ which have a strict delay requirement, but also serves sources $j \in J_2$ which have a much less stringent delay requirement. Then two constraints of the form

$$\sum_{j \in J_1} B(A_j) \leq K_1 \qquad \sum_{j \in J \cap J_2} B(A_j) \leq K_2 \qquad (1.5)$$

will generally be needed to ensure that both sets of requirements are met, where B_1 and B_2 are calculated using different values of the space and time scales s and t appearing in expression (1.4) (Bean 1994; Elwalid and Mitra 1995; de Veciana and Walrand 1995; Kelly 1996). If the less stringent delay requirement becomes very weak, corresponding to a very large buffer and almost no sensitivity to delay, then $s \to 0$ in (1.3), and

$$B_2(A_j) \to E(A_j), \qquad (1.6)$$

the mean load produced by source j. The second constraint of (1.5) then becomes the simple constraint that the mean loads of all sources should not exceed the capacity of the resource, the minimal constraint necessary for the queue to be stable.

Under specific modeling assumptions on sources it is often possible to refine the constraints (1.2), (1.5) by numerical computations (Gibbens and Hunt 1991; Elwalid and Mitra 1995). The effective bandwidths defined by the more refined constraints may no longer have the simple analytical forms (1.3) and (1.4), but share a qualitatively similar dependence on the statistical properties and performance requirements of the sources.

To develop some understanding of this dependence, let us consider the very simple case of an on/off source of peak rate h and mean rate m, for which

$$P\{A = 0\} = 1 - \frac{M}{h}, \qquad P\{A = h\} = 1 - \frac{M}{h},$$

The effective bandwidth (1.3) of such a source is then

$$B(h, M) = \frac{1}{s} \log \left[1 + \frac{M}{h} (e^{sh} - 1) \right] \qquad (1.7)$$

and, with s replaced by st, this expression provides a bound on the effective bandwidth (1.4) of any source with peak rate h and mean rate m. For fixed h the function (1.7) is increasing and concave in m, while for fixed m it is increasing and convex in h. As s → 0 (corresponding to a very large capacity C in relation to the peak h), the effective bandwidth approaches m, the mean rate of the source. However as s increases (corresponding to a larger peak h in relation to the capacity C), the effective bandwidth increases to the peak rate h of the source.

Next we consider how an effective bandwidth might be used for charging and connection acceptance control. One possible charging mechanism might assess the effective bandwidth of a connection, using an empirical average to replace the expectation (1.4), and then charge according to the assessment. Apart from the difficulty of interpreting this tariff to users, there is a conceptual flaw, which can be illustrated as follows. Suppose a user requests a connection policed by a high peak rate, but then happens to transmit very little traffic over the connection. Then an *a posteriori* estimate of quantity (1.4) will be near zero, even though the *a priori* expectation may be much larger, as assessed by either the user or the network. Since tariffing and connection acceptance control are primarily concerned with expectations of *future* quality of service, the distinction matters.

An alternative charging mechanism might calculate the largest possible effective bandwidth subject to the agreed policing parameters, and charge accordingly. For example, the expression (1.7) might be evaluated with h and m set equal to a peak and sustainable cell rate respectively. This tariff is certainly easier to explain, but severely penalizes users whose mean traffic may be unpredictable and not easily characterized by policing parameters.

Instead our approach is to regard the effective bandwidth as a function of both static parameters (such as the parameters of leaky bucket regulators) and dynamic parameters (such as duration and volume); to police the static parameters and measure the dynamic parameters; to bound the effective bandwidth by a linear function of the measured parameters with coefficients that depend on the static parameters; and to use such linear functions as the basis for simple charging and connection acceptance mechanisms. In the next two sections we illustrate this approach.

Charging Mechanisms

In this section we consider the case of delay-sensitive connections, where statistical sharing is important over short time scales, comparable to or less than round-trip delay times across the network. Examples include the variable bit rate service class of ATM standards, and some of the proposals for real-time services over the Internet.

Known Peak Rate, Unknown Mean Rate

Consider first the case of an on/off source with a known (and perhaps policed) peak rate h, but with a mean rate that may not be known with certainty, even to the user responsible for the source. Assume, however, that the user has a prior distribution G for the mean rate M of the connection. The distribution G may represent very vague information, or might be constructed by recording past observed mean rates. Then the expected mean rate of the connection is

$$E_G M = \int_0^h x dG(x).$$

If the network knew the prior distribution G for the mean rate M, then the network would determine the effective bandwidth of the connection, from equations (1.3) and (1.7), as

$$\frac{1}{s} \log E \ e^{sA} = \frac{1}{s} \log E_G E(e^{sA} \mid M) = \frac{1}{s} \log E_G \left[1 + \frac{M}{h} (e^{sh} - 1) \right]$$

$$= \frac{1}{s} \log \left[1 + \frac{E_G M}{h (e^{sh} - 1)} \right]. \tag{2.1}$$

But expression (2.1) is just the effective bandwidth if M is not random, but identical to its mean value under G. We see that since the source is on/off with known peak rate, the network need only know $E_G M$, the user's expected mean rate; further detail about the distribution G does not influence the effective bandwidth, and would be superfluous for the network to even request.

How, then, should the network encourage the user to assess and to declare the user's expected mean rate? We next investigate whether the charging mechanism might be used to provide the appropriate amount of encouragement.

Suppose that, before a connection's admission, the network requires the user to announce a value m, and then charges for the connection an amount f (m; M) per unit time, where M is the measured mean rate for the connection. We suppose that the user is risk-neutral and attempts to select m so as to minimize $E_G f$ (m; M), the expected cost per unit time: call a minimizing choice of m, say, the best declaration for the user. What properties would the network like the best declaration to have? First of all, the network would like to be able to deduce from the user's expected mean rate $E_G M$. A second desirable property would be that the expected cost per unit time under the best declaration be proportional to the effective bandwidth of the connection (or, equivalently, equal to the effective bandwidth under a choice of units). In Kelly (1994a) it is shown that these two requirements essentially characterize the tariff f (m; M) as

$$f(m; M) = a(m) + b(m)M, \qquad (2.2)$$

defined as the tangent to the curve B(h, M) at the point M = m (see Figure 1). By a simple differentiation of the function (1.7), the coefficients in expression (2.2) are given by

$$b(h, m) = \frac{e^{sh} - 1}{s[h + M(e^{sh} - 1)]}, \qquad a(h, m) = B(h, m) - mb(h, m) \qquad (2.3)$$

where we now make explicit the dependence of the coefficients on the peak rate h.

Observe that the choice of m simply labels the choice of a linear function (2.2), and that the presentation of tariff choices for a given peak rate h may be entirely couched in terms of pairs (a(h, m), b(h, m)), giving a charge per unit time and a charge per unit volume respectively, with no mention of the word "mean." It is not essential to provide the user with a continuum of tariff choices: the relevant functions may be well approximated by a small number of tangents, especially if the capacity C is large in relation to the peak rate h. Later, in the following section, we shall see that connection acceptance control is also primarily concerned with tangents rather than their points of contact with effective bandwidth functions, and that any inaccuracies in the choice of tangent by a user cause the connection acceptance control to accept less, just as they cause the user to be charged more.

In Figure 1, the effective bandwidth is shown as a function of the mean rate M for a given peak rate h. The user is free to choose a

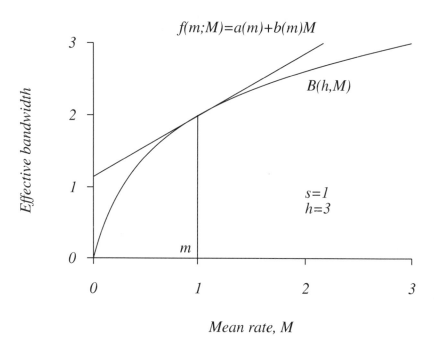

Figure 1
Implicit Pricing of an Effective Bandwidth.

tangent to this curve, and is then charged an amount a(m) per unit time, and an amount b(m) per unit volume.

Under the tariff f, the user has no incentive to "cheat" by choosing a tangent other than the tangent that corresponds to the user's expected mean rate. The property that the expected cost per unit time under the best declaration is equal to the effective bandwidth has several further incentive compatible properties: the benefit to a user in reduced charges of either shaping traffic to have a different peak or mean or of better characterizing traffic through improved prediction of statistical properties is exactly the expected reduction in the effective bandwidth required from the network. Thus users are not encouraged to do more work determining the statistical characteristics of their connections than is justified by the benefit to the network of better characterization.

If we do not insist on these further incentive compatible properties, but require only that the best declaration for the user be the user's expected mean rate, then many tariff structures are possible: it would be sufficient for the family (2.2), as m varies, to form the envelope of a strictly concave function of M. We shall see later, in the next two sections, that while connection acceptance control places a special emphasis on the particular concave function B(h, M), further incentive issues may justify the simultaneous use of a modified function for tariffing.

A Numerical Example

We now illustrate the formulae (2.3) with a numerical example. Suppose that the predominant traffic offered to a link with a capacity of 100 megabits per second falls into three categories, with peak and mean rates as described in Table 1. Then the choice $s = 0.333$ in expression (1.3) is reasonable (Kelly 1994b). Note that almost all of the charge for these three service types arises from the variable charge b(h, m).

While the predominant traffic may be of types 1, 2 and 3, connections are not constrained to just these types. For example, a connection with a known peak rate of 2 megabits per second could select any pair (a(2, m), b(2, m)) from Figure 2, or a connection with a

263

Charging and Accounting for Bursty Connections

Table 1.
Typical Charges for Traffic with Low Mean Rates

Service type	Rate (Mbps)		Charge	
	Peak	Mean	fixed (s)	variable (Mbit)
1	0.1	0.04	2.7×10^{-4}	1.0
2	2.0	0.02	1.3×10^{-4}	1.4
3	10.0	0.01	1.1×10^{-3}	7.9
	h	m	a(h, m)	b(h, m)

known peak rate of 10 megabits per second could select any pair
(a(10, m), b(10, m)) from Figure 3. As Figure 2 illustrates, the user
can choose a lower charge per megabit, with a higher charge per
second. As Figure 3 highlights, the charge per second is typically
higher with a peak rate of 10 megabits per second than with a peak
rate of 2 megabits per second; this is because statistical sharing of
the resource is harder.

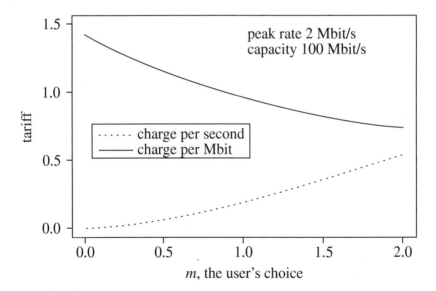

Figure 2.
Tariff Choices, for a Peak Rate of 2 Mbps

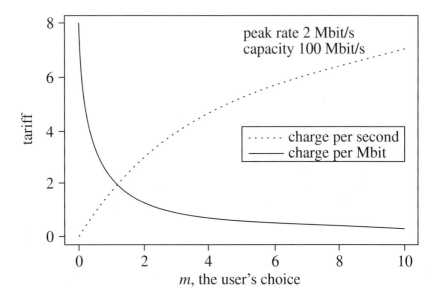

Figure 3.
Tariff Choices, for a Peak Rate of 10 Megabits per Second

Tariffs may be calculated for sources with other peak rates. For a peak rate of 0.1 megabits per second, the bandwidth B(h, M) is almost linear in M, producing a variable charge b(h, m) per unit of traffic that is almost constant in m. Since statistical multiplexing is efficient for sources with such low peak rates, very little incentive need be given to determine mean rates accurately. Peak rates above 2 megabits per second produce more concave effective bandwidths and hence more incentive to accurately estimate the mean. The various charges shown in Table 1 above and Table 2 below are expressed in the same units (of resource usage per second or per megabit) and are directly comparable with each other.

Observe that the total charge for service type 1 is higher than that for service type 2: for these service types at this resource statistical sharing is relatively easy, and the advantage of a lower mean rate outweighs the disadvantage of a higher peak rate. The total charge for service type 3 is, however, more than twice as high as for service

Table 2.
Charges for Traffic with Higher Mean Rates

Service type	Rate (Mbps)		Charge	
	Peak	Mean	fixed (s)	variable (Mbit)
4	2.0	1.0	0.2	1.0
5	10.0	1.0	1.7	2.2
6	10.0	2.0	3.0	1.3
	h	m	a(h, m)	b(h, m)

types 1 and 2: statistical sharing becomes more difficult with a peak rate as high as 10% of the capacity of the resource. Observe that for the three service types shown in Table 1 almost all of the total cost to the user arises from the variable charge. For the service types shown in Table 2 much more of the total cost arises from the fixed charge, more than half in the case of service type 6.

The above charges can be compared with those that might be appropriate if the link were entirely loaded by delay-tolerant traffic (that is, traffic whose effective bandwidth approaches its mean rate, (1.6), and for which the average utilization could reasonably exceed 90%). A variable charge of about 0.5 per megabit would recover from such traffic about the same total revenue as could be recovered from a link loaded with high-priority traffic from the categories shown in Table 1. Note that delay-tolerant traffic does not directly substitute for high-priority traffic until its volume exceeds a certain level, about 50 megabits per second for the numerical example of this subsection. There are two distinct constraints in (1.5): when the first constraint is tight and the second is not, then the link is unable to accept any more high-priority traffic and yet is capable of accepting more delay-tolerant traffic.

Unknown Peak and Mean Rate

Next consider the case of an on/off source where the peak rate as well as the mean rate may not be known with certainty. Let G be the joint prior distribution for the peak rate H and the mean rate M. If the network knew the prior distribution, then it would determine the effective bandwidth of the call, from equations (1.3) and (1.7), as

$$\frac{1}{s}\log E_G\, e^{sA} = \frac{1}{s}\, E_G E(e^{sA}\mid H, M) = \frac{1}{s}\log E_G\left[1 + \frac{M}{H}(e^{sH} - 1)\right].$$

The network thus needs to know just the quantity $E_G Z$ where

$$Z = 1 + \frac{M}{H}(e^{sH} - 1). \tag{2.4}$$

Suppose the network charges an amount $f(z; M, H)$ per unit time, where z is chosen by the user, and M and H are subsequent measurements of the mean and peak rates respectively. In Kelly (1994a) it is shown that the optimal choice for the user is $z = E_G Z$, and with this choice the expected cost per unit time is equal to the effective bandwidth of the call, if and only if

$$f(z; M, H) = \hat{a}_z + \hat{b}_z Z \tag{2.5}$$

where the right side of equation (2.5) is the tangent to the curve $B(Z) = s^{-1}\log Z$ at the point $Z = z$.

We may rewrite the form (2.5), using the definition (2.4), as

$$f(z; M, H) = a_z + M b_z(H) \tag{2.6}$$

where

$$a_z = s^{-1}(\log z - z^{-1}) \qquad b_z(H) = \frac{e^{sH} - 1}{szH} \tag{2.7}$$

The form (2.6) is linear in the measured mean M, with a peak dependent charge of $b_z(H)$ per unit of carried traffic. The function $b_z(\cdot)$ is increasing and convex: hence a connection that is more uncertain about its peak rate will prefer to choose a higher value z, thus incurring a higher charge per unit time and a lower charge per unit of carried traffic.

The tariff structure (2.6)-(2.7) subsumes the simpler structure (2.2)-(2.3): if a user knows its peak rate H, but not the mean M, then its optimal choice of z under the structure (2.6)-(2.7) incurs charges identical to those incurred with an optimal choice of m under the structure (2.2)-(2.3). Note that although the function (2.5) is linear in Z, the function (2.6) is nonlinear in H and M. Difficulties with the structure (2.6)-(2.7) become apparent for networks comprising multiple heterogeneous resources, where a distinct choice of z may be required for each resource: for the simpler structure (2.2)-(2.3) a single choice of m suffices.

Connection Acceptance Control

In this section we outline how the framework of the second and third sections allows the development of connection acceptance control mechanisms sympathetic to statistical sharing. Again, our emphasis will be on the case where statistical sharing is important over short time scales, comparable or less than round-trip delay times across the network.

Suppose that a resource has accepted connections $1, 2, \ldots, J$, and write (a_j, b_j) for the coefficients $(a(h, m), b(h, m))$ describing the choice of a tangent (2.2), (2.3) to the effective bandwidth function of connection j (see Figure 1). Suppose that the resource measures the arriving workload $A_j[t]$ from connection j over a period of length t (the same length t as appears in the definition (1.4)), and let $M_j = A_j[t]/t$. Define the *effective load* on the resource to be

$$(a_j + b_j M_j). \tag{3.1}$$

Then a connection acceptance control may be defined as follows. A new request for a connection should be accepted or rejected accordingly as the most recently calculated effective load lies below or above a threshold value, with the proviso that, if a request is rejected, then later requests are also rejected until either a short interval has elapsed or an existing connection has terminated.

If admitted calls have high peak-to-mean ratios, as for the service types in Table 1, then the above control may amount to comparison of $\Sigma_j b_j M_j$ with a threshold, where b_j is the variable charge for call j. It may seem that such a call admission control is naively straightforward: after all, the measurements M_j will be highly variable, according to whether the source is on, off, or somewhere in between. In Gibbens et al. (1995) it is shown that such a simple call admission control can be both robust and efficient: an example is analyzed where a 1 in 10^9 condition on loss rates is combined with a utilization at least 97% of that achievable when mean rates are known.

Both the charging mechanisms of the second section and the connection acceptance control described above use bounding tangents to the effective bandwidth function. If the same tangents are used for both purposes, then the effective load has a natural interpretation as an aggregate charge at the resource over a recent short period. But there is no necessity for identical tangents to be used for charging and for connection acceptance. Thus users choosing a small peak rate might be offered no further choice of tariff, so that for charging purposes the effective bandwidth function is bounded by a single tangent. In contrast, the resource might choose its tangent to the effective bandwidth function at the point where the mean rate is the long-term observed average for traffic with that peak rate. Or, if distinct effective bandwidth functions are used for charging and connection acceptance control, then the resource might still choose its tangent according to the user's declaration of expected mean rate.

Distinct effective bandwidth functions might be appropriate for charging and connection acceptance control since the two areas have quite different time scales and requirements for precision. Connection acceptance control must use accurately calculated effective bandwidths based on the buffer sizes, port speeds and other features of current hardware to make decisions on connections as they request connection, otherwise quality-of-service guarantees on loss rates may be compromised. While charges need to be precisely defined, they influence users' behavior and software application design over much longer time scales where features of hardware may evolve. Thus tariff design might include consideration of the possible effective bandwidth functions appropriate to future hardware and network scale.

A fuller discussion of connection acceptance control would consider multiple constraints of the form (1.5), network routing, and the shadow prices associated with different physical and logical resources (cf. Kelly 1988). The analysis and implementation of dynamic routing schemes often use Lagrange multipliers or shadow prices for each of the internal resources of the network, but only certain aggregates of this network detail might usefully influence charges to users. For example, competition between network providers might appear to users as a choice between routes, and averaged congestion measures might motivate a predictable time-of-day element to charges for delay-sensitive connections. We shall see in the sixth section that there are other ways of providing dynamic feedback on congestion for users able to respond to such feedback.

Incentive Issues

Adaptation

Until now we have supposed that the choice of tariff is made once, at the start of a connection. Might it be worthwhile for a connection to vary this choice over its duration? Changes in the tariff regime might be made over time intervals longer than round-trip delay times but shorter than a connection. Such changes would incur additional control and complexity overhead, but might allow more efficient statistical sharing through a more precise indication of short-term statistical characteristics. Where statistical sharing is easy we might expect there to be little benefit, but there may be circumstances in which a connection can make good short-term predictions that might be helpful to the network.

It is relatively easy to describe a mechanism that allows these various trade-offs to be assessed. Suppose that a connection may change its choice of tariff regime at any time, but must pay a fixed charge c every time this choice is exercised. Equivalently, we allow a connection to become a sequence of shorter-duration connections, but charge c for the setup costs incurred by the network for each connection. Then a user is able to make its own evaluation of the benefit of changing the choice of tariff, and to assess whether the benefits of short-term prediction of its load outweigh the setup charge c.

Incentives to Split Traffic

The independence of loads produced by different sources is an essential feature of the analysis leading to the constraints (1.2), (1.5), and to the concept of an effective bandwidth. But might a user split a connection with a high effective bandwidth into multiple connections, such that the sum of the effective bandwidths is smaller, in order to pay less? This is an important issue: users should *not* be encouraged to produce correlated sources. Fortunately there seem to be several mitigating factors.

To understand why an incentive to split traffic may exist, consider an effective bandwidth of the form (1.7) for a resource with a fixed capacity C. This expression is more than doubled if the peak h and mean m are both doubled, reflecting the fact that statistical sharing becomes harder as the peak-to-capacity ratio increases. Conversely, if capacity were to increase, while peak and mean remained constant, then effective bandwidth would decrease, illustrating the economies of scale of statistical sharing itself. Finally, if capacity C, peak h, and mean m were all to double, then the effective bandwidth would be exactly doubled (as is clear from scaling arguments for very many resource models; in expression (1.7) the space scale s would be halved).

For connection acceptance control it is important to use effective bandwidths calculated for current resources, where the effective bandwidth function increases faster than linearly with the peak for a given mean-to-peak ratio. But, as discussed in the previous section, prices influencing longer-term user behavior may need to consider the future network scale. In particular, larger users should not be deterred if their attraction to a network allows the capacity of the network to increase proportionately. Indeed, if the cost of capacity were to rise *less* than linearly with capacity, there would be a clear rationale for having the effective bandwidth function used for pricing increase *less* than linearly with the peak, for a given mean-to-peak ratio. A simple compromise might be constructed as follows: calculate time and volume charges for a typical peak-to-capacity ratio, and then scale these charges to be proportional to the peak for a given mean-to-peak ratio (so that $a(h, m) = ha(m/h)$, $b(h, m) = b(m)$). Such charges lessen the incentive to split traffic and simplify the presentation of tariffs while retaining a (weakened) incentive for a user to lower the peak rate of a connection.

As well as transmission and buffering resources, a connection also uses other resources of the network. We have already discussed setup costs incurred per connection. Additionally, in an ATM network, a connection holds a Virtual Circuit Indicator (VCI) for its duration. If a rent is charged for use of a VCI, then the charge per unit time of the connection is increased, and this further lessens the incentive to split traffic.

Finally, we note that there may be occasions when it is to the joint advantage of network and users for traffic to be split: for example, if the network is able to route correlated traffic streams over disjoint paths.

Discussion

We have discussed several incentive compatibility issues and seen that compromises may be necessary between the incentive given to users to lower peak rates and to split traffic, as well as between the effective bandwidth functions used for charging and connection acceptance control. Simplicity and predictability of tariffs are other important issues. For example, suppose that users choosing a small peak rate relative to capacity are offered no further choice of tariff, corresponding to the bounding of the effective bandwidth function by a single tangent. Then this tangent might be chosen with predictability in mind. Thus, the tangent to the effective bandwidth function at the point where the parameter M is equal to the peak rate, or a sustainable cell rate has the property that the charge to a user is bounded above in terms of the peak rate or the sustainable cell rate respectively. This will not overly penalize users whose mean traffic may be not easily characterized by policing parameters. Precisely where the various compromises should be drawn may not yet be clear, but the theory of the second and third sections does at least provide a framework for discussion of the several trade-offs involved.

Delay-tolerant Traffic

The third and fourth sections above have concerned delay-sensitive traffic, and we have seen that charging schemes based on measurements of time and volume can encourage the coordination of users and the network, and allow statistical sharing over short time scales. In this section we consider traffic less sensitive to delay, arising from applications that have been termed elastic (Shenker 1995). Statistical sharing is somewhat simpler for such traffic since flows may be coordinated over time periods longer than round-trip delay times across the network, and since delay itself is available to convey control information. On the other hand, the aims of pricing may be more complex, and may include providing feedback to users on network congestion and the revelation of user valuations. We shall describe a simple scheme based on measurements of time and volume that can again achieve almost all of what could be expected of any scheme.

We shall describe the scheme in terms of the Available Bit Rate (ABR) service class of ATM standards. This service class assumes that a connection responds to rate control messages from the network, but that a user may choose a Minimum Cell Rate (MCR) below which the connection will not be asked to fall. The essence of the scheme is that traffic up to the MCR is charged at one rate, while traffic above the MCR is charged at a lower rate. If a resource within the network has spare capacity beyond that required for high-priority and MCR traffic, then it may be shared among ABR connections, in proportion to their MCRs. Thus the choice of MCR by a user buys a share of spare capacity, as well as providing a Minimum Cell Rate.

More precisely, we suppose that there is a charge of a times the chosen MCR per unit time, and additionally a charge of b per unit volume, where b may be zero. Thus traffic above the chosen MCR is charged at a lower rate, possibly a substantially lower rate. To illustrate the properties of this scheme, consider a typical ABR application, such as a file transfer of a given size. By choice of MCR a user can obtain an upper bound on the time taken to transfer the file, although the user would expect a much faster transfer if the network were lightly loaded. Note the important feature that both the time taken to transfer the file *and* the total charge to transfer the file will be larger when the network is congested since the higher charge a applies to a larger volume of the transfer. Users may, of course, complain that they are charged more for a slower service, but this is the key characteristic of any incentive-compatible scheme designed to ease congestion. At times of congestion the user can speed up file transfers by increasing the chosen MCR for connections: each user is able to act according to its own trade-off between delay and cost.

Note that users and network can achieve a coordinated response to congestion without the need for the charges a and b to depend upon the level of congestion or even upon factors such as the time of day. The key point is that for traffic that is not highly delay sensitive, both price and delay are available as coordination signals (cf. Shenker et al. 1996). The scheme described here allows delay to carry feedback on network congestion to users; the charges a and b turn the delay signal into a price signal with many of the attractive properties of the "smart market" of MacKie-Mason and Varian (1995). In particular, the price signal encourages the revelation of user preferences.

There are several other ways to describe the above scheme, both practically and theoretically. The scheme closely resembles some of the existing tariffs for Frame Relay, where the committed information rate plays a similar role to the minimum cell rate. It can be described in terms of the effective bandwidths of the second section, where the charges a and b play the role of the respective shadow prices for the two constraints (1.7). It would be interesting to explore further relationships with the expected capacity service of Clark (1996), where packets tagged *out* might correspond naturally with traffic charged at the rate b = 0.

The approach of the previous sections could be readily integrated with the above scheme to price traffic below the MCR, and this may be worthwhile if the statistical properties of users' traffic are such that MCRs are frequently not filled. Similarly, the approach outlined in the fourth section will have relevance for the statistical multiplexing over short time scales of delay-tolerant traffic that is bursty within its rate control envelope. A fuller discussion of rate control for delay-tolerant traffic would depend upon implementation details, and particularly upon the allocation of buffering across the network, but it seems unlikely that this level of network detail could usefully influence the structure of tariffs.

A Unified Pricing Model

The essence of the pricing model developed in the third and sixth sections is as follows. The cost of a connection is given by the expression

$$a(x)\ T + b(x)\ V + c(x) \tag{4.1}$$

where T is the duration of the connection (measured in seconds, hours or months), V is the volume of the connection (measured in megabits or gigacells), and x describes tariff choices allowed to the user by the network at the time of connection acceptance. The tariff choice x includes the service class (for example, variable bit rate or available bit rate), the traffic contract parameters (such as the peak cell rate or minimum cell rate), and further choices which might allow a user to lower the "per unit time" rate $a(x)$ at the cost of raising the "per unit volume" rate $b(x)$, as described in the third section above. The charge per connection is $c(x)$.

The above scheme thus makes a distinction between static and dynamic parameters of a connection. The static parameters contained in x may be many and varied, but are fixed for the duration of the connection: the dynamic parameters T and V are measured in real time. The cost of a connection to the customer and the connection acceptance decisions of the network are based on both static and dynamic parameters, but in a very restricted manner: through linear functions of the dynamic parameters, with coefficients that depend on the static parameters.

For expositional convenience we have called a, b and c charges, and expression (4.1) the cost, but these are really measured in units of resource usage. The conversion of such units into monetary units and a final bill is likely to involve many other factors (e.g., customer discounts, marketing promotions, and subscription charges) whose discussion seems not so inextricably linked with statistical sharing.

We have suggested that for delay-sensitive traffic the conversion might depend upon the time of day, but that for delay-tolerant traffic statistical sharing is possible without a dependence upon the time of day, much less upon dynamic estimates of network load.

Currently the CA$hMAN project, a consortium of network operators, equipment manufacturers, and theoreticians, is examining the implementation of the above and other approaches to the pricing of ATM networks. Key issues explored in the early experiments include the following (Songhurst 1996a, 1996b). Is it feasible for the time T and volume V measurements to be made in hardware? Where should the cost be calculated, and how can it be transferred around the network, both for accounting purposes and to provide feedback to the user? What is the response of customers to the tariff structure, and can a user or application designer make good use of the feedback on resource usage provided by charges? Can the information on statistical characteristics conveyed through tariff choices be of assistance to the connection acceptance mechanisms of the network, and should the intelligence required to make tariff choices be provided by a user, an application, or a device elsewhere in the network that is knowledgeable about the traffic patterns usually generated?

Conclusion

Statistical sharing over several time-scales is a key feature of the Internet, and is likely to be an essential aspect of future ATM networks. In this chapter we describe how usage-sensitive pricing can encourage statistical sharing, and we provide a quantitative framework for the discussion of pricing issues in systems where statistical sharing is important.

In particular we describe a simple charging and accounting mechanism for real-time bursty connections, based on the concept of an effective bandwidth. The mechanism performs the dual role of conveying information to the network that allows more efficient statistical sharing, and information to the user about the resource implications of differently policed connection requests. The resulting tariff takes a strikingly simple form: a charge $a(x)$ per unit time, a charge $b(x)$ per unit volume of traffic carried, and a charge $c(x)$ per connection, where the triple $(a(x), b(x), c(x))$ are fixed at the time of connection acceptance as a function of the connection contract x. This form of tariff is also able to reveal user preferences concerning delay tolerant traffic, and thus promises to provide a unified charging mechanism over a wide range of quality of service classes.

The major issues for usage-sensitive pricing may be categorized under four headings.

Incentive compatibility. Users of a multiservice network will make quality-of-service choices, and the network will enforce priorities. Pricing is the major method of communication between users and network concerning the consequences of these actions. For example, prices will generally give some incentive to shape traffic: it is important that this incentive be compatible with the efficient operation of the *entire* system, comprising users and network.

Accounting and transaction costs. Such costs are a major deterrent to usage-sensitive pricing schemes. A less obvious, but ultimately more significant, cost may be that poorly designed tariffs impede innovation or network usage by making uneconomical potentially important classes of application. The Internet has allowed the organic development of applications in a highly distributed manner: well-designed charging schemes should encourage similarly decentralized decisions about resource allocation.

Commercial reality. Pricing schemes must be stable under competition, and under resale. The various economies of scale and scope present in communication networks make this a challenging issue, and more work is clearly needed in this area. The issue interacts with the major topic of this chapter since important economies of scale and scope are provided by statistical sharing.

Technical feasibility. Any usage-sensitive pricing scheme must be capable of implementation in hardware and systems: for example, the time scales imposed by speed-of-light constraints on round-trip delay times must be respected.

In this chapter we have described how usage-sensitive pricing can encourage the efficient statistical sharing of scarce network resources required by many users, and have outlined a time- and volume-based charging mechanism which is both incentive-compatible and simple enough to integrate with network control. The theoretical basis for the mechanism provides some prospect that the disparate issues outlined above may be treated in a coherent way.

Bibliography

Bean, N. 1994. Effective bandwidths with different quality of service requirements. In *IFIP transactions, integrated broadband communication networks and services*, ed. V.B. Iverson. Amsterdam: Elsevier. 241–252.

Clark, D.D. 1996. A model for cost allocation and pricing in the Internet. In *Internet economics*, ed. Lee McKnight and Joseph Bailey. Cambridge, Mass.: MIT Press.

Courcoubetis, C., and R. Weber. 1996. Buffer overflow asymptotics for a switch handling many traffic sources. *Journal of Applied Probability* 33.

De Veciana, G., and J. Walrand. 1995. Effective bandwidths: Call admission, traffic policing and filtering for ATM networks. *Queuing Systems* 20: 37–59.

Elwalid, A., and D. Mitra. 1995. Analysis, approximations and admission control of a multi-service multiplexing system with priorities. In *Proceedings of IEEE INFOCOM*: 463–472.

Gibbens, R.J., and P.J. Hunt. 1991. Effective bandwidths for the multi-type UAS channel. *Queuing Systems* 9: 17–28.

Gibbens, R.J., F.P. Kelly, and P.B. Key. 1995. A decision-theoretic approach to call admission control in ATM networks. *IEEE Journal of Selected Areas in Communication* 13: 1101–1114.

Guérin, R., H. Ahmadi, and M. Naghshineh. 1991. Equivalent capacity and its application to bandwidth allocation in high-speed networks. *IEEE Journal of Selected Areas in Communication* 9: 968–981.

Hui, J.Y. 1988. Resource allocation for broadband networks. *IEEE Journal of Selected Areas in Communication* 6: 1598–1608.

ITU Recommendation I371. 1995. Traffic control and congestion control in B-ISDN. Geneva, Switzerland.

Kelly, F.P. 1988. Routing in circuit-switched networks: Optimization, shadow prices and decentralization. *Advances in Applied Probability* 20: 112–144.

Kelly, F.P. 1991. Effective bandwidths at multi-class queues. *Queueing Systems* 9: 5–16.

Kelly, F.P. 1994a. On tariffs, policing and admission control for multiservice networks. *Operations Research Letters* 15: 1–9.

Kelly, F.P. 1994b. Tariffs and effective bandwidths in multiservice networks. In *The fundamental role of teletraffic in the evolution of telecommunication networks*, ed., J. Labetoulle and J.W. Roberts. (editors). Amsterdam: Elsevier. 401–410.

Kelly, F. P. 1996. Notes on effective bandwidths. In *Stochastic networks: Theory and applications*, ed. F.P. Kelly, S. Zachary and I. Ziedins. Oxford: Oxford University Press. 141–168.

MacKie-Mason, J.K., and H. Varian. 1995. Pricing the Internet. In *Public access to the internet*, ed., B. Kahin and J. Keller. Cambridge, Mass.: MIT Press. 269–314.

MacKie-Mason, J.K., L. Murphy, and J. Murphy. 1996. The role of responsive pricing in the Internet. In *Internet economics*, ed., Lee McKnight and Joseph Bailey. Cambridge, Mass.: MIT Press.

Shenker, S. 1995. Service models and pricing policies for an integrated services Internet. In *Public access to the internet*, ed., B. Kahin and J. Keller. Cambridge, Mass.: MIT Press. 315–337.

Shenker, S., D. Clark, D. Estrin, and S. Herzog. 1996. Pricing in computer networks: Reshaping the research agenda, *Telecommunications Policy*, 23, April, 183–201.

Songhurst, D. 1996a. Charging schemes for multiservice networks. In *Proceedings of the 13th UK Teletraffic Symposium* London: The Institution of Electrical Engineers.

Songhurst, D., ed. 1996b. Experiment design for round I. The CA$hMAN Consortium (http://www.isoft.intranet.gr/cashman/).

Acknowledgments

The support of the Commission of the European Communities ACTS project AC039, entitled Charging and Accounting Schemes in Multiservice ATM Networks (CA$hMAN), is acknowledged. This chapter has benefited from the questions and criticisms of participants at the Internet Economics Workshop, of members of the COST 242 project, and especially of colleagues in the CA$hMAN project, to all of whom I am grateful.

Responsive Pricing in the Internet

Jeffrey K. MacKie-Mason, Liam Murphy, and John Murphy

Introduction

The Internet continues to evolve as it reaches out to a wider user population. The recent introduction of user-friendly navigation and retrieval tools for the World Wide Web has triggered an unprecedented level of interest in the Internet among the media and the general public, as well as in the technical community. It seems inevitable that some changes or additions are needed in the control mechanisms used to allocate usage of Internet resources. In this chapter we argue that a feedback signal in the form of a variable price for network service is a workable tool to aid network operators in controlling Internet traffic. We suggest that these prices should vary dynamically based on the current utilization of network resources. We show how this responsive pricing puts control of network service back where it belongs: with the users.

A communications network is as good, or as bad, as its users perceive it to be. Network performance should therefore be measured in terms of overall user satisfaction with the service they receive. However, network performance is usually expressed in terms of network engineering measures such as average packet delay or loss rate. These engineering measures are an imperfect reflection of overall user satisfaction because user requirements vary widely, in every service dimension and over time.

Example 1: Some real-time interactive applications are able to tolerate relatively frequent packet loss without significant quality degradation, whereas some command and control functions require essentially lossless transmission.

Example 2: Interactive communications usually have an upper limit on total delay and delay variation corresponding to the limits of human perception (e.g., 400–500 milliseconds maximum delay, with maximum variation an order of magnitude lower), whereas some off-line data transfers are essentially insensitive to delays.

Example 3: Packet delay or loss may be valued differently by different users even if they are running the same application. Similarly, a user's valuation of quality of service (QOS) may vary depending on destination or time of day.

Example 4: Some users want deterministic worst-case performance guarantees, whereas others are satisfied with average-case statistical guarantees. Some users may be content with "best effort" service, for which the network offers no guarantees on loss or delay, especially if there are periods in which network utilization is low enough that even "best effort" traffic is reliably transferred.

Accounting for individual QOS requirements makes network operation and control considerably more complicated. In practice, user objectives are averaged across all users and over time. These averaged objectives are reduced to engineering measures and then are used to drive the network control process (see Figure 1): the users are not in the loop when making operational decisions.

In an effort to reflect variations in QOS requirements, many researchers divide usage into classes according to application requirements and traffic characteristics; for example, real-time video, real-time audio, one-way video playback, or off-line file transfer. Each class is then regarded as having a single representative user for analytical and control purposes. However, this approach ignores substantial heterogeneity within application classes and across users.

Heterogeneity across time means that a user's valuation of a given application will be different at different times, and thus the user's requirements for network performance for the same application will

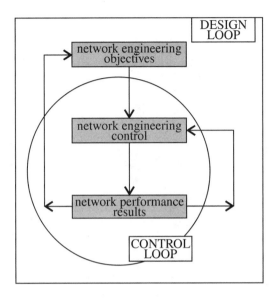

Figure 1
Network Design and Control Loops (a)

vary over time. Heterogeneity across users means that different users will differently value a given application and its QOS. A common—but we believe erroneous—assumption is that video applications should receive network priority because the performance degrades more drastically with delay than for, say, a World Wide Web session. In fact, some users may place sufficiently high value on low-latency Web usage that total user valuation of the network would be increased by giving higher priority to their Web sessions than to some video sessions. Therefore we think it is increasingly important for network operators to develop flexible tools that can support heterogeneity in usage types and user valuations.

One such tool is the ever-increasing intelligence located within the users' end-stations. It is already feasible for many traffic sources and sinks to do some basic processing on the transmitted data; for example, Transmission Control Protocol (TCP) congestion control schemes (Jacobson 1988) respond to network feedback by adjusting the traffic inputs. And as technology advances, these capabilities will continue to expand. This intelligence represents a network resource

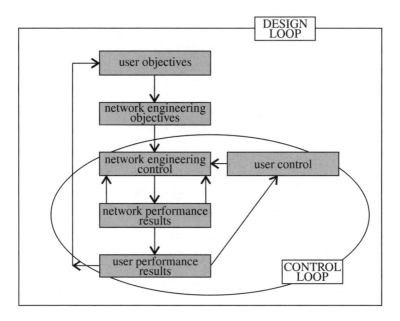

Figure 2
Network Design and Control Loops (b)

that, if properly managed, could enable a "tighter" network control loop than before.[1]

As a natural extension of existing network feedback control mechanisms, we propose bringing users back into the loop and thereby ensuring that performance measures are user-oriented (see Figure 2). We propose a form of feedback which we call responsive pricing and argue that it represents a particularly useful mechanism for maximizing network value. Users would gain by obtaining service more closely matched to their needs; network operators would gain through improved network utilization and increased user satisfaction with the service they receive. In particular, responsive pricing helps network operators by its "value discovery" function: it reveals how the valuations for QOS differ across time, users, and applications. Summary network engineering measures will continue to be

1. Our emphasis on increasingly controlling network congestion at the periphery echoes the views expressed by Dave Clark in his contribution to this volume (Clark 1996).

important, but we believe that user preferences should be the primary consideration driving resource allocation and congestion control schemes.

Two Definitions of Efficiency

In focusing on user preferences, we need to distinguish two very different notions of efficiency. *Network efficiency* refers to the utilization of network resources, such as bandwidth and buffer space. *Economic efficiency* refers to the relative valuations users attach to their network service.

If a network can maintain a target level of service while minimizing the resources needed to provide this service, we say that its operation is network efficient. For example, by statistically multiplexing bursty transmissions, the bandwidth required can often be reduced from that of a pure circuit-switched approach while still meeting the delay requirements of the applications.

If no user currently receiving a particular QOS values it less than another user who is being denied that QOS, we say that operation is economically efficient. For example, if one user is willing to pay x per second for undelayed access to a 1 Mbps link, and a second user is willing to pay only x/2, and if only one of them can be accommodated, then in an economically efficient network the bandwidth will be allocated to the first user (whether or not this user actually pays anything).

An obvious question is, why will either type of efficiency continue to be important? Some observers have suggested that the widespread deployment of fiber-optic lines and continuing exponential decreases in processor and memory costs will result in these network resources becoming essentially "free," and thus efficiency in their use will not be important in the future and all users will always be accommodated. We do not believe these arguments apply in the short or medium terms, if indeed they will ever apply. User demands are increasing exponentially, so that it is not clear when—if ever— network resources will be "free." We share the dream of ubiquitous, two-way broadband connectivity at low or zero cost, but believe we must wait at least a few decades to achieve it despite astonishing technological advances. Consider the cost of providing gigabit bandwidth not just to every home in the industrialized world, but for the other three-quarters of the planet's population as well. Add to that the cost of gigabit mobile communication that will follow each person around town, country, and world. Also, experience suggests that application developers will have little difficulty in designing new services that use up all the available resources.

For the foreseeable future, we will continue to live in a world characterized by network resource scarcity. We will move most quickly toward "free" service if we use our scarce network resources —whether public or private—efficiently in economic terms. The greater the value that users receive from scarce network resources, the more they will have to invest in building better and faster networks. Meanwhile, if commercial providers are not responsive to user valuations, they will not succeed in a competitive market. The same considerations apply even to private-access networks: the ultimate goal is to maximize some human measure of the value of using the network, such as profits, sales, shareholder value, and so on.

Feedback and Adaptive Users

Feedback is a well-established method of improving network efficiency. Users of current data networks respond to multiple forms of feedback on various time scales. On the longest time scale users decide whether or not to use a particular network, perhaps based on the network's charging structure or their previous experience with it. At the connection level, if a user observes that the network is usually heavily loaded at certain times of the day and lightly loaded at others, she may schedule her network usage accordingly. On these longer time scales, user responses are usually determined on economic grounds (although not always explicitly). For example, deciding whether or not to set up a connection involves weighing the expected value of using the network against the cost (in money, time, and/or degraded quality) of doing so. Most people are familiar with the decision that it is not "worthwhile" to use a network during busy periods, but instead to do something else and defer their network usage, without necessarily recognizing this process as economic decision-making.

During a connection, adaptive users can adjust their traffic inputs or QOS demands to respond to feedback signals from the network about the current state of network resources. TCP applications use various congestion control algorithms such as slow-start (Jacobson 1988) to adjust their input rates to the currently available bandwidth. The ATM Forum is developing an Available Bit Rate (ABR) service in which users who respond "appropriately" to dynamic feedback get loss guarantees from the ATM (Asynchronous Transfer Mode) network (Newman 1994). Since it is already accepted that user responses can be automated using preprogrammed network interfaces, fairly sophisticated user behavior can be envisaged, and feedback strategies need not be limited by human user response times. The issue becomes one of choosing a feedback signal to modify user behavior in some desired manner.

Adaptive users can help to increase network efficiency if they are given appropriate feedback signals. When the network load is high, the feedback should discourage adaptive users from inputting traffic; when the load is low, the feedback should encourage these users to send any traffic they have ready to transmit. In this way, many of the congestion problems that occur if the offered load is regarded as fixed can be avoided. One possible feedback signal is a price based on the level of network load: when the load is high, the price is high, and vice versa. Similarly, by associating a cost measure with network loading, all users can be signaled with the prices necessary to recover the cost of the current network load. Price-sensitive users—those willing and able to respond to dynamic prices—increase economic efficiency by choosing whether or not to input traffic according to their individual willingness to pay the current price. Users who value network service more will choose to transmit, while those who value it less will wait for a lower price. When the network is lightly loaded, the price will be close to zero and all users can input traffic.

Price signals thus have the potential to increase both network and economic efficiency, though whether a particular pricing scheme increases either notion of efficiency depends on the implementation (see the fifth section below). In a public network, where the users cannot be assumed to be cooperative, the more traditional feedback schemes as currently used in TCP/IP networks are not robust to user manipulation: it is relatively easy to program a host to ignore the feedback signals. Of course, it would be just as easy to ignore price signals; but since users would be liable for charges they incurred, there is some incentive to respond.

Price as a Form of Feedback

Congestion control and feedback control are difficult problems in network operations. Perhaps because of the technical challenges involved, most researchers have ignored two key issues (or relegated them to "policy issues") which are nevertheless crucial. First, how should congestion be defined and measured? This is a difficult question because individual user requirements vary considerably, so that one user may think the network is congested while another does not; also, because in internetworks the responsibility for detecting congestion may be distributed among several network operators, each of which applies a different test at their bottleneck points. This problem will become more difficult in a multiple-QOS network, in which several different performance characteristics are relevant to different applications (e.g., maximum delay, delay jitter, packet loss rate).

Second, how should limited resources be allocated under congestion? Currently, randomization with first in, first out queuing is used, but some proposals call for users to indicate the relative priority of their traffic—leading to the problem of providing incentives so that all users will not choose the highest priority.[2]

Charges to an Internet user could have several components, such as a connection fee, a charge per unit time or per unit of bandwidth, premium charges for certain services, and so on. In this chapter we focus attention on only one type of pricing: a responsive component that varies with the state of network congestion. By responsive pricing we do not mean a charge that counts the number of bytes or packets regardless of the network conditions.[3] On the contrary, we propose charging only when network congestion indicates that some

2. See, for example, Bohn et al. (1993); MacKie-Mason and Varian (1995a); Gupta et al. (1996); and Cocchi et al. (1992).

3. We use "packet" in a generic sense to mean a unit of data transmitted by a user.

users may be experiencing QOS degradation, with the size of the charges related to the degree of congestion. If the network is lightly loaded and all users are getting acceptable QOS, the responsive prices would be zero.

Proposing a scheme to allocate network resources and service priorities is not a radical departure: allocation occurs today in the Internet. However, the current allocation is implemented on a first come, first served basis, without any consideration for whether some users value immediate access more highly than others. Given the heterogeneity of user requirements for network performance, responsive pricing would improve economic efficiency by inducing users with low-priority traffic to delay it until a burst of congestion eases. Such time-smoothing would not upset users who can tolerate high latency, while it would improve the network's value to users who get the greatest benefits from immediate access.

Let us clarify one point: when most people think of prices, they think in monetary terms, e.g., dollars and cents. However, there is nothing inherently monetary in applying pricing principles to communication networks. As long as the appropriate cost and valuation functions can be defined, a pricing mechanism can be applied even if money is not directly involved. For example, in a private network where one organization controls all the users, the "prices" would be control signals that summarize the state of network resources. In this case, the users (or their applications) are cooperative and can be programmed to obtain a desirable traffic mix.[4]

We recognize that many people are concerned about the use of pricing in network operations. Concerns range from questions about the feasibility and overhead of usage-sensitive pricing to more philosophical issues such as profit opportunities and fairness. While some of these concerns may or may not be borne out by future developments, others are based on misconceptions of what is being proposed or on other nontechnical grounds. We do not expect that decisions on pricing will be made solely on technical grounds, but

4. Control theorists will recognize "prices" as the cost variables or shadow values that provide the correct signals to optimize the allocation of resources in the network—in this case, that optimize a function of user valuations of network performance.

we do believe that a clear understanding of the nature of what is being proposed is necessary on all sides. Therefore we first describe a framework for responsive pricing, and some of our work on analyzing and simulating various implementations. We then address some of the objections often raised in discussions of dynamic network pricing.

Modeling User Adaptation to Feedback

Our focus is on the interaction between user behavior and the efficiency of the network. Therefore, we want to model traffic types that a user can adapt to the state of the network. In this section we discuss the nature of such adaptive applications.

There are several ways in which a user can adapt her traffic load to the network state. Not all of these are equally obvious to the network. For example, a user may have a Constant Bit Rate (CBR) application that cannot tolerate either delay or loss. If the user does not like the service offered by the network, she may adapt by connecting to a different network, so that the original network never sees the load at all.

Alternatively, the user may decide to make a connection and use it for a CBR and delay-intolerant application. However, depending on the state of the network and the service guarantees it offers, the user may adapt the traffic at source. For example, she could reduce the number of packets transmitted by accepting lower fidelity or precision. Or she could delay making the connection to a different time. In these cases, the network merely sees a CBR source; it does not directly observe that the user has adapted.

In another case, a user may offer a load to the network, but accept a "best effort" service quality. In this case, the user is abdicating the adaptation to the network. If the network accepts all best effort traffic, then the offered load is not adapted to the network state. Rather, the burden the traffic imposes is adapted through varying the delay and packet loss. This form of adaptation can be quite costly if a higher-layer protocol is resending lost packets: congestion breeds congestion.

Even without pricing, users obviously adapt their network usage in several ways. We propose taking advantage of this natural adaptability to improve efficiency over a short time horizon. We have elsewhere (MacKie-Mason et al. 1995; Murphy and Murphy 1995) described several different types of adaptive users. So far we have modeled inelastic and elastic user types.

An *inelastic* application requires a delay guarantee, but can tolerate loss and is adaptive. For example, this might be the second level of a two-level codec for video. The first level is likely to contain the minimum necessary information, and would be transmitted as a nonadaptive application. The second level consists of enhancement information. It is not essential that all of the information be delivered, and it is possible for the user to vary the amount of information transmitted in response to feedback. However, a delay guarantee is required: if the information does not arrive before the playback point, it is considered useless.

Elastic users wait until feedback from the network indicates that they can input traffic, then they transmit and require that their cells are not lost in the network. Each elastic user decides individually what her transmission criteria are, e.g., the maximum price per cell she is willing to pay. A possible example of an elastic user type would be a non-real-time data transfer with no ARQ capability, so that already-transmitted cells are not buffered at the sender.

With these two types we have heterogeneity across applications, and thus are modeling an integrated services network. Further, we are able to model within-type heterogeneity by specifying users of a given type who value their QOS differently. For our preliminary results see Murphy et al. (1996).

Responsive Pricing Schemes

In our simulations we have been comparing three different schemes for allocating a simple network's resources. The first is a conventional approach that makes no use of feedback and user adaptation to the network state. The second is a closed-loop form of feedback and adaptation; the third is a closed-loop variation we call "tight loop" because it shortens the delay in the control loop.

No Feedback

Our proposal to improve network efficiency through involving the users in session control is somewhat novel, and certainly controversial. Most in the network engineering community seem to assume that a network will (and should?) be tuned for efficiency given a set of admitted user connections. The only room for interaction with the users in this setting is through the connection setup negotiation. Therefore, as a baseline, we simulate a network that does not provide feedback: users do not adapt to the network state.

A fixed number of inelastic sources are always admitted and active. In addition, a number of elastic applications are active at any given time. To simplify, the number of new elastic connections each period is held constant, but the number of packets to be delivered by each connection is random, so the number of active connections in any given period after the first will be random (as varying numbers of connections are completed). The distribution of elastic message sizes is chosen so that the average load being added to the network in each period is within the tolerance for a reasonable call admission algorithm. However, sometimes the amount of active elastic traffic will be large, and the network will suffer some performance difficulties (packet delays and losses).

Closed-loop Feedback

Our first feedback network uses a simple scheme (Murphy and Murphy 1994; Murphy et al. 1994). The network state is measured by buffer occupancy at the gateway. This occupancy is converted into a price per packet, which is then transmitted back to each active adaptive application. The applications then decide on how many packets to send during the next interval, as described above.

In this network, users send some packets in period t, and network performance is affected by the aggregate number of packets received during an interval. At the end of period t the network sends a signal back to users based on the network utilization in period t. Users then decide how many packets to send in period t+1, based on their observed period t performance and their application requirements. This is a closed-loop feedback system with at least a one-period lag between the state of the network and the effect on the user inputs.

Smart Market Pricing

A "smart market" approach to adaptation has been proposed in MacKie-Mason and Varian (1995a). A user sends packets to the network interface which include in each header a token indicating how much the user is willing to pay to get that packet onto the network in the current interval. Then, during the pricing interval, the network gateway sorts the "bids" on the incoming packets, and admits to the network only as many as it can accommodate without degrading performance below some bound.[5] The gateway admits packets in descending order of their bid. Users are charged not the amount that they declared they were willing to pay, but the value of the minimum bid on a packet that is admitted to the network. Thus users pay just the congestion cost (the amount that the highest-value denied packet would have paid for immediate transport), but they get to keep all of the excess value that they attribute to delivery above the cutoff bid. This form of pricing by auction has several nice properties, described in MacKie-Mason and Varian (1995a).

We call this mechanism a tight loop because the user sends willingness to pay along with the packet, and the network admission and pricing is determined based on those reports and the current state of network congestion, without creating a feedback delay. In practice, there might be a one-period delay to allow the gateway to determine the approximate cutoff bid from packets presented in the prior interval.

5. In practice, the gateway would probably estimate the cutoff bid that would admit the number of packets that can be accommodated using recent information on the bid distribution and perhaps a sample of newly arriving packets. Then the gateway would merely route incoming packets into two (or more) queues—one for immediate handling, and one for buffering and reentry in the next bid period. When the number of packets being held back exceeded buffer capacity, some would be dropped.

Preliminary Simulation Results

To give a sense of the gains that are possible with responsive pricing, we offer some preliminary results that compare no feedback to the closed-loop pricing scheme.

Source Type		%Loss	User Value	%Decr. Value	%Incr. Value
Unpriced	Inelastic	0	240		
	Elastic	30.4	146		
	Combined	**19.1**	**386**		
Priced	Inelastic	4.4	239		
	Elastic	0.1	204		
	Combined	**1.7**	**443**	**91.0**	**14.8**

Figure 3
Performance and Economic Gains from User Feedback (preliminary)

In the simulations we have generated 20 video sources with random frame sizes to represent the inelastic traffic, and between 1 and 39 elastic data sources with random frame sizes, with the number of active flows at a given moment chosen randomly. Under these conditions, our network capacity has experienced an average of 80% utilization. When closed-loop pricing is implemented, packet loss drops from 19% to under 2%, while the net benefits perceived by the users increase by nearly 15%.[6]

Objections to Responsive Pricing

We explore here some common arguments against responsive pricing in network operations and offer some counterpoints. Previous work along these lines is found in MacKie-Mason and Varian (1995b) and Murphy and Murphy (1995a).

---

6. See Gupta (1996) for related simulation results. They show a greater improvement due to the type of pricing they simulate. Of course, our results and theirs are illustrative, as they depend on the reasonableness of the many simulation approximations and parametrizations.

Responsive Pricing in the Internet

Myths

Why do we need to introduce prices? The Internet is free now—let's keep it that way.

The Internet is not free now, though it seems that way to many users whose universities or organizations pay the access fees. The issue is not whether Internet usage should be priced: it already is. The issue is how the Internet should be priced so that its value to users is maximized.

Network resources will soon be essentially free, therefore Internet congestion and the accompanying QOS degradation will not be a problem in the future.

This represents an optimistic view of the future, but we do not believe that this will come true in the short or medium term, if ever. See our arguments on why efficiency will continue to be important in the second section above.

With any form of responsive pricing, it's the small users who will suffer the most. Rich users can behave as they want since they have the resources, and could effectively limit the network access of smaller users. The role of the Internet as a medium for information exchange between all comers will be lost!

Absolutely not! Quite the opposite. Suppose that the network is supported only by connection fees. The connection fee will then be set based on the average usage for a connection of a given size. Then the small users will be paying more than their share to support the heavy users. A corollary to this myth is that the user cost of the Internet will increase if responsive pricing is introduced. The whole purpose of responsive pricing is to make the network more efficient, and to raise the value for users. Thus, if implemented intelligently, we will get more value out of a network of given cost. For a network of fixed size, we can lower the connection fees by an amount equal to the congestion fees and still recover costs, so total outlays are the same but the network has higher value. Or we can use the congestion revenues to invest in a bigger, more valuable network facility. It is also worth remembering that with responsive pricing, you pay for your actual usage in terms of the cost it imposes on other users. If all you want to use the Internet for is email and netnews, your charges under responsive pricing would be zero because these are flexible applications and do not require real-time performance or guaranteed bandwidth. As for rich users being able to afford to ignore dynamic prices, this is true under any pricing scheme and is a larger issue concerning the distribution of wealth in a society.[7]

Responsive pricing is just another way for network operators to make more money. Users will lose out as network operators maximize their profits.

It's true that there is the potential for profiteering whenever prices are charged, especially when the conditions under which prices are set are not immediately accessible to ordinary users. But in a competitive environment, the market disciplines network operators whose revenues exceed actual cost by more than the minimal amount necessary to stay in business. Of course, market discipline is limited in the case of a monopoly provider or a cartel of price-fixing providers. But then the outcome depends on policy and regulatory decisions rather than on the specific pricing scheme.

Objectives for Responsive Pricing

If congestion is caused by bandwidth-intensive users such as real-time video, why don't we just keep these users off the Internet, or limit their number so that they don't cause congestion problems?

Keeping these users off the Internet means keeping the Internet low-tech and continuing the "best effort, no guarantees" paradigm. That is, can't we do better than a network that cannot support reasonable quality for real-time video and audio? This runs contrary to the trend toward integrated-services networks, and may cause the Internet to miss out on innovative information transfer and retrieval mechanisms. Apart from the administrative issues, why should "low-tech" users be allowed to veto "high-tech" users? What will the general public want when they come on-line? Which administrative bodies do we want to empower with rationing authority?[8]

7. We do not mean to dismiss income distribution problems as unimportant, but rather to say that network pricing (or nonpricing) is not the right venue for solving them.

8. It is interesting to note that for a while in 1995 the EUNet backbone in Europe administratively forbade unrestricted use of the CU_SeeMe video-conferencing software, requiring that users apply in writing, in advance, for permission to establish a session.

Why won't some nonpricing scheme be enough? Administrative controls can be used to impose some appropriate notion of fairness, for example; or users can choose a traffic priority level that matches their requirements.

Who decides what is fair? The network operator can; but according to a user-oriented objective, fairness should be determined collectively by the users. We might all agree that telesurgery is more important than email, but what about interactive video games versus email? Also, every time a new application is developed it has to be slotted into the priority order, an increasingly complex process. Furthermore, the value of an application to a given user will vary over time. Priorities for different applications will sometimes—perhaps usually—incorrectly order valuations. Suppose the network simply supports priority levels and allows users to choose their own level. Why wouldn't they all choose the highest priority? To guard against such abuses, there would have to be some penalty for "inappropriate" declarations, implying the need to define "appropriate" priority levels or to assign increasing charges to higher priorities (e.g., Bohn et al. [1993]). A user's choice of priority level would then be based on economic considerations: balancing the benefits of higher priority against the costs and/or the penalties for inflating an application's perceived priority level. This is the essence of a pricing scheme.

Bits/bytes/cells/packets are not the correct units to charge for—it's information that users care about. Any scheme that proposes to look inside every packet to determine how it relates to other packets is likely to be too complex to be justified. Also, lower-layer mechanisms (such as Ethernet collisions) or packet losses requiring retransmissions make it difficult to predict how much "raw" data has to be transferred to transmit a given amount of information. Should users be charged for retransmissions that they have no control over, or packets that are dropped by the network?

Our proposal involves pricing for transport, not for content. The "importance" of a particular packet, and its relation to other packets, is a higher-layer issue determined by the application (or ultimately by the users). We are not proposing that the network be aware of these issues; on the contrary, with responsive pricing it is up to the users to decide how packets are used to transfer information. It is true that in general it is impossible to determine beforehand exactly how many packets are required to transmit a block of information, but again, this is a higher-layer issue. Indeed, there will be some efficiency gains from providing a financial incentive to software developers to make more efficient use of network packet transport. The important question is whether the users or the network should bear the uncertainty arising from variations in congestion. If the network is expected to offer a "file transfer" service, the file transfer charge per megabyte could be computed by averaging over many such transfers. If the user is expected to pay for all transmitted packets, she could define a maximum number of packets she is willing to transmit per megabyte of information, and invoke an application-layer process if this threshold is exceeded.

Once a network is installed, any load-dependent costs of transferring data are minimal—the fixed costs of network management and maintenance dominate. These fixed costs can be efficiently recovered through connection fees and capacity prices (proportional to the size of the access link). Why implement an elaborate pricing mechanism to recover the relatively small variable costs?

Our point is not about current cost recovery. Most network production costs can and should be recovered through connection fees and capacity prices. We are concerned about the *congestion* cost that one user's traffic imposes on other users sharing the resources. Bandwidth or buffer space occupied by one user's traffic is not available to other users. When this reduces other users' quality of service (through increased delays, loss rates, blocking probabilities, and so on), they suffer congestion costs that may translate into significant actual costs of service degradation. One mechanism to capture these costs is a price that is sensitive to some indicator of congestion, such as load.

Why are we so concerned with modifying individual user behavior anyway? Surely one user can't do that much damage to the Internet?

One user, or a relatively tiny number of users, can now do a lot of damage to the Internet. A single interactive video connection can take up as much bandwidth as thousands of traditional Internet applications. Without some incentives to take other users into account (and/or penalties when they are not), a small fraction of the user base could bring large regions of the Internet to a standstill. In any case, the collective behavior of lots of individuals, acting without concern about the effects of their traffic on others, can easily lead to congestion. We think it most natural and efficient to attack the problem at its source, but it may be that feasible responsive pricing schemes are more practical if imposed at a higher level of aggregation.

There is already a penalty for heavy network usage: my application runs more slowly. Why should I pay again, in real money?

Your application running more slowly represents a penalty to you, but what about other users' applications which are also running more slowly? In order to efficiently share resources, you have to be made aware of the costs your usage imposes on other users. If there is enough of the shared resources, these congestion costs can be insignificant. But we believe that the Internet cannot rely on these costs being essentially zero, at least not for the foreseeable future. Meanwhile, some forms of responsive pricing give the user a choice: either pay in delay, or pay in money to avoid delay. This choice is available on a gross scale today: we can use the Internet with uncontrolled delays, or use a low-delay private leased network. We think it is possible to offer this pay-or-delay choice to users within the Internet, making them better off by giving them a wider range of service choices.

How Would It Work?

Most users will want to know their charges in advance, and will not want to deal with prices that change during the lifetime of a typical connection. Why won't flat-fee prices (per minute connected, or per kbps of the access link) be enough?

We are not advocating that all users must face responsive prices. Any user can choose not to pay dynamic prices, even if their application is adaptive. They would then be charged according to some other pricing scheme. For example, a user might be allowed to pay zero responsive prices in exchange for getting only best effort service with lower priority than other users who pay a positive price. In any realistic pricing scheme it would be possible for users to set the maximum charge they are willing to pay, which is what is usually required for budgetary purposes. We should also point out that

298

MacKie-Mason, Murphy, and Murphy

flat-fee pricing is really long-term usage pricing, so even "flat" fees include a usage-based component: it is just averaged over a period much longer than a connection lifetime.[9]

Even if we want to allocate according to congestion costs, how can the network determine what actual costs the current load is imposing on users who probably have widely varying service requirements? Getting users to reveal these costs is likely to be extremely complicated, if not impossible.

It is true that providing users with the right incentives to reveal their actual costs of service degradation is complicated. It is not impossible, however: truthful revelation is one of the properties of the smart market mechanism in MacKie-Mason and Varian (1995a). With any prices that increase with the degree of congestion in the network, users will be induced to prioritize their traffic. Only users who value their traffic at least as much as the current price will transmit. If congestion remains unacceptably high, then the associated price is too low; conversely, if capacity is unacceptably underutilized, the price is too high. Thus, through a process of experimentation and dynamic adjustment, the network can shape the price schedule so that users approximately reveal their valuations for uncongested service through their responses to the price feedback.

Suppose we institute some form of responsive pricing, and users (especially the high-bandwidth ones who will pay the most) leave the Internet and use other networks. Won't that reduce the value of being on the Internet, perhaps to the point where even small users leave and join the other networks?

We are discussing only charging users for the amount of congestion cost they impose on other users. Users get to decide whether they want to pay money to avoid congestion, or not pay money and bear congestion delays; in the current Internet, everyone is forced to accept the latter alternative. Costs are not just monetary: if the cost of congestion delay is severe, then we can expect that some users are already being driven away. Indeed, many network applications are restricted to private leased-line networks to avoid Internet congestion (e.g., most video-conferencing). By allowing transport priori-

---

9. This assumes that the flat fees are set to recover some function of the usage cost, as they would be in a competitive market for service provision.

ties to be sorted based on who suffers the most from congestion delay, we will increase the value of the network, which should spawn additional growth and new uses.

Feasibility

Dynamic pricing schemes are unworkable in practice due to the overheads involved in accounting and billing for usage on such a detailed level. In addition, a significant portion of the revenue raised is needed to defray the cost of doing dynamic pricing in the first place!

The costs of dynamic pricing may outweigh the benefits for a particular implementation, but we do not believe this is necessarily true for all dynamic pricing schemes. In particular, on-line pricing mechanisms may reduce the actual cost to an acceptable level; there is no reason to think that current billing and accounting costs in other industries, such as telephone or electricity networks, will necessarily apply to dynamic pricing in the Internet. In particular, since data networks have vast distributed computing power in the form of smart end-user devices at the periphery, it may be possible to design distributed billing systems that have very low cost for large numbers of small transactions.

Dynamic pricing is impractical because users cannot respond to prices that are updated many times per second. If the update interval is increased to the minimum period in which users can respond, congestion can arise and disperse in between price updates, so that prices no longer influence user behavior.

Our scheme assumes an intelligent network interface at price-sensitive user sites, so the processing necessary to respond to dynamic prices would be done automatically based on preprogrammed user preferences. For example, a user could have a default preference in her email program that instructed the software to hold outgoing email whenever the price exceeds 0.01 cents per packet. Such software would play a similar role to current TCP implementations that respond to network feedback by adjusting their traffic inputs, except that the feedback in our case is the current price.

Charging for transmission fails to capture cases where the benefit of a transfer is with the receiver. If senders are charged for receiver-initiated transfers, we could see a drastic reduction in the number of open-access servers with a corresponding decrease in the value of using the network.

The problem of allocating the benefits of a particular information transfer is a higher-layer issue. We do not believe that associating the charge for a transmission with the sender constrains the actual flow of money in any way. It is easy to imagine multiparty connection protocols that initially negotiate each party's responsibility for the total charge, or "reverse-charges" servers that only transmit data once the receiver has indicated willingness to pay the resulting transmission costs. Just as in telephony, we can expect "800," "900," and other billing services to arise.

Cultural Effects

By introducing responsive pricing, the traditional Internet culture (which emphasizes openness and sharing) will be destroyed, and it will become just another commercial service.

It is true that by changing the pricing scheme used in the Internet, the culture will also change. However, the culture is changing anyway due to the strains imposed by the demands of the ever-increasing user population. The question is, how can this change be managed so that overall user satisfaction with the Internet is maximized? Insisting that the Internet remain a connection-fee-only network consigns it to ever-lessening value as usage and congestion increases, and new, QOS-sensitive applications are developed that cannot be successfully implemented in a first come, first served network. Many users are already fleeing the increasingly noisy Internet; shifting some responsibility for congestion control out to the users, and treating them as smart rather than dumb devices, will help preserve those parts of the Internet that users most value preserving.

We don't know what the future Internet will look like, so it would be a mistake to adopt a responsive pricing scheme that is so controversial—it could stifle innovation and cause the Internet to miss out on opportunities to enhance its value to society.

Equally, by not introducing some additional forms of congestion control, the Internet may miss out on future growth and improvements. For example, the Internet may be consigned to missing the widespread deployment of real-time interactive video if better mechanisms for controlling congestion are not developed. We propose one particular form of congestion control based on economic principles of pricing for resource allocation. Price is one possible feedback signal which has some attractive properties (compactness, quantifiability, etc.). Economists have developed a large body of theory of pricing mechanisms, and there is a lot of experience with the use of prices in real-world markets. However, we do not rule out the possibility that there are other feedback mechanisms that, for one reason or another, may be preferable in communication networks.

Conclusions

Many proposals have been made to incorporate feedback into network control and resource allocation schemes, such as TCP congestion control and avoidance algorithms or ABR service in ATM networks. We suggest taking these proposals one step further by explicitly defining how that feedback is generated by the network, and what form it takes. In responsive pricing, the network announces a price that is based on the cost of using network resources, and price-sensitive users adjust their traffic inputs based on this price and their own specification of how valuable network service is to them.

What we propose is to give users incentives to consider the effects of their usage on other users. While users may or may not behave "considerately" in a privately-owned network, it appears that some incentives will always be necessary in commercial networks. We also address the issue of user valuation of the service, and allow for some sources to have more demanding traffic than others regardless of the type of applications involved. Simulations show that it is possible to gain both network efficiency and economic efficiency by using pricing. In other words, the network actually carries more traffic and carries more important traffic from the users' point of view.

References

Bohn, R., H.-W. Braun, K. Claffy, and S. Wolff. 1993. Mitigating the coming Internet crunch: Multiple service levels via precedence. Technical report, University of California at San Diego, San Diego Supercomputer Center, and National Science Foundation.

Clark, D. 1996. A model of cost allocation and pricing in the Internet. In *Internet economics*, ed. Lee McKnight and Joseph Bailey. Cambridge, Mass.: MIT Press. Available from URL: http://www.press.umich.edu:80/jep/works/ClarkModel.html.

Cocchi, Ron, Deborah Estrin, Scott Shenker, and Lixia Zhang. 1992. Pricing in computer networks: Motivation, formulation, and example. Technical report, University of Southern California. Available from URL: ftp://ftp.parc.xerox.com/pub/net-research/pricing2.ps.Z.

Gupta, Alok, Dale O. Stahl, and Andrew B. Whinston. 1996. A priority pricing approach to managing multi-service class networks in real time. In *Internet economics*, ed. Lee McKnight and Joseph Bailey. Cambridge, Mass.: MIT Press. Available from URL: http://www.press.umich.edu:80/jep/works/GuptaPrior.html.

Jacobson, V. 1988. Congestion Avoidance and Control. Proceedings of the ACM SIGCOMM '88 Symposium.

MacKie-Mason, J. and H. Varian. 1995a. Pricing the Internet. In *Public access to the Internet*, ed. B. Kahin and J. Keller. Englewood Cliffs, NJ: Prentice-Hall. Available from URL http://www.spp.umich.edu/ipps/papers/info-nets/Pricing_Internet/Pricing_the_Internet.ps.Z

MacKie-Mason Jeffrey K., and Hal R. Varian. 1995b. Some FAQs about usage-based pricing. *Computer Networks and ISDN Systems* 28. Available from URL: http://www.spp.umich.edu/ipps/papers/info-nets/useFAQs/useFAQs.html. Also in Proceedings of WWW '94, Chicago, Illinois, and in Proceedings of the Association of Research Librarians 1994.

MacKie-Mason, J., J. Murphy and L. Murphy. 1995. ATM efficiency under various pricing schemes. Proceedings of the 3rd International Conference on Telecommunications Systems Modelling and Analysis, Nashville, March 1995.

Murphy, J., and L. Murphy. 1994. Bandwidth allocation by pricing in ATM networks. *IFIP Transactions C: Communication Systems*, No. C-24: 333–351. Available from URL http://www.eeng.dcu.ie/murphyj/band-price/band-price.html.

Murphy, L., and J. Murphy. 1995a. Feedback and pricing in ATM networks. Proceedings of the IFIP TC6 Third Workshop on Performance Modelling and Evaluation of ATM Networks, Ilkley, England, July 1995. 68/1–68/12. Available from URL http://www.eeng.dcu.ie/murphyj/brad-price/brad-price.html.

Murphy, L., and J. Murphy. 1995b. Pricing for ATM network efficiency. Proceedings of the 3rd International Conference on Telecommunication Systems Modelling and Analysis, Nashville, March 1995. 349–356. Available from URL http://www.eeng.dcu.ie/murphyj/atm-price/atm-price.html

Murphy, J., L. Murphy and E.C. Posner. 1994. Distributed pricing for embedded ATM networks. Proceedings of the International Teletraffic Congress ITC-14, Antibes, France, June 1994. 1053–1063. Available from URL http://www.eeng.dcu.ie/murphyj/dist-price/dist-price.html.

Murphy, L., J. Murphy and J. MacKie-Mason. 1996. Feedback and efficiency in ATM networks. *Proceedings of the International Conference on Communications (ICC '96).*

Newman, P. 1994. Traffic management for ATM local area networks. *IEEE Communications Magazine* (August): 44–50.

Acknowledgments

We would like to thank the contributors to the com-priv Internet mailing list and some of the attendees of the MIT Internet Economics Workshop for their vigorous objections to usage-based pricing.

User Control and IP Allocation

Ketil Danielsen and Martin Weiss

Introduction

The Internet is a global interconnection network for computers
running the TCP/IP protocol suite. Allocation of network resources
is primarily controlled by first in, first out rationing and adaptive
routing at the IP (Internet Protocol) network layer, and window-
based network congestion control at the TCP (Transmission Control
Protocol) transport layer (Clark 1989; Jacobson 1988). This collection of control mechanisms has been successful at providing high
and stable throughput during congested periods and, with some
modifications, scaled well to both increasing link capacities and a
richer interconnection structure. Despite continuous efforts to minimize such effects as biases in both average throughput and drop
rates to individual TCP conversations (Floyd and Jacobson 1992;
Mankin 1990), the allocation system remains unable to individualize
allocation levels to the applications. Hierarchical link-sharing has
been proposed to guarantee minimum allocations to classes of users,
protocols, or organizations, while at the same time allowing for
alternate use of unused allocations (Floyd and Jacobson 1995). Re-
placement of IP's datagram service with resource reservation service
was proposed in Braden et al. (1994). Ultimately, however, the objective of a production Internet is to provide maximum value to its
users. Neither of these practices offers any tangible user involvement
in the real-time allocation process. This chapter proposes real-time

control modes in which the user can influence his allocation of network resources so as to direct quality in his preferred direction.

Users Involvement

Users of the Internet make choices based on their individual value of information and the cost of waiting for responses to the various information requests. Their selections of Internet server to use, time to submit request, the size of the request, and potential abortion of submitted requests have an indirect influence on their individual allocation levels as well as externality effects on concurrent users sharing the same resources. As such, the system is slowly self-regulating at the user level, complemented with faster regulation at lower layers, such as round-trip time window adjustments at the transport layer.

With recent proposals to charge users for the network resources they consume, an alternate opportunity emerges for control of IP allocation that can individualize allocations at the user level. Briefly stated, the proposals promote a slowly changing fee per unit for production cost recovery and a rapidly changing congestion fee per unit for dynamic balancing of usage value and waiting cost. High uncertainty as to the magnitude and variation of network expenditures motivates users to bound these.

The design of an Expenditure Controller Interface (ECI) will be proposed, via which the user can specify a real-time upper bound on his network expenditures. The user's decisions will be based on quality perceived and expenditure feedback. Since the bound regulates the flow of IP packets from the user's active application, the ECI and the user together form a response to the pricing process and contribute to load regulation on the current IP path.

Computational Markets

In general, the coupling of congestion fees and users with appropriately designed ECIs defines a real-time market for resources whose potential use for computer networks was noted in Braden et al. (1994) and Estrin and Zhang (1990). Current work has described the potentially very efficient Smart Market trading mechanism in which users submit sealed bids per packet and the service center decides job schedule and optimal price. This mechanism has been examined for energy networks in Rassenti et al. (1994) and IP networks in MacKie-Mason and Varian (1994). Related mechanisms for access to distributed and parallel CPU (Central Processing Unit) resources were demonstrated with favorable experimental results in Waldspurger et al. (1992). Economic models have been developed under the assumption that the price coordinator has estimates on users' valuation on waiting time (Stahl and Whinston 1994). Dynamic pricing was shown, via simulation, to improve on net consumer surplus produced in general multi-service networks (Gupta et al. 1996) and on cell drop rates in an Asynchronous Transfer Mode (ATM) network (Murphy and Murphy 1994). These studies emphasize the market mechanism rather than user involvement, and assume that "smart agents" operate on behalf of the user.

Human Process Control

Direct user involvement for real-time price-quality control in digital telephony was proposed in Danielsen (1993). In an environment where price and quality change frequently, and telephones have speech compression equipment that removes quiet periods, the user would regulate the price-quality relationship by talking more or less. The costs could be controlled by shifting speech activity to periods when talking is cheaper. The user's real-time decisions were motivated by real-time feedback; costs of talking were displayed and speech quality was detected in the form of the received earpiece speech quality.

Hume et al. (1995) studied the use of human control of multiple file transfer scheduling over a congestible and dynamically priced network. In their evaluation, process control problems appear to be advantageously automated when the task involves highly procedural observation, storage, and computation with quickly changing numerical input data, whereas the selective and inductive behavior so characteristic of humans appears better suited to high-entropy tasks that are hard to characterize. Their work demonstrates the use of ecological interface design theory to significantly improve the operator's ability to schedule file transfers within the deadline and monetary budget.

Quality Control

Drawing from this, it appears that control of expenditure in real time falls within the domain of control problems better suited for automation. Expenditure is the price × usage integral over time, where price changes very rapidly and the usage is generally unobservable by the end-user. The proposed ECI will automatically ensure that the expected expenditure rate does not go beyond a user-specified upper bound. Our design leaves the setting of the upper bound for the user. Optimal setting of this bound depends on the individual quality preferences of the user and trends in the price-quality relationship. Users perceive quality differently depending on the type of application they are running.

Recent trends have favored an approach in which the application specifies its service requirement to the network using the service descriptors available from the network interface. The service requirement, which is asked for by a request-response-type application (e.g. telnet, FTP and World Wide Web navigators), is based on studies of human preferences for response times to various types of information requests. For continuous media, the service requirement is based on the user's tolerance to noise in the received information (see Braden et al. [1994] for details). Preprogramming service requirements may be a technically favorable solution to provide the average user with the average preferred service quality, but allows for suboptimal over- or underprovisioning of resources to nonconforming users.

The proposed ECI requires no user quality specifications to performs its role. All that is needed is the upper limit on expenditures, which in turn bounds network resource usage. This is a sufficient approach because response time can be reduced by increasing the processing resource allocation to a user (Touch and Farber 1994), and noise can be reduced by allocating either more buffers or processing resources to the user (Low and Varaiya 1991).

Since the user at any time can adapt his expenditure rate control policy to his current private quality preferences and financial budget, the ECI is an application-independent quality-control methodology.

Accounting and Billing

Computational markets rely on usage-sensitive prices to be computed by the service center (i.e., an IP packet switch) and endpoints represented by users to respond. Sufficient user incentives to regulate in real time can be preserved through reliable billing, which requires an accounting mechanism such as in Brownlee (1995) and Mills et al. (1991), and virtually instantaneous expenditure feedback, which requires the ECI to know the current usage-sensitive price and billing rule.

A standard IP billing format is not defined yet. Locally implemented solutions for cost recovery are used in Chile (Baeza-Yates et al. 1993) and New Zealand (Brownlee 1996). Based on the accounting architecture, the local Internet Service Provider (ISP) can bill for all incoming and/or outgoing packets, but not identify the originator of an end-to-end call, which complicates billing of the calling party. Higher-level distribution mechanisms for IP expenditures are likely to emerge. A possible scenario is that the user is billed for his outgoing traffic, as suggested in Mills et al. (1991), and that the price he pays per packet is billed only once.

For congestion control purposes, IP may exercise upstream price control between switches. This form of control, which was elaborated on in Jain (1990), Lehr and Weiss (1995), and Shenker et al. (1995), can be used for internal regulation, between adjacent switches, or externally between adjacent Autonomous Systems (AS). In either case, the user pays the price of the closest IP switch subject to usage-sensitive pricing, and the price may reflect both congestion cost as well as forwarding costs to neighboring switches. The purpose of the ECI is to facilitate efficient load control for high-frequency pricing mechanisms, so it is largely irrelevant to our approach where the price is computed as long as the ECI knows the rule according to which it will be billed.

User Control Modes

This section describes end-user control modes for two important forms of price-based allocation, general usage-based pricing with periodic price changes, and the Smart Market. Initially, we discuss some known problems with usage-based pricing, or measured rate services as they are also known.

Measured Rate Services

From the typical Internet user's standpoint, network load as measured in bits, bytes, packets, or channels is a hardly a comprehendible input good. Rather, the user often considers each information request as a single input unit and qualifies its value with such quality parameters as response time and noise in the received response (Clark 1996; Jain 1991).

Applications translate each information request into one or more data channels in space/time. Pricing mechanisms that require the end user to acknowledge the setup and price of each channel (as in Edell et al. [1995] and Perez and Aldana [1996]) may easily overwhelm the user in addition to presenting uncomprehendible units to the average end-user. These two problems repeat themselves more severely when the pricing units reduce to packets, bytes, or bits.

Indications of "discomfort" with measured rate services have been voiced on various technical Internet mailing lists and in other media (Baeza-Yates et al. 1993; Wilson 1994). Users seem to prefer a pricing structure in which the organization pays a capacity-dependent monthly fee for access without any fee for usage (see MacKie-Mason and Varian [1992] for a review of such flat-rate pricing practices). This is somewhat reminiscent of the debate over mandatory local measured telephone service that took place in the early to mid-1980s.

Wenders (1987, chapter 3) argues that pricing in telecommunications must be separated into usage and access pricing components.[1]

---

1. Note that these components interact with each other. As the price of access decreases, we can expect an increase in usage, and vice versa.

More germane to this discussion, Wenders (1987, chapter 5) argues for mandatory local measured service. Under this pricing regime, access prices are lowered, allowing for an increased number of users on the network, while the usage charges suppress usage. This has the effect of reducing the usage costs (because of suppressed traffic) even when the costs of the measuring equipment are included. While Wenders considers peak-load pricing, not dynamic pricing as we do, and while a telephone call is a more tangible commodity to the end-user than a packet as part of an application, his analysis is nonetheless instructive.

Analogies

When a user specifies an upper expenditure limit via the ECI, he constrains the flow of IP packets from his application without actually knowing by how much. He can only observe quality effects from the action. In a useful analogy, the accelerator pedal serves as the user tool for speed control in a car. Unaware of the actual gas consumption rate, the user has to *learn* the short-run relationship between action and quality and, in the longer run, the relationship between driving habits and monetary outlays. We expect this to hold true for users of the ECI as well. Over repeated trials users will learn how to operate effectively in their self-interest.

Simplicity of the ECI is deliberate for the initial design although "smart agents" can reduce the mental burden on the user, and have been called for in general computational economies (Gupta et al. 1996; Stahl and Whinston 1994; Waldspurger et al. 1992). We choose to fit the control problem within what we think are current ranges of human capability and trust that automation of subtasks will be pursued in future works.

The ECI Model

A user will choose to submit an information request if his expected net benefit is positive. Let v be the information value of the information item when successfully received by the user, $C(T)$ be the congestion cost from having to wait T time units for the response, and P be the IP expenditure. Since neither T nor P is known perfectly ahead of the submission, the user must deal with expectations, and submit if $v - C(\hat{T}) - \hat{P} \geq 0$, and form those expectations through learning.

A congestion-priced resource is assumed to announce a new usage-sensitive price at fixed intervals in time. In response to this price process, and while awaiting a response to a submitted request, the user controls three variables: a budget unit m > 0; a current budget multiplier $u \in (0, 1, \dots, K)$; and a budget period length k > 0. The ECI ensures that IP packets are not submitted when $\hat{P} > \tilde{P}$, where $\hat{P}$ is predicted period expenditure and $\tilde{P} = mu$ is period expenditure bound set by the user. While all three elements can be specified by the user at any time, it is expected that the user rarely will specify k, occasionally will specify m, and use u as the real-time control tool. Perhaps the simplest control interface is binary, with K = 1. The user either allows for expenditure ($u = 1$ and $\tilde{P} = um = m$) or not ($u = 0$).

Estimation Noise To estimate $\hat{P}$ the ECI must know the current packet price and have a rule for determining how many more packets will be charged for within the current period. With an ECI-to-switch network latency of Δ, the ECI knows the price Δ time units in the past and will be charged the price Δ time units into the future. Also, the billing policy affects $\hat{P}$ if, for example, the user is to be billed for both incoming and outgoing traffic.

The ECI can provide better safeguards against average expenditure rate overruns by allowing the negative or positive surplus a from the previous period to carry over to the next. That is, the expenditure limit for the successive period becomes $\tilde{P} + a$ rather than $\tilde{P}$. Allowing for surpluses to carry over will increase the chances for the ECI to meet the user's expenditure in the long run over multiple pricing periods.

Transparency The control interface (k, m, u) rules out the need for the user to know about any network-related loading units. The ECI estimates $\hat{P}$ and communicates this to the user across the control interface whereas q is the subjective quality measured by the user.

In cases where it is possible, the user can benefit from knowing the portion of the request that has been acknowledged, $\delta \geq [0,1]$.

For larger response times, in bulk transfers, this would be the number of units successfully transferred divided by the bulk size. This information is already supplied by newer applications.

User Control in the Smart Market

The discussion so far has assumed that the ECI is periodically informed of changes in the usage-sensitive unit price, delayed by Δ. In the Smart Market, each packet is charged a per-packet price, which in turn is recomputed periodically and cannot be publicized ahead of service if recomputation intervals are very small. Expenditure feedback in this case cannot be collected from the switch's billing system. Instead, an alternative mechanism will be described that does not rely on instantaneous expenditure feedback from the network.

Each IP packet submitted for service has a bid $\tilde{p}$ in its header. Let the set $A(t)$ contain the packets awaiting service at time t at the IP switch. The next served packet is the one with the highest bid, for which the originating user will be charged a price equal to the lowest bid in $A(t)$, which is at most equal to the bid of the packet served. The Smart Market thus guarantees an upper bound on the packet charge.[2]

A user can control the upper expenditure bound to $\tilde{P}$ for N packets by setting $\tilde{p} = \tilde{P}/N$. Since N is unobservable, as discussed above, the ECI for a Smart Market must provide for both real-time expenditure feedback, as well as a real-time controllable $\tilde{p}$ through which the user can manipulate quality. While this is in line with the original Smart Market proposal, its proponents suggest reverse packets to carry the realized prices (MacKie-Mason and Varian 1994). However, not all flows experience frequent reverse traffic, so the expenditure feedback must constitute an upper bound. The ECI knows how many packets were submitted at which bids and, due to

2. This is an approximate form of a Vickrey auction, the auction form on which the Smart Market idea is based. While the Vickrey auction assumes instantaneous arrivals of all competing packets (Rassenti et al. 1994), this approximation considers the current waiting line $A(t)$ that was formed by the preceding queue arrivals. In general, $A(t)$ is the set on which, at any time t, the price setter bases his pricing decision, and does not necessarily have to equal the current queue.

the price guarantee, knows this upper bound. Long-run differences between bidding levels and packet charges, as materialized in periodic billing information, are likely to influence the behavior of the user: for example, the user may bid higher for better quality, or use more resources.

Other Technologies

There is no inherent dependency on charging unit in the ECI approach since only expenditure feedback is essential to create incentives for end-user regulation. User involvement as discussed here can be used for real-time purchase of goods in other systems such as connection-oriented networks. When rate is dynamically priced (Murphy and Murphy 1994), the user can regulate his rate requirement in real time. In a more complex situation when both rate and buffers are priced (Low and Varaiya 1993), the user may control both or some composite thereof. Again, both rate and buffer allocation form incomprehendible input goods, so the user has to learn the price-quality relationship and therefore relies on explicit expenditure feedback from the ECI and implicit quality feedback through the application.

Implementation

An implementation of the ECI requires modifications at both the application and transport level. The following figure illustrates one candidate implementation.

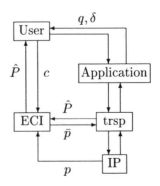

The user perceives quality q from the application and possibly δ, the completion ratio of a bulk transfer. He applies control c toward the ECI, which is (k, m, u) for the general expenditure rate controller, or $\tilde{p}$ for the Smart Market expenditure per-request controller. His decisions are based on expenditure feedback $\hat{P}$, which is a fairly accurate xp in the general case, or an upper bound $x\tilde{p}$ for the Smart Market; x is actual usage as reported by TCP. The ECI may supply $\hat{P}$ via a textual or a graphical information display and receive c via keyboard entries or window selections.

Although TCP currently defers IP submissions when the congestion window or the receiver window is empty, it must now perform an additional test on an ECI-controlled variable $\tilde{x}$. ECI updates $\tilde{x}$ every k time units as $\tilde{x} = \tilde{P}/p$ where $\tilde{P}$ = um and p is the prevailing network price. If surplus carryover is allowed, the ECI sets $\tilde{x} = (\tilde{P} + a)/p$ where a is the surplus of the previous period.[3]

In the additional test, TCP will submit an IP packet if $\tilde{x} > 0$ and, if so, decrease $\tilde{x}$ by one. In the Smart Market, the user does not need to constrain usage rate, so $\tilde{x} = \infty$, but $\tilde{p}$ must be known by TCP for insertion into the IP header. A TCP that serves multiple users must be able to identify which $\tilde{x}$ to test and update, or for the Smart Market, which $\tilde{p}$ to insert.

An implementation needs to address, among other issues, how to facilitate interprocess communication between the ECI and the communication software, and allow a study of perturbations to the fine-tuned TCP and UDP transport protocol operation.

Communicating User Input to the Kernel TCP, UDP, and IP are parts of the kernel and any user input has to be communicated via system calls. IP is normally accessed by the application via sockets, so

---

3. This scheme resembles the Leaky Bucket traffic shaper in that it restricts burstiness of the output traffic (as described, for example, in Bala et al. 1990). At a rate of 1/k, the shaper generates $\tilde{x}$ new permits (with or without carryover). Burstiness in the outgoing IP traffic can increase with increases in user-controlled u, m or k. If carryover is allowed, it may be desirable to specify (by the system, not the user) an upper limit B on how much the period budget can accumulate to, the maximum burst that can emanate is B/p within a period. The modified budget update rule is then that the ECI sets $\tilde{x} = \min[B/p, (\tilde{P} + a)/p]$. The utility of the expenditure bounder as a traffic shaper may be low since the short time scale window adjustment procedures mentioned earlier will limit bursts in times of congestion.

user-to-kernel communication can be established by extending the socket structure with needed state variables and accessing these via the setsockopt() and getsockopt() system calls.

In general, there are multiple users, each operating one ECI. Each user starts multiple applications which in turn may establish multiple sockets to communicate remotely. The user's ECI must know the socket handler for each of the user's sockets to ensure that the user control is applied to all IP traffic that generates monetary charges toward that user.

When the user controls limit the usage limits to $\tilde{x}$, the ECI communicates $\tilde{x}$ with a setsockopt() call. To provide expenditure feedback, the ECI applies a getsockopt() on each of its supporting sockets and multiplies the usage by the current price level to get expenditure. Usage is the difference in usage limit as reported between successive calls. TCP decreases the usage limit $\tilde{x}$ by one for each unit consumed and will submit datagrams as long as $\tilde{x}$ is positive for that datagram's socket.

In the Smart Market case, the user controls $\tilde{p}$, the bid level that is to be associated with all IP packets originating from the user's applications. One implementation is to have the IP header carry the bid, as proposed by MacKie-Mason and Varian (1995). More detailed, the IP header has an 8-bit Type of Service (TOS) field that is set to the socket's TOS for each IP packet submitted. To alter this to $\tilde{p}$, the ECI uses setsockopt(), whereas to provide expenditure feedback, the ECI performs a getsockopt() and uses the differential between successive calls to find interval usage. Accumulated expenditures then must be increased by the interval usage times the current bid level. Again, this is an upper bound on expenditures that may have to be adjusted periodically with periodic charging information from the ISP.

Performance and Configuration The existing TCP/IP communications subsystem is a fine-tuned system and the proposed changes have been found, in simulations and experiments, to have some major effects. One effect of a real-time controllable $\tilde{p}$ is that the bid-queuing subnetwork may deliver packets out of the original order. While TCP ensures proper ordering, other transport protocols do not (although these are typically used by applications that do not require full order preservation). Second, TCP uses incoming acknowledgment packets to clock its output packet rate. If the user throttles TCP from sending packets, eventually there will be no incoming acknowledgment packets and TCP will lose its clock. The slow-start clock probing technique should therefore be run in the event that all data packets are acknowledged (Jacobson 1988).

On a longer time scale, the question arises about the extent to which existing networks have to be reconfigured to accomodate a usage-sensitive pricing system and ECI control at endpoints. Reconfiguration is only needed in the elements of the network that are going to be priced and in those that are going to host users that will be charged for use of these priced elements. If usage-sensitive prices are used for backpressure control within an Autonomous System, as discussed above, end-user-controlled ECIs will have to be installed only for end systems within the AS, whereas an automatically controlled ECI will be needed in the AS-to-AS connecting switch. Adoption of ECI-based resource allocation can therefore take place in steps, AS by AS.

Related Work and Conclusion

Incentive-based allocation has received considerable attention from various groups, and some very recent work promotes ideas of user involvement similar to those laid out in this chapter. First, the idea of incentive control extends to non-price-based ones where the end-users face some form of social pressure which in turn motivates self-regulation. This may be particularly effective in user groups where users know each other and can observe each other's contribution to the system load. The expected expenditure in selecting actions will depend on who the user thinks will receive quality degradation and the type of social contract that exists between these two individuals (Estrin and Zhang 1990). Prototype work on social regulation was undertaken in a RACE initiative, but without reports on welfare effects (MITS 1995).

R & D for Advanced Communications Technologies in Europe

When the individual load contribution is invisible, as for IP networks, the regulating effect of any social contract vanishes and necessitates price-based regulation. Among recent proposals two specifically promote user involvement in the allocation process. MacKie-Mason et al. (1996) envision users who periodically decide period usage based on the reported price per unit, i.e., per IP packet. Via simulations the authors estimate positive benefits from real-time user involvements. Clark (1996) provides a simple mechanism that IP networks can use to support service descrimination. In his model, users will contract with ISPs on the basis of a usage profile. He assumes that the ISPs will be able to communicate the implications of a transmission-rate-based usage profile to end-users in such a way that users can define their needs in terms of such a profile, even though it is not clear how this will be done. When usage exceeds the profile, the network will drop this traffic first if congestion exists in the network.

Our work resides at a layer above either of these mechanisms. These proposals assume that users can specify certain network-level parameters, whereas we think that users want to regulate parameters they can relate to, and that expenditure is a natural parameter for users who are subject to dynamic price-based allocation. An Expenditure Controller Interface is therefore proposed to allow users to bound expenditure. The ECI will subsequently transform user-level controls into network-level service requests. Users will, at their own pace, regulate their expenditure rates to maximize their net benefits. At the same time, the ECI operates at a much faster rate as an agent for the user in responding to signals from a high-frequency network-service price process.

Expenditure control input from the user is a representative that the ECI has to translate into a network-level period request, such as usage limits and packet rates (as in the above-mentioned proposals), packet bid levels (as in the Smart Market case), or more sophisticated service request formats (as in connection-oriented ATM networks). The ECI model provides distributed resource control in line with traditional Internet design philosophies (Clark 1989), and is, we think, by its analogies relatively simple to learn and use. Finally, experiments on a closed IP network using NetBSD and 4.4 BSD (the Berkeley version of Unix) communication protocols are currently being performed to determine the welfare effects of allowing the user to influence allocation via an Expenditure Controller Interface.

References

Baeza-Yates, R., J.M. Piquer and P.V. Poblete. 1993. The Chilean Internet connection, or I never promised you a rose garden. In *Proceedings of INET'93*.

Bala, K., I. Cidon and K. Sohraby. 1990. Congestion control for high speed packet switched networks. In *IEEE Infocom'90*: 520–526.

Braden, R.T., D. Clark, and S. Shenker. 1994. Integrated services in the Internet architecture: An overview. RFC1633: Internet Request For Comment. Available from http://www.ietf.org.

Brownlee, N. 1995. NeTraMet and NeMaC. Network Traffic Meter and NeTraMet Manager/Collector, ver. 3.2. Tech. report, Computer Centre, University of Auckland.

Brownlee, N. 1996. New Zealand's experiences with network traffic charging. In *Internet economics*, ed. L. McKnight and J. Bailey. Cambridge, Mass.: MIT Press.

Clark, D. 1996. A model for cost allocation and pricing in the Internet. In *Internet economics*, ed. L. McKnight and J. Bailey. Cambridge, Mass.: MIT Press.

Clark, D. 1989. Design philosophy of the DARPA network protocols. *ACM Computer Communications Review*.

Danielsen K. 1993. Price-quality telephony. Working Paper, Information Science Department, University of Pittsburgh.

Edell, R.J., N. McKeown and P.P. Varaiya. 1995. Billing users and pricing for TCP. *IEEE Journal on Selected Areas in Communications*.

Estrin, D., and L. Zhang. 1990. Design considerations for usage accounting and feedback in internetworks. *ACM Comparative Communications Review*, 20(5): 56–66.

Floyd, S., and V. Jacobson. 1992. On traffic phase effects in packet-switched gateways. *Journal of Internetworking: Research and Experience*, 3(3): 115–156.

Floyd, S., and V. Jacobson. 1995. Link-sharing and resource management models for packet networks. *IEEE/ACM Transactions on Networking*.

Gupta, A., D.O. Stahl and A.B. Whinston. 1996. A priority pricing approach to manage multi-service class networks in real-time. In *Internet economics*, ed. L. McKnight and J. Bailey. Cambridge, Mass.: MIT Press.

Hume, S., M. Lewis and C. Edlund. 1995. Operator performance at network scheduling with dynamic pricing and limited capacities. In *1995 Conference on Systems, Man and Cybernetics*.

Internet Requests for Comment. http://www.ietf.org.

Jacobson, V. 1988. Congestion avoidance and control. *ACM Comparative Communicative Review* (ACM SIGCOMM '88): 314–329.

Jain, R. 1990. Congestion control in computer networks. *IEEE Network;* 4(5): 24–30.

Jain, R. 1991. *The art of computer systems performance analysis.* New York: Wiley & Sons.

Lehr, W. and M.B. Weiss. 1995. The political economy of congestion charges and settlements in packet networks. In *Proceedings of the 1995 Telecomunications Policy Research Conference*

Low, S.H., and P.P. Varaiya. 1991. A simple theory of traffic and resource allocation in ATM. *IEEE Globecom:* 1633–1637.

Low, S.H., and P.P. Varaiya. 1993. A new approach to service provisioning in ATM networks. *IEEE/ACM Transactions on Networking.,* 1(5): 547–553.

MacKie-Mason, J.K., L. Murphy, and J. Murphy. 1996. The role of responsive pricing in the Internet. In *Internet economics,* ed. L. McKnight and J. Bailey. Cambridge, Mass.: MIT Press.

MacKie-Mason, J.K., and H.R. Varian. 1995. Pricing the Internet. In *Public access to the Internet,* ed. B. Kahin and J. Keller. Cambridge, Mass.: MIT Press.

MacKie-Mason, J.K., and H.R. Varian. 1994. Economic FAQs about the Internet. *Economic Perspectives.*

Mankin, A. 1990. Random drop congestion control. *ACM Comparative Communicative Review (SIGCOMM'90).*

Mills, C., D. Hirsch, and G. Ruth. 1991. Internet accounting: background. RFC1272: Internet Request For Comment. http://www.ietf.org.

MITS. 1995. D17: Metaphors for PSCS. Technical report, European RACE Initiative.

Murphy, J., and L. Murphy. 1994. Bandwidth allocation by pricing in ATM networks. In *Proceedings of IFIP Broadband Communications '94,* Paris.

Perez, M., and C. Aldana. 1996. Priority pricing on the Internet. In *4th International Conference on Telecom Systems, Modelling and Analysis:* 311–318.

Rassenti, S., V. Smith and K. McCabe. 1994. Designing a real time computer assisted auction for natural gas networks. In *New directions in computational economics,* ed. W.W. Cooper and A.B. Whinston. Amsterdam: Kluwer Publishers.

Shenker, S., D. Clark, D. Estrin and S. Herzog. 1995. Pricing in computer networks: Reshaping the research agenda. In *1995 Telecomunications Policy Research Conference.*

Stahl, D.O., and A.B. Whinston. 1994. A general equilibrium model of distributed computing. In *New directions in computational economics,* ed. W.W. Cooper and A.B. Whinston. Amsterdam: Kluwer Publishers.

Touch, J.D., and D.J. Farber. 1994. An experiment in latency reduction. In *IEEE Infocom.*

Varian, H.R. The Information Economy. http://www.sims.berkeley. edu/~hal/

Vickrey, W. 1961. Counterspeculation, auctions and competitive sealed tenders. *Journal of Finance,* 16: 8–37.

Waldspurger, C.A., T. Hogg, B.A. Huberman, J.O. Kephart, and W.S. Stornetta. 1992. Spawn: A distributed computational economy. *IEEE Transactions on Software Engineering.*, 18(2): 103–117.

Wenders, J.T. 1987. *The economics of telecommunications.* Cambridge, Mass.: Ballinger.

Wilson, D.L. June 1994. Metering the Internet—users campaign to retain current pricing system. *The Chronicle of Higher Education:* A17–A19.

Acknowledgments

The authors wish to acknowledge valuable discussions with Sam Hume and Dr. Michael Lewis. Ketil Danielsen was supported through grant #100249/410 from the Royal Norwegian Council for Industrial Research. Hal Varian's information server, The Information Economy, has been of great value. NetBSD is generously made available at www.netbsd.org.

Priority Pricing of Integrated Services Networks

Alok Gupta, Dale O. Stahl, and Andrew B. Whinston

Introduction

In the near future a collection of computer networks are going to provide a wide variety of services with an even wider set of user demands with respect to these services. The research community has had a considerable amount of experience with the Internet, and a significant amount of research is being conducted to explore efficient management of the resources (routers, communication links, and even data communication protocols) of these networks. These networks will significantly change the Internet, both technically and in terms of the kinds of services being offered. Today, common examples of Internet services include electronic mail, File Transfer Protocol (FTP), Telnet, Internet Relay Chat (IRC), Gopher, and the World Wide Web, plus limited experience with real-time audio/video services such as MBONE. With the advent of the Web, access to information on the Internet has become easier and more user-friendly—not to mention highly data intensive. The availability of user-friendly interfaces and the high speed of access coupled with higher awareness about these services have already started creating congestion problems on the Internet.

In the near future, personal publishing via the Web or its descendants and an increased number of real-time audio/video applications such as teleconferencing may be offered through public data networks such as the Internet. This will create significant congestion problems on the network, resulting in the degradation of service quality.[1] At present the Internet backbone is comprised of T1 and T3 lines with data transmission speeds of 1.5 megabits per second and 45 megabits per second respectively, which are orders of magnitude greater compared with a couple of years ago when almost the entire backbone was running at 56 kilobits per second. In the next five years, this increase in capacity may grow to gigabit ranges. However, the number of servers and users have both increased by several orders of magnitude in the last three years and, as mentioned earlier, the services provided on the network have become much more data intensive.

We believe that the arguments in favor of simply overprovisioning the capacity of the Internet are erroneous. There are both physical and cost limitations to providing capacity, whereas at the application level the desire for additional capacity seems boundless. Furthermore, future applications on the Internet will inherently have different quality-of-service requirements.[2] Thus it is essential that appropriate resource management techniques be developed and tested for a multi-service class network.

There are, however, several complications in providing resource management schemes that will be universally accepted. The matter is further complicated because different parts of the network will be owned by different entities and, even though different networks owners may be forced to carry packets from other networks via legislation or by mutual agreement, the required quality of service (in terms of response time) may not be available to packets from other networks. The need to deliver different service requirements to different services and users, and for multiple network providers' incentives to deliver desired service quality, indicates that the current nonpriority "best effort" model of the Internet may not be sufficient to sustain a multiservice or integrated service computer network. This, however, does not mean that separate (proprietary) networks have to be developed and maintained for different kinds of services. The positive network externalities of interconnectivity,

1. In this chapter we use the words service quality and service requirement to mean the response time delivered or needed for a particular service.

2. We will elaborate on this further in the next section.

the efficiencies of operation due to availability of different types of services and the potential to provide interoperability between these services, may outweigh the benefits of separate networks—if the negative network externalities or the performance considerations can be addressed.

We believe that a viable approach should have the following characteristics: (1) the network should reduce the excess load from the user end without wasting network resources (for example by congesting routers) when users can reschedule without any loss in their value; (2) the network should take the impact of the current load on future arrivals into account; (3) pricing should preferably be coarser than packet-level pricing so that it is easier and less costly to implement; (4) the load status of the network nodes (routers, gateways) should be taken into account in the decision-making process of users; (5) the approach should be implemented in a completely decentralized manner, thus not requiring any central governing body and allowing for interaction with other possible resource management schemes; (6) the approach should result in effective load management; (7) the network should have multiple priorities to take into account the differing quality of service required by different applications and users; and (8) the approach should be implemented in such a way that users have incentives to make the right decisions and service providers have incentive to provide the right level of service.

In rest of this chapter we present a detailed discussion of the issues relevant for the management of an integrated service computer network and propose a priority-pricing scheme which has the potential to address many of the required attributes for a resource management scheme. In the following section we discuss the future of the computer networks, the different types of services and their network resource requirements, and the interaction of different players that will constitute the electronic marketplace. In the third section we provide the details of our priority-pricing scheme and discuss the potential of this approach in facilitating electronic commerce. In the fourth section we explain how our pricing approach can be implemented in real time. In the fifth section we provide detailed results from our extensive simulation study, and in the sixth section we discuss issues related to actual implementation in a data communication network. We conclude with directions for future research.

The Future of the Computer Networks

At present various types of communication networks provide a wide range of telecommunications services, such as voice communications on telephone networks, business transactions on proprietary or leased networks, and data communication on private/public computer networks. However, a computer's ability to transfer any kind of data in digital form and then transmit/receive it enables a variety of services to be offered or tested over public computer networks. In the near future it is conceivable that a single network architecture may be able to handle different types of data communication requirements imposed by different services. Figure 1 illustrates a conceptual figure of such a network (note that users may be on servers themselves and may be accessing services on other servers, or pro-

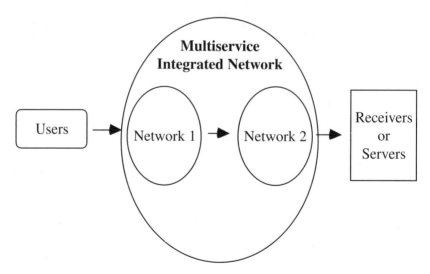

Figure 1
A Multiservice Integrated Network with Multiple Infrastructure Providers

viding services to other servers or users). In this section we examine the types of data communication networks that might be integrated, types of services that may be offered along with their service requirements, and the question of how an appropriately designed pricing policy may help to manage the resources in such an environment.

By a single network architecture we mean that the users may have a single interface to a communication network through which they will be able to access any application. Clearly this requires a tremendous amount of interoperability within the physical infrastructure and between the different parties involved, such as service providers, infrastructure providers, and software developers. There is a relatively strong consensus that packet-switching technology will be the technology of choice to meet this interoperability requirement (Shenker 1995). Within packet-switching technology, however, there are several protocols which may be chosen as a communication protocol including TCP/IP, ATM, and User Datagram Protocol (UDP). There are several ways to achieve technological interoperability among competing technologies, e.g., by enveloping[3] packets in an appropriate protocol or by using multiple protocol routers. However, for the purpose of this chapter we focus on: (1) the rationale for providing interoperability between services and thus for the technology[4]; (2) the mechanism needed to provide this interoperability; and (3) the incentive for infrastructure providers to provide appropriate service levels to users from different subscriber bases.

To understand the aforementioned issues we first have to understand the types of services and applications which may have to be provided or for which this *single* data communication network will be used. These services range from simple email to multimedia real-time teleconferencing. However, from our point of view, it hardly matters what applications do; the important aspect is the service requirement. For example, whereas email may be considered to have relatively small sensitivity to delay, a voice conversation

---

3. Enveloping refers to a technique in which packets of one type are packaged in the packets of another type for transmission purposes; for example, at present the MBONE packets that are normally in UDP format may be enveloped within TCP/IP.

4. We address this relationship later in this section.

may be extremely delay-sensitive. It is possible to define several categories of service quality depending upon the required response time by an application; Figure 2 provides one such categorization which is based on the delay requirements of an application. Other categorizations may be defined by taking into account the data requirement (or size) of different applications (for example, see Shenker 1995); however, for the purpose of our discussion this categorization is sufficient.

Another important aspect of application requirements is sensitivity to lost packets. Typically, in a TCP/IP network, the receiving application waits until it receives all the packets before presenting it to the user because the traditional alphanumeric data is rather sensitive to incomplete information. In some future applications (e.g., real-time video) some packets may be dropped (and not resent) without much loss in presentation because of redundancy in the data. However, some applications may be real-time as well as very sensitive to dropped packets (e.g., audio conversations—except for the silences of human speech). The different delay requirements coupled with the sensitivity to lost packets will virtually force future data communication networks to support multiple service classes with multiple data transfer protocols.

Bohn et al. (1994) suggest a voluntary precedence level choice for different applications dependent upon their delay requirements and loss sensitivity. In their scheme, the user's traffic is monitored after some time interval (say, monthly), and the user may be penalized if she does not choose appropriate precedence for her application.

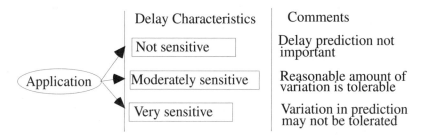

Figure 2
Relationship Between Delay Characteristics and Delay Prediction

There may be a lack of incentive to provide multiple precedence networks on the part of network providers under this scheme since the providers may not be appropriately rewarded for providing multiple service classes.[5] Moreover, it would be a mistake to categorize the service requirements by just looking at the appearance or title of an application; rather, we must look at the context in which an application is used. For example, email-based real-time transaction systems are being developed by some researchers (see Kalakota et al. 1995), as well as email-based Electronic Data Interchange (EDI) systems. Clearly in such applications even email cannot tolerate a significant delay. We believe only users can truly know what level of service is tolerable for their purposes and service providers should only play a passive role in deciding the service quality—which can only be ensured through a proper incentive mechanism.

The next part of the problem arises from the fact that the Internet of the future will comprise several multi-service class data communication networks. Besides the technological issue of interoperability, one has to provide enough incentive for these individual networks to provide similar service class levels across the whole network. Specifically, why will a network provide a high service class to a request from another network without proper incentive, and if a price is quoted, how will a network requesting a service class know whether it is fair?

In the next section we introduce a priority-pricing model that has the potential to be a good resource allocation mechanism in real time. It can be implemented in a completely decentralized manner in which individual networks need to worry only about the loads on their systems to compute near-optimal prices. Users of the network services will make myopic decisions which will lead to socially optimal choices. The priority classes can be associated with the service classes. Table 1 provides a hypothetical example where there are four user priority classes available[6] in a multiple service class network

---

5. Even if this approach is interpreted as a "ticket" approach where network providers sell these tickets for accessing different service classes, the larger question remains—i.e., how to price these tickets for appropriate incentives.

6. There may be more priority classes than users are allowed to use in order to perform important network management tasks, which may indeed take precedence over any other usage.

Table 1
A Hypothetical Example Associating Priority Classes to Service Classes

Priority Class	Service Class
1 - Highest Priority	Real-time services with no tolerance for lost packets
2	Real-time services that are relatively tolerant to lost packets
3	Higher best effort level
4 - Lowest Priority	Lower best effort level

where highest priority is associated with continuous real-time data that is sensitive to dropped packets, second priority is for continuous real-time data that is relatively tolerant to dropped packets, third priority is for higher-level best effort service, and lowest priority is for lower-level best effort service. Multiple-level best effort service may provide a finer division of delay requirements which consumers may want. In our opinion, relative flexibility in performance constraints for lower-priority classes is an important element. Another scheme which divides services into essentially two classes is presented by Wang, Peha, and Sirbu (1996).

Priority-Pricing Approach

In Gupta, Stahl, and Whinston (1996a) we present a priority-pricing mechanism for network computing in which the priority prices are essentially a congestion toll, or, in other words, a priority price at a node is the collective system valuation of access to that node in a particular priority. In this model, user service requests are modeled as a stochastic process and network nodes are modeled with priority queues. An incoming request is associated with an instantaneous value for the service and a linear rate of decay (delay cost) for this value. A user request can be fulfilled through several alternatives, each associated with a price and expected performance (waiting time). A user is interested in the lowest total cost for a service, including the cost of delay, since it maximizes the user's value for the requested service. Since the total cost includes the delay cost, the total cost reflects the user's performance requirement (e.g., a large delay cost implies low tolerance for delays). An optimal choice is reflected by a choice of an alternative in a particular priority class, dependent upon the user's instantaneous value and delay cost.

This model is based on general equilibrium theory in economics, but departs from the Arrow-Debreu framework in a manner that makes the results computationally practical. In a pure Arrow-Debreu model, a commodity would be defined for every contingency and every moment in time. Given stochastic demands for computational services, the full state-space model would be much too large for practical purposes. In lieu of state-contingent equilibrium prices, we introduce the concept of a "stochastic equilibrium" in which (1) average flow rates of service requests are optimal for each user given the prices and anticipated delay, and (2) the anticipated delays are the correct *ex ante* expected delays given the average flow rates. Furthermore, an optimal stochastic equilibrium is one which maximizes the net social benefits. We derive a formula that characterizes the priority prices that support an optimal stochastic equilibrium.

This equilibrium concept (and associated results) has significant informational and computational implications. First, it allows the decentralization of the resource allocation process to the user level and reduces the information required for the user's decision to current rental prices and current expected delays. The administrative and communication costs of distributing this information pale in comparison to the associated costs of the extremely large number of Arrow-Debreu contingency markets (or even spot auction markets). Second (as presented in more detail later), prices can be adjusted in real time in a manner that pushes them into (and keeps them in) a neighborhood of theoretically optimal prices, and this process can be decentralized as well. Again, the computational and communication costs of this mechanism pale in comparison to those of fixed-point algorithms for Arrow-Debreu equilibrium prices.

Although it might be impossible to achieve exact optimal pricing in practice for a volatile environment such as the Internet, we contend that it is possible to compute near-optimal prices in real time. As a result of this near-optimal pricing, users with different values for the same service will choose different ways or times to obtain the same service. This, in turn, can substantially reduce peak loads and will achieve better distribution of the load over time.

These results are based on an objective function which maximizes collective benefits of the system and its users. The natural question to ask is: Why should network service providers be concerned about collective benefits of the system? The primary reason is that the market on the Internet can essentially be viewed as a service industry, and customer satisfaction is directly related to the market share in the service industry. The issue of interoperability with other subnetworks also may force these providers to look for a socially optimal choice since without interoperability a subnetwork will become a deserted information island with little value.

From a practical standpoint these results are significant. The priority prices at the servers decentralize the management and accounting problems, and give the users or their clients access to an evaluation mechanism to decide what kind of service they want, when they want it, and at what priority. At the server level, priority pricing will allow the management to assess the queues and delays more accurately and design their systems accordingly. Priority prices will also enable servers to maintain or delete different classes of services depending on the type of traffic they experience. At the network level, priority prices will allow for a better load distribution because excessively loaded and thus highly priced servers would be avoided by users; thus priority prices will foster proper incentives to provide equivalent classes of services across the network.

The price at a particular server for a particular priority class can be represented by the following system of equations (see the appendix for the mathematical model):

$$r_{mk}(q) = \Sigma_l \, \Sigma_q] \partial \Omega_1 / \partial \chi_{mkq}] \, \Sigma_i \, \Sigma_j \, \delta_{ij} \, x_{ijlm} \qquad (1)$$

where:

- $r_{mk}(q)$ is the price of a job sized q at server m for priority class k;
- χ_{mkq} is the arrival rate of jobs sized q at machine m in priority class k;
- Ω_l is a continuously differentiable, strictly increasing function of arrival rate χ_{mkq} and capacity v_m, which provides the waiting time at a server m for priority class l;
- δ_{ij} is the delay cost parameter of consumer i for service j; and
- x_{ijlm} is the flow rate of service j for consumer i with priority k at server m.

Let us briefly interpret this equation. The first term on the right side $(\partial\Omega_1/\partial\chi_{mkq})$ is the derivative of waiting time with respect to the arrival rate of jobs sized q. Since the waiting time is a strictly increasing function of this arrival rate, an increase in the arrival rate of a certain priority class increases the prices for that priority class. The second term $(\Sigma_i\ \Sigma_j\ \delta_{ij}\ x_{ijlm})$ can be interpreted as the accumulated delay cost of the system; an increase in this cost increases the price. Since the jobs in the highest priority class impose delays on the jobs in all other priority classes, whereas the jobs in the lowest priority classes impose very little delay on the jobs in other priority classes, the prices for higher priority classes are higher than those of lower priority classes. These prices are optimal congestion tolls. Other approaches to congestion tolls are provided by Mendelson and Whang (1990), Stahl and Whinston (1991), MacKie-Mason and Varian (1994), Shenker (1995), and MacKie-Mason et al. (1996).

Clark (1996), who provides an "expected capacity" allocation proposal, argues that a priority scheme will result in lower throughput for lower priority classes. In our scheme, facing the priority prices and expected throughput times, users will adjust their demand in a manner that increases the value of the throughput while decreasing the volume, thus increasing social welfare. Clark's assertion that the "highest priority can pre-empt all the available capacity" may be true for voluntary priority classification schemes such as the one suggested by Bohn et al. (1994). However, in our scheme the choice of priority is inseparable from bearing the cost (via prices) of that choice. While the highest priority could still dominate in our scheme, that will happen only when it is the socially optimal resource allocation and will not arise by user manipulation.

The optimal prices can only be computed if the optimal arrival rates are known and true equilibrium waiting times are known. We propose an iterative approach in which the current estimates of the prices are computed given the historical information on flow rates and waiting times. This iterative approach can be implemented and analyzed by using simulation techniques by which we estimate the prices using the transient information to guide the system toward a stochastic equilibrium. In the next section we first introduce the iterative approach and the conceptual model of the Internet that we

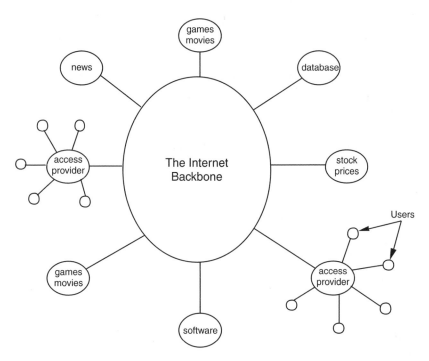

Figure 3
A Conceptual Model of The Internet

are using to evaluate our pricing scheme, and then we present the simulation model that we are using to estimate the prices and calculate the benefits.

Iterative Price Computation and the Simulation Model

Figure 3 presents a conceptual model of the Internet. Essentially, we model the Internet infrastructure as a black box, i.e., we aggregate the total delay at the server such that it appears that delay is only suffered at the server.[7] The users are connected to the Internet through access providers (which we can also consider as a service).

7. This assumption is used to simplify the model; however, the results presented here can easily be extended to cases in which the delay is suffered at multiple nodes as shown in Gupta, Stahl, and Whinston (1995).

The access providers and the service providers (e.g., offering news, movies, video-conferencing, and databases) are "directly" connected to the Internet through a data pipeline of a certain capacity. In this model, the capacity of the data pipeline is essentially the bottleneck for the service providers.[8] In the absence of any pricing mechanism as more users demand a service, the quality of the service (in terms of data transfer rates) suffers.[9] Furthermore, as congestion increases at the data pipeline, the backbone also experiences more load because of the resending of lost packets. The network service providers are able to monitor the loads at different servers, and they impose prices according to the load imposed by the servers on the backbone due to the congestion at their gateways.

The prices are computed based on the system of equations presented in the previous section. However, since these prices are not estimated at the equilibrium conditions, they are approximate at any given time. We implement the following iterative equation to update the prices at any given time $(t+1)$:

$$r_{mk}^{t+1} = \alpha \, \hat{r}_{mk}^{t+1} + (1 - \alpha) \, r_{mk}^{t} \tag{2}$$

where:

- α is a number between $(0,1)$;
- $\hat{r}_{mk}^{t+1}$ is the estimated new price at time $(t+1)$ using equation (1); and
- r_{mk}^{t} is the implemented price during the time $(t, t+1)$.

The idea behind updating the price this way is to provide a shield against local fluctuations in demand and the stochastic nature of the process. A lower value of the parameter α means that the price adjustment will be gradual in time, whereas a higher value will result in potentially large changes in the prices from period to period. In

---

8. From the users' perspective, in reality, the bottleneck is either the server's pipeline or the slowest data communication link in their path to the server.

9. Note that some users might decide not to get the service because of the excessive delays; however, users with negligible delay costs will try to obtain the service regardless of the delays. Thus with no pricing mechanism, the services can potentially be accessed only by the users who value it the least.

our experience with the simulations we have found that smaller values of α, of the order of 0.1, result in reasonably quick convergence and higher stability in prices.

We test our pricing mechanism by using a simulation platform. The objectives of the simulations are twofold: (1) to provide a sense of the degree of improvement an appropriately designed pricing scheme may provide; and (2) to gain insight into the real-time implementation of a pricing mechanism. Very little is known about the performance and/or design of feedback mechanisms to control the processes in real time. To our knowledge, our effort is the first systematic, theoretically supported approach to such real-time problem-solving. We have gained valuable insights and have developed several mechanisms for consistent predictions in real time. The details of these approaches are beyond the scope of this chapter and will be presented in future papers. However, we present a sketch of the overall approach as well as some results.

Figure 4 provides a flow diagram of the simulation model we are using at present. The arrival rates of the system are price/cost sensitive; to explore the effect of scaling, we vary a parameter X_o. Suppose with X_o the optimal arrival rates of jobs entering the system is x_o. As we increase X_o to X_o', the service requests increase and more users try to enter the system. However, the prices also increase, resulting in an optimal arrival rate of x_o', which usually is not directly proportional to the increase in X_o. Alternatively, we can interpret X_o as the arrival rate of the system that would occur if there were free access and zero expected waiting times (i.e., the hypothetical uncongested arrival rate or the demand for network services). Note that realized arrivals into the system are always less than X_o. Figure 5 graphically illustrates the above-mentioned phenomenon.

Upon the arrival of a service request, the type of service required is identified; a service is characterized by the amount of computational cycles required at a server. Next the current estimates of prices and predicted waiting times are obtained for all the servers offering the particular service. The user then evaluates the total expected cost of this service in terms of her delay cost and the service cost against her value of the service. If the total cost of the service is higher than her value for the service, the user quits the system.

Priority Pricing of Integrated Services Networks

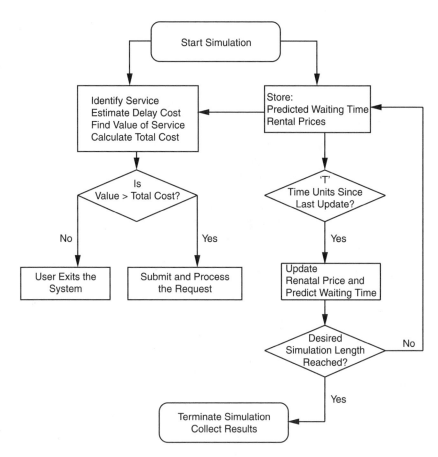

Figure 4
Flow Chart of the Simulation Model

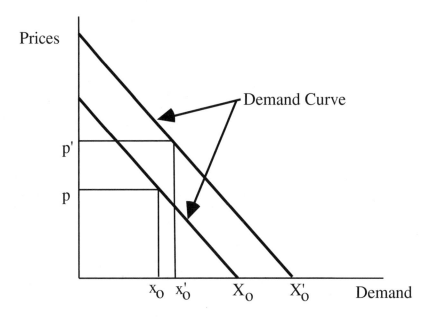

Prices

p'

p

x_O x_O' X_O X_O' Demand

Demand Curve

Figure 5
Effect of Scaling Parameter X_O

Otherwise she submits a request to obtain the service.[10] We generate user values and delay costs from normal distributions. The mean delay costs are set to be less than 1% of the mean job value.

A user's request is sent to the server that was chosen as the least cost server. For example, if a service is available at five servers, then the user estimates the total cost of the service by adding his expected delay cost and network services cost at all five servers and chooses the one where the total cost is expected to be the smallest. If the server queue is empty, the request is immediately processed. However, if some job requests exist in the server queue, then the requests are handled in a first in, first out manner by priority class.

The estimates of waiting times and prices are updated every T units of time. Although we can conceivably update the expectations whenever a request is made, we find three major arguments for

10. Realistically, this work would be done by a smart agent on the user's machine. We discuss this and more implementation issues later in the chapter.

less frequent updates in stochastic systems: (1) estimating waiting times and prices over a longer time period provides more stable results; (2) once we are in the vicinity of the stochastic equilibrium, the small fluctuations in prices will not warrant frequent updates; and (3) the computational effort required in recomputing the prices and waiting times at each request might negate any benefits derived from pricing. However, as other parameters are changed, the update interval also must be changed for any cross-comparison of results.

The results presented here are based on a model that has 50 servers and 100 services. The capacity of the data pipelines at the servers, which are generated through a random process, are among the following: (1) 128 kilobits per second; (2) 256 kilobits per second; (3) 384 kilobits per second; (4) 1.544 megabits per second; (5) 4.0 megabits per second; and (6) 10.0 megabits per second. The first three choices here represent two, four, or six multiplexed Integrated Services Digital Network (ISDN) data channels respectively; the fourth choice is the capacity of a T1 line; and the fifth and sixth choices are typical of those achieved via Frame Relay or Switched Multimegabit Data Services (SMDS) connections. The size of each service is also randomly generated to be in the range of 10 kilobits— 15 megabits (or 1.22 kilobytes—1.8 megabytes); however, the distribution is chosen such that there is a higher number of smaller services to simulate a more realistic service request distribution. Figure 6 displays the service size distribution. A server can provide several of the 100 services. A service can be provided on up to 25 servers; the exact number of servers on which a service is available is generated randomly from a discrete uniform distribution. Figure 7 displays a sample of a service directory that provides information on how many and which services are available on a server, where a service is available and on how many servers. The service directory and the network configuration, in terms of service sizes and server capacities, were kept constant for all the results reported here.

We examine this system under the following pricing policies:

(1) *Free-usage policy.* Under this policy there are no usage-sensitive charges. There may be a monthly connection charge; however, users are not billed for usage in any way.

Gupta, Stahl, and Whinston

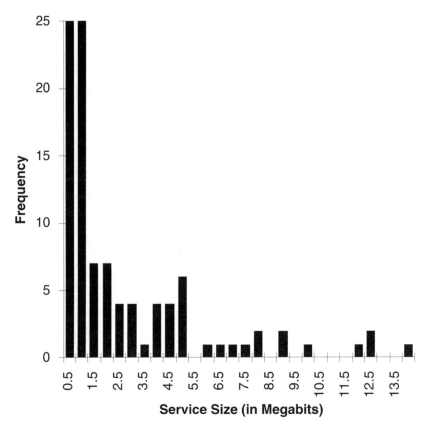

Figure 6
Distribution of Service Sizes Used in the Simulation

(2) *Priority-pricing policy.* As mentioned earlier, this is a usage-sensitive pricing scheme in which users are billed for the bits they transfer.

(3) *Flat-rate pricing policy.* Under this policy, at a given server, every job is charged the same amount regardless of its size. This kind of pricing policy results, for example, in time-based charges in which the amount of data one transfers in a given period of time does not matter.

We compare these three pricing policies under different sets of load conditions by simulating higher loads as higher arrival rates to

Services → Servers ↓	1	2	3	→	98	99	100	Total Number Services
1	0	1	1		0	0	0	20
2	0	0	0	→	0	0	1	16
3	0	0	0		0	1	0	12
↓	↓	↓	↓	↓	↓			↓
46	1	0	0		0	0	0	32
47	1	0	1		1	0	1	4
48	0	0	1	→	0	0	0	22
49	0	0	0		0	0	0	11
50	0	0	0		0	0	0	19
Number of Servers Offering the Service	12	5	16	→	1	2	10	

Figure 7
A Service Directory

the system. A higher arrival rate induces more load on the system and helps in understanding the behavior of a network with fixed capacity under increasing load. Specifically, we examine this model for an arrival rate of 10 to 500; this captures the system behavior under virtually no queues (at the arrival rate of 10) and under extremely long queues (at the arrival rate of 500).[11]

We present our results under two sets of conditions. First we compare the results for all three pricing policies when the perfect information regarding the waiting times is available.[12] However, providing perfect information in any realistic situation is not practical because of the excessive cost involved in computing new information for every new request; furthermore, several requests can be

11. The arrival rate refers to the arrival rate of service requests and uses units of requests per second. The distribution of the service sizes is shown in Figure 6. Therefore, the arrival rate in bits per second can be obtained by multiplying the request arrival rate by average service size.

12. Note that the perfect waiting time information scenario is the best-case scenario for our implementation of the free-access policy because users first check where can they get the fastest service and exact information.

submitted virtually at the same time making this information invalid even it was financially possible to provide perfect information. Thus we also provide results for the case when perfect information regarding the waiting time is not available and only an estimated (or predicted) waiting time is known. In the latter case, both prices and predicted waiting times are updated at the same time, whereas in the former case, only prices are updated after a fixed interval of time while implementing our pricing policy.

Simulation Results

In this section, we provide some results from our simulation testing that compare the benefits derived from different pricing policies with the benefits of providing multiple service classes. We also present some robustness results against customer misrepresentation and discuss the implications of these results. The results presented here are suggestive of the benefit of applying a priority-pricing scheme to Internet services. Essentially, without a pricing mechanism, users with zero or low delay cost have nothing to discourage them from overutilizing the services; however, with a pricing mechanism, they prefer to use only the services for which their value is higher than the cost. In addition, they choose an appropriate service class based on their service requirements. Service providers have incentives to provide multiple service classes because they can simultaneously generate higher revenues and provide better service overall.

First we present results for the case in which perfect information regarding delays is available. As mentioned earlier, exact information cannot be provided in real-world implementations. We provide these results as a benchmark case since these conditions constitute the best-case scenario for free access and flat-rate pricing. It is quite difficult to assess good flat-rate prices in a large network such as the one modeled here; poorly chosen flat-rate prices may in fact provide inferior performance to that of free access. To obtain estimates of good flat-rate prices we collected the average price information during simulation runs with our pricing scheme and then used these average prices as flat-rate prices for the simulations. Since the waiting times in lower priority classes in a network with multiple priority

Priority Pricing of Integrated Services Networks

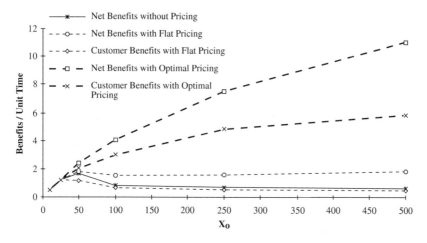

Figure 8
Net and Customer Benefits with Perfect Delay Information

classes depend on the future arrivals in higher waiting classes during their stay in the queue, it is not possible to assess exact waiting times for a network with priority classes. Thus for this case we restrict our attention to simulation results with just one priority class.

Figure 8 presents the results from the simulation with exact waiting time information. The net benefits[13] per unit of time and customer benefits[14] per unit of time are presented for all three pricing policies. The results indicate that as the load on the system increases, our dynamic pricing approach performs better than either the free-access or the flat-rate pricing strategy. Our pricing approach not only is significantly better in terms of net benefits, but the customer benefits are also significantly higher. In fact, our pricing approach delivers higher customer benefits than the net benefits with flat pricing. Figure 8 also suggests that a flat-pricing scheme may be found which is better than free access in terms of net benefits (i.e., it provides additional revenue for service providers) and is comparable in terms of customer benefits and thus customer satisfaction.

13. Net benefits = total value - total delay cost.

14. Customer benefits = net benefits - total price. Note that with free access, net benefits = customer benefits.

Anther important point to realize is that when the network load is low, our pricing scheme delivers the same performance as zero pricing, i.e., the prices adjust according to the load on the system. This is a significant and desirable characteristic of any pricing scheme because it allows for a self-adjusting real-time implementation of our optimal-pricing scheme in data networks where prediction of load is extremely difficult.

Next, we present results for the case in which perfect delay information is not known, but after fixed intervals of time (periods) when prices are updated, future waiting times are estimated. These estimated waiting times are then used by customers to evaluate their service needs. Our experience with the pricing strategies has revealed that it is not possible to predict delay with free access with the same accuracy as with our pricing approach; hence the performance with free access deteriorates exponentially (see Gupta, Stahl, and Whinston 1996b). Thus we do not present results using free access and flat pricing with predicted delays; instead we concentrate on providing results with priority classes.

Figure 9 presents net and customer benefits per unit of time for a nonpriority and a two-priority network. Other details such as customer arrivals, delay costs, and service requirements were kept the

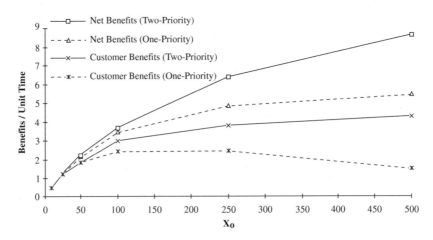

Figure 9
Performance of a One-Priority and a Two-Priority System

same in the simulation runs across these two situations by generating random numbers from the same streams for each parameter in both cases.

Figure 9 indicates that for quite a large range of load a two-priority system performs better than a one-priority system in terms of both net and customer benefits. As the load increases, the net benefits tend to increase; a similar trend can be seen with customer benefits. However, in a fixed-capacity network benefits may only increase in value up to a certain load by using any pricing scheme—we call this the *critical load*. Beyond the critical load a network's performance deteriorates and the only way to increase benefits beyond this point is to increase network capacity. By using our approach and simulation modules it is possible to compute these critical loads and to compare them to the mean loads of any network in order to make rational capacity-expansion decisions.

Some large customers may thus have an incentive to misrepresent their needs in an attempt to artificially increase or decrease prices by providing incorrect information about their delay costs. In economics this is called an incentive compatibility problem. On a data communication network with different customers such as the Internet it is difficult to envision a price scheme that would be absolutely incentive compatible as compared to a centrally managed system (see, for example, Mendelson and Whang 1990). However, we contend that it is more important to have a robust pricing scheme that deviates little from its performance in the case of misrepresentation as compared to correct representation. A robust system may also allow us to avoid any direct query regarding customers' value of delay for pricing purposes since surrogate estimation schemes can be designed for this purpose.

Figure 10 provides a comparison of our pricing policies with and without misrepresentation of delay costs. In the misrepresentation case, customers overquote their value of delay to the network by a mean factor of 125%. It is clear from the figure that very little may be gained from misrepresentation; in fact, performance in a two-priority system is virtually identical. We think that Figure 10 provides evidence that our pricing approach and its implementation is quite robust against misrepresentation of delay cost. This has encouraged

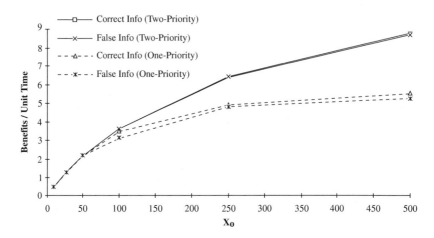

Figure 10
Net Benefits With and Without Misrepresentation

us to develop a surrogate scheme for estimating average delay cost. We are in the initial development process of this surrogate scheme and will present these results in the future.

Implementation Issues

A detailed discussion on implementing a secure priority-pricing mechanism is presented in Gupta et al. (1996c). This paper develops an "Intranet"[15] resource management application using four key components:

(1) *A third-party authentication system.* Such authentication systems (such as Kerberos or SESAME) provide transaction security and data integrity while transmitting data via a public network. Third-party authentication mechanisms can provide centralized service databases and may provide the ability to interact with search engines for undefined services. We propose development of front-end or user interface that will make the access to authentication mechanism transparent to users.

---

15. The term "Intranet" is usually used for a corporate-wide wide area network, parts of which may communicate with each other via public data networks such as the Internet.

(2) *A topology management application.* Such applications (such as IBM's NetView or Hewlett-Packard's OpenView) monitor network traffic and sample performance data. A topology management application monitors service requests on local servers for arrival rates and actual wait times in each priority class. It may also be designed to accumulate totals by service class or for specific server for use by service providers in making capital investment decisions. With some interface modification a topology management application could also interact with performance-forecasting and price computing mechanisms, that use the collected data to forecast performance.

(3) *A performance database.* This database keeps the information obtained from forecasting and price-computing mechanisms. It can be accessed via an authentication mechanism and plays a central role in cost optimization for user service requests by interacting with a cost-optimization module.

(4) *A payment and accounting mechanism.* Design of an efficient payment and accounting mechanism is one of the major concerns in implementing a pricing mechanism. For example, should the infrastructure providers be involved in the accounting of every transaction by receiving payment from each individual and passing it on to the service providers? In our view, revenue collection should be left to the service providers, which in turn can make payments to the infrastructure providers for their services on an aggregate level. This scheme lends itself to a hierarchical accounting system in which the method of accounting in each layer of the hierarchy is "almost" independent of the others; for example, at the lowest level some servers may charge individuals a fixed amount for providing access to the network and other basic services.

Most of the interaction among these various components of a price implementation mechanism will be achieved by platform-independent "software smart agents." Dramatic advances in the field of distributed artificial intelligence are allowing researchers to build increasingly competent "software smart agents" (Etzioni and Weld 1994; Greif 1994; Genesereth and Ketchpel 1994; and Maes 1994). These agents will soon be used in great numbers to facilitate use of many Internet services (Reinhardt 1994; and Wayner 1994). The shift to this new computing paradigm forces us to confront choices regarding how to restructure the user-computer interaction so as to incorporate a new entity that will introduce a complementary style of interaction. Instead of user-initiated interaction via commands and/or direct manipulation, the user will be engaged in a cooperative process in which the user and the software agents both initiate communication, monitor events, and perform tasks.

We are investigating the various subdomains within our pricing model that could be efficiently implemented using software agents for introducing effective usage-based pricing of network services. We will focus on the problem of using software agents to facilitate several aspects of our current research by introducing them in the implementation of our pricing model. We think that software agents could be effectively utilized to manage the individual networks providing Internet services, to maximize the efficiency of the network servers, and to operationalize the user/network interface.

Summary and Conclusions

In this chapter we provide a glimpse of the future of the Internet. The Internet is going to provide a diverse group of services to an even more diverse group of users and their service requirements. The only possible way to realize such a network is by allowing a multi-service class network with possibly a diverse group of data transmission protocols to cater to different service requirements and/or specifications.

We present a priority-pricing approach to manage a multi-service class network. This pricing scheme can be implemented in real time and in a completely decentralized setting. We are developing and testing the implementation by simulating a network of diverse server capacities and service requirements. The simulation involves the feedback of information regarding the expected network performance in the future. The success of any real-time pricing scheme will depend on the reasonable prediction of expected performance. Through our simulation studies we have developed mechanisms that predict these expectations with reasonable accuracy and will provide important guidelines in actual implementations.

Our simulation results provide evidence that significant advantages can be gained by using a priority-pricing approach in data networks. We contend that priority pricing will allow the dynamic management of bandwidth in multiple class networks. Revenue will provide incentives for network service providers to offer appropriate service classes, and cost will provide incentives for customers to choose appropriate service classes. Furthermore, our implementation seems to hold up against misrepresentation, which has encouraged us to develop surrogate estimation procedures for which no user input other than service requirements is required.

Our simulation platform is a powerful tool for exploring various pricing strategies, regulatory impact, and infrastructure investment.[16] It can provide guidelines for capacity expansion and information restructuring. We can also use it to explore the effect of using different pricing strategies by different network entities.

In future research we will concentrate on the development of better estimation techniques and the development and testing of accounting and billing procedures. Specifically, we will evaluate the relative strengths and weaknesses of various accounting and billing schemes by testing their impact on actual processing of data. We will also test the effects of different market structures that may arise in electronic commerce.

Appendix: Mathematical Model

Notation

δ_{ij} Delay cost of customer i for service j

$r_{mk}(q)$ Rental price at server m in priority class k, for q bits

q_j Number of bits associated with service j

$\tau(j, m, k)$ Expected throughput time for service j at server m, in priority class k

---

16. If private infrastructure providers are not provided with appropriate incentives through optimal pricing, then they may have incentives for underprovision of capacity as discussed by Crawford (1996).

p_{ijkm} Probability that customer i will request service j at server m, in priority class k

X_o Demand scaling parameter

λ_{ij} Fraction of X_o associated with customer i for service j

Benefit Maximization

$$B(p, w) \equiv X_o \int\int \Sigma_i \Sigma_j \Sigma_k \Sigma_m \lambda_{ij} [V_{ij} - \delta_{ij} \tau(j, k, m)] \, p_{ijkm} \, dF(V_{ij}, \delta_{ij}) \tag{A1}$$

subjected to

$$w_{mk} \equiv \Omega_k(\chi_m; v_m) \tag{A2}$$

where

χ_m is the matrix of service request arrival rate by job size and priority, and

v_m is the capacity at the server m.

Customer Optimization

The customer costs are optimized as follows:

$$c_{ij}^* (r, w \mid \delta_{ij}) \equiv \min_{m,k} \{\delta_{ij} \tau(s, k, w) + \Sigma_m r_{mk}(q_j)\} \tag{A3}$$

Then the probability that a customer will submit their job is given by

$$p_{ijkm}(r, w \mid V_{ij}, \delta_{ij}) = \begin{cases} 1 \text{ if } V_{ij} > c_{ij}^* (r,w \mid \delta_{ij}) \\ 0 \text{ if } V_{ij} < c_{ij}^* (r,w \mid \delta_{ij}) \end{cases} \tag{A4}$$

The resulting stochastic arrival rate to the system is then

$$x_{ijkm} = X_o \lambda_{ij} \int p_{ijkm} \, dF(V_{ij}, \delta_{ij}) \tag{A5}$$

References

Bohn, R., H.W. Braun, K.C. Claffy, and S. Wolff. 1994. Mitigating the coming Internet crunch: multiple service levels via precedence. Technical report, University of California.

Clark, D.D. 1996. A model for cost allocation and pricing in the Internet. In *Internet economics*, ed. Lee McKnight and Joseph Bailey. Cambridge, Mass.: MIT Press.

Cocchi R., D. Estrin, S. Shenker, and L. Zhang. 1993. Pricing in computer networks: Motivation, formulation, and example. *IEEE/ACM Transactions on Networking* 1(6): 614–27.

Crawford, D. 1996. Pricing network usage—a market for bandwidth or market for communication? In *Internet economics*, ed. Lee McKnight and Joseph Bailey. Cambridge, Mass.: MIT Press.

Cronin, M. 1994. *Doing business on the Internet: How the electronic highway is transforming American companies*. New York: Van Nostrand Reinhold.

Etzioni, Oren and Daniel Weld. 1994. A softbot-based interface to the Internet. *Communications of the ACM* 37(7): 72–76.

Genesereth, M.R. and S.P. Ketchpel. 1994. Software agents. *Communications of the ACM* 37(7): 48–53.

Greif, Irene. 1994. Desktop agents in group-enabled products. *Communications of the ACM* 37(7): 100–105.

Gupta, A., D.O. Stahl, and A.B. Whinston. 1996a. An economic approach to network computing with priority classes." *Journal of Organizational Computing and Electronic Commerce*. Forthcoming.**

Gupta, A., D.O. Stahl, and A.B. Whinston. 1996b. *IMPACT: How IC^2 research affects public policy and business markets: Pricing of services on the Internet*. Forthcoming.

Gupta, A., D.O. Stahl, and A.B. Whinston. 1996c. Managing computing resources in intranets: An electronic commerce perspective. CISM, University of Texas at Austin. Mimeo.

Kalakota, R., J. Stallert, and A.B. Whinston. 1995. Solving operations research problems using a global client/server architechture." CISM, University of Texas at Austin. Working paper.

MacKie-Mason, J.K., and H.R. Varian. 1995. Pricing the Internet. In *Public access to the Internet*, ed. B. Kahin and J. Keller. New York: Prentice-Hall.

MacKie-Mason, J.K., L. Murphy, and J. Murphy. 1996. The role of responsive pricing in the Internet. In *Internet economics*, ed. Lee McKnight and Joseph Bailey. Cambridge, Mass.: MIT Press.

Maes, Patti. 1994. Agents that reduce work and information overload. *Communications of the ACM* 37(7): 31–40.

**A version of this paper is available in postscript form on the World Wide Web server of the Center for Information Systems Management (CISM), University of Texas at Austin. The URL for linking to this server is http://cism.bus.utexas.edu. The paper is under the title of "CISM Working Papers," and it can be viewed with a postscript viewer or it can be downloaded and printed on any postscript printer.

Mendelson, H. 1985. Pricing computer services: Queuing effects. *Communications of the ACM* 28: 312–21.

Mendelson, H., and S. Whang. 1990. Optimal incentive-compatible priority pricing for the M/M/1 queue. *Operations Research* 38: 870–83.

Reinhardt, A. 1994. The network with smarts. *BYTE*, (October): 51–64.

Shenker, S. 1995. Service models and pricing policies for an integrated services Internet. In *Public access to the Internet*, ed. B. Kahin and J. Keller. New York: Prentice-Hall.

Stahl, D., and A.B. Whinston. 1991. A general equilibrium model of distributed computing. Center for Economic Research Working Paper 91-09, Department of Economics, University of Texas. Also in *New directions in computational economics*, ed. W.W. Cooper and A.B. Whinston, 175–89. The Netherlands: Kluwer Academic Publishers.

Spigai, Fran. 1991. Information pricing. *Annual Review of Information Science and Technology* 26: 39–73.

Wang, Q., J.M. Peha, and M.A. Sirbu. 1996. The design of an optimal pricing scheme for ATM integrated-services networks. In *Internet economics*, ed. Lee McKnight and Joseph Bailey. Cambridge, Mass.: MIT Press.

Wayner, Peter. 1994. EDI moves the data. *BYTE* (October): 121–128.

Optimal Pricing for Integrated Services Networks

Qiong Wang, Jon M. Peha, and Marvin A. Sirbu

Introduction

The economics of providing multiple types of services through a single network is a question of growing significance to network operators and users. As a result of the rapid development of packet-switching technology, it is becoming increasingly efficient to provide different telecommunication services through one integrated services network instead of multiple single-service networks, such as telephone networks for voice communications, cable networks for broadcasting video, and the Internet for data transfer. In a packet-switched integrated services network, any piece of information, regardless of whether it is voice, image, or text, is organized as a stream of packets and transmitted over the network. By controlling the packet transmission rate and packet delay distribution of each packet stream, the network can use a single packet transmission technology to provide a variety of transmission services, such as telephony, video, and file transfer.

While integrating multiple services into a single network generates economies of scope, heterogeneous services complicate pricing decisions. For example, users watching high-definition television

The research reported in this chapter was supported in part by the National Science Foundation under grants NCR-9210626 and 9307548-NCR. The views and conclusions expressed here are those of the authors and should not be interpreted as representing the official policies, either expressed or implied, of the National Science Foundation or the U.S. government.

(HDTV) through the network require up to tens of megabits per second transmission capacity, while users who make phone calls only send/receive tens of kilobits per second; telnet users require mean cell transmission delay to be kept below a few tens of milliseconds, but email senders will tolerate longer delay; Web browsing generates a very bursty cell stream, while constant-bit-rate file transfer results in a very smooth cell stream; to carry a voice conversation with acceptable quality under certain encoding schemes, packet loss rate (i.e., the percentage of packets that are allowed to miss a maximum delay bound; usually 30–50 milliseconds for voice conversation) should not exceed 5%, while to carry video service, packet loss rate should be kept much lower (Peha 1991).

Asynchronous Transfer Mode (ATM) technology has emerged as an appropriate basis for integrated services networks. ATM networks have the capability to meet the strict performance requirements of applications like voice and video, and the flexibility to make efficient use of network capacity for applications like electronic mail and Web browsing. The use of fixed-length packets (cells) also facilitates the implementation of high-speed switches. As a result, telephone and cable TV networks will adopt cell-switching technology as they expand the range of services that they offer. The Internet has already begun to offer new services like telephony, but without the guarantee of adequate performance that telephone customers have come to expect. Eventually the Internet will also employ protocols that differentiate packets based on the type of traffic that they carry, and guarantee adequate quality of service appropriate for each service. This could be done by adopting ATM technology, or by adding the capability to guarantee performance through use of protocols like the Resource reSerVation Protocol (RSVP) (Zhang et al. 1993). This chapter will focus on ATM-based integrated services networks since the technology is available today, but trivial extensions would enable the same approach to be applied to any integrated services network that offers quality of service guarantees.

Since there are great differences among the services offered by ATM networks, one might ask whether the prices of these service should also differ, and if so, how? There is some literature on how to price a network that offers heterogeneous services. Cocchi et al.

(1993) study the pricing of a single network that provides multiple services at different performance levels. They give a very impressive example which shows that in comparison with flat-rate pricing for all services, a price schedule based on performance objectives can enable every customer to derive a higher surplus from the service and, at the same time, generate greater profits for the service provider. Dewan and Mendelson (1990) and Whang and Mendelson (1990) have developed a single queuing model in which the network is formulated as a server (or servers) with limited capacity, and consumers demand the same service from the server but vary in both willingness to pay for the service and tolerance for delay. Based on that model, they discuss the optimal pricing policy and capacity investment strategy. MacKie-Mason and Varian (1994) suggest a spot-price model for Internet pricing. In their model, every Internet packet is marked with the consumer's willingness to pay for sending it. The network always transmits packets with higher willingness to pay and drops packets with lower willingness to pay. The network charges a spot price that equals the lowest willingness to pay among all packets sent during each short period. The major benefit of this approach is that it provides consumers with an incentive to reveal their true willingness to pay, and based on that information, the network can resolve capacity contention in transmitting packets in a way that maximizes social welfare. In Gupta, Stahl, and Whinston (1996), priority-based pricing and congestion-based pricing are integrated. In their pricing model, services are divided into different priority classes. Packets from a high-priority class always have precedence over packets from a low-priority class. The price for each packet depends not only on the packet's priority level, but also on the current network load.

In the optimal pricing models mentioned above, the fact that different applications may have different performance objectives was usually *not* considered. For example, Dewan, Whang and Mendelson's work (Dewan and Mendelson 1990; Whang and Mendelson 1990) assumes that the consumer's willingness to pay depends only on expected mean delay, and Mackie-Mason (1996) assumes that consumers do not care about delay—only whether or not their packets are eventually transmitted. There is no way, for example, to accommodate a service that would impose a maximum delay limit. These formulations also do not consider the case of heterogeneous data rate and burstiness. Consequently, pricing policies developed in these studies cannot be applied to ATM integrated services networks in which services differ from each other in terms of performance objectives and traffic pattern (data rate and burstiness). Some of these factors are discussed in Cocchi et al. (1993); however, they do not discuss procedures for designing an optimal pricing scheme. Gupta, Stahl, and Whinston (1996) consider different services that are divided into different priority classes; however, none of these services can be guaranteed a given performance objective under their pricing scheme.

In this chapter, we analyze the problem of pricing and capacity investment for an integrated services network with guaranteed quality of service. Based on an optimal control model formulation, and the demand elasticities of users, we develop a three-stage procedure to determine the optimal amount of capacity and the optimal price schedule. We show that pricing a network service is similar to pricing a tangible product, except that the marginal cost of producing the product is replaced by the opportunity cost of providing the service, which includes both the opportunity cost of reserving and the opportunity cost of using network capacity. Our findings lay out a framework for making investment and pricing decisions, as well as for the analysis of related economic trade-offs.

The Network Service Model

Network capacity is often subadditive, leading to conditions of natural monopoly for an integrated services network operator. In the model which follows, we assume a single profit-maximizing monopolist is operating the network. In this chapter, we consider only a point-to-point single-link network. This frees us from network routing details and allows us to focus our attention on the economic principles for designing pricing policy. The capacity of that link is denoted as C_T, whose unit is the maximum number of cells that can be transmitted over the link per unit of time.

The network is used for providing multiple services. Quality of service is measured by the distribution of cell delay time, where lost cells are considered as being delayed infinitely. A service will be labeled as a "guaranteed" service if during each session the network makes a commitment to meet some prespecified delay objectives. These guarantees are typically expressed in stochastic, not absolute terms; e.g., no more than 5% of the cells will be delayed for more than 30 milliseconds, or the average delay will be less than 200 milliseconds. If no such guarantee is made, the service is considered as best-effort service. Telephone calls, high-definition television, and interactive games typically require some type of guaranteed service, while e-mail is usually specified as a best-effort service.

In our pricing model, the network service provider attempts to maximize profit, which is the sum of profits from guaranteed services and best-effort service. In establishing a tariff for network service, one might charge for access independent of any usage, capacity reservation for guaranteed services, and actual usage. In this chapter, we assume dedicated access is priced at average cost, and the cost of all shared network facilities is recovered through a combination of reservation and usage prices. This assumption allows us to consider reservation and usage prices independent of access prices.

Service Model for Guaranteed Services

Guaranteed services differ from each other significantly in terms of performance objectives, traffic pattern (data rate and burstiness), and call duration distribution. For example, HDTV service has a much stricter performance objective and a 500-times higher mean data rate than telephone service. An HDTV session can take hours to complete, while telephone calls usually last only minutes. The transmission rate of the former (if the data stream is compressed) is also much burstier than that of the latter, which may not be compressed.

In this chapter, we assume the network offers N guaranteed services. Within the same service category i (i = 1, N), calls require the same performance objective, exhibit the same intercell arrival statistics, and have call duration drawn from the same distribution.

We assume the price for a call using guaranteed service is determined by service type i, call starting time, and service duration. For a call of service i which begins at time t, $p_i(t)$ is the price which will

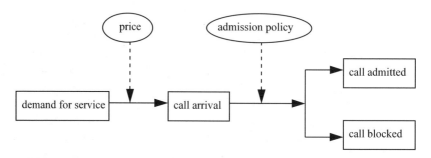

Figure 1
Call Admission Process for Guaranteed Services

be charged for each unit of time that the call lasts. A consumer will be charged a price equal to $p_i(t)$ times the call duration if the call starts at time t. We shall also assume that for calls of a given service, call duration is independent of price.

We define $\lambda_i[p_i(t), t]$ as the arrival rate of calls for service i given that the price of a call which starts at t will be $p_i(t)$ throughout the call.[1] We also assume that at any given price $p_i(t)$, and any given time t, call arrivals form a Poisson distribution, i.e., the number of calls arriving within any period is independent of the number of calls that arrived within previous periods. Note that we have also assumed no cross-elasticity of demand between different services, which may not be realistic. We leave that enhancement for future research.

To meet guaranteed performance objectives, the network can only carry limited numbers of calls simultaneously. These numbers are determined by the performance objectives and traffic patterns of each service. To avoid accepting more calls than they can handle, ATM integrated services networks enforce an admission policy by which a network monitors its current load and decides whether an incoming call should be admitted or rejected (Peha 1993). This

1. The consumer thus expected to pay $\dfrac{p_i(t)}{r_i}$ if call length has a mean value of $\dfrac{1}{r_i}$. It is more typical for a provider to define a price schedule $R_i(t)$ where a call is charged $R_i(t)$ at each instant it is in progress. Our formulation of $p_i(t)$ is related to $R_i(t)$ by $\dfrac{p_i(t)}{r_i} = \int_{t}^{+\infty} R_i(\tau)e^{-r_i(\tau-t)}d\tau$ when call length is exponentially distributed.

process is shown in Figure 1. For the purpose of this chapter, we assume calls are not queued if they cannot be admitted immediately.

For each service i (i = 1, N), we assume the call duration is exponentially distributed with departure rate r_i. Define $q_i(t)$ as the number of calls under way of service i at time t, and $\bar{q}_i(t)$ as the expected value of $q_i(t)$. Under the assumptions we made about call arrival and departure processes, the rate of change of $\bar{q}_i(t)$ should follow:

$$\frac{d\bar{q}_i}{dt} = (1 - \beta_i)\lambda_i(p_i, t) - r_i\bar{q}_i(t)\bar{q} \qquad i = 1, N \tag{1-1}$$

where β_i is the blocking probability.

Since both call arrival and departure are stochastic, unless the network has an infinite amount of capacity, there will always be a possibility of blocking calls. A high blocking probability gives consumers an unpleasant experience with the network and externally reduces demand, but a lower blocking probability also means more capacity will lay idle most of the time. From a network operator's perspective, the blocking probability should be kept at a desired level at which any marginal revenue increase from increasing demand by reducing blocking probability can no longer offset the marginal loss from letting more capacity lay idle. Values of desired blocking probability are usually determined during the process of making long-term capacity investment decisions. In the following, we will show how keeping blocking probability at the desired level will affect short-term pricing decisions:

Suppose the network only offers one service; then the blocking probability at each time can be determined by:

$$\beta = \frac{\dfrac{\rho^H}{H!}}{\displaystyle\sum_{i=0}^{H} \dfrac{\rho^i}{i!}} \tag{1-2}$$

where β is the blocking probability, H is the maximum number of calls that can be carried by the network, and ρ is the product of call arrival rate and expected call duration.

Wang, Peha, and Sirbu

Let $\tilde{\beta}$ be the blocking probability that the network operator desires to maintain. From (1-2), H can be uniquely determined by the desired blocking probability $\tilde{\beta}$ and the network load ρ, i.e., $H = d(\rho, \tilde{\beta})$. In other words, to keep blocking probability at a desired level under given load ρ, the network should be designed to carry H calls. This requirement can be translated into a demand for network capacity: define $\theta(H)$ as the amount of capacity needed to carry H calls, and $\alpha(\rho, \tilde{\beta}) = \theta[d(\rho, \tilde{\beta})]$. Thus $\alpha(\rho, \tilde{\beta})$ can be interpreted as the amount of capacity needed to keep blocking probability at $\tilde{\beta}$ when the network load is ρ.

Since at each time the network load is related to the expected number of calls in progress by $\rho = \dfrac{\overline{q}}{1 - \tilde{\beta}}$, we can also express the amount of capacity needed as a function of expected number of calls in progress as $A(\overline{q}, \tilde{\beta}) = \alpha\left(\dfrac{\overline{q}}{1 - \tilde{\beta}}, \tilde{\beta}\right)$. $A(\overline{q}, \tilde{\beta})$ increases with $\overline{q}$. $A(\overline{q}\,\tilde{\beta})$ is defined as the amount of capacity required to carry an average of $\overline{q}$ calls with blocking probability $\tilde{\beta}$. If capacity required exceeds total capacity C_T, the network either has to admit more calls than it can handle, thus failing to meet some quality of service guarantee, or exceed the desired blocking probability.

At each time t, $\overline{q}(t)$, the expected number of calls in progress, is a function of previous and current prices. Therefore, in the short term, prices should be set such that the reserved capacity can never go above total capacity, i.e.:

$$A[\overline{q}(t), \tilde{\beta}] \leq C_T \qquad \text{at all t} \tag{1-3}$$

Equation (1-3) defines the "admissible region constraint" (see Hyman et al 1993; Tewari and Peha 1995), which specifies the maximum number of calls that can be carried under a given amount of network capacity and a given blocking probability.

The definition of the admissible region constraint can be extended to a multiple services scenario in which the reserved capacity is a function of the expected numbers of calls in progress for all services, which is shown below:

$$A[\overline{q}_1(t), \ldots, \overline{q}_N(t); \tilde{\beta}_N(t)] \leq C_T \tag{1-4}$$

Optimal Pricing for Integrated Services Networks

Service Model for Best-effort Service

Without a performance guarantee, cells of best-effort service will be put in a buffer and transmitted only when there is remaining capacity after the needs of guaranteed services have been met. If there is not enough buffer space for all incoming cells, some of them will be dropped.

In our model, users of best-effort service are charged on a per-cell basis. We assume all cells of best-effort service share a buffer of size B_s. The willingness to pay for sending each cell is revealed to the network. At each time t, the network sets a cut-off price, $p_b(t)$, which is a function of both current buffer occupancy and predicted willingness to pay values of future incoming cells. A cell will be accepted if and only if the willingness to pay for that cell is higher than $p_b(t)$, and $p_b(t)$ will also be the price charged for sending that cell. Accepted cells will be admitted into the buffer as long as the buffer is not full. Once admitted into the buffer, cells will be eventually transmitted according to a sequence dictated by some scheduling

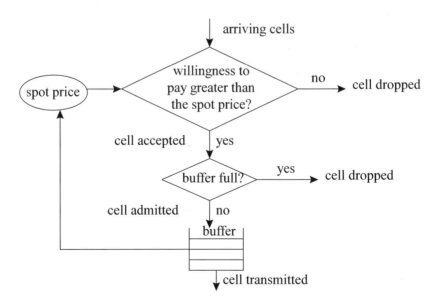

Figure 2
Service Model for Best-effort Service

algorithm, such as first come, first served or cost-based scheduling (Peha 1996).

If we assume that at time t, the arrival process of cells of best-effort service is a Poisson distribution with expected value $\lambda_b(0, t)$, the acceptance of cells is also a Poisson distribution with expected value $\lambda_b[p_b(t), t]$. Define $s_b(t)$ as the instantaneous transmission rate of best-effort service at that time, then:

$$s_b(t) \leq C_T - s[q_1(t), q_2(t), \ldots, q_N(t)] \tag{1-5}$$

where $s[q_1(t), q_2(t), \ldots, q_N(t)]$ is the instantaneous transmission rate of all guaranteed services, which is a function of numbers of calls in progress. Equation (1-5) implies the instantaneous transmission rate of best-effort service cannot exceed the total bandwidth left after transmitting all guaranteed services.

If one accepts the assumptions that: (1) accepted cells constitute a Poisson random process; (2) the instantaneous transmission rate depends on the bandwidth left by guaranteed services, which is also random; and (3) the buffer size is limited, and there is a possibility that even accepted cells (i.e., cells with willingness to pay higher than the cut-off price) can be dropped because the buffer can become temporarily full. Define $\upsilon(t, \Delta t)$ as the number of cells actually admitted into the buffer during the interval [t, t+Δt); then the instantaneous admission rate can be defined as:

$$\omega_b(t) = \lim_{\delta t \to 0} \frac{\upsilon_b(t, \Delta t)}{\Delta t} \tag{1-6}$$

$\omega_b(t)$ is a random variable and we assume its expected value is $\varpi_b(t)$, then

$$\varpi_b(t) \leq \lambda_i[p_b(t), t] \tag{1-7}$$

Define $q_b(t)$ as the number of cells in the buffer at time t, then:

$$\frac{dq_b(t)}{dt} = \varpi_b(t) - s_b(t) \tag{1-8}$$

and

$$s_b(t) \leq q_b(t) \leq B_s \tag{1-9}$$

Optimal Pricing for Integrated Services Networks

The Optimal Pricing Policy

In this section, we will discuss the profit-maximizing pricing policy for network operators. We formulate an optimal control model to derive the pricing policy, and discuss how to solve this model through a three-stage procedure.

The Optimal Pricing Model

Assume a network operator wants to maximize total profit over a period composed of multiple identical business cycles (such as days). The cycle length is T. Her rational behavior would be to choose a price schedule for each type of guaranteed service $p_i(t)$, and best-effort service $p_b(t)$, and the amount of bandwidth C_T to maximize the following objective:

$$\int_0^T \left\{ \sum_{i=1}^{N} (1 - \tilde{\beta}_i) \frac{\lambda_i[p_i(t), t]}{r_i} p_i(t) + \varpi_b(t)p_b \right\} dt - K(C_T) \qquad (2\text{-}1)$$

under constraints:

$$\frac{d\overline{q}_i}{dt} = (1 - \tilde{\beta}_i)\lambda_i(p_i, t) - r_i\overline{q}_i, \ \overline{q}_i \geq 0 \quad i = 1, N \qquad (2\text{-}2)$$

$$A[\overline{q}_i(t), \ldots, \overline{q}_N; \tilde{\beta}_1(t), \ldots, \tilde{\beta}_N(t)] \leq C_T \qquad (2\text{-}3)$$

$$\frac{dq_b(t)}{dt} = \omega_b(t) - s_b(t) \qquad (2\text{-}4)$$

when $q_b(t) = B_s \quad \omega_b(t) \leq s_b(t)$ \qquad (2-5)

$$0 \leq \theta_b(t) \leq B_s \qquad (2\text{-}6)$$

$$s_b(t) \leq C_T - s[q_1(t), q_2(t), \ldots, q_N(t)] \qquad (2\text{-}7)$$

when $q_b(t) = 0 \quad \omega_b(t) \geq s_b(t)$ \qquad (2-8)

$$q_i(0) = q_{i0}, \ i = 1, N \qquad (2\text{-}9)$$

Wang, Peha, and Sirbu

Interpretations of these constraints are the same as discussed in the previous section, and definitions of variables can found there and in the following list:

Variables of guaranteed services:

N	number of different services;
$p_i(t)$	unit price for service i, as a function of call starting time t;
$\lambda_i(p_i, t)$	call arrival rate of service i at time t, when price is p_i;
r_i	call departure rate of service i;
$q_i(t)$	number of calls of service i in progress at time t;
$\overline{q}_i(t)$	expected value of $q_i(t)$;
$s[q_1(t), q_2(t), \ldots, q_N(t)]$	total data rate of all guaranteed services at time t;
$\overline{s}[\overline{q}_1(t), \overline{q}_2(t), \ldots, \overline{q}_N(t)]$	average total data rate of all guaranteed services at time t;
$\widetilde{\beta}_i(t)$	desired blocking probability for service i at time t;

Variables describing best-effort service:

$p_b(t)$	price for admitting one cell into the buffer at time t;
$q_b(t)$	queue length of best-effort service at time t;
$s_b(t)$	cell transmission rate at time t;
$\lambda_b[p_b(t), t]$	cell accepting rate, i.e., arrival rate of cells with willingness to pay higher than $p_b(t)$;
$\omega_b(t)$	admission rate of cells at time t;
$\overline{\omega}_b(t)$	expected value of $\omega_b[p_b(t), t]$;

Other variables:

T	duration of business cycle;

$C_T T$ total bandwidth;

$K(C_T)$ amortization of capacity investment cost over one cycle;

B_S buffer size.

In (2-1), $(1 - \beta_i)\lambda_i$ $(p_i, t)dt$ is the expected number of calls of service i that will be admitted during the period [t, t+dt). Multiplying this number by the unit price, $p_i(t)$, and expected call duration, $\frac{1}{r_i}$, yields the expected revenue from all calls of service i admitted in that interval. At time t, the network also charges a price for each cell of best-effort service that enters the buffer, and $\varpi_b(t)dt$ is the expected number of cells that will enter the buffer at that time. Thus $\varpi_b(t)p_b(t)dt$ is the expected revenue from best-effort service at t. The total expected profit is calculated by summing up expected revenue from all services, accumulated over all time in [0, T], minus the amortized capacity cost. At this point, we assume zero discount rate for simplicity.

The Solution: A Three-Stage Procedure

Though it would be ideal to solve the model defined in (2-1)—(2-8) directly to get the analytical form of the optimal pricing trajectory $(p_i(t), p_b(t))$ and the optimal amount of bandwidth C_T, it is mathematically intractable. Therefore, we construct a three-stage procedure to find a near-optimal solution. At each stage, we will make some simplifying assumptions, or treat some variables as constants, and solve part of the problem. The solution obtained at one stage will be used either as an input to the next stage or as a feedback for modifying assumptions made in the previous stage. This process is iterated until prices stabilize at a near-optimal level.

The three-stage procedure is defined as follows: at the first stage, we solve a long-term optimal investment problem to find the optimal amount of total bandwidth C_T, as well as the desired blocking probability $\tilde{\beta}_i(t)$, which we expect will vary with time of day. Using these values as inputs, we develop the optimal pricing policy at the second stage. The result shows that the optimal price for a service should

Wang, Peha, and Sirbu

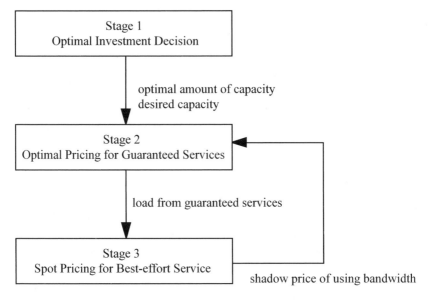

Figure 3
The Three-stage Procedure

be a function of the opportunity cost of providing that service. The opportunity cost is determined by both the service characteristics and the shadow prices of reserving/using network bandwidth. We give trial values to shadow prices and set up a price schedule for each guaranteed service accordingly. Based on these price schedules, the traffic load from guaranteed services can be determined. Under a given traffic load from guaranteed services, at the third stage, we formulate a more precise model to describe the cell flow of best-effort service at each moment. The spot price for best-effort service is then derived to maximize the revenue from best-effort service. From these spot prices, we can then decide the instantaneous value of using network bandwidth. This information is used as feedback to the second stage for adjusting the trial value of shadow prices we previously calculated, so the price schedule for guaranteed services can be refined. The process is iterated until both the price schedule for guaranteed services and the spot price for best-effort service stabilize.

In the next section, we will discuss the implementation details at each stage, and interpret the economic implications of our results.

Implementation of the Three-Stage Procedure

Stage 1: Optimal Investment

At this stage, we formulate and solve an optimization problem to determine the optimal amount of total bandwidth C_T, and the desired blocking probability of each guaranteed service at each time, $\tilde{\beta}_i(t)$, $i = 1, N$. The formulation of the problem is as follows:

Divide $[0, T]$ into M time intervals, each lasting w_m, $(m = 1, M)$.

Take the average arrival rate $\lambda_{im} = \dfrac{\displaystyle\int_{[m-1, m)} \lambda_i(\tau)d\tau}{w_m}$ as the arrival rate for all time during that interval. Average arrival rate λ_m is determined by price p_{im}. We also assume that calls admitted during the interval $[m-2, m-1]$ will have no influence on traffic load within the interval $[m-1, m]$. β_{im} is the blocking probability during the interval $[m-1, m]$, which is a function of network loads within that interval.

At this stage we ignore blocking due to finite buffer space for best-effort traffic. Then the expected cell acceptance rate equals the expected cell admission rate, i.e., $\lambda_{bm}(p_{bm}) = \varpi_{bm}$. In other words, all cells with a willingness to pay higher than the cut-off price are assumed to be able to enter the buffer. To keep the queue length in the buffer reasonably short, we assume the expected cell admission rate equals the expected cell transmission rate, i.e. $\varpi_{bm} = \bar{s}_{bm}$. Consequently, $\lambda_{bm}(p_{bm}) = \bar{s}_{bm}$.

The network operator controls p_{im}, p_{bm}, and C_T to maximize total profit, i.e.,

$$\max_{p_{im}, p_{bm}, C_T} \sum_{m=1}^{M} w_m \left[\sum_{i=1}^{N} \frac{(1 - \beta_{im})\lambda_{im}(p_{im})p_m}{r_i} + p_{bm}\lambda_{bm}(p_{bm}) \right] - K(C_T) \tag{3-1}$$

$$\text{such that } \bar{q}_m = \frac{(1 - \beta_{im})\lambda_{im}(p_{im})}{r_i} \tag{3-2}$$

Wang, Peha, and Sirbu

$$\beta_m^\rho = A(\overline{q}_{im}, i = 1, N, C_T),\qquad\qquad(3\text{-}3)$$

where $\beta_m^\varpi = (\beta_{1m}, \ldots, \beta_{Nm})$

$$\overline{s}[(1 - \beta_{im})\overline{q}_{im}, i = 1, N] + \lambda_{bm} \le T, \qquad m = 1, M\qquad(3\text{-}4)$$

This is an optimization problem with $(N+1)M+1$ controlling variables. It can be solved either by nonliner optimization techniques or generic algorithms such as simulated annealing. The resulting C_T and β_m will be considered as optimal values for the total amount of capacity and for blocking probability in each period.

The solution we have obtained so far is not truly optimal because we have made several simplifications. One simplification is that we assume the traffic load in any period has no influence on the traffic load in succeeding periods. We have also ignored the fact that the arrival rate may change continuously over time within each period by using a single value λ_b as the arrival rate for all time in a period $[m\text{-}1, m)$. Both simplifications will cause inaccuracy in our results. Interestingly, the effects of these two simplifications depend on how we divide $[0, T)$ into different intervals. If we divide $[0, T)$ into longer intervals, i.e., w_m is larger, the effect of not considering the relationship between traffic load in different periods will be smaller and the effect of ignoring the change of arrival rate within a period is more serious. If we choose a smaller w_m, the effects will go in the opposite direction. Therefore w_m should be chosen to minimize the total negative effect of these two simplifications.[2]

Stage 2: Optimal Pricing

We now allow the arrival rate to change continuously over time, consider the dependency of traffic load at different times, and derive the optimal pricing policy at this stage. We will continue to assume that for best-effort service, cell admission rate equals cell transmission rate at all times, and ignore blocking of best-effort traffic. As a result, $\lambda_b(p_b, t)$, the arrival rate of cells for which the willingness to pay is above the cut-off price $p_b(t)$ at time t, is used both as the

---

2. It is preferable to choose a larger w_m if call arrival rate is stable over time and call duration is long, and a smaller w_m if arrival rate is sporadic and call duration is short.

average rate of cell admission into the buffer and the average rate of cell transmission out of the buffer at time t for best-effort service in the problem formulation.

Given the amount of bandwidth C_T and optimal blocking probability $(\tilde{\beta}_i(t), i = 1, N)$ calculated at the first stage, we can simplify the optimal pricing model defined in (2-1)–(2-9) as follows:

$$\max_{p_i(t), p_b(t)} \int_0^T \left\{ \sum_{i=1}^{N} [1 - \tilde{\beta}_i(t)]\lambda_i(p_i, t)\frac{p_i}{r_i} + \lambda_b(p_b, t)p_b \right\} dt \qquad (3\text{-}5)$$

subject to: $\dfrac{d\overline{q}_i}{dt} = [1 - \tilde{\beta}_i(t)]\lambda_i(p_i, t) - r_i\overline{q}_i(t) \quad i = 1, N,$ \qquad (3-6)

$$A[\overline{q}_1(t), \ldots, \overline{q}_N; \tilde{\beta}_1(t), \ldots, \tilde{\beta}_N(t)] \le C_T \qquad (3\text{-}7)$$

$$\lambda_b(p_b, t) + \overline{s}[\overline{q}_1(t), \ldots, \overline{q}_N(t)] \le C_T \qquad (3\text{-}8)$$

$$q_i(0) = q_{i0}, i = 1, N \qquad (3\text{-}9)$$

We assume that the optimal solution exists for this pricing model. The optimal solution to equation (3-5) through (3-9) must obey the following proposition, which yields the optimal pricing policy:

Proposition: The optimal pricing policy

Suppose $p_i^*(t)$, $p_b^*(t)$ are the optimal solutions to the pricing model defined in (3-5)–(3-9), then:

(1) $\quad p_i^*(t) = \dfrac{\varepsilon_i(p_i^*, t)}{1 + \varepsilon_i(p_i^*, t)} * h_i(t) \quad$ and $\quad p_b^*(t) = \dfrac{\varepsilon_b(p_b^*, t)}{1 + \varepsilon_b(p_b^*, t)} * l_2(t)$ \qquad (3-10)

if $l_2(t) > 0$ and $h_i(t) > 0$, $i = 1, N$

or

(2) $\quad p_i^*(t) = \dfrac{\varepsilon_i(p_i^*, t)}{1 + \varepsilon_i(p_i^*, t)} * h_i(t) \quad$ and $\quad p_b^*(t) = p_b^0(t)$ \qquad (3-11)

if $l_2(t) = 0$ and $h_i(t) > 0$, $i = 1, N$

or

(3) $\quad p_i^*(t) = p_i^0(t) \quad$ and $\quad p_b^*(t) = p_b^0(t)$ $\hfill$ (3-12)

if $\quad l_i(t) = 0, i = 1, N$

where: $\quad p_i^0(t)$ maximizes $p_i(t)\lambda_i(p_i, t)$, $\quad p_i^0(t)$ maximizes $p_b(t)\lambda_b(p_b, t)$,

$$\varepsilon_i(p_i^*, t) = \frac{\partial \lambda_i}{\partial p_i} * \frac{p_i^*}{\lambda_i}, \qquad \varepsilon_b(p_b^*, t) = \frac{\partial \lambda_b}{\partial p_b} * \frac{p_b^*}{\lambda_b} \qquad (3\text{-}13)$$

$$h_i(t) = \int_t^T \left[\frac{\partial A}{\partial \overline{q}} l_1(\tau) + \frac{\partial \overline{s}}{\partial \overline{q}_i} r_i e^{-r_i(\tau-t)} d\tau \qquad i = 1, N \right. \qquad (3\text{-}14)$$

$l_1(t)$ is the Lagrangian multiplier of constraint (3-7),

$l_2(t)$ is the Lagrangian multiplier of constraint (3-8).

In the following subsections, we discuss the economic implications of this policy and how to decide the optimal pricing schedule for guaranteed services based on the policy.

Economic Implications The pricing policy shown in (3-10) is designed for situations in which the network capacity is tightly constrained. If the network operator prices services without considering capacity constraints, in the case of guaranteed services, either the network cannot meet performance requirements, or some services will experience a blocking rate beyond the designed value. For best-effort service, if the number of cells admitted exceeds the number of cells transmitted, the queue would grow without bound. Our proposition shows that under these scenarios, the network operator's optimal strategy is to attach an opportunity cost to each service ($h_i(t)$ for guaranteed service i, and $l_2(t)$ for best effort service), and price a network service in the same way as a tangible product, except that the marginal production cost should be replaced by opportunity costs.

We now explain the rationale for using $h_i(t)$ as the opportunity cost for providing guaranteed service i, and $l_2(t)$ as the opportunity cost for providing best-effort service, beginning by explaining the

Lagrangian multipliers of the two capacity constraints. The economic implication of the Lagrangian multiplier of a resource constraint is the maximum value that can be derived from having one more unit of the constrained resource, i.e., the shadow price of consuming one unit of that resource. In our case, $l_1(t)$, $l_2(t)$ are the shadow prices of reserving and using one unit of bandwidth, respectively. Since we measure the bandwidth in terms of the number of cells that can be sent per unit of time, at time t, when one cell of best-effort service is sent, one unit of bandwidth is consumed. Therefore, the unit opportunity cost for best-effort service at time t is just the shadow price of using one unit of bandwidth at that time, i.e., $l_2(t)$.

To meet performance requirements for guaranteed services, the network needs to reserve some capacity each time a call is admitted. At each moment, part or all of reserved bandwidth will actually be used by guaranteed services. Consequently the opportunity cost should include two components: the opportunity cost of reserving the bandwidth, and the opportunity cost of using it. In our formulation, at time t, the former equals the shadow price for reserving one unit of bandwidth, $l_1(t)$, times the marginal increase of the amount of reserved bandwidth for admitting one more call, $\dfrac{\partial A}{\partial \overline{q}}$; and the latter equals the shadow price for using one unit of bandwidth, $l_2(t)$, times the marginal increase of bandwidth usage which results from admitting one more call, $\dfrac{\partial \overline{s}}{\partial \overline{q}_i}$. The total opportunity cost for a call is thus the sum of these two components, accumulated over all time. Since the service duration is an exponentially distributed random variable, the total cost, $h_i(t)$, is estimated by taking mathematical expectation, using the distribution function of the call duration $r_i e^{-r_i t}$.

Equation (3-10) is appropriate when the number of guaranteed calls that can be admitted while meeting performance requirements is still limited, but there is more than enough capacity to carry the cells from all guaranteed calls that are admitted, as well as all of the best-effort traffic that the network wants to carry. This situation might occur, for example, if the guaranteed calls are extremely bursty, or if their performance requirements are extremely strict, i.e.:

$$\lambda_b(p_b, t) + \bar{s}[\bar{q}_i(t), \ldots, \bar{q}_N(t)] < C_T$$

As a result, at time t, the shadow price of using the bandwidth $l_2(t)$ equals 0, and the optimal pricing policy should follow (3-10), i.e., the network operator should set the price to maximize total revenue from best-effort service without considering the constraint on data rate.

Equation (3-11) specifies the pricing policy for the situation when there is an excessive amount of bandwidth. In this case, even if the network operator maximizes revenue without considering capacity constraints, she can still meet performance objectives for all services, keep blocking probability below the desired level, and have more transmission capacity for best-effort service than is needed. As a result, both the opportunity costs for guaranteed services and the opportunity costs for best-effort service equal zero (i.e., $h_i(t) = 0$, $l_2(t) = 0$). This only happens when capacity is not constrained for both reservation and use for all time, or in other words, the capacity is overprovisioned. Since we have assumed that the capacity, C_T, is set at the optimal level in the first stage, this cannot occur.

The Optimal Pricing Schedule for Guaranteed Services As shown in (3-10), (3-11), the optimal price for guaranteed services depends on the ε_i, which is the demand elasticity; $\dfrac{\partial A}{\partial q_i}$, which reflects traffic characteristic and performance requirements; as well as $l_1(t)$, $l_2(t)$, the shadow prices for reserving and using bandwidth, respectively, i.e.:

$$p_i(t) = \frac{\varepsilon_i}{1 + \varepsilon_i}\, h_i(t)$$

$$\text{where} \quad h_i(t) = \int_t^T \left[\frac{\partial A}{\partial \bar{q}_i} l_1(\tau) + \frac{\partial \bar{s}}{\partial \bar{q}_i} l_2(\tau) \right] r_i e^{-r_i(\tau - t)} d\tau$$

To find $p_i(t)$, values of $l_1(t)$, $l_2(t)$ need to be determined. At this point, we assume the values of $l_2(t)$ have been estimated and given as $\hat{l}_2(t)$. (This prior estimation will be modified by the feedback from the third stage). We then set $l_1(t)$ to the trial value $\hat{l}_1(t)$, and construct the following procedure to find the optimal value for $p_i(t)$, as well as to modify the estimate of $l_i(t)$:

1) Calculate the optimal pricing schedule for guaranteed services by:

$$\hat{h}_i(t) = \int_t^T \left[\frac{\partial A}{\partial \overline{q}_i} \hat{l}_1(\tau) + \frac{\partial \overline{s}}{\partial \overline{q}_i} \hat{l}_2(\tau) \right] r_i e^{-r_i(\tau-t)} d\tau \quad \text{and} \quad \hat{p}_i(t) = \frac{\varepsilon_i}{1 + \varepsilon_i} \hat{h}_i(t)$$

2) The call arrival rate of guaranteed services i at time t is then $\hat{\lambda}_i[\hat{p}_i(t), t]$. Given $\hat{\lambda}_i[\hat{p}_i(t), t]$ and the total amount of bandwidth, C_T, the expected number of calls in progress, $\hat{q}_i(t)$, and the blocking probability, $\hat{\beta}_i(t)$, can be determined.

3) If $l_1(t)$ is underestimated, $\hat{p}_i(t)$ will be lower than its optimal value, so call arrivals will be higher than the optimal level, which leads to the situation that blocking probability is higher than the desired level, i.e., $\hat{\beta}_i(t) > \tilde{\beta}_i(t)$ at some t. If $l_1(t)$ is overestimated, $\hat{p}_i(t)$ will be lower than its optimal value and $\hat{\beta}_i(t) < \tilde{\beta}_i(t)$.

4) Increase or decrease $\hat{l}_1(t)$ by Δl_1, depending on whether it is over- or underestimated. Go to the first step to calculate $p_i(t)$.

The process is iterated until $\hat{\beta}_i(t) = \tilde{\beta}_i(t)$ or is within a tolerable error band.

The price schedule for guaranteed services is based on the given estimates of $l_2(t)$, i.e., the shadow price for using the bandwidth. This estimate was given arbitrarily at the beginning, and needs to be modified by using feedback from the third stage.

Spot Pricing

Given the prices for guaranteed services obtained at the second stage, the distribution of available capacity for best-effort service as a function of time can be determined as $C_T - s[q_1(t), \ldots, q_N(t)]$. At each instant, the network operator will set $p_b(t)$, the spot price for admitting cells of best-effort service into the buffer to maximize:

$$\int_{t}^{T} p_b(t) * \omega_b(t)dt \tag{3-15}$$

under constraints:

$$\frac{dq_b}{dt} = \omega_b(t) - s_b(t) \tag{3-16}$$

$$s_b(t) ,= C_T - s[q_1(t), \ldots, q_N(t)] \tag{3-17}$$

$$0 \le q_b(t) \le B, \tag{3-18}$$

when $\quad q_b(t) \le B, \quad \omega_b(t) \le s_b(t) \tag{3-19}$

when $\quad q_b(t) = 0 \quad \omega_b(t) \ge s_b(t) \tag{3-20}$

Given $\omega_b(t)$, $s_b(t)$ are random variables with complicated distributions, the problem in (3-15)–(3-20) cannot be solved directly. However, through simulation, we can design heuristic rules that indicate how the spot price, $p_b(t)$, should be set based on current buffer occupancy and the expected distribution of willingness to pay of cells arriving in the future.

As soon as the spot price, $p_b(t)$, is determined, a new estimate of $l_2(t)$ can be constructed. This can be done by using the proposition above that defines the optimal pricing policy. Equation (3-10), i.e.,

$p_b^*(t) = \dfrac{\varepsilon_b(p_b^*, t)}{1 + \varepsilon_b(p_b^*, t)} * l_2(t)$ applies when the bandwidth is fully used,

and Equation (3-11), i.e., $l_2(t) = 0$ applies otherwise. The new estimate can then be used as feedback to revise the optimal pricing schedule for guaranteed services.

The optimal pricing policy is reached by iterating the second and the third stages until both the price schedule for guaranteed services and the expected spot price for best-effort service stabilize.

Conclusions and Future Work

In this chapter, we discuss the optimal pricing policy for integrated service networks with guaranteed quality of service based on ATM technology. By formulating the pricing decision as a constrained control problem and developing a three-stage procedure to solve that model, we find there is great similarity between the optimal pricing policy for network services and the optimal pricing policy for conventional products. We demonstrate that under capacity constraints, the service provider should consider the opportunity cost incurred by serving a customer. This opportunity cost should be used to determine the price of a network service in the same way as the marginal production cost is used to determine the price of a conventional product. Since demand for network services usually changes with time of day, we will develop a time-varying price schedule (i.e., price as a function of time of day) instead of giving a single price for each service. We derive the mathematical expressions that calculate opportunity costs for different services offered by a single integrated services network, and explain the implications of these expressions.

Though our procedure is designed to maximize the service provider's profit, a similar approach can be used to maximize other objectives, such as social welfare.

Note that the pricing policy developed in this chapter optimizes the profit for providing integrated services under the assumption that the demand for each service is independent of the prices of any other services. In future work, we will relax that assumption and consider the cross-elasticity effect among services. Even in the absence of the cross-elasticity effect, the price of one service can also affect the demand for another service if the network adopts a three-part tariff pricing scheme, under which users are not only charged for each service based on reservation and usage, but also pay a flat subscription fee (e.g., an access charge). In this case, the network operator may maximize profit by setting reservation or usage prices for each service different from the optimal values derived in this chapter. As another example, in the presence of positive network externalities, it can be optimal to price access below average cost, recovering the balance from the increased demand for usage which results from a larger network population. This chapter considers neither three-part tariff nor positive demand externalities. The design of an optimal pricing schedule that takes these factors into consideration is an interesting issue that remains to be explored.

References

Cocchi, R., S. Shenker, D. Estrin, and L. Zhang. 1993. Pricing in computer networks: Motivation, formulation, and example. *IEEE/ACM Transactions on Networking* 1(6) (December): 614–27.

Dewan, S. and H. Mendelson. 1990. User delay costs and internal pricing for a service facility. *Management Science* 36(12): 1502–1517.

Gupta, A., D.O. Stahl, and A.B. Whinston. 1996. Priority pricing of integrated services networks. *Internet economics,* ed. Lee McKnight and Joseph Bailey. Cambridge, Mass.: MIT Press.

Hyman, J.M., A.A. Lazar, and G. Pacifici. 1993. A Separation principle between scheduling and admission control for broadband switching. *IEEE Journal on Selected Areas in Communications* 11(4) (May): 605–616.

Kamien, M.I. and N.L. Schwartz. 1981. *Dynamic optimization: The calculus of variations and optimal control in economics and management.* North Holland: Amsterdam.

MacKie-Mason, J.K., and H.R. Varian. 1994. Pricing the Internet. In *Public Access to the Internet,* ed. B. Kahin and J. Keller. Edglewood Cliffs, N.J.: Prentice-Hall.

Pappas, J.L., and M. Hirschey. 1987. *Managerial economics,* 5th ed. Dryden Press: Hinsdale, IL.

Peha, J.M., and F.A. Tobagi. 1996. Cost-based scheduling and dropping algorithms to support integrated services. *IEEE Transactions on Communications* 44(2) (February): 192–202.

Peha, J.M. 1993. The priority token bank: Integrated scheduling and admission control for an integrated-services network. *Proceedings of IEEE International Conference on Communications,* ICC-93, Geneva, Switzerland: 345–51.

Peha, J.M. 1991. *Scheduling and dropping algorithms to support integrated services in packet-switched networks.* Ph.D. dissertation, technical report No. CSL-TR-91-489, Computer Systems Laboratory, Stanford University.

Tewari, S., and J.M. Peha. 1995. Competition among telecommunications carriers that offer multiple services. *Proceedings of 23rd Telecommunications Policy Research Conference,* Solomon Island, Maryland.

Whang, S., and H. Mendelson. 1990. Optimal incentive-compatible priority policy for the M/M/1 queue. *Operations Research* 38: 870–883.

Zhang, L., L. Deering, D. Estrin, S. Shenker, and D. Zappala. 1993. New resource reservation protocol. *IEEE Network* 7(5) (September): 8–18.

Internet Commerce

Internet Services: A Market for Bandwidth or Communication?

David W. Crawford

Introduction

This chapter examines proposed congestion pricing schemes for allocating traffic on the Internet, such as those proposed in MacKie-Mason and Varian (1995), Cocchi et al. (1992), and Gupta, Stahl, and Whinston (1996). I apply two basic formulations of an Internet pricing model. In the first formulation, the task is to allocate only network usage, i.e., consider a market for bandwidth. This formulation ignores what it is that users want to send through the Internet; bandwidth is the only good considered, and can be considered from the perspective of either sender or receiver. In the second formulation, the task is to simultaneously allocate both rights to information which can be sent over the Internet and the resources to be used for transmission, i.e., consider a joint market for information and for bandwidth. I will call this second formulation, the combination of information and bandwidth, a *market for communication*. This formulation should be considered simultaneously from the perspective of both sender and receiver. The relationship between these two formulations is shown in Figure 1. Both formulations—as a joint market for information and bandwidth, and as a market for bandwidth alone—address the possibility that both the sender and the receiver have a preference for the receiver receiving information.

The Internet and its predecessors, ARPANet and NSFNET, were funded by federal government agencies, the Department of Defense and the National Science Foundation (NSF); individual users still are

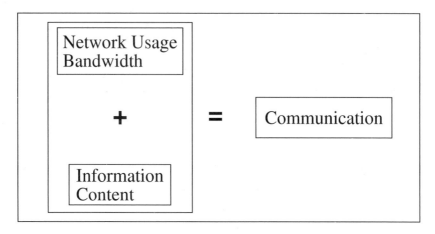

Figure 1
Bandwidth, Information, and Communication

not charged for their own use of these networks, and generally remain unaware of the impact of their use on network performance and the value of the network enjoyed by other network users. The number of people on the Internet is widely reported to have grown at a rate of approximately 10 percent per month since 1990,[1] when the Commercial Internet Exchange (CIX) was established; since then, commercial sites and their customers have been able to connect to the Internet, and their commercial traffic has not been disallowed by the NSF's now-defunct Acceptable Use Policy, which forbade commercial traffic. Rapid growth in the number of users, the proliferation of on-line graphic images, audio files, and especially the one-button, click-to-download user interfaces are factors that are increasing the demand for transmission capacity, and thus increasing the opportunity cost of misallocating transmission capacity. The phasing out of federal funding for Internet operation in the United States necessitates some form of alternative funding, such as revenue from users.

One motivation for imposing a pricing scheme is to give information to the sender of the value they give to other people. It is

1. See, for example, the MIDS Internet Demographic Survey at http://www.mids.org/ids3/index.html.

assumed that a system that grants users the power to cause congestion also provides them with the power to reduce congestion and thereby avoid needless or inefficient harm. A generous user who is willing to use a system after hours needs to know when that actually occurs. A less socially benevolent user, if offered a discount for after hours usage, may reschedule her use not out of charity or concern for the public good, but because it is in her interest to save money. Finally, a user who decides to save money by using resources when they are cheap must have sufficient knowledge about the system to know which actions to take in order to do so. A user who submits her contributions to a mailing list at night will not have any benevolent impact if her software accumulates mail until 9:00 AM and then transmits her spool of messages.

A potential pitfall of introducing a dynamic pricing scheme is that not only the behavior of consumers may be affected, but also the behavior of providers. Profit-seeking providers will have as much knowledge, interest, and power in the system as any consumer.

This chapter has three objectives. The first is to characterize congestion pricing as part of an optimal pricing scheme for network usage. The charge to users can in principle be based on any observable characteristic of or behavior by the user. Suitable behavioral characteristics on which to base a pricing scheme include: (a) access; (b) capacity; (c) usage; and (d) priority of service. Observable nonbehavioral characteristics include factors such as whether a user is a nonprofit or for-profit institution, and the age of an individual user. Nonbehavioral characteristics such as these could be used in setting prices, e.g., by giving discounts to senior citizens or to nonprofit institutions. Similarly, lump sums or rebates could be given to particular classes of consumers in order to create a uniform price market. Such schemes of nonbehavior-based price discrimination will not be considered in this chapter.

Access and capacity charges do not depend on whether or how much the user utilizes the system, so these two charges can be combined into one lump-sum charge for each user called the fixed charge, π. The usage and the priority charges depend on how and how much the user uses the system, and can be combined into one charge called the variable charge, p. Together, the fixed charge, π, and the variable charge, p, form a two-part tariff. If the usage charge is considered in isolation, there appears to be an incentive to set that part of the tariff higher than if both parts are considered simultaneously. For example, if p was *a priori* set to 0 as a simplification of the analysis, the apparent optimal value of π becomes larger. Therefore I model both the fixed charge and the variable charge simultaneously.[2]

Second, the question of incidence and liability for network usage costs are two distinct issues. The liability for communication costs (obligation to collect and submit the communication cost) may be imposed by the network owner on senders (sellers of information) and/or on receivers (buyers of information). Different liability allocations will result in different compliance (accounting, collection, and verification) costs. The liability should be imposed so as to minimize such compliance costs. Third, and lastly, many people see analogies between the Internet and the interstate highway system, as suggested by the nickname Information Superhighway and as demonstrated by the use of extended metaphors such as on ramps, road kill and speed bumps. Fiber-optic links are called pipes; and analysis of the Internet lends itself to many analogies to other network resources. This chapter also explores the specific characteristics of various networks that make them similar or dissimilar to the Internet.

The Multi-Part Tariff: Access, Capacity, Usage, and Congestion

The short-run costs of operating the Internet backbone are all either sunk (because they are due to past decisions) or fixed (because they do not depend on the quantity of information sent). Here the short run is defined as the duration of time from the present until just before new capital goods can be bought and installed. Thus sunk and fixed costs may include the construction and configuration of lines, switches, and routers, or the leasing of these assets. Once such costs have been incurred, the cost to their owner providing an

2. If the service provider is using two-part pricing, by limiting the analysis to only one of the two parts—the congestion price—capacity provided is underestimated and congestion is overestimated.

additional unit of bandwidth is zero, as long as the total bandwidth used is between zero and the capacity of the system. Additional usage, beyond the capacity of the present system, is by definition impossible during the short run.

A congestion pricing scheme will generate congestion revenue only if there is congestion, i.e., if demand for bandwidth at zero price exceeds the bandwidth capacity. In Figure 2, for the smaller supply, the price where quantity demanded equals quantity supplied is positive; but for the larger supply, a zero price allows all demand to be met. If the only revenue generated by a communication re-source is due to congestion pricing, the owner of the resource has a strong incentive to increase her revenue by causing congestion, for example, by withholding capacity. In Figure 3, the gain in revenue from a higher per-unit price more than offsets the loss in revenue due to fewer units of bandwidth sold; the marginal revenue from increasing the price is positive. The supplier will keep reducing the quantity of bandwidth offered to the market until reaching the

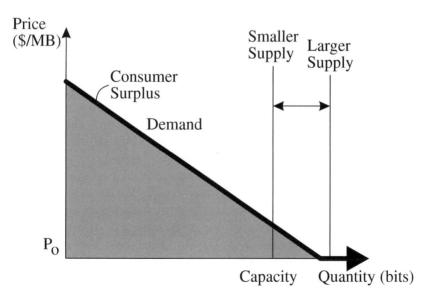

Figure 2
No Congestion

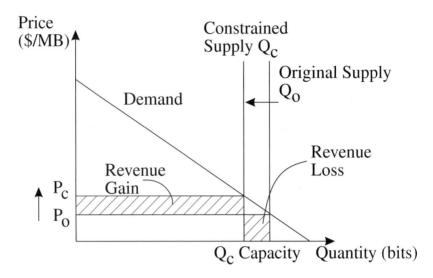

Figure 3
Reduced Capacity

quantity where marginal revenue equals marginal cost, which in this environment equals zero. At this point, the revenue gain due to a higher price per unit is just equal to the revenue loss from selling one less unit. (See Figure 4).

On the Internet, capacity can be underprovisioned or hidden from routers for strategic reasons. Analogously, one could cause congestion in a road network by hiring construction crews to pose by their equipment and install bogus detour signs. On the Internet, congestion could also be caused by what the "pseudo-augmentation" of demand whereby the apparent demand is increased by some form of supplier self-dealing. Similarly one could cause congestion in a road network by hiring a few cars and drivers to feign breakdowns in strategic locations, or by hiring many cars and drivers to drive about.

The optimal increase in demand shown in Figure 5 results in the same quantity legitimately consumed as does the optimal decrease in supply shown in Figure 4. But unlike cars and drivers and road crews, the packets that travel on the Internet are essentially costless

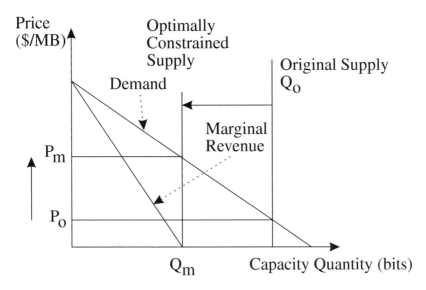

Figure 4
Optimally Reduced Capacity

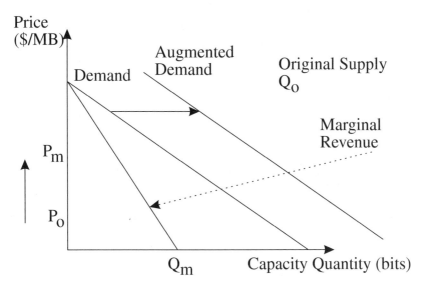

Figure 5
Augmented Demand

to both generate and discard. Demand could be legitimately augmented by providing access to more users or greater advertising of the benefits of Internet use. Pseudo-augmentation could be caused by the supplier of the bandwidth or her collaborator buying bandwidth solely to drive up the price. The collaborator would be refunded the entire cost of units purchased, so there would be no net cost to the collaborator.

This kind of long-run scheme would work easily on the Internet since it costs nothing to generate and request transmission of huge files (or numerous packets), or to dispose of them upon receipt. In the financial world, self-dealing (whereby the owner of securities buys back a portion of her own holdings in order to manipulate the apparent market price) is generally illegal. Such a long-run scheme for raising the price by pseudo-augmenting demand would not work in most other contexts because there is a real cost of generating the articles sold or transmitted, and there is a further cost of then storing or disposing of them after they arrive at their destination. Furthermore, there may be a social stigma associated with wasting or hoarding a scarce resource.

Of the various strategies to reduce the quantity actually delivered to consumers in the market, underinvesting in capital by underbuilding capacity is the most attractive steady-state solution, because presumably the smallest system is the cheapest to build, yet it yields the same revenue as the other strategies. However, the notion of a steady state is not applicable to the Internet or the computer industry because both demand and consumer technology continue to grow rapidly.

The strategy of building capacity and hiding it is appealing because it accommodates growth in demand. As demand grows, less capacity must be hidden, and the supplier can claim credit for innovation and efficiency as the quantity of information transmitted increases. This would be like an environmental engineer, when faced with a mandate to reduce emissions by half, declaring, "This is the benchmark-setting period—let's run dirty today." The strategy of pseudo-augmenting demand is less appealing because the growth of official quantity consumed will be underreported and will hide the growth of the company providing bandwidth.

There are several means of discouraging monopolistic inefficiencies from withholding capacity: revenue-neutral congestion pricing, unitizing the network, a multi-part tariff, competition for bandwidth provision. These alternatives are discussed below.

Revenue-Neutral Congestion Pricing

Rather than allowing the network owner to keep congestion pricing revenue, the revenue could be given to displaced users. This is called a revenue-neutral process because the revenue is collected from and given to the users, leaving the network owner unaffected. This procedure is not quite analogous to the practice of compensating passengers who are bumped from an overbooked airplane; it would be identical if the passengers who were not bumped were taxed to pay for the bumping compensation.[3]

This kind of compensation system needs to block further entry by consumers once it is recognized that the system is overbooked or congested. The revenue-neutral congestion pricing rule removes the network owner's interest in having network congestion occur.

Unitizing the Network

Users can form a cooperative to manage a public good. The revenue from operation is divided among the users according to some agreed upon formula. This kind of system has been used extensively to manage oil reserves and aquifers with multiple well-owners drawing from the same source (Libecap 1989). The unitized network curtails the incentive to cause congestion because the same agents both suffer from congestion and share in congestion pricing revenues.

A Multi-Part Tariff

The charge to users can in principle be based on any observable characteristic of or behavior by the user. Suitable behavioral

---

3. If ticket prices for flights were set with the possibility of bumping compensation in mind, then the situations would be perfectly analogous. The good represented by an airline ticket would then be a large chance of a journey as scheduled and a small chance of a delayed journey plus some bonus.

characteristics on which to base prices include access, capacity, usage, and priority.

• *Access:* whether the user is in fact connected to the system.

• *Capacity:* the maximum rate at which a user can move information through the system, regardless of whether the user actually uses the capacity—essentially this is a standby charge for having the option to use available capacity.

• *Usage:* a charge for the actual quantity of information sent through the system.

• *Priority:* a charge for displacing, or having the option to displace, other users in the event of congestion.

The access and capacity charges do not depend on whether or how much the user uses the system, so these two charges can be combined into one lump-sum charge for every user called the fixed charge, π. The usage and priority charges, which depend on how and how much the user uses the system, are variable; they can be combined into one charge called the variable charge, p. Together π and p form a two-part tariff. The optimal solution for the network owner is to set π equal to the consumer's surplus (See Figure 2), and to set p equal to the marginal cost. If there is congestion, the unserved users have been displaced. The marginal cost is presumed to equal the highest value that a displaced user put on not being displaced. In an economically efficient allocation, the highest value that a displaced user put on not being displaced is bounded by the lowest value a non-displaced user put on not being displaced. If there is congestion and the buyers bid for usage, the marginal cost is equal to the highest rejected bid. If there is no congestion, no bids are rejected, no user is displaced, and the marginal cost is zero.

If we assume that the consumer surplus is increasing with bandwidth capacity purchased, then the strategy of using a two-part tariff is normatively appealing because users pay a fixed fee based on their usage. Using bandwidth capacity purchased as a measure of size, we find that large sites would pay higher fixed fees than small sites. Sites of all sizes pay fees which vary with usage—the greater the usage, the higher the usage fee. However, once packets are admitted to the system, each packet is routed the same way, and all originator sites are treated alike.

The difficulty with the two-part tariff approach lies in the fact that all consumers do not have the same demands, and thus will have different surpluses even if all are charged by the same price list. It may be difficult to discern a consumer's surplus, and many consumers may have a surplus that is far from typical. This difficulty could be overcome if the supplier could identify consumers with high demand and justify charging them a higher price, and prevent resale by consumers paying low prices to consumers paying high prices. Since the proposed system has elicited bids for service, those bidding relatively high amounts can be presumed to be those with a high demand. The fact that such consumers have less chance of being displaced (by more valuable customers), and therefore have less chance of having their service interrupted, helps to justify charging them a higher fee (Wilson 1989). If low-bidding customers engage in resale, they will require larger-capacity connections, and may need to bid higher in order to obtain additional bandwidth. In doing so, they will reveal themselves as having higher demand than those to whom they would resell. Clearly, the opportunities for arbitrage in such a system are rather limited. Also, it is technically feasible to block much resale of capacity.

If only one part of the two-part tariff, the variable charge, is considered in isolation, there appears to be an incentive for the supplier to withhold capacity. Therefore, both the access charge and the congestion charge should be modelled simultaneously. Or the congestion charge should be modelled as a parameter for maximizing value to consumers, and the profit maximization problem of the bandwidth provider should be ignored.

Incidence and Liability for Transmission Costs

Assuming compatibility and interoperability problems could be overcome, competition among multiple suppliers would drive out monopolistic profits. If one supplier withheld bandwidth, another would be willing to provide it.

The cost of network usage, T, can be modeled as a difference between the price the buyer pays for the information received, Pb, and the price the seller receives for the information sent, Ps, so that

$$Pb - Ps = T$$

Consider, for example, phoning an out-of-town information service to learn the instantaneous price of a security. There will be the cost of the service, say $0.25, and the cost of the phone call, say $0.75. How might you pay? Consider three possible ways of charging for the call and for the information.

1. You could call a long-distance toll number to learn the instantaneous price of a security and be billed twice: once by the telephone company for $0.75, and once by the company you called for $0.25.

2. You could call a 1-800 toll-free number and be billed once for $1.00 by the company you called, which receives the $1.00 and then remits $0.75 to the telephone company and retains $0.25 for itself.

3. You could call a 1-900 toll number and be billed once for $1.00 by the telephone company, which would retain $0.75 for itself and then remits $0.25 to the company you called.

All three examples involves you paying $1.00, the phone company retaining $0.75 and the company you called retaining $0.25. However, the activities of accounting, billing, remitting, collecting, and retaining money are performed differently, so the cost of the transactions may be different in each of the examples.

The liability refers to the obligation to submit T to the transmission provider. The incidence of a transmission fee refers to the change in prices from a datum of content market with a zero transmission charge, where the price for both buyer and seller is P. The buyers may see their price increase by Pb – P and the sellers may see their price decrease by P – Ps upon imposition of a transmission fee T.

Seller incidence IS refers to the portion of the transmission fee paid by the seller:

$$IS = \frac{P - Ps}{T} = \frac{P - Ps}{Pb - Ps}$$

Buyer incidence IB refers to the portion of the transmission fee paid by the buyer:

$$IB = \frac{Pb - P}{T} = \frac{Pb - P}{Pb - Ps}$$

Note that IS + IB = 1 is an identity.

$$IS + IB = \frac{P - Ps}{Pb - Ps} + \frac{Pb - Ps}{Pb - Ps} = \frac{(P - Ps) + (Pb - P)}{Pb - Ps}$$

$$IS + IB = \frac{-Ps + Pb}{Pb - Ps} = 1$$

Collecting a transmission fee is analogous to collecting a sales tax in a retail store. In the retail industry, where buyers greatly outnumber sellers, and sellers are less mobile than buyers, it is presumed more efficient to hold sellers liable for the tax; this division of labor reduces the number of agents to be monitored for compliance and evasion.

Returning to the specific context of the Internet, providers of files (e.g., FTP archives or World Wide Web sites) already assume the costs of disk space, access and capacity, and file maintenance. In some cases—for example, files offered to provide technical support or advertising—the provider would be willing to incur the additional cost of transmission. In other cases—for example, the distribution of shareware or noncommercial documents—the consumer would be willing to pay an additional charge for transmission. In all cases, the file is made available and the buyer pays Pb and the seller keeps Ps. Implementing this system as a seller-liable system would be easy since the seller is the sender of the files; depending on incidence, this might require the seller to collect a charge from the buyer. Implementing this system as a buyer-liable system would require a charge-back accounting system in which the file sent by the seller has its transmission cost billed to the buyer. The buyer-liable system has a greater security-related obstacle in that it must verify that the buyers actually requested the files for which they are charged trans-mission costs.

We could extend this analysis to cover the messages that the receiver sends to the sender to acknowledge receipt. An explicit hybrid
liability scheme is also possible in which the buyer and seller agree
to some allocation of the transmission costs. For example, the buyer
may agree to pay $0.10 and the seller may agree to pay the remain-
der of the transmission charge. Any system that bills the receiver for
transmission cost will be easier to implement if the receiver is already
paying for the content. It is likely that there will be more cases of
receivers paying senders to send files than senders paying receivers
to receive files; thus most file transfer transactions would be file
senders collecting money from file receivers. In these cases, it seems
appropriate for the sender to collect additional money to cover the
receiver's incidence of transmission cost. We could extend the current analysis to include transactions in which the receiver sends a
"message received" acknowledgment to the sender. Assuming that
most file transactions are of the paying to receive mode rather than
the paying to send mode, a sender-liable system seems likely to
minimize the transactions costs. Given that the Internet has negligible storage capacity relative to bandwidth, for a collect on delivery
or postage due type of system to be feasible, the potential recipient
of data needs to agree to pay for the transfer. For example, a receiver's server could be configured to accept and pay for incoming
data from any addresses on a preferred list.

How Are Networks Similar or Different?

A network is a set of nodes and arcs; each arc links two nodes. The
use or function of a network is to allow some object to be sent from
one node to another node. An arc may be directional, which implies
that sending is possible in only one direction. There may be more
than one arc linking two nodes. The object transported may be
water, oil, or gas in the case of pipeline commodity networks; planes,
trains, and automobiles in the case of transportation networks. The
planes, trains, and automobiles also include passengers and freight
as objects transported. In the case of information networks, such as
computer data or telephone networks, the object transported is a
bundle of information. A postal system may be considered a network; objects sent via mail may be considered information. In a

commodity network (oil, gas, water, or electricity), the objects transmitted are generic and perfectly interchangeable. In an information network (mail, phone, computer data), the objects sent may be individualized and not interchangeable. Clark (1996) provides a framework for users to reserve bandwidth. It is not important whether the sender or the receiver has reserved the bandwidth, only that the bandwidth has been reserved.

Example: Water transport network technology

input: x = water at node A at time t1

output: y = water at node B at time t2

production function: f (x) = y

Note that in the water network example above, both the input and the output are time stamped. If $t1 < t2$, then the flow is from A to B. Generally network flows are reversible, so it is important to keep track of the direction of flows and the time at which an object is at a particular node. A factor common to all types of networks is that their capacity to produce cannot be stored, so capacity unused today cannot be saved for use tomorrow. Note that the storage of a network's capacity to transmit is distinct from the storage of objects transported over the network. For example, if a milkman takes one day off and does not use his capacity to deliver milk for a day, his capacity to deliver milk is not stored and accumulated, giving him double delivery capacity on the following day. However, the undelivered milk may be stored.

The use of the network in the example above can be formally expressed as the set of all possible transportation activities. For instance, a postal network can be represented as a mapping from and to the space generated by the Cartesian product of all possible pieces of mail, all possible locations of mail, and all possible instants of time. Of course, this may not be the most parsimonious representation. For a communication network, discrete pieces of information may be represented by flashes of light or voltage fluctuations on a wire, mail trucks on a road, or packages inside the mail truck. Though computers can send data over phone lines by using modems, the terms "telephone network" and "computer data network"

are not usually synonymous. The cost of operating a network typically depends on the amount of traffic it bears; the Internet is an
exception. The phenomenon of more users increasing operation
costs is a negative externality. In the case of increased connectivity,
having more users is a positive externality because more people are
reachable.

Store and Forward

Above it was stated that no networks can store its capacity. However,
the good transmitted on a network may itself be storable. For instance, a mailbox is a node in a mail network. The mailbox sends (is
emptied) once or twice a day, but may receive incoming mail hundreds of times per day. When it is not being emptied, the mailbox is
storing mail. Nodes on gas, water, or oil networks may have storage
reservoirs. Many data networks have a store-and-forward architecture. However, electricity itself is not storable, so nodes in an electric
network cannot be used for storage. At a low-level protocol, the
Internet does not store and forward, but Internet-based applications
such as USENet do.

Net Flow vs. Total Flow

The commodity networks do share a common property in that one
unit transferred from node B to node A is a perfect substitute for a

Table 1
Comparison of Networks: Network Type vs. Characteristics

Network Type	Characteristic				
	Store and Forward	Net Flow or Total Flow	Frictional Loss	Self-powering	Measure of Capacity
Mail	yes	total	possible	no	letters/day
Electricity	no	net	yes	yes	power (MW)
Data	possible	total	possible	possible	bits/second
Telephone	no	total	no	no	calls
Road	yes	total	possible	yes	trucks/hour
Water	yes	net	yes	no	kg/second
Gas/Oil	yes	net	yes	possible	kg/second

unit already at node A. Noncommodity transportation networks (planes, trains, and automobiles) do not share this perfect substitution regardless of the origin of property. In communication networks, each unit of information has a source node (author) and receiver node (reader). Receiving mail (unless there is cash in the envelope) or phone calls intended for another party is typically useless both for the sender and for the recipient. In communication, there are intermediate cases such as broadcasting, in which watching the president deliver the State of the Union Address on channel 2 is a perfect substitute for watching the same event on channel 3. In this case, if the cable company makes a mistake and sends the signal for channel 2 on channel 3, you are no worse off.

In commodity flow networks only net transfers between two nodes during a particular period or net transfer rates at a specific time matter. In information networks (data, mail), the total number of objects transferred between nodes matters. Compare the following two cases.

Example 1. Suppose we pump 50 units of water from node A to node B. The net transfer between nodes is 50 units from node A to node B.

Example 2. Suppose we pump 80 units of water from node A to node B and simultaneously pump 30 units of water through the same pipe from node B to node A. The net transfer between nodes is 50 units from node A to node B.

Both of these examples describe the same net flow of water. Example 2 may appear to be an inefficient use of the network, but since we are considering net flows, and the second case is identical to the first case in terms of net flow, the second case is as efficient as the first case.

Frictional Losses

In a pipeline network transporting water, gas, or oil, flow is induced by increasing pressure at source nodes and/or decreasing pressure at sink nodes. In electricity networks, flow is induced by increasing voltage at source nodes and/or decreasing voltage at sink nodes. Gas and oil networks have frictional losses, and pumps may be used to overcome such losses, but it is not necessarily gas that is used to power pumps in a gas network to overcome friction, or oil-powered pumps used in an oil network. An electricity network has losses that are analogous to friction: the resistance or impedance of the wires. In an electricity network, electricity itself is used to overcome this resistance. The electricity used up in an electricity network is like milk drunk by a milkman who drinks more milk the longer and more tiring his route. But an electricity network has in-kind losses, so what comes out at one end is less than what went in at the other end.

Self-Powering

If the material used to overcome frictional losses is the same as the matter transported on the network, the network is self-powering. Modelling a self-powering network is more difficult than modelling an externally powered or frictionless network. Communication networks may be externally powered. For example, the mailman provides the energy to sort and move mail; the mail itself is not energized. But we may think of the bandwidth used to carry header data as frictional loss encountered when sending a data payload over a computer network.

Measuring Network Capacity

Gas and oil may be measured by mass, number of molecules, volume at some pressure and temperature, or energy content at some pressure and temperature. Electricity is measured in terms of energy. Road networks are measured in number of trips or number of passenger miles.[4]

Quantifying communication is more problematic than quantifying electricity or water because one knowing wink or nudge can tell an

4. Why doesn't Negroponte use "electrons not atoms" as a mantra instead of "bits not atoms" (Negroponte 1995)? One explanation is that the electrons are the signal and the bits are the content. So "bits not atoms" represents two transformations: the first from physical goods to information goods, and the second from a particular media (say, wires) to a non-media-specific communication.

informed party as much at a longwinded explanation. Suppose you wish to tell someone which horse you think will win a race against seven other horses. You might transmit the DNA genetic code of the winning horse; that would be a lot of information. If the horses have proper and unique English names, you might transmit the name of the horse, "Sir Ed, 3rd." If the horses have numbers, you might transmit "1." That is very little information, but in this context, "1" identifies the horse as well as its complete genetic code.

In this example, we need to indicate one of eight possible states of the world, since there are eight horses. If we start with a set of eight horses and make three binary decisions to partition the set of still contending horses, we will have uniquely identified a particular horse. If each horse has a unique indicator, then by making three binary decisions on the set of indicators, we will have uniquely identified a particular indicator, and by the uniqueness of the indi-cator, we will have identified a particular horse. The lesson here is that we can measure information as the number of binary decisions needed to get from some set of possible states of the world that is common knowledge to the knowledge that one particular state of the world is true. In the eight-horse race, the amount of information needed to identify a particular horse is three binary decisions, or three bits.

To write a document on a computer, we commonly use an exten-sion of the Roman alphabet called ASCII, which has 128 characters (a, . . . , z, A, . . . , Z, 0, . . . , 9, and control characters and punctua-tion), or a large alphabet which may have a few hundred characters. An ancient computer might have used an alphabet of 38 characters (A, . . . , Z, 0, . . . , 9) and therefore would need six bits per charac-ter of telegram style all capital English ($38 < 2^6 = 64$). A modern computer with a character set of 256 needs eight bits per character ($2^8 = 256$). Newer alphabets are much larger: Apple Computer's QuickDraw GX alphabet has 65,000 possible characters (Arnold 1994). Ultimately we can determine the amount of information native in each character by counting the number of pixels per char-acter in the display or the number of dots per character at the printer and then multiply that number by the number of states (colors and intensity) of the display pixels or printer dots. For example, a 600 dot per inch (dpi) display with 16 million possible colors displaying six characters per inch needs

$$\frac{(600 \text{ dpi horizontal})(600) \text{ dpi vertical})(16 \times 10^6 \text{ colors})}{6 \text{ characters per inch}}$$

$$\leq 2^{21} = 2 \text{ million bits.}$$

These examples show why saving the same content as different file types may result in different file sizes. The trend toward much larger symbol sets allows much more richly formatted text, but at a cost of longer files. A more detailed discussion of measuring information can be found in Cover (1991).

This analysis is germane to Internet pricing, because unitized systems such as America Online have been designed to send graphical icons once and save them locally; then subsequent invocations of the icon need only pass a cryptic abbreviated reference to the icon, not the icon itself. However, the user who has stored the icon sees the icon, not the cryptic reference.

The World Wide Web system is not organized to store icons with common identifiers, but instead uses a system called Hyper Text Markup Language (HTML) which allows for very abbreviated formatting commands to be sent, such as <strong> emphasis </strong>, which sends the word emphasis with information that the recipient's system should emphasize the word using, for example, underlining, boldface, or italics, as determined by the recipient's system. HTML does not tell the recipient's system how to render boldface or italic text; that ability is already known to the local system. The ability of smart receiver systems to perform computation to determine how to display information given a few concise clues allows the files transmitted to be much smaller than those that would allow a dumb display system to display identical images. The trade-off here is that by conserving bandwidth, we use more processing power. The incentives for conserving bandwidth depend on the pricing of both computation and bandwidth.

However, counting bits is not the best way to measure Internet transmission rates. Measuring communication in terms of bits transmitted is reminiscent of how the output of television factories was measured in the Soviet Union: not by counting televisions sets produced or by totalling sales revenue, but by adding up the weight of the televisions. This kind of quantification is somewhat useful, but subject to easy manipulation, and most important, is without reference to the value received by the consumer. However, until there is data that elucidates the value received by the consumer, we will continue to do best by counting communication bit by bit.

Conclusion

For an analysis of the incidence of transmission costs for senders and receivers of information, it is best to consider both allocation of both bandwidth and rights to information. This formulation is called a market for communication. The market for communication is an appropriate framework when the content and its transmission is paid for.

For an analysis of the provider's behavior under congestion pricing, the content market can be ignored, but the access and capacity charges must be considered jointly with the usage and priority charges. This formulation is called a market for bandwidth. The market for bandwidth is an appropriate framework when no economic transaction is necessary to acquire content.

The market for bandwidth is also a more appropriate framework than the market for communication if the price of the content is not likely to vary over time or among different users. Like other pricing schemes discussed in this book, either market scheme requires some sort of pricing allocation scheme to be effectively implemented at congestion points to determine which transmissions have priority.

References

Arnold, Kandy. 1994. GX will provide printing power. *MacWeek*, August 15.

Bellamy, John. 1991. *Digital telephony.* New York: John Wiley and Sons.

Bergseth, F. R., and S. S. Venkata. 1987. *Introduction to electric energy devices.* Englewood Cliffs, N.J.: Prentice Hall.

Clark, David C. 1996. A model for cost allocation and pricing in the Internet. In *Internet economics,* ed. Lee McKnight and Joseph Bailey. Cambridge, Mass.: MIT Press.

Cocchi, R., D. Estrin, S. Shenker, and L. Zhang. 1992. Pricing in computer networks: Motivation, formulation, and example. Technical report, University of Southern California.

Cocchi, R., D. Estrin, S. Shenker, and L. Zhang. 1991. A study of priority pricing in multiple service class networks. In *Proceedings of SIGCOMM '91*. Available from: ftp://ftp.parc.xerox.com/pub/net-research/pricing-sc.ps.

Cover, Thomas M. and Joy A. Thomas. 1991. *Elements of information theory*. New York: John Wiley and Sons, Inc.

Fudenberg, Drew and Jean Tirole. 1992. *Game theory*. Cambridge, Mass.: MIT Press.

Kahn, Robert E. 1994. The role of the government in the evolution of the Internet. *ACM Communications* 37(8): 15–19.

Laffont, Jean-Jacques and Jean Tirole. 1993. *A theory of incentives in procurement and regulation*. Cambridge, Mass.: MIT Press.

Libecap, Gary D. 1989. *Contracting for property rights*. Cambridge, New York: Cambridge University Press.

MacKie-Mason, J. K., and H. Varian. 1995. Pricing the Internet. In *Public access to the Internet*, ed. Brian Kahin and James Keller. Cambridge, Mass.: MIT Press.

MacKie-Mason, J. K., and H. Varian. 1994. Economic FAQs about the Internet. *Journal of Economic Perspectives* (Fall); anonymous ftp, gopher, or World Wide Web at http://gopher.econ.lsa.lsa.umich.edu (version: April 4, 1994).

MacKie-Mason, J. K., and H. Varian. 1993. Some economics of the Internet. Technical report, University of Michigan.

Negroponte, Nicholas. 1995. *Being digital*. New York: Alfred A. Knopf.

Gupta, A., D. O. Stahl, and A. B. Whinston. 1996. A priority approach to manage multi-service class networks in real-time. In *Internet economics,* ed. Lee McKnight and Joseph Bailey. Cambridge, Mass.: MIT Press.

Wilson, R. 1989. Efficient and competitive rationing. *Econometrica* 57: 1–40.

Acknowledgments

I would like to thank participants in the Experimental Economics Workshop at the University of Arizona, John Hawkinson, and Dale O. Stahl for useful comments and suggestions. Remaining misconceptions and errors are the fault of the author.

Internet Payment Services

B. Clifford Neuman and Gennady Medvinsky

Introduction

In the past couple of years, the number of users and organizations reachable through the Internet has increased dramatically. Many organizations now see the Internet as an efficient means to reach potential customers. Most commerce on the Internet today consists of the interactive dissemination of advertising material through World Wide Web home pages and product databases. In most cases, the actual purchase of the product occurs outside the network. Nevertheless, we have started to see some commercial transactions on the Internet.

This chapter discusses some of the desired characteristics of payment systems for open networks, and describes the NetCheque and NetCash systems developed at the University of Southern California.[1] It also examines the benefits and drawbacks of alternative approaches, and describes how the different methods can be used together to provide financial infrastructure for the Internet.

Requirements

Important characteristics for an Internet payment system include security, reliability, scalability, anonymity, acceptability, customer

1. NetCheque® is a registered trademark of the University of Southern California.

base, flexibility, convertibility, efficiency, ease of integration with applications, and ease of use. Some of these characteristics, like anonymity, are more important in some communities, of for certain kinds of transactions, than they are in others. These characteristics are presented for discussion and comparison. The NetCheque and NetCash systems meet some of these characteristics better than other systems, but make trade-offs with respect to some of the other characteristics.

Security

Since payments involve actual money, payment systems on the Internet will be a prime target for criminals. And since Internet services are provided today on networks that are relatively open, the infrastructure supporting electronic commerce must be usable and resistant to attack in an environment where eavesdropping and modification of messages are easy.

Reliability

As more commerce is conducted over the Internet, the smooth running of the economy will come to depend on the availability of the payment infrastructure, making it a target of attack for vandals. Whether the result of such an attack or simply poor design, an interruption in the availability of the infrastructure would be catastrophic. For this reason, the infrastructure must be highly available and should avoid presenting a single point of failure.

Scalability

As commercial use of the Internet grows, the demands placed on payment servers will also increase. The payment infrastructure as a whole must be able to handle the addition of users and merchants without suffering a noticeable loss of performance. The existence of central servers through which all transactions must be processed will limit the scale of the system. The payment infrastructure must support multiple servers, distributed across the network.

Anonymity

For some transactions, the identity of the parties to the transaction should be protected; it should not be possible to monitor an individual's spending patterns, nor to determine one's source of income. An individual is traceable in traditional payment systems such as checks and credit cards. Where anonymity is important, the cost of tracking a transaction should outweigh the value of the information that can be obtained by doing so.

Acceptability

The usefulness of a payment mechanism is dependent upon what one can buy with it. Thus a payment instrument must be widely accepted. Where payment mechanisms are supported by multiple servers, users of one server must be able to transact business with users of other servers.

Customer Base

The acceptability of a payment mechanism is affected by the size of the customer base, i.e., the number of users able to make payments using the mechanism. Merchants want to sell products, and without a large enough base of customers using a payment mechanism, it is often not worth the extra effort for a merchant to accept the mechanism.

Flexibility

Payment mechanisms can appropriately meet variations of the guarantees needed by the parties to a transaction, the timing of the payment itself, requirements for auditability, performance requirements, and the amount of the payment. The payment infrastructure should support several payment methods, including instruments analogous to credit cards, personal checks, cashier's checks, and even anonymous electronic cash. These instruments should be integrated into a common framework.

Convertibility

Users of the Internet will select financial instruments that best suit their needs for a given transaction. It is likely that several forms of payment will emerge, providing different trade-offs with respect to the characteristics just described. In such an environment, funds represented by one mechanism should be easily convertible into funds represented by others.

Efficiency

Royalties for access to information may generate frequent payments of small amounts. Applications must be able to make these "micropayments" without noticeable performance degradation. The cost per transaction of using the infrastructure must be small enough that it is insignificant even for transaction amounts on the order of pennies.

Ease of Integration

Applications must be modified to use the payment infrastructure in order to make a payment service available to users. Ideally, a common Application Programming Interface (API) should be used so that the integration is not specific to one kind of payment instrument. Support for payment should be integrated into request-response protocols on which applications are built so that a basic level of service is available to higher-level applications without significant modification.

Ease of Use

Users should not be constantly interrupted to provide payment information and most payments should occur automatically. However, users should be able to limit their losses. Payments beyond a certain threshold should require approval. Users should be able to monitor their spending without going out of their way to do so.

Payment Models

Most recently proposed, announced, and implemented Internet payment mechanisms can be grouped into three broad classes: electronic currency systems, credit-debit systems, and systems supporting secure presentation of credit card numbers. In less common use are forms of payment that can be described as direct transfer or as the use of a collection agent.

Electronic Currency

With electronic currency systems such as Chaum's DigiCash system (Chaum 1992), which is currently being tested on the Internet, and USC-ISI's NetCash system (Medvinsky and Neuman 1993), customers purchase electronic currency certificates from a currency server. They pay for the certificates through an account established with the currency server in advance, or by using credit cards, electronic checks, or paper currency accepted through a reverse automatic teller machine. Once issued, the electronic currency represents the value, and may be spent with merchants who deposit the certificates in their own accounts or spend the currency elsewhere.

An important advantage of electronic currency is its potential for anonymity. In Chaum's approach, one cannot identify the client to which a certificate was issued even if all parties collude. However, a client attempting to spend the same certificate twice gives up enough information to determine his identity.

ISI's NetCash provides a weaker form of anonymity. If all parties collude, including the currency servers involved in the transaction, it is possible to determine who spent a certificate. However, the client gets to choose the currency server it uses and can select one it trusts not to retain information needed to track such transactions.

An important disadvantage of electronic currency mechanisms is the need to maintain a large database of past transactions to prevent double spending. In Chaum's approach, it is necessary to track all certificates that have been deposited. With ISI's approach, it is necessary to keep track of all certificates that have been issued, but not yet deposited.

Credit-debit Instruments

In payment mechanisms that use the credit-debit model, including CMU's NetBill (Sirbu and Tygar 1995), First Virtual's InfoCommerce system, and USC-ISI's NetCheque system, customers are registered with accounts on payment servers and authorize charges against those accounts. With the debit or check approach, the customer maintains a positive balance that is debited when a debit transaction or check is processed. With the credit approach, charges are posted to the customer's account and the customer is billed for or subsequently pays the balance of the account to the payment service. The implementation of the electronic payment instrument is the same for both approaches. An important advantage of the credit-debit model is its audibility. Once a payment instrument has been deposited, the owner of the debited account can determine who authorized the payment, and that the instrument was endorsed by the payee and deposited. This is extremely important for payments by businesses, and it is desired by many individuals for a significant percentage of their transactions. This model does not typically provide anonymity, though it may be extended to do so (Low, Maxemchuk, and Paul 1994; Medvinsky and Neuman 1993).

For credit-debit or electronic currency systems to move beyond trials with play money, a separate tie to the existing banking system is needed to convert account balances and electronic currency to and from real money in a customer's or merchant's bank account. Though funds can circulate electronically, such an outside connection is required to settle imbalances between the funds spent and received electronically by an individual. The form and timing of such transfers is a contractual issue between the payment service provider and the customer or merchant, and is beyond the scope of this chapter. How these transfers are made is an important distinguishing characteristic of different payment services.

Secure Credit Card Presentation

Secure credit card transactions constitute the third class of network payment services. Most network payment systems presently in use follow this model. For secure network credit card transactions, a customer's credit card number is encrypted using public key cryptography so that it can only be read by the merchant, or in some approaches by a third-party payment processing service.

The biggest advantage of this approach is that the customer does not necessarily need to be registered with a network payment service; all that is needed is a credit card number. This provides a much larger customer base for merchants accepting this method of payment. Encryption using this approach prevents an eavesdropper from intercepting the customer's credit card number. In approaches where the credit card number and amount are encrypted using the public key of a third-party payment processing service, the merchant doesn't see the card number either, providing some protection against fraud by the merchant.

It is important to note, however, that without the registration of customers, the encrypted credit card transaction does not constitute a signature; anyone with knowledge of the customer's credit card number can create an order for payment, just as they can fraudulently place an order over the telephone. More recent examples of secure presentation, including Mastercard and Visa's SET specification, provide for a customer signature, but in order to do so, they require advance registration by the customer. Finally, because payments processed using the secure presentation model are processed as standard credit card charges, costs are high enough that this method is not suited for small payments (e.g., one or two pennies).

Direct Transfer and Collection Agents

In the direct transfer payment model, the customer and merchant are registered with accounts on a payment server in much the same way as in the credit-debit model. To make a payment, the customer directs the payment server to transfer funds to the merchant's account. The merchant then provides the product or service after verifying that the transfer has occurred.

When using a collection agent, the customer contacts the merchant and is provided with purchase information which is then presented to a third party who collects payment and provides the customer with a receipt. The customer presents the receipt to the merchant who then provides the product or service. This is the approach taken by the OpenMarket payment system (Gifford et al. 1995). The method by which the customer pays the collection agent may take any form, including those already discussed. In this sense, the collection agent is not a true payment model, but instead provides the means of integrating several forms of payment with the services provided by the merchant.

The NetCheque System

The NetCheque (Neuman and Medvinsky 1995) service is a distributed accounting service supporting the credit-debit model of payment. Users of the NetCheque service maintain accounts on accounting servers of their choice. A NetCheque account works in much the same way as a conventional checking account: account holders write electronic documents that include the name of the payer, the name of the financial institution, the payer's account identifier, the name of the payee, and the amount of the check. Like a paper check, a NetCheque payment instrument bears an electronic signature, and must be endorsed by the payee, using another electronic signature, before the cheque will be paid.

As a distributed accounting service, NetCheque exchanges properly signed and endorsed cheques between accounting servers to settle accounts through a hierarchy, as shown in Figure 1. In addition to improving scalability and acceptability, clearing between servers allows organizations to set up accounts in their own in-house accounting servers with accounts corresponding to budget lines. Authorized signers write cheques against these accounts, while the organization maintains a single account with an outside bank, integrating its own internal accounting system with the external financial system.

The NetCheque accounting system was originally designed to maintain quotas for distributed system resources (Neuman 1993), resulting in frequent transactions for small amounts. Thus, it is well suited to support small payments needed for some kinds of electronic commerce. Handling micropayments requires high performance which is obtained through the use of conventional, instead of public-key, cryptography. This gives up some support for independent verification of payment documents at each stage in the payment pipeline.

Implementation Overview

The NetCheque system is based on the Kerberos system (Neuman and Ts'o 1994), and the electronic signature used when writing or endorsing a cheque is a special kind of Kerberos ticket called a proxy (Neuman 1993). The cheque itself contains information about (1) the amount of the cheque; (2) the currency unit; (3) an expiration date; (4) the account against which the cheque was drawn; and (5) the payee or payees, all of which is readable by the bearer of the cheque; as well as (6) the signatures and endorsements accumulated during processing, which are verifiable by the accounting server against which the cheque was drawn. The Kerberos proxy used as a signature is based on conventional cryptography. It may be replaced by a signature using public key cryptography with a corresponding loss of performance.

To write a cheque, the user calls the write cheque function, specifying an account against which the cheque is to be drawn, the payee, the amount, and the currency unit. Defaults for the account and currency unit are read from the user's chequebook file. The write cheque function generates the cleartext portion of the cheque, obtains a Kerberos ticket that will be used to authenticate the user to the accounting server, generates an authenticator with an embedded checksum over the information from the cheque, and places the ticket and authenticator in the signature field of the cheque. The cheque is then base 64 encoded and may be sent to the payee through electronic mail, or transferred in real time as payment for services provided through an on-line service.

The deposit cheque function reads the cleartext part of the cheque, obtains a Kerberos ticket to be used with the payer's accounting server, generates an authenticator endorsing the cheque in the name of the payee for deposit only into the payee's account, and appends the endorsement to the cheque. An encrypted connection is opened to the payee's accounting server and the endorsed cheque is deposited. If the payee and the payer both use the same accounting server, the response will indicate whether the cheque cleared.

If different accounting servers are used, the payee's accounting server places a hold on the funds in the payee's account and indicates to the payee that the cheque was accepted for collection. The payee has the option of requesting that the cheque be cleared in real time, though we expect there may be a charge for this service. If a cheque accepted for collection is rejected, the cheque is returned to the depositor, who can take action at that time. As a cheque is cleared through multiple accounting servers, each server attaches its own endorsement, similar to the endorsement attached by the payee.

In some cases the payee's and payer's accounting servers can settle the check directly, bypassing higher levels of the hierarchy. This is possible when the cheque is drawn on an accounting server that is trusted to properly settle accounts. Such trust must be based on certificates of insurance (Lai, Medvinsky, and Neuman 1994) representing endorsement of the accounting server in much the same way that the Federal Deposit Insurance Corporation (FDIC) insures banks in the United States. In such cases, the hierarchy would still be used to settle any imbalance between credits and debits for each

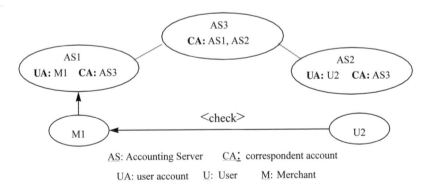

AS: Accounting Server   CA: correspondent account

UA: user account   U: User   M: Merchant

Figure 1
An Accounting Hierarchy

accounting server at the end of the day, but the cost of these transfers would be amortized over the day's transactions.

To determine account balances and find out about cleared cheques, authorized users can call the statement function which opens an encrypted connection to the accounting server and retrieves the account balance for each currency unit, together with a list of cheques that have been recently deposited to, or drawn on and cleared through the account. The entire cheque is returned, allowing the user's application to extract whatever information is needed for display to the user, or for integration with other applications.

The NetCash System

NetCash (Medvinsky and Neuman 1993) is an electronic currency service that supports real-time electronic payments with provision of anonymity across multiple administrative domains on an unsecure network. NetCash strikes a balance between unconditionally anonymous electronic currency, and signed instruments analogous to checks that are more scalable but identify the principals in a transaction. It does this by providing the framework within which electronic currency protocols can be integrated with the scalable, but non-anonymous, NetCheque service described in the previous section.

Currency issued by currency servers is backed by account balances registered with the NetCheque accounting system, which is used to clear payments across servers and to convert electronic currency into debits and credits against customer and merchant accounts. Though the balances backing the currency are stored in named accounts, the accounts are registered to the currency servers, and not to end-users, preventing the identification of the end-user during currency transactions.

When NetCash is used in combination with the NetCheque system, service providers and their users are able to select payment mechanisms based on the level of anonymity desired, ranging from non-anonymous and weakly anonymous instruments that are scalable, to unconditionally anonymous instruments that require more resources of the currency server.

NetCash Anonymity

The anonymity provided by NetCash is weaker than the unconditional anonymity provided by Chaum's DigiCash system (Chaum 1992). In particular, at the point that a client purchases coins from a currency server by check, or cashes in coins, it is possible for the currency server to record which coins have been issued to a particular client. It is expected that currency servers will not do so, and it is likely that the agreement with clients will specifically preclude it. Additionally, the client can choose its own currency server, and will select one that it believes it can trust.

Once coins have been purchased, they can continue to circulate without identifying the intermediaries. Although the currency server is involved each time a coin changes hands, and could conceivably track which coins are exchanged for others though it is prohibited from doing so, it will not know the identity of the intermediaries until one of the parties chooses to identify itself when converting coins. The longer the chain of intermediaries, the more difficult it is to determine who made a particular purchase.

Although coins may be transferred in our scheme without interaction with the currency server, when coins are used in this manner, no assurances exist that a coin has not been double spent. Thus, among a group of individuals who trust one another (or each other's tramper-proof hardware), off-line coin transfer is possible. Parties to a transaction would need to eventually verify and exchange their coins to limit their vulnerability to double spending.

We believe that the vast majority of transactions on the Internet will not require anonymity, and that for most of the transactions that do require anonymity, the level of anonymity provided by NetCash is sufficient. Where unconditional anonymity or completely off-line operation is required, the NetCash framework can be extended to integrate exchanges from Chaum's protocol or from other electronic currency mechanisms. Such exchanges could be applied to only those transactions that require them, while still providing scalability, acceptability, and interoperability across mechanisms.

Status

A binary release of the NetCheque system is available for several platforms. The release contains programs for writing, displaying, and depositing cheques, and for retrieving account statements. Cheques may be cleared across multiple accounting servers. The NetCash prototype has been integrated with the NetCheque system and is available as an integral component of our payment system software.

Summary and Discussion

The NetCheque system is a distributed payment system based on the credit-debit model. The strengths of the NetCheque system are its security, reliability, scalability, and efficiency. Signatures on cheques are authenticated using Kerberos. Reliability and scalability are provided by using multiple accounting servers. NetCheque is well suited for clearing micropayments; its use of conventional cryptography makes it more efficient than systems based on public-key cryptography. Though NetCheque does not itself provide anonymity, it may be used to facilitate the flow of funds between other services that do provide anonymity.

The principle weakness of NetCheque at this time is its small initial customer base. Individuals or companies must be registered as NetCheque users before they can make payments. However, once registered with one server, cheques written by the user may be cleared through other NetCheque servers that have an agreement with the customer's server, either directly, or as a member of a clearinghouse.

NetCash provides scalable electronic currency that is accepted across multiple administrative domains. The NetCash service relies on NetCheque to tie together independent currency servers and to back the currency issued by such servers. NetCash provides a practical level of anonymity that is less absolute than that provided by the DigiCash system. The principal strengths of NetCash over other currency services are its scalability and efficiency.

Ease of integration and ease of use should be addressed for all applications in a mechanism-independent manner so that the effort spent integrating payments with an application and developing user interfaces is not duplicated for each payment service. There is a need for a common API and user interface for all of the evolving payment services. There is also a need for conversion-of-payment instruments between payment services. The NetCheque system has been designed to clear payments between NetCheque accounting servers, and is well-suited for clearing payments between servers of different types.

An Internet payment system should have the properties of security, reliability, scalability, acceptability, flexibility, convertibility, and efficiency, and it should provide for the possibility of anonymity. For a variety of purposes, the NetCheque and NetCash systems discussed in this chapter will satisfy the needs of future customers and suppliers in electronic markets such as the Internet.

References

Chaum, David. 1992. Achieving electronic privacy. *Scientific American* (August): 96–101.

Gifford, D., A. Payne, L. Stewart, and W. Treese. 1995. Payment switches for open networks. In *Proceedings of IEEE Compcon '95.*

Lai, Charlie, Gennady Medvinsky, and B. Clifford Neuman. 1994. Endorsements, licensing, and insurance for distributed system services. In *Proceedings of the Second ACM Conference on Computer and Communications Security.*

Low, Steven H., Nicholas F. Maxemchuk, and Sanjoy Paul. 1994. Anonymous credit cards. In *Proceedings of the Second ACM Conference on Computer and Communications Security.*

Medvinsky, Gennady, and B. Clifford Neuman. 1993. NetCash: A design for practical electronic survey on the Internet. In *Proceedings of the First ACM Conference on Computer and Communications Security.*

Neuman, B. Clifford. 1993. Proxy-based authorization and accounting for distributed systems. In *Proceedings of the 13th International Conference on Distributed Computing Systems.*

Neuman, B. Clifford, and Gennady Medvinsky. 1995. Requirements for network payment: The NetCheque perspective. In *Proceedings of IEEE Compcon '95.*

Neuman, B. Clifford, and Theodore Ts'o. 1994. Kerberos: An authentication service for computer networks. *IEEE Communications* 32(9).

Sirbu, Marvin, and J. Douglas Tygar. 1995. Netbill: An electronic commerce system optimized for network delivered information and services. In *Proceedings of IEEE Compcon '95*.

Acknowledgments

The authors are grateful to Celeste Anderson, Charlie Lai, Paul Mockapetris, Brenda Timmerman, and Brian Tung for their comments on drafts of this chapter. This research was supported in part by the Advanced Research Projects Agency under NASA Cooperative Agreement NCC-2539 and through Ft. Hauchuca under Contract No. DABT63-94C-0034. The views and conclusions contained in this chapter are those of the authors and should not be interpreted as representing the official policies, either expressed or implied, of the funding agencies. Figures and descriptions in this chapter were provided by the authors and are used with permission.

This chapter is predominantly drawn from B. Clifford Neuman and Gennady Medvinsky, Requirements for network payment: The NetCheque perspective, in *Proceedings of IEEE COMPCON'95*, 1995. This paper was used almost in its entirety; additional material (the discussion of NetCash) was drawn from Gennady Medvinsky and B. Clifford Neuman, NetCash: A Design for Practical Electronic Currency on the Internet, in *Proceedings of the First ACM Conference on Computer and Communication Security*, 1993. These papers are reprinted here with the permission of their publishers.

Endorsements, Licensing, and Insurance for Distributed Services

Charlie Lai, Gennady Medvinsky, and B. Clifford Neuman

Introduction

In distributed systems, local applications rely on remote servers to provide file storage, computation, authentication, authorization, and other functions. Such servers should be judged by their users, or users' organizations, to be secure and competent to perform the offered services. In smaller systems, users have confidence in service providers governed by the same administrative body to which they belong. When a system spans administrative boundaries, applications may rely on servers provided by other organizations. Users rarely understand the policies of remote organizations, making it hard to assess confidence in such foreign servers. Without sufficient assurance, users may limit their interactions to only those servers within their own administrative domain, limiting sharing—a principal benefit of a distributed system.

In the "real world," consumers rely on endorsements, licensing, liability insurance, and surety bonding to compensate for such lack of confidence. For example, the American Automobile Association provides endorsements for hotels and restaurants using a five-diamond scale, and the Better Business Bureau provides information about local businesses. In computer systems, these assurances can be represented by certificates digitally signed by the endorser, licensing authority, or insurance provider. Such assurance credentials would be granted to a server after it meets the requirements set by the organization issuing the credentials (Neuman 1991).

A license is a credential that indicates a service provider is legally authorized to provide a service. It indicates that the service provider has been found to meet certain minimal qualifications required by law, and that the service provider is subject to regulation and sanctions if found to be violating the law. The extent to which licensed service providers are monitored varies depending on the service, but is usually minimal. Licenses usually are issued by governmental bodies, are rarely revoked, and are on occasion obtained fraudulently. A license rarely provides information about the quality of a service.

An endorsement provides assurance that a service provider meets more rigorous requirements determined by the endorser, and usually provides information about the quality of a service provider, often as compared with other service providers. One's confidence in an endorsed service provider depends in part on one's confidence in its endorsers. In addition to services, endorsements may apply to products. For example, Underwriters Laboratories endorses products as compliant with established safety standards.

While an endorsement or license assists in determining the level of risk involved in dealing with a service provider, a liability insurance policy or surety bond provides a client with a means to recover damages in the event of a loss that is the fault of the service provider.

When a user deals with an insured or bonded service provider, the risk of malfeasant or misfeasant behavior on the part of the service provider is partially shifted from the client to the insurance provider. Premiums for insurance are based on the level of risk assumed by the insurance provider. To be competitive, the parties insured may adopt policies that reduce this premium, potentially resulting in improved security for the distributed system as a whole.

This chapter describes a method to electronically represent endorsements, licenses, and insurance policies, and discusses the means by which clients use such items when selecting service providers. We begin our discussion with the principles of liability insurance and surety bonding, which are the more general mechanisms described in this chapter. The next section continues with a discussion of endorsements and licensing. The design of the system is presented, server selection policies are described, and the implications of trusting insurance providers and endorsers themselves are discussed. The chapter continues by describing how the proposed mechanisms can improve confidence in several distributed system services and by discussing similarities with mechanisms already in use. The chapter concludes with a brief summary.

Liability Insurance

Today, three basic types of insurance exist: (1) personal insurance, which protects the life of the insured; (2) casualty insurance, which protects the property of the insured; and (3) liability insurance. Liability insurance does not cover personal losses of the insured; instead, the insured is covered for any legal obligation to pay damages inflicted upon a third party. Liability insurance providers agree to "assume loss or liability imposed by law with respect to certain property, rights, or liability caused by specified risks or hazards. The party to be insured against loss or liability is called the 'assured' or 'insured,' and the causes of damage, loss or liability are 'risks' or 'hazards'" (Long 1992).

A liability insurance contract is an agreement between an insurance provider and the insured. This contract, called a policy, specifies the obligations of the parties involved. The policy covers damages inflicted by the insured upon a third party if the damages were caused by an accident or occurrence. The words "accident" and "occurrence" do not include damages caused willfully by the insured. Liability insurance does not relieve the insured from responsibility for committing malicious acts (Long 1992).

Surety bonding closely resembles liability insurance. The major distinction is that a liability insurance policy represents an agreement between two parties, and a surety bond represents an agreement among three parties: the surety, the obligee, and the principal. The surety (insurance provider) agrees to be responsible to the obligee (the party insured) for the conduct of the principal (the service provider). In other words, a surety bond guarantees to a prospective client the performance of a service provider. A surety bond also indemnifies the insured for any damages resulting from dishonest acts of the service provider. Unlike the coverage provided by liability insurance, these acts may be intentional or unintentional in nature. As a result, surety bonding provides greater coverage for clients than does liability insurance (Porter 1970).

Due to the similarities between surety bonding and liability insurance, we will use the term insurance to encompass both for the remainder of the chapter.

When a policy is requested, insurance providers calculate the risk to be assumed by a liability insurance policy and fix the premium at an adequate level to reflect this risk. If the insured's situation or position changes, altering the assumed risk, the insurance provider has the right to alter the policy or charge a different premium (Long 1992). Insurance providers will need to assess a service provider's procedures, past behavior, etc., to determine whether to insure the service provider and to set a premium.

Because issuing policies requires an assessment of the assumed risk, and settling claims requires judgment, neither of which are easily automated, we will leave such issues outside the system where they may be handled by the insurance agent, the adjuster, the injured party, and possibly the judicial system. In this chapter, we concern ourselves with "proof of insurance," the mechanism by which users of a service verify that adequate coverage is in force.

Today, policies are written agreements certified by the signatures of the parties. In a computer system, the terms and the parties to such an agreement must be easily interpretable. For our purposes, the electronic representation of an assurance policy will include the following information:

1. The names of the parties in a form suitable for authentication. Specifically:

• the name of the insurance provider;
• the name of the service provider; and
• a description of the obligee if a surety bond.

2. The subject of the insurance and the insured risks.
3. The period the policy is in force.
4. The limits of liability, possibly as:

• an individual limit per occurrence or party;

• an aggregate limit of liability; or

• possibly no limit (if endorsement or license).

5. Any other conditions pertaining to the insurance.

The standard representation of each of the elements of a policy is required so that applications can easily determine if the right kind of insurance is in place. For general coverages, the hazards insured against are determined by the category of the service provider. Several categories have been defined, including authentication, security, electronic currency, accounting/payment, data storage, and computation. The insured risks are standard for each of these service categories and are described in Table 1. Additional coverages may apply, e.g., service availability. Such "special" coverages have a registered meaning, known to applications that require such coverage.

Licensing and Endorsements

Other mechanisms may be used to assess confidence in the service provider. For example, although prospective clients may not trust a service provider, confidence in the provider may be elevated through endorsements from trusted and well-known organizations. Such organizations may officially endorse a service provider when they have found the service provider to be competent, trustworthy, and providing a high quality of service. Examples of organizations that issue

Table 1
Common Hazards and Assurances

Subject/Risk	G/S	Description of Hazard or Occurrence
AUTHENTICATION	General	Issue of improper credentials or disclosure keys
SECURITY	General	Improper mediation of access
CURRENCY	General	Issue of unbacked currency (including counterfeit)
ACCOUNTING	General	Error in account maintenance, insufficient reserves
INSURANCE	General	Insufficient reserves to cover expected losses
STORAGE	General	Unauthorized disclosure of data, or loss of data
COMPUTATION	General	Unauthorized disclosure of data or computation, loss of integrity of computation
AVAILABILITY	Special	Failure to meet specified availability metric
ASSURANCE	Special	Failure to meet specified quality rating

endorsements today include the American Automobile Association, which provides endorsements for hotels and restaurants using a five-diamond scale; the Better Business Bureau, which provides information about local businesses; and Underwriters Laboratories, which certifies that products meet certain safety standards. Endorsements do not provide compensation for damages incurred while interacting with service providers; instead they provide a mechanism for clients to better evaluate (and therefore reduce) the risk involved in dealing with service providers.

Similarly, users can require presentation of licenses from service providers proving the legal authority to offer a particular service. Issuance of a license might require a service provider to follow certain policies protecting its customers. In addition, before issuing a license, the licensing agency might verify that the party is competent to perform the service, as is done for licenses to practice medicine or law. Like endorsements, licensing does not provide compensation for damages, but it does provide prospective clients a simple means to reduce the likelihood of relying on illegitimate service providers.

The concept of an insurance policy, surety bonding, licensing, and endorsements are the same, differing solely in the limits and source of compensation in the event of a loss. Licensing usually provides no compensation by the licensing authority, endorsements provide no contractual liability on the part of the endorser (although they might be sued anyway), and insurance and surety bonding provide contractual liability by the insurance provider.

Implementation

The characteristics of insurance policies, endorsements, and licenses have already been described. To incorporate such mechanisms into a distributed system, we first define the basic representation of assurance credentials.

Representation of Assurance Credentials

An assurance credential can be an insurance policy, a surety bond, a license, or an endorsement. We represent such a credential as a restricted proxy (Neuman 1993). A proxy is a token that enables one principal to operate with the privileges of another principal. A restricted proxy is a proxy that allows the exercise of such privileges for a particular purpose, subject to a specified set of conditions and restrictions. We use the term proxy in the remainder of this chapter to mean a restricted proxy.

Figure 1 shows the proxy encoding of an assurance credential. When used to represent an assurance credential, the authority granted by a proxy is the right to assert that such an assurance is in force. The terms of the credential, i.e., the assurances provided, are encoded as restrictions, some of which were described in Table 1. The principal on whose authority a proxy is granted is referred to as the grantor. For assurance credentials this will be the insurer, the endorser or the licensing agent. The proxy is signed by the grantor. This is represented abstractly in the figure by square brackets; the encryption keys used for the signature depend on the proxy implementation. The grantee or delegate is the principal to whom the proxy is issued, in this case the service provider. Although Neuman (1993) calls the verifier of a proxy the end-server, such terminology is confusing here since the verifier of an assurance credential is the client of the service provider; consequently, we will use the term verifier instead.

CERTIFICATE	Class:	Insurance, endorsement, or license
	Quota:	Limit of liability $1M (optional)
	Subject:	Currency (as per Table 1)
	Grantee:	CurrencySever1
	Proxy Key:	K_{Proxy}

$K_{grantor}$

| PROXY KEY | K_{proxy} |
| GRANTOR | Insurance agent, endorser, or license agent |

Figure 1
Assurance credential represented as proxy

Proxies can be divided into two classes: bearer proxies and delegate proxies. Bearer proxies have an associated proxy key that is used by the bearer to prove to the verifier possession of the proxy. To present a bearer proxy to the verifier, the grantee sends the certificate to the verifier and uses the proxy key to partake in an authentication exchange using the underlying authentication system. Delegate proxies have a list of delegates encoded as a restriction. They can only be used by one of the named delegates, which must send the certificate part of the proxy to the verifier and authenticate itself under its own identity. The verifier validates the certificate and checks to see that the delegate is included in the list of delegates. Both forms of proxies are suitable for representing assurance credentials, but the greater accountability of a delegate proxy (i.e., the identification of the delegate) makes it a better choice for most situations.

Proxies may be implemented using either conventional or public-key cryptography. Both implementations are described in Neuman (1993). By defining assurance credentials as proxies, we free our mechanisms from dependence on a particular encryption algorithm. We also inherit the infrastructure needed to verify such credentials, and a structured framework within which the characteristics of the credential may be enumerated.

Service providers use proxies to demonstrate proof of insurance or endorsement. A client may request presentation of an assurance credential from a service provider, or may retrieve the credential from a separate directory service. Assurance credentials requested from the service provider may be bearer proxies, while those retrieved from a separate directory service must be delegate proxies.

Verification

When an assurance credential is received from a service provider or retrieved from a directory service, the client validates the credential in two steps. First, the proxy is verified cryptographically. The details of this verification will depend on the proxy mechanism used (e.g., public key vs. conventional cryptography, and bearer proxy vs. delegate proxy) and may require further interactions with other servers.

Endorsements, Licensing, and Insurance for Distributed Services

Second, the restrictions, hazards, and assurances present in the proxy are extracted and compared against the user's and application's policy for server selection. Finally, the service provider must authenticate itself to the client using the underlying authentication protocol used by the system, possibly as part of a mutual authentication protocol in which the client and service provider prove their identities to one another.

Figure 2 shows the messages needed to retrieve and verify assurance credentials. Depending on the proxy mechanism used, some of the messages may be skipped. It is assumed that assurance credentials are issued to the grantee in advance, based on external agreements and evaluations by the grantor. It is further assumed that a client has settled on a candidate service provider and knows what assurances are required. In message 1, the client requests proof of assurance from the candidate service provider. The assurance is presented to the client in message 4 in a form that varies with different proxy implementations. Refer to Neuman (1993) for details.

If the service provider requires a separate credential for each client (which will be the case in a conventional cryptography

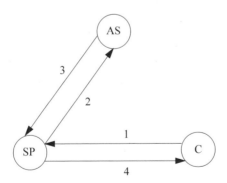

1. Client (C) requests proof of assurance from service provider (SP)
2. SP requests credentials from authentication server (AS)
3. AS returns assurance credentials to SP
4. SP sends assurance credentials to client and authenticates to client

Figure 2
Obtaining Proof from Service Provider

implementation), it requests and retrieves such a credential in messages 2 and 3. In such an implementation, the service provider sends a less specific credential to an authentication server, with the name of the prospective client. The authentication server returns a new credential derived from the original one, encrypted in a key that may be verified by the client. Messages 2 and 3 will be absent in a public key implementation, possibly replaced by messages between the client and an authentication server to verify the public key of the grantor of the assurance.

After validating assurances from the service provider, clients may cache the assurance until its expiration, saving repeated requests on subsequent dealings with the same service provider.

Alternative Implementations

Alternative assurance mechanisms are possible. For example, one could require the client to contact the grantor of the assurance directly through an integrity-protected channel. This would provide for faster cancellation of assurance credentials but would make the assurance grantor a bottleneck, possibly affecting the performance and availability of the system. It is the concept of assurance that is important, and the benefits of one implementation over another will depend on environmental assumptions including the real-time availability of insurers and endorsers.

Server Selection Requirements and Preferences

To utilize assurance credentials, distributed applications must be modified to request specific credentials, verify the credentials, and decide whether those credentials are sufficient according to a user-specified server assurance policy. A user's server assurance policy identifies the assurances required for each class of application and identifies the assurance grantors whose assurances will be accepted. Usually a user's organization will provide a default configuration for use by its members. Users may extend the default settings, and may define their own configuration for nonbusiness use. Such configuration information may be maintained in a configuration database, a distributed directory service, or a configuration file accessed by each application at run time.

The server assurance criteria will be different for different classes of applications. For example, banking servers may require proof of insurance issued by the Federal Deposit Insurance Corporation (FDIC), while insurance providers may require the combination of a particular rating by an endorsement institution and a license from the state insurance commissioner.

Because the server assurance criteria defines a subset of network servers with which a user can interact, it defines a custom view of the network. Information about the assurances available for each service provider could be stored in directory service entries for each service provider, making it easier for applications to choose candidates that meet the assurance criteria (Neuman, Augart, and Upasani 1993). Similarly, some endorsers might provide directories of endorsed service providers making it even easier to identify candidate providers. Such directory service entries might be advisory only, with proof of assurance presented by the service provider as described in the previous section.

A Framework for Building Confidence

Presence of assurance credentials should not by itself improve confidence in a service provider. The contribution of such credentials toward improving confidence in a service provider must depend in part on one's confidence in the endorser or insurance provider itself. There are many insurance companies, many organizations granting endorsements, and many jurisdictions issuing licenses. It is not practical to list all such assurance providers as part of each user's server assurance criteria. Instead, such criteria may identify organizations authorized to grant assurances for other assurance providers. For example, a user's server assurance criteria might require a service provider to present a business license from an agency with competent jurisdiction, of which only local agencies are listed directly; licenses for foreign license agencies may require assurance credentials for the licensing agency itself.

Lai, Medvinsky, and Neuman

Such transitive assurance is common in the insurance industry. Insurance companies are rated and endorsed by agencies such as A.M. Best. In many jurisdictions, insurance companies must also be affiliated, with a portion of every premium dollar going to the jurisdiction to make good on claims with insurance companies that fail. This backing constitutes insurance of the insurance provider itself.

Transitive assurance may extend to an arbitrary depth, but longer chains generally promote less confidence. Where assurance is rated, heuristics are needed for deriving the combined assurance rating from the metrics and limits associated with the individual credentials involved. Such heuristics are a topic for further study.

Though confidence in an endorser or insurance provider is important, self-endorsement and self-insurance are also meaningful. Self-endorsement or self-insurance is analogous to marketing claims and warranties today. While such claims by a service provider might not instill as much confidence as outside endorsements and insurance, they can assist the user in differentiating between a production service and a prototype. They also allow a service provider to make claims regarding the efforts made to keep the service available.

As insurance, licensing, and endorsements are integrated with distributed system services, networks of assurance relationships will evolve. Figure 3 shows how such a network might appear. Dark arrows indicate a dependence on the correct operation of the destination of the arrow. Light arrows indicate that the source of the arrow will provide assurance for the service provider to which the arrow points. Dashed arrows indicate implied confidence.

In this example, client C requests service from service provider S2. To provide this service, S2 subcontracts to service provider S1. C's confidence in the composite service depends on the assurance provided for both S1 and S2.

To improve customer confidence, S1 and S2 obtain a liability insurance policy from insurance provider I1. As long as C has confidence in I1 it is assured that C will be compensated in the event of damages caused by S1 or S2. In this example, C does not have confidence directly in the insurance provider, but will accept the endorsement of E3, an organization that rates insurance companies.

Endorsements, Licensing, and Insurance for Distributed Services

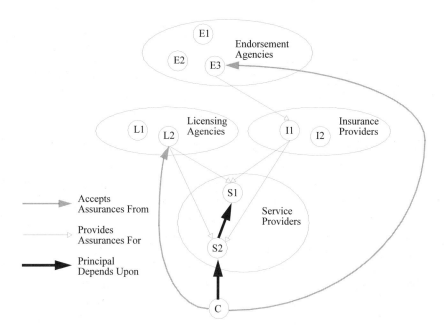

Figure 3
A Network of Trust Relationships

Client C will also find that service providers S1 and S2 are licensed by licensing agency L2, indicating that L2 has found each server competent in offering its services. The licensing authority L2 has not been endorsed directly, but is recognized as the appropriate licensing agency by C.

It is unlikely that the network of assurance relationships will be strictly hierarchical, though the network will contain components that are hierarchical. By not imposing a hierarchy, clients gain greater flexibility in specifying server selection policies.

Relationship to System Services and Other Work

Users require confidence in the distributed system services they use. This section discusses some of these services, shows how assurance credentials affect confidence in the service provider and, in some cases, describes confidence mechanisms already used by the service.

Authentication

An authentication server certifies the association of encryption keys to individuals. The credentials issued by authentication servers are subsequently used to authenticate users to one another. In essence, an authentication server issues assurance credentials where the assurance provided pertains solely to the identity of the individual. Cross-realm authentication allows individuals registered with one authentication server to prove their identity to those registered with different authentication servers. Global cross-realm authentication is supported by several authentication systems (Neuman and Ts'o 1994; Tardo and Alagappan 1991), and techniques for assessing confidence in foreign authentication servers has been discussed widely in the literature (Birrell et al. 1986; Gligor, Luan, and Pato 1992; Lampson et al. 1992).

Most approaches require a hierarchical organization of realms, with trust relationships following the hierarchy. Assurance of the authority of an authentication server is provided by credentials issued by other servers in the hierarchy. A problem with the hierarchical organization of realms is that different administrative bodies with different policies control the authentication servers, making it difficult to assess confidence in the authentication process as a whole.

In practice, it has been difficult to establish a complete hierarchy for authentication servers precisely because the level of confidence required for participating realms is not well understood, and organizations that have the stature to serve as realms near the root of the hierarchy are concerned about liability. Some systems, including Pretty Good Privacy (PGP) (Zimmerman 1994), loosen the requirements, allowing users to certify the keys of other users, avoiding the need for a complete hierarchy. Like the assurance mechanisms described in this chapter, PGP users identify other users whose certifications they trust. Unlike endorsements, certifications in PGP pertain to identity only. Endorsements of the certification procedures of other users are not public.

Insurance, licensing, and endorsements provide a better means to assess confidence in the certification policies of an intermediate realm. Insurance provides a means of recovering damages that result from faulty certifications, making individuals and other service providers more willing to rely on such certifications. The procedures of such authentication servers may be assessed by independent auditors, resulting in an endorsement that improves confidence by parties that trust the independent auditor.

Electronic Currency

Currency servers issue electronic currency and provide services for currency exchange (Chaum, Fiat, and Naor 1988; Medvinsky and Neuman 1993). Currency servers for a distributed system will be governed by multiple administrative bodies and may exist in different jurisdictions. As with paper money, electronic currency should be backed, directly or indirectly, by real value. This backing is jeopardized by counterfeit currency, faulty accounting procedures, or fraud.

Today, paper currency is trusted because there are relatively few issuers, mostly sanctioned by national governments. There may be many more issuers of electronic currency, many of which will be less trusted. Users must be more cautious when dealing with electronic currency, and should not blindly trust unknown currency servers.

Using the assurance mechanisms described in this chapter, backing of a currency may be represented by insurance with an aggregate liability limit equal to the amount of backing. The assurance credentials would be granted by the bank, accounting service, or any other body that maintains the assets backing the currency. The records and procedures of the currency server would be endorsed by independent auditors. These auditors can attest to the amount of currency in circulation and can verify that currency servers only issue properly backed currency.

Accounting

Accounting servers maintain account balances for users, track consumption of resources, maintain quotas, and more generally act as electronic banks (Neuman 1993). The confidence of users in such

Lai, Medvinsky, and Neuman

services may be derived from insurance analogous to FDIC insurance of banks in the United States. The required level of assurance will depend in part on the kinds of balances maintained. A high level of assurance may be required for services that maintain large positive balances for its customers, while less assurance may be necessary for services that grant credit or maintain debit balances for customers (which are collected after the purchase or service has been provided).

Status

Authentication credentials in version 5 of Kerberos, a distributed authentication mechanism, provide preliminary support for restricted proxies. The assurance mechanisms described in this chapter are not yet implemented. Work is under way to develop distributed accounting and currency services. The assurance mechanisms described here are an important part of the implementation of those services.

Discussion and Conclusions

As a distributed system spans organizational boundaries and users interact more frequently with outside service providers it becomes increasingly difficult to determine the appropriate level of confidence to place in the service provider. Without a method to assess the integrity and competence of service providers, sharing across organizations will be reduced. It is this sharing that is typically one of the strengths of a distributed system.

This chapter examined the use of licensing, endorsements, and insurance as a mechanism for addressing this problem. The approaches are similar and may be implemented electronically as a single mechanism, but with different parameters. Together, these approaches provide clients with several options for assessing confidence and evaluating the risks incurred when interacting with service providers. Clients may determine whether a service provider has been endorsed by a respected organization, or whether the service provider is licensed or insured. The degree of assurance required will differ from client to client, and from application to application.

Service providers will obtain insurance policies, surety bonds, licenses, and endorsements to offer prospective clients greater assurance in their ability to conduct their trade. With a financial incentive to improve the security and reliability of their systems, service providers will finally have a means to justify investment in security. With a basis for selecting service providers, users will finally have a means for choosing servers that can meet their operational and security requirements.

References

Birrell, Andrew D., Butler W. Lampson, Roger M. Needham, and Michael D. Schroeder. 1986. A global authentication service without global trust. In *Proceedings of the IEEE symposium on security and privacy.*

Chaum, D., A. Fiat, and N. Naor. 1988. Untraceable electronic cash. *Proceedings Crypto '88.*

Gligor, Virgil D., Shyh-Wei Luan, and Joseph N. Pato. 1992. On inter-realm authentication in large distributed systems. In *Proceedings of the 1992 IEEE symposium on research in security and privacy.*

Lampson, Butler W., Martin Abadi, Michael Burrows, and Edward Wobber. 1992. Authentication in distributed systems: Theory and practice. *ACM Transactions on Computer Systems* 10(4): 265–310.

Long, Rowland H. 1992. *The law of liability insurance,* Volumes 1 and 2. Oakland, Calif.: Mathew Bender and Company. See in particular pages 1.2 and 13.7.

Medvinsky, Gennady, and B. Clifford Neuman. 1993. NetCash: A design for practical electronic currency on the Internet. In *Proceedings of the first ACM conference on computer and communications security.*

Neuman, B. Clifford. 1991. Protection and security issues for future systems. In *Proceedings of the workshop on operating systems of the 90s and beyond,* Lecture Notes in Computer Science No. 563: 184–201.

Neuman, B. Clifford. 1993. Proxy-based authorization and accounting for distributed systems. In *Proceedings of the 13th international conference on distributed computing systems.*

Neuman, B. Clifford, Steven Seger Augart, and Shantaprasad Upasani. 1993. Using Prospero to support integrated location independent computing. In *Proceedings of the Usenix symposium on mobile and location-independent computing.*

Neuman, B. Clifford, and Theodore Ts'o. 1994. Kerberos: An authentication service for computer networks. *IEEE Communications* 32(9).

Porter, David. *Fundamentals of bonding, a manual of fidelity and surety.* Indianapolis, Ind.: The Rough Notes Co., Inc., 9–11.

Tardo, Joseph J., and Kannan Alagappan. 1991. SPX: Global authentication using public key certificates. In *Proceedings of the IEEE symposium on security and privacy.*

Zimmermann, Philip. 1994. *PGP user's guide,* Volumes 1 and 2. Distributed with PGP 2.6.

Acknowledgments

Steven Augart, Celeste Anderson, Sridhar Gullapalli, Shai Herzog, Katia Obraczka, Jon Postel, and Stuart Stubblebine provided discussion and comments on drafts of this chapter.

Previously appeared as: Charlie Lai, Gennady Medvinsky, and B. Clifford Neuman, "Endorsements, Licensing, and Insurance for Distributed System Services," in *Proceedings of the 2nd ACM Conference on Computer and Communication Security,* November 1994. It is reprinted here with permission.

Information Security for Internet Commerce

Lee McKnight with Richard Solomon, Joseph Reagle, David Carver, Clark Johnson, Branko Gerovac, and David Gingold

Introduction

Internet privacy and security are of growing importance to businesses, nations, and, last but not least, people.[1] New applications, new users, and improved access have enabled the Internet to become an important medium for communication, information dissemination, and commerce. Security policy for the Internet, however, is not yet well developed. In part because of the lingering effects of the Cold War, work on the intersection of Internet commerce and Internet security policy has been largely avoided by researchers and policy analysts. Nevertheless, even on an insecure

1. An earlier draft of this chapter, titled "Strategies for Federal R&D on Heterogeneity and Information Security," was presented at a July 1995 workshop on "America in the Age of Information: A Forum on Federal Information and Communications R&D" sponsored by the Committee on Information and Communications, National Science and Technology Council, and the National Coordination Office for High Performance Computing and Communications. This chapter draws upon work partially funded by the Sloan Foundation, National Science Foundation grant NCR-9509244, and Defense Advanced Research Projects Agency contract N00174-93-C-0036. This chapter draws extensively on the research and insights of the participants in the Internet economics and the Internet privacy and security workshops, held at MIT in March 1995 and May 1996, respectively, both with the support of the National Science Foundation and the Federal Networking Council. Feedback on these issues from the members of the Federal Networking Council and Federal Networking Council Advisory Committee is gratefully acknowledged. Please consult (http://rpcp.mit.edu/Workshops/cfp.html) for Internet economics and Internet privacy and security workshop notes and other information. Any errors of fact or by omission are the lead author's sole responsibility. Views expressed here are the personal views of the authors, and not of their sponsoring institutions.

Internet, entrepreneurs and technologists are finding market opportunities arising from Internet commerce (Kalakota and Whinston 1996).

The lack of cohesive national policies disadvantages corporations competing in a global market with foreign firms free of restrictions limiting use of information security technologies. Furthermore, an alarming disarray of protocols that do not interoperate, become static, and ultimately fail to provide real information security has created a confusing and precarious environment for users worldwide.

A development path for Internet commerce must be found which satisfies at the same time the national security interests of governments and the privacy and security concerns of users (FNC/RPCP 1996). There are reasons for optimism. Businesses have a strong incentive to seek to profit from users (consumers) while cooperating —and competing—in the provision of privacy and security. Governments have an interest in continuing to stimulate the development of security, privacy, and electronic commerce technologies to gain the benefits of efficiency and new capabilities from computing and networking technologies, while lessening the risks from failures in the computing infrastructure, whether from physical damage, errors, or intentional attacks (NSTC 1996). And users of Internet commerce have an interest in being able to trust the security of their transactions (Reagle 1996). Privacy is a more complex issue, affected by the nuances of individuals, cultures and national laws, applications, and networks, but it cannot be ignored in the development of advanced information and communications systems.[2]

In this chapter we explore these issues and their implications for Internet commerce. First, we identify factors encouraging Internet commerce development by the private and public sectors. We discuss why there is a misalignment inhibiting the growth of Internet commerce. We propose a balanced government role to promote Internet commerce that differs from the polarized suggestions of intelligence and security agencies, on the one hand, and cyberlibertarians, on the other. Instead of advocating either a laissez-faire or a regulatory

---

2. Concerns about the threat to privacy of advanced networks are not limited to the Internet, but extend to other digital systems. See, for example, Kerber (1996).

role, this chapter argues that governments may best help Internet commerce develop by participating in and facilitating understanding of Internet commerce requirements and funding information security development testbed projects.

Private Development of Internet Security Mechanisms

Commercial development of standards and products to support Internet commerce is accelerating, but the lack of widespread adoption of them underscores the barriers still present which inhibit commercial Internet services. Two critical areas of development include information security technology and electronic payment mechanisms. Without security, information technologies cannot realize their full potential for customers, and suppliers fear falsified or tampered transactions (Cheswick and Bellovin 1994). Security in information technology allows for reliable electronic payment mechanisms, which in turn enable Internet commerce.

Information Security Products

Many different products have been developed to improve information security, but security requires an integrated approach to be successful (NRC 1991). Security at any layer reduces the possibility of unauthorized users intercepting data, but it does not eliminate it. People are at the highest layer of developing secure transactions, and typically, where people are involved, transactions are the least secure. For example, how often do we, as customers, write down a password or hand our credit card to a clerk we don't know? Both actions reduce security.

However, the difficulty of achieving end-to-end security does not mean that private development in information security products should be halted. And even if we trust another person on the Internet, using no information security technology may still be a bad idea. For example, the paths taken by many of the Internet data transmissions we send and receive are not known to us. Someone we don't know may "see" our packets as they traverse their network.

To promote information security for transmissions, there are two layers where private development is helping: the network layer and the application layer. An example of a network-layer security protocol is the Secure Sockets Layer (SSL) developed by Netscape. SSL is a security protocol which was built into the Netscape Navigator and Commerce Server in the mid-1990s to allow for the authentication of customers of Internet stores and for the encryption of payment information such as credit card numbers. Although the 40-bit key initially used was weak, little could be done to strengthen the protocol since export restrictions disallowed the use of longer keys.[3] Key length regulation is an important factor in limiting the trust users place in Internet commerce systems.

The export (non-U.S.) version of Netscape's server and browser software was not equipped with the Secure Sockets Layer due to U.S. government policy.[4] Because the information market is a global market, most Netscape browsers are the "weakened" applications. This poses a risk to the users of electronic commerce as well as to the technological strength of the United States. Companies in other countries are developing their own versions of SSL and similar technologies and may benefit from fewer export restrictions than Netscape faces. These companies can develop stronger products for sale worldwide.

Application-layer security (security above the network layer) programs include Pretty Good Privacy (PGP)[5] and the MIT-developed Kerberos. PGP uses a combination of private and public key encryption for users to encode documents that can only be opened with a particular password-protected private key.[6] In 1995, Phil Zimmer-

3. For example, in 1995 two members of the Internet mailing list "cypherpunks" broke the 40-bit RC4 key, an algorithm used by Netscape's Secure Socket Layer.

4. U.S. federal policy on security technologies is currently evolving. At the time of this writing (Fall 1996), new rules facilitating export of particular security technologies including longer keys are being implemented, as are new private sector developments. In particular, in 1996 authority for export licensing of cryptographic products was transferred from the State Department to the presumably more business-oriented Department of Commerce. It is too soon to say whether these changes will be sufficient to alleviate the constraints lack of security imposes on Internet commerce, but we have our doubts.

5. For more information on PGP, see Garfinkel (1995).

6. Private key encryption includes a pair of "keys" (a string of bits that, when added to an algorithm, transforms an encrypted file to a decrypted file or vice versa). The private key decrypts a document and a public key encrypts a document. The public key is used by the sender to encode bits that are sent to you and decrypted by your private key.

mann, the author of PGP, announced the release of the telephony application PGPfone, which will allow users to conduct encrypted voice communications over normal phone lines and eventually over the Internet. Kerberos allows for authentication of users by a secure server and uses private key security (Steiner, Neuman, and Schiller 1988; Kohl and Neuman 1993). Using Kerberos, users can gain access to a password-protected server without that password traversing the network or without having it read by the server. A benefit of PGP is that there is no trusted party or server required to guarantee security.

Payment Mechanisms

Private developments to enable Internet commerce include a number of payment mechanisms. The heterogeneity of payment mechanisms in the physical world (e.g., cash, check, credit card, and debit card) has parallels in the digital world.[7] Information security technologies are needed in order to make a payment mechanism that people trust—a mechanism that is not susceptible to fraud. Sirbu and Tygar (1995) argue that security and privacy issues must be addressed to ensure the integrity of electronic commerce systems which eventually lead to the adoption of payment mechanisms. Just as there is a variety of payment mechanisms in the physical world, many different electronic payment mechanisms are also being developed.

NetBill (Sirbu and Tygar 1995), for example, is designed for anonymous, high-volume, low-price transactions—similar to cash transactions in the physical world. Aggregation of transactions allows for a billing system that can recover its costs even if the price is as low as a fraction of a penny. The system employs digital signatures, encrypted goods delivery, and pseudonyms to support anonymity. Moreover, NetBill recognizes the importance of interoperability by being built upon a foundation of standard interfaces and open protocols.

7. The chapter by Neuman and Medvinsky in this volume discusses some of the critical requirements for these payment mechanisms. See also Reagle (1996).

For transactions that do not require anonymity, have a higher transaction value, and are therefore able to warrant higher transaction costs, a system such as NetCheque (Neuman and Medvinsky 1995) or NetCash (Medvinsky and Neuman 1995) may be appropriate. NetCheque is a system that supports payment for access to National Information Infrastructure (NII) services. It uses technology such as Kerberos encryption for a secure, reliable, and efficient system design. NetCheque was created to meet many electronic payment criteria; for example, the system must be flexible enough to support many different payment mechanisms, sufficiently scalable to support multiple independent accounting services, efficient so as to avoid delays, and unobtrusive so that users will not be constantly interrupted.[8] A fraction of each transaction is paid to the NetCheque system (Bailey et al. 1996).

Credit cards will certainly have a presence on the Internet. Banking is just one, but perhaps the most obvious, of the industries affected by Internet electronic payment mechanisms (Crede 1995). For example, in 1995, an announcement regarding electronic commerce was made by 14 banks and financial institutions that formed a company under the name of SmartCash. Participants include Master Card, Bank One, and the Bank of America. The goal of the program was to provide smart cards that could hold immense amounts of information and security functionality. Also, efforts are being made to standardize SmartCash's system with those being developed by others, such as Europay and Visa.[9] However, the ability of SmartCash to interoperate with Europay is not only a technical issue, but also depends on the public policies of each country in which Europay operates.

Public Policy

From a policy perspective, when considering information security policy decisions and Internet commerce the role of government, the role of users, and the role of the Internet in a global economy must

8. More information on NetCheque and NetCash is found in the chapter by Neuman and Medvinsky in this volume.

9. Reuters, August 16, 1996.

all be taken into account. The previous section discussed significant research under way on architectures for billing and electronic payment mechanisms. Commercial development of such systems is also accelerating, as one can read in the daily business press. These developments would not be possible without information security technologies, which in turn are affected by public policy.

The United States has pursued a domestic cryptographic policy that some argue violates its citizens' right to privacy. Also, a foreign export policy thought by many industry leaders to be damaging the competitiveness of American companies.[10] The long- running "Clipper Chip" debate of the 1990s illustrated this concern over cryptographic policy. Many argued that a mandatory requirement to disallow citizens from using all cryptography other than that to which the government would have backdoor access would be a violation of civil rights.

The Clinton administration contended that it was never its goal to disallow other forms of cryptography (like PGP), but merely to make the Clipper protocol the required protocol for communications with the federal government. However, in 1995, the Electronic Private Information Center (EPIC) under the Freedom of Information Act obtained and made public files from the FBI. One of the files submitted to the White House National Security Council in February 1993 was entitled "Encryption: The Threat, Applications and Potential Solutions" and was endorsed by the Federal Bureau of Investigation, the National Security Agency, and the Department of Justice. The document states, "Technical solutions, such as they are, will only work if they are incorporated into all encryption products. To ensure that this occurs, legislation mandating the use of government-approved encryption products or adherence to government encryption criteria is required."[11]

10. See, for example, an open later to the Honorable Lee Hamilton, Chairman of the House Foreign Affairs Committee, at http://www.eff.org/pub/Crypto/ITAR_export/hamilton_eff_industry.letter. The National Research Council (among others) has sought to help government, industry, and the public understand each others' interests and concerns with regard to encryption technology.

11. Other similar documents confirmed that recommendations were being made contrary to the public statements of those organization at that time. "FBI Documents—Clipper Must Be Mandatory," Clari News Services, August 8, 1995, available from clari.nb.govt.

While there may be some promise that public key cryptography could resolve some information security problems, the government's first response to these application areas was a return to the Clipper/Capstone proposal. In mid-August 1995, Ray Kammer of the National Institute of Standards and Technology and Michael Nelson of the White House Office of Science and Technology Policy announced that the administration would propose to allow the use of 64-bit keys in international products if those products had a key escrow system similar to the one proposed in the original Clipper/Capstone initiative. Industry responded favorably to the administration's movement on this issue, but Robert Holleyman, president of the Business Software Alliance, stated that, though it was a step in the right direction, the 64-bit limit was "unnecessary and incompatible with the whole purpose behind key escrow systems which will allow lawful government access and, importantly, assure users the privacy and security they need for their communications."[12] There has been further constructive interaction between business groups and the U.S. government, but there is not yet a U.S.—much less an international—consensus on the proper treatment of security technologies and Internet commerce.

A public policy allowing only certain kinds of encryption is misguided. It will, for example, hinder the ability of U.S. firms to globally implement secure tools for Internet commerce (e.g. authentication and payment). Specifically, the ability of U.S. government approved tools to interoperate with other Internet commerce platforms will remain limited if the U.S. encryption export policy does not change further. U.S. cryptographic policies are one of the major roadblocks to Internet commerce development.

Defining the State Role

The public and private sectors are on different paths in developing Internet commerce, as shown above. However, the U.S. government may be able to change some of its roles to align the public and

12. "White House Offers Encryption Compromise," Clari News Services, August 22, 1995, available from clari.nb.govt.

private sectors. In particular, we have discussed the vision of an Open Communications Infrastructure (OCI) in our research (Neuman et al. 1997), and we believe this vision for public policy will help bridge the gap that currently exists between the public and private sectors in Internet commerce development.

In this section, we explore possible roles for the U.S. government to promote electronic commerce. We begin with the roles described by Neil et al. (1995) in their discussion of the high-definity television (HDTV) standardization effort. In Table 1, we list the five potential roles for the state (U.S. government): funder, facilitator, judge or arbiter, partner, and legitimizer. We describe each of the roles in greater detail and discuss how these roles are viewed by the two poles (laissez-faire and controlling) of political views. In the final column, we examine how the OCI approach could be embodied by the state for each of these roles.

Table 1 indicates that the laissez-faire and controlling approaches are too extreme to help develop an Open Communications Infrastructure. The OCI approach promotes market development when possible, but also encourages state participation to prevent a market failure (Neuman et al. 1997). Market failures can occur when a market is dominated by a monopoly, public good characteristics lead to underdevelopment, or a market has high coordination costs. Participation of the state when a market failure is evident allows for development without hindering innovation and competition.

But how can this OCI approach affect Internet commerce? The public development of information security technology and electronic payment methods offers an example, particularly as such systems may require interoperability. Certainly it is difficult to promote interoperability when there are significant barriers to competing in global markets. Part of the solution relates to the domain of the World Trade Organization (McGovern 1995). The other part calls for governments to develop better domestic public policies.

Perhaps the most important domestic policy limiting Internet commerce concerns the regulation of Internet security. Clipper Chip-like solutions that have been promoted as magic bullets to solve the heterogeneous problems concerning security for Internet commerce are insufficient and untested. The emphasis on one solution

Table 1.
Alternative Public Roles in Internet Commerce

Role	Description	Laissez Faire	Controlling	OCI Approach
Funder	The state funds technology development either directly, through grants or subsidized loans, or indirectly, through tax credits and loan guarantees.	Private sector solely funds technology development.	Funds public good technologies and promotes technology transfer.	Shares funding of some pre-competitive technologies.
Facilitator	State actors consciously choose goals and set about enabling the private sector to realize them. The most obvious example of this role is legislation, but the executive branch also has the capacity to do this.	Government does not get involved in research and development.	Government organizes industries and coordinates actions of private sector companies.	Shares information between private sector companies and promotes interindustry development.
Judge or Arbiter	This is the "traditional" role of the government in telecommunications development. The state (e.g., the Federal Communications Commission) chooses between two or more proposed standards, with many cases settled in the courts.	Standards and interoperability are decided by the marketplace.	Government sets standards after a careful review process.	No standard is "forced" by the government, although openness is encouraged, and the emphasis is placed on antitrust policy.
Partner	Public and private sector co-develop the technology by sharing resources and vision.	Only defense-related partnering is allowed.	A wide spectrum of public and private goods is supported by partnering.	Partnering exists for development of some technologies that would not be developed due to market failure.
Legitimizer	The state may give its blessing to the concerns of a special interest group by supporting its policy documents.	The government does not legitimize any interest group.	The needs of disadvantaged groups are legitimized.	The state recognizes issues to grow the economy.

Source: Adapted from Neil, McKnight, Bailey (1995).

for all may prevent new developments from being adopted by the wider marketplace. Without giving up the Clipper Chip development, the U.S. government may look at its use as just one of many security technologies of an integrated solution. Export policy for encryption technology is also myopic and needs to be re-examined.

The other aspect of domestic policy affecting Internet commerce is coordination of private efforts. While this does not mean the government should be picking winners and losers, it may address areas of pre-competitive technology by using its leadership role to fund research and development. The government operates many Internet Protocol (IP) networks that interconnect with the Internet; these networks may become early adopters of Internet commerce products to grow the market and promote open standards.

Analysis

Paradoxically, Internet commerce requires both openness and privacy, as well as ubiquitous access and security. Several points about Internet economics and its effects on market opportunities for Internet commerce should be pointed out in this context. The growth and benefits of the Internet are explained by a combination of economic, technical, and policy factors: positive economic network externalities such as the bandwagon effect, economies of distribution and scale, and statistical sharing[13]; other benefits include the interoperable and layered approach of the Internet, and its distributed peer-to-peer architecture employing statistical sharing.[14] Unfortunately, information security does not necessarily exhibit positive network effects; instead, it takes knowledge, foresight, and technical

---

13. Statistical sharing is the ability of networks to allocate bandwidth to users based upon the users' needs. It does not allocate a fixed bandwidth for all users so that the bursty nature of the traffic can be accommodated. As the bursty traffic gets aggregated by all users, better performance can be realized. For example, when user A is idle, more bandwidth can be given to user B who is making a large file transfer.

14. This definition of the critical features of the Internet as well as other findings discussed in this chapter are partially a result of the authors' work in organizing an Internet Economics Workshop (hereinafter referred to as "the workshop") sponsored by the National Science Foundation and Advanced Research Projects Agency. The workshop was held in Cambridge, Massachusetts, at MIT on March 9 and 10, 1995.

McKnight et al.

skill to design an effective and secure infrastructure, which may, however, dampen growth.

The popular expectations raised by the Internet's abundant information resources and new market potential cannot be fully realized until the alarm expressed by some federal agencies, businesses, and the public over the lack of an understood and accepted security policy also has been addressed. The information security needs of users can be served by a thoughtful, scalable framework architecture, which will exhibit positive network externalities: enabling some secure transactions or offering enhanced privacy to some Internet users may encourage others to adopt the same or similar methods to engage in Internet commerce. This would enable the marketplace for Internet commerce to grow, which in turn would encourage more people and businesses to adapt their consumption or business practices to the services offered through Internet commerce, and so on (FNC-SWG 1996).

Internet commerce implies the development of a new marketplace and a new economy, which therefore raises the issue of how to evaluate that marketplace from an analytical, economic, and technological point of view. Perhaps in no other market is the underlying technology such an integral part of the market it will be built on. A very large portion of the expenditures and profits concerning the networked world currently relates to infrastructure.[15] One cannot simply create a product, conduct marketing research, price the product, and present it to consumers. Rather, it is the real demand— which is very different from the assumed or perceived demand—that guides which infrastructure or product is the most efficient and cost effective.

Furthermore, research and development funding can have a substantial impact on what occurs in the marketplace within a matter of

15. In "Computer Networking: Global Infrastructure for the 21st Century," Vint Cerf stated that, "Although not easy to estimate with accuracy, the 1994 data communications market approached roughly $15 billion/year if one includes private line data services ($9 billion/year), local area network and bridge/router equipment ($3 billion/year), wide area network services ($1 billion/year), electronic messaging and online services ($1 billion/year), and proprietary networking software and hardware ($1 billion/year). Some of these markets show annual growth rates in the 35–50% range, and the Internet itself has doubled in size each year since 1988."

a few years, given the rapid rate of innovation in this sector. To examine one quirky example, in 1985, the National Center for Supercomputing Applications was asked to conduct research on high-performance computing and communications with funding from the federal High Performance Computing and Communicating HPCC program and other corporate and government support.[16] Capitalizing on work previously done by the European high energy physics laboratory CERN in 1989 on HTTP HyperText Transfer Protocol, the NCSA offered the world the Mosaic browser in 1992. In a few short years the result hardly needs explaining: the use and expansion of and the excitement over future applications for the World Wide Web are phenomenal. Returning to our point, the economics of such a new and dynamic environment is simply not well understood, as is made clear by Bailey et al. (1996). Which form of pricing is the most efficient? Flat-rate pricing requires a fee to be paid to connect, but does not meter usage. Usage-sensitive pricing meters usage and a fee is paid for each bit sent and/or received. Transaction-based pricing determines price by the characteristics of a transaction and not by the number of bits sent and/or received. The appropriate model very much depends on user behavior, which in turn is affected by the biases of the technology in use.

Clark offers an example of such ambiguity resulting from user behavior in his chapter in this book when he introduces "expected capacity": during periods of congestion users have a pragmatic expectation about what they can do, based on what has happened in the past. If one could measure such expectations, one could actually assess the needs of users and charge them differently. User behavior is based on provisioning, which in turn is based on the amount of network bandwidth. Perhaps in order to maximize the utility of all involved one should set cost according to the expected capacity.

Not only is user behavior at the personal level important, but so too are the ethos and culture of the user base as a whole. Mitch Kapor argued that the "Internet culture" has relied on collaboration and is likely to lead to better overall results (Bailey et al. 1996). Admittedly, there will always be misbehaving or malicious users.

16. For details, see http://www.ncsa.uiuc.edu/General/NCSAIntro.html.

Nevertheless, a system would be designed very differently depending on whether criminals were the norm or exception. Based on this principle, Kapor and others posed the following questions. Does the federal government's cryptographic policy presume that the infrastructure should be built under the assumption that a portion (even if very small) of users will be malicious or conduct illegal activities? Will the commercialization and privatization of the Internet break down its cooperative nature and the assumption that the "netizen" one meets is a good citizen? Is it economically feasible to retain the Internet culture and support for heterogeneity? One would hope the previous culture of the Internet will continue to grow. The Internet has thrived because of a culture of cooperation. Significant positive network externalities associated with being on the Internet have translated into powerful economic incentives to cooperate. These incentives bring perceived benefits to individual users and have until now provided sufficient motivation to avoid worst-case abuses.

Thus the challenge is not only to develop effective Internet pricing and security mechanisms, but to do so without losing the benefits of positive network externalities currently gained through interoperability, cooperation, statistical sharing, and the peer-to-peer architecture of the Internet. Achieving economic efficiency without inciting users to abandon the Internet's core technical and cultural approach is the challenge that faces policymakers, businesses, and the public.

Internet commerce requires security, privacy, and intellectual property protection. Similar to other Internet services, the electronic commerce architecture may only succeed if it lays the foundation for a competitive market. If possible, electronic payment should reach everyone without requiring merchants to vie for electronic storefront space.

A great deal of significant work has been done by researchers and developers of systems such as those mentioned above. However, there is also a great deal of work yet to be done in the technical and engineering fields to make these systems efficient. Of equal importance is the work that members of the policy, economic, and business communities must do to properly understand what has previously occurred on systems such as the Internet and how these lessons may be properly applied toward the future. Economists will have to come to a new understanding of Internet utility and pricing models; businesses will have to adapt their marketing, customer service, product support, and sales infrastructure to a digital marketplace; and policymakers will have to realize—among other things—the international aspects of the new market.

Significant opportunities to address these issues exist. However, the government's actions have continued to be heavily influenced by enforcement and intelligence agencies in ways that are contrary to the expressed interests of many researchers, civil liberty groups, and leaders in the information technology industry. All constituents should have ample opportunity to discuss the full range of cryptographic policy initiatives.

Conclusions

Commerce and information security are of concern to the public, businesses, government, researchers, and users of the rapidly expanding Internet.[17] The sometimes heated and wide-ranging debate concerning cryptographic policy, content controls, commerce and interoperability on the Internet tends to divert attention from the need for a reasoned assessment and understanding of the true dynamics of nurturing a diverse global marketplace on the Internet. Lost in the debate is a principle we consider particularly important given the nature of information technology: that a policy consistent with user requirements and market acceptance provides economic benefits. In some cases, the "economic pie" can be expanded—or shrunk—by corporate or government actions, inevitably affecting all.

Information security is compromised if government policies and corporate initiatives ignore user requirements and the basic principles of Internet economics. This in turn may limit market acceptance of new research, services, applications, and technologies.

17. For a reasoned treatment and approach to public-private interaction on security technology and policy development, see FNC-SWG (1996).

For example, unintended results from ill-formed laws may severely limit economic benefits gained from the billions of dollars of U.S. government-sponsored research that created and sustained the Internet. Furthermore, in the guise of enhanced security and advanced features, proprietary systems and partitioned markets may lead to a lack of interoperability that further compromises prospects for society to realize the aforementioned benefits. Many of these problems could be avoided by an open policymaking process that is informed by collaborative research and development activities.

It would be ironic indeed if the United States, which founded and sustained the precursors of the emerging electronic marketplace, namely the Internet, forced those new opportunities offshore. Aside from affecting the U.S. balance of trade, jobs and opportunities for further innovation could be lost. If not adapted to business and user needs at the end of the millennium, the information security policies of the Cold War era, which provided much of the motivation for the critical federal research and development support of the Internet and its predecessors, the NSFNET and ARPANET, may cripple the development of commercially acceptable levels of security for electronic marketplace transactions.

The Internet may not only have an impact on society, but may also become an integral part of our lives if it guides our cars, provides our entertainment, and allows us to pay our bills. Consequently, there are many questions and thorny problems—all of which interrelate in a delicate web of mutual influence. Since there are so many questions, the most important issue is which questions need to be answered now rather than later? We believe that the security infrastructure that will form the basis of the new digital marketplace must be addressed now.

An infrastructure that is full of holes, plagued by fraud, rife with spies, and lurching upon a single leg for lack of interoperability, is the consequence of a shortsighted policy. This chapter, as well as the previously mentioned Internet Economics and Internet Privacy and Security Workshops, all reached the same conclusion: that understanding issues related to information security and the economics through which information infrastructure is developed is of pivotal importance to the future of Internet commerce, and to society. An intensified dialogue among industry, academia, government, and the public on information security and Internet commerce issues is clearly needed.

References

Bailey, Joseph P., Sharon Gillett, David Gingold, Brett Leida, Douglas Melcher, Joseph Reagle, jae Hun Roh, Russell Rothstein, and Grady Seale. 1996. Internet economics workshop notes. *Journal of Electronic Publishing*, http://www.press.umich.edu/jep.

Committee on Information and Communications, National Science and Technology Council. 1995. America in the age of information. National Coordination Office for HPCC, Executive Office of the President, Office of Science and Technology Policy. (March 10).

Cheswick, William R., and Steven M. Bellovin. 1994. *Firewalls and Internet security: Repelling the wily hacker.* Reading, MA: Addison Wesley.

Crede, Andreas. 1995. Electronic commerce and the banking industry: A study of Japanese, US, and UK owned banks in London. Paper presented at the International Communications Association Annual Meeting (May 25–29).

Dam, Kenneth W., and Herbert S. Lin, editors. 1996. *Cryptography's role in securing the information society.* Washington, D.C.: National Academy Press.

Federal Networking Council Security Working Group, (FNC-SWG). 1995. Draft federal Internet security plan (FISP). National Performance Review. http://www.fnc.gov//fisp_sec_contents.html.

Federal Networking Council/Research Program on Communications Policy (FNC/RPCP). 1996. Report on the workshop on Internet privacy and security. Center for Technology Policy, and Industrial Development, Massachusetts Institute of Technology, Groton, Massachusetts (May 20–21).

Garfinkel, Simson. 1995. *PGP: Pretty good privacy.* Sebastopol, CA: O'Reilly & Associates, Inc.

Kalakota, R., and A. B. Whinston. 1996. *Frontiers of electronic commerce.* Reading, MA: Addison Wesley.

Kerber, Ross. 1996. Privacy concerns are roadblocks on 'Smart' highways. *The Wall Street Journal* (December 4).

Kohl, John, and Clifford Neuman. 1993. The Kerberos network authentication service (V5). Request for Comment 1510. (September).

McGovern, Edmond. 1995. *International trade regulation.* Globefield, UK: Globefield Press.

Medvinsky, Gennady, and Clifford Neuman. 1993. NetCash: A design for practical electronic currency on the Internet. ACM Conference on Computer and Communications Security.

Neil, Suzanne C., Lee W. McKnight, and Joseph P. Bailey. 1995. The government's role in the HDTV standards process: Model or aberration? in *Standards policy for information infrastructure*, ed. Brian Kahin and Janet Abbate. Cambridge, MA: MIT Press.

Neuman, C., and G. Medvinsky. 1995. Requirements for network payment: The NetCheque perspective. Proceedings of IEEE Compcon '95.

Neuman, W. Russell, Lee McKnight, and Richard Jay Solomon. 1997. *The Gordian knot: Political gridlock on the information highway.* Cambridge, MA: MIT Press.

National Research Council (NRC). 1991. *Computers at risk: Safe computing in the information age.* Washington, D.C.: National Academy Press.

National Science and Technology Council NSTC. 1996. *High performance computing and communications: Advancing the frontiers of information technology. Supplement to the president's FY 1997 budget.* A Report by the Committee on Computing, Information, and Communications.

Reagle, Joseph. 1996. Trust in a cryptographic economy and digital security deposits: Protocols & policies. MIT Master's thesis.

Sirbu, M., and J. Tygar. 1995. NetBill: An Internet commerce system optimized for network delivered services. Carnegie Mellon University.

Steiner, Jennifer, B. Clifford Neuman, and Jeffrey I. Schiller. 1988. Kerberos: An authentication service for open network systems. In *Proceedings Winter USENIX Conference.*

Internet Economics and Policy

The Economic Efficiency of Internet Public Goods

Martyne M. Hallgren and Alan K. McAdams

Introduction

In 1994, debate was in full force over commercialization of the Internet. At one extreme were the proponents of the classic market approach who revere the genius of the market exchange system. It was time, they said, for the government, in the form of the National Science Foundation (NSF), to step aside and let the free market, that system of entities which produce and ·exchange goods in markets, determine the future growth and direction of the Internet. At the other extreme were the evangelists, who saw the Internet as a great equalizer in the new information economy; they claimed that only strong government intervention and subsidy would allow the Internet's full potential to be realized.

With the National Science Foundation stepping back from supporting commodity interregional connectivity by ending the services known as the NSFNET backbone in 1995, there is a temptation to claim that the classic market proponents indeed have won the debate. The rhetoric of the press and the hype of commercial advertisements would appear to support the claim: not only should market forces determine outcomes, but they now do.

In this chapter, we demonstrate that such a claim is inconsistent with the fundamental economic characteristics of the Internet and thus that "the market" would be an inappropriate mechanism to drive the future development of the Internet. The Internet was not, and could not have been, created by "the market" or by firms operating through the market. Similarly, the perceptions of the evangelists represent a fundamental misreading of the past development of the Internet. While it could have been created fundamentally by the government, it was not—as is clearly noted in the introduction to this book. Universities played the major role and paid the major portion of the costs of developing the Internet. Not only is this what happened, but also it is what should have happened in accord with fundamental economic precepts.

Universities operating under their resource allocation incentive structure (captured through the shorthand phrase "publish or perish") created the reality that we know today as the Internet. In doing so, universities integrated their campus infrastructures, innovations (some developed under government subsidy), as well as products purchased through the market structure.

Economic reality is more complex than either extreme position (market pricing vs. full government subsidy) might suggest. Goods of different economic characteristics exist simultaneously in all real economies. Efficiency requires different solutions to allocation problems for goods of different economic characteristics. The Internet is much more than a simple connection. All of its components—the technology; the consumers; the suppliers of the myriad forms of computer, communication, information, and human creativity—are continually changing. The economy based on those components is as complex as the components themselves. To attempt to use a single model to explain and efficiently allocate such a diverse, dynamic, complex set of elements is not just inappropriate, it is impossible.

This chapter builds on the same basic economic foundation as Hallgren (1994) for understanding what economists call "public goods" as contrasted with "private goods" and understanding the mechanisms that result in their efficient allocation in the economy. Specifically, we examine public and private goods and some in between, plus the allocation mechanisms that are appropriate for each. We examine two Internet "goods," neither of which can be efficiently allocated through markets: the first is a widely used piece of Internet routing software called GateDaemon (or GateD—read: gated-dee), and the second is (uncongested) computer networks. We consider

Cornell University's implementation of a funding model for GateD based on its economic characteristics as an economic public good. Computer networks have the same economic characteristics and for efficiency must be allocated in the same way. Then we turn to congested networks—an intermediate form of economic good explained, discussed, and analyzed below. Much study, both economic and technical, is being undertaken on network congestion and its effects (Kelly 1996; Crawford 1996). We explore congestion based on its economic characteristics and examine ways to deal with its intermediate nature—one solution for which is clearly the preferable choice under the real-world conditions of the Internet. We conclude with a summary of the model for the efficient allocation of public goods that we call the University Model, and with its extensibility.

Economic Definitions: Public Goods, Private Goods

It is important to recognize that there is more than one kind of economic good in the world. ("Good" is a generic term that is used to encompass both items and services that are exchanged, as well as things that can be either "good" or "bad" from society's viewpoint.) It might be a desktop computer, a piece of software, a book, or a service. But no matter what it may actually be, the principles presented below apply to all within a given class.

There are private goods and public goods. An economic public good does not necessarily imply something provided by a government. *NYPD Blue*, a TV program broadcast by ABC Television, has the economic characteristics of a public good, for example. A public good has a precise economic definition based on the characteristics of the good itself, not the characteristics of the provider.

A public good is nondepletable (Baumol and Oates 1975). This means that when it is used by one person, what is available to others is not depleted in quality or quantity. A public good is nonexcludable (Baumol and Oates 1975). What is available to one is available to all. This means that the use of the good by one person will not exclude others from its benefits in any way. Simply putting an antenna on my roof, turning on my TV set, and watching the broadcast of *NYPD*

Blue, does not mar your reception: my reception of the signal does not "deplete" the signal available to you; neither does my viewing of the program somehow "exclude" you from doing the same at the same time in your own home.

The most commonly used example of a public good is national defense. National defense also is both nondepletable and nonexcludable. Everyone in the country, including newcomers and newborns, is protected simultaneously and to the same degree by national defense (whatever it is). Because your neighbor is protected does not mean you are protected any less. The resource is not depleted by being used by your neighbor; and because your neighbor partakes of its benefits does not mean that you or others are excluded from the same benefits.

Private goods, in contrast, are both depletable and excludable (Baumol and Oates 1975). An example of a private good is a candy bar. When one person purchases a candy bar, the number of candy bars is reduced or depleted by one, and there is one less bar available for the next person. If a person eats the candy bar, then all other persons are excluded from receiving its benefits.

Economic Definitions: Externalities

There is a third class of economic goods that falls between pure private goods and pure public goods. These are goods with externalities. An unintended "spillover" of any good is called an externality (Baumol and Oates 1975). If the spillover is positive (e.g., a research breakthrough opening a new avenue of commerce to all), then it is a positive externality, a benefit; if the spillover is negative (e.g., pollution from automobiles), then it is a negative externality, a cost to society. In some cases, the positive economic spillover may actually be of more benefit than the intended benefit of the good to its original creator, as often occurs with research. But, since it is unplanned and cannot be captured by the creator, it is often hard to quantify.

Externalities are themselves of two economic types. Public good externalities are unintended spillovers that are neither depletable nor excludable. They are themselves "public goods" (or "bads," as with pollution), but since they are not intended by those who create them, they are public good externalities, rather than "plain old" public goods. An example is U.S. national defense that simultaneously "spills over" to protect a nation or group whose protection was not intended by the United States when it determined its expenditure on defense.

Unlike the case of public good externalities that differ from plain-old public goods only by the intent of their creator, private good externalities represent a fundamentally different class of economic good: it is a good that is a half-step from a public good toward a private good. Private good externalities are externalities that are depletable, but not (effectively) excludable. An example of a private good externality is an underground oil pool that can be accessed from multiple surface locations. The pool is depletable, but not effectively excludable. Under current international law, ocean fishing has the characteristics of an economic private good externality—unfortunately.

Network congestion is another example of a private good externality (Katz and Shapiro 1985, 1986)—an example that we deal with extensively below. When a network is initially built, made available to users, and not congested, it has the characteristics of a public good: it is nondepletable and nonexcludable. When a new user sends traffic over the network, current users see no difference in performance to them: their service is nondepletable. Then too, anyone at a network node can make use of the network: it is nonexcludable. But as more and more users access the network to use it in many different ways, users are likely to experience "performance degradation"; the network begins to experience congestion. At that point, an additional user's traffic does make a difference to the performance achieved by current users; the economic characteristics of the service have changed—the network is nonexcludable, but it is now depletable. A good with these economic characteristics meets economists' definition of a "private good externality."

Principles for Efficient Pricing of Public and Private Goods

Once it is understood that there are both public goods and private goods (among others) in an economy, the next step is to understand how to allocate each kind of good efficiently. A basic economic principle for efficient pricing—pricing that maximizes social benefit for any type of good—is: price must be equal to "society's" marginal cost, the cost of providing the good to the next user. For private goods, efficient allocation is achieved at a price determined at equilibrium in a competitively structured market at the point that supply equals demand. Price equates to marginal cost (i.e., the determinant of the industry's supply curve) through the "invisible hand" of market forces (Smith 1910). Effective competition ensures that the "right" level of output is achieved. That level is equal to the most efficient output point for each firm in the market—their minimum average cost point—which simultaneously is the marginal cost of the good.

Prices determined in markets are symmetrical. In other words, the producer receives the same price as the buyer pays. When a private good is allocated through a competitive market at equilibrium, the pricing is efficient as well as symmetric. The price equals the marginal cost of producing the good; in economic terms, this "cost" includes a "normal return on investment": a sufficient incentive to the private firm to continue production of the good.

As we noted above, a public good is a good that, once produced, is undiminished by being used by one or more users, and it is available to all. This means that, by definition, the marginal cost of supplying the public good to the next user is zero. Given that the requirement for efficient pricing of a public good is the same as that for any other good, the efficient price must equal the marginal cost of the good. In the case of a public good, the efficient price is zero!

The "kicker" in the definition of a public good in the paragraph above comes with the words "once produced." How do you get the good produced if you are "selling" it at a price of zero? To get the good produced in the first place is often quite costly, as it is for *NYPD Blue* (millions of dollars), for national defense (trillions of dollars), or the Internet (indeterminate). The producer must be paid "enough" to produce the good; but efficient allocation requires that the good be given away. It is impossible to retain an efficient price for the user and deliver a public good through what we normally call a market. For society to receive full benefit of the good, a different method of pricing must be found.

In the case of a public good, asymmetric pricing must be used: the price paid to the producer must be different from the price paid by the consumer. This type of pricing requires formal or informal economic "taxes" to generate enough resources to get the good produced and still be able to provide it to users at a price of zero. For example, for commercial television, the economic "tax" is informally added to the price the consumer pays in the market for the goods advertised; for public television, the "tax" is raised through pledge drives. (And both involve a costly, negative, public good externality—watching the commercial through which the tax is raised.) Note again that economic taxation does not require involvement by a government agency, as might be one's initial reaction to the concept of a tax. Any method an organization uses to implement asymmetric pricing should be recognized as a form of economic taxation. It is a means of collecting, from whatever sources, funds that can be used for production of a particular public good. The organization collects the tax with one hand, then pays the money to those who produce the public good (e.g., the military-industrial complex for national defense) and then, with the other hand, provides the good "free" to the country. It is important to recognize that the tax itself cannot be tied to the use of the public good, or it becomes a de facto price, greater than the marginal cost of zero.

What is GateDaemon?

As the first organization to manage the NSFNET, Cornell University had to find a way to connect this new network to existing (and future) networks. It therefore created gateway software—GateDaemon (GateD)—to accomplish the task. GateD is a modular software program that implements multiple routing protocol families on a UNIX-based hardware platform (Hallgren and Honig 1993). It is the heart of an Internet Protocol (IP) router. The router is a critical element of a packet-switched network. It links organizations together as it transfers blocks of information from one place to another. Originally developed to link the early regional networks with the original NSFNET backbone, GateD was designed to listen to different routing protocols and choose the best route for traffic to a given network destination. Cornell has chosen to make GateD freely available through a File Transfer Protocol (FTP) to the worldwide Internet community. The NSF supported the initial development of GateD with federal tax dollars, making it possible for Cornell to price this software in accord with its economic characteristics: it is a nondepletable, nonexcludable good—a public good—that is priced to users at its marginal cost to society—zero. There is a significant cost of getting GateD produced; once a given release is produced, it costs essentially zero to make it available over the network to the next user.

The GateD project continues its history of being the routing arbitration software used between and among organizations for complex routing situations that cannot be handled (at a given date) by commercial products. It is a de facto reference implementation for many routing protocols. It can be used with independently developed routing protocol implementations in interoperability tests. It is a research and prototyping implementation, allowing the community to focus on resolving critical problems such as scaling. It is important to understand that the value of GateD comes not only from its functionality at a given point, but also from the continuing development of enhanced functionality, plus maintenance updates and bugfixes that are an integral part of the "product."

A Public Good for the Internet

GateD is an example of an Internet economic public good that has been allocated with economic efficiency—through asymmetric pricing—in practice. Its value to one user is not diminished by making it available to other users. In fact, that value is enhanced—one of many positive externalities that arise from wide use and connectivity of networks.

The outcomes of following the pricing strategy appropriate to the economic characteristics of GateD are identifiable and significant. The commercial market for IP routers is flourishing, thanks in part to GateD. Several organizations (U.S. and non-U.S.) use GateD to jump-start and enhance their own development efforts for their networks or for new, value-added router products. These physical routers themselves are private goods: they are depletable and excludable; they are efficiently allocated through competitive markets and symmetric pricing. Their economic value is enhanced by the presence of GateD—an economic public good that is efficiently allocated through asymmetric pricing that no "market" can bring about.

Conditions of Use of GateD

As part of the conditions of use by those organizations that intend to redistribute the GateD software in their own products, there is the requirement to sign a redistribution license stipulating that major enhancements the licensee introduces into the software must be turned back to Cornell for inclusion in the product for public distribution. Commercial companies that use GateD in their products thus become part of the community collaboration, contributing to the public distribution of the software rather than simply taking from it.

For those organizations wishing to utilize an existing hardware platform as a router through which to connect into the Internet, GateD can be downloaded and installed directly, providing a (financially) low-end entry, thus linking that organization into the Internet without necessitating the purchase of a new router.

Because of its widespread use both as publicly available software and as the heart of many private good commercial products, GateD is a powerful deployment mechanism for necessary routing enhancements needed to sustain the current growth of the Internet. For example, its implementation of Border Gateway Protocol 4 (BGP4) (Rekhter and Li 1994) and Classless Inter-Domain Routing (CIDR) was among the first in the U.S. portion of the Internet. Versions of GateD incorporating these features could be (and were) downloaded at no fee and loaded into gateway hardware to provide these enhanced capabilities.

GateD's widespread use has guaranteed a level of interoperability between and among networks whose routers are based on it, or that have tested against it. Here, an unanticipated level and scope of interoperability has developed. GateD has created a worldwide de facto standard, in large part because it is a quality product and is priced at zero.

Implementing an Asymmetric Pricing Model

Cornell University's goal for the GateD project was to provide the community with a freely available state-of-the-art software implementation that supported the most current routing protocols for the Internet community while focusing on the most critical new functionality needed by the Internet. As noted, initial funding came from the National Science Foundation. Then, as with so many important projects, more groups demanded greater functionality and applied significant pressure to the project, to the point that the demands far exceeded the resources available at Cornell. Given the financial constraints on universities, Cornell could not use internal funds to meet these demands. A knee-jerk response might have been to make GateD a commercial product and distribute it through the market. However, that would violate the rules for efficient allocation of goods with public goods characteristics, and it could more than proportionally have undermined the spillover benefits that were catalyzed by its free distribution.

To keep the GateD software freely available requires classic asymmetric pricing. Instead of marketing the software as a product with a licensing or royalty fee, Cornell has created a consortium to raise the necessary funding for GateD. This has answered the needs of the community, while remaining consistent with the economic characteristics of the good. It permits a zero-price to the user, while sufficient resources are generated to pay for continuing development. As noted earlier, a funding mechanism had to be found that was independent of the use of the product; that is, it must not become a de facto software price.

Cornell's strategy is to look both to government and to other organizations for funding through lump-sum contributions (e.g., membership fees). It uses no fees tied to use (e.g., usage-sensitive pricing) or to number of implementations. Nor is GateD access tied to membership in the consortium. It continues to be given away free.

The National Science Foundation and other grant-giving agencies that have funded GateD recognized it as an important element of Internet infrastructure. However, even though direct and spillover benefits far exceed the cost of funding the project, this was not the basis on which the NSF did so. Instead, with each new grant, the NSF required a detailed project plan describing technical enhancements that are of value to the U.S. infrastructure effort.

In something of a partial departure from the pure model for public goods, Cornell has also focused some of its fund-raising efforts on those organizations that benefit directly and indirectly from having GateD freely available. The Cornell GateDaemon Consortium, an international affiliates program, fosters and expands the already successful community collaborations centering on the development of the GateDaemon software. Prospective members for the consortium come from industry, government, and academia. Membership fees—the consortium's equivalent of taxes—are collected by Cornell and are used directly to support the development effort.

GateD Consortium: Successful or Not?[1]

There are at least two ways to judge the success of the consortium and its asymmetric funding strategy. Clearly the GateD software satisfies the economic definition of a public good with public good externalities. In practice, it is easy to see the economic benefits derived from the availability of GateD and, given enough time and effort, those benefits could be quantified. That Cornell has been able to get funding from the National Science Foundation, itself funded through public taxation, and attract members to the

---

1. Because of a shift in its technical strategy toward Asynchronous Transfer Mode (ATM) to support an integrated voice, data, and video environment and the resources this required, Cornell University was faced with a choice of closing down the GateD project and consortium, or finding another organization to assume the leadership role and responsibilities for existing licenses and agreements. After a lengthy and careful selection process, in September 1995, Cornell University announced that Merit Network, Inc., of the University of Michigan was assuming the technical and legal leadership for both the technical project and the consortium. Merit formally agreed to continue the consortium and the asymmetric pricing model as Cornell had defined them for not less than one year after it assumed the project.

consortium, a form of private taxation, is further proof that this model can work.

The current challenge for the consortium is to generate enough funding to increase the development staff resources in order to deliver critical enhancements and updates to the community in a timely fashion. This does not happen automatically. It requires considerable effort to convince individual organizations in the Internet community to voluntarily pay the membership fees—i.e., economic taxes. Often firms do not perceive an economic incentive to join the consortium. Since the software is already available to them for free, many organizations are content to be free riders, the classic problem of dealing with public goods (Gibbons 1992), especially with public good externalities, when the providing agency does not have the power to impose taxes. This is the bad news. The good news is that even by freeloading, these organizations nonetheless have helped establish GateD as a de facto standard for Internet connectivity—a huge spillover benefit.

As a further compromise to help overcome the free-rider problem, Cornell has used targeted benefits as direct and measurable incentives for organizations to join the consortium. A firm that bases its private good product on GateD is given the opportunity to attend technical briefings or utilize a technical residency at Cornell, for example. It can quantify these benefits and recognize them as product development or professional development for its staff. Paradoxically, this in effect modifies the process: in other words, Cornell has found it necessary to sweeten the consortium with private goods-style benefits to induce organizations to pay "taxes" (greater than the costs of providing those particular benefits) and sufficient to support the continuing development of this public good with its strong public good externalities.

Computer Networks as Public Goods

The services of uncongested computer networks have the same economic characteristics as GateD. Once a network is fully enabled and up and running, its use by the next user implies costs to society that are essentially zero. The network service is neither depletable (up to the point of congestion) nor excludable (by definition of the network). Therefore the price to the user for efficient allocation of an uncongested network is also zero.

This is the approach that has historically been used with the Internet. Resources, mainly provided by universities (about 97% of the total costs of the Internet), have been cobbled together in response to the catalyst of some government funding (3% of the total) to enable the worldwide Internet to be offered to users for free.

The Economics of Congestion

Congestion on a computer network means that the network is experiencing performance degradation. As noted above, it then takes on economic characteristics that are consistent with a private good externality: it is depletable, but not excludable. Once congestion occurs, a decision point has been reached. Decision-makers now can choose to transform the private good externality in either direction as shown in Figure 1. They could choose the option we recommend: transform its characteristics from those of a private good externality back into those of a public good by acting to overcome its depletability—by expanding its bandwidth, for example. Or they could introduce an institutional constraint of some sort to remove the depletability by making the resource excludable: "enough" current users would have to be excluded from the network to remove or obviate the congestion. In effect, this is a process of introducing one characteristic of a private good, excludability, in exchange for removing the other, depletability. The result of this process we call the creation of an "impeded public good."

The institutional change that removes depletability, but simultaneously brings about excludability, can be achieved either through pricing or through an administrative limitation on entry, or by introducing a combination of the two. In the latter case, an administrative limitation could be combined with a "white market" through which those with an administrative permit for entry can trade their permit in exchange for financial considerations to persons who place a higher value on it. Whatever the institutional change, that change

Economic Characteristics of the Good

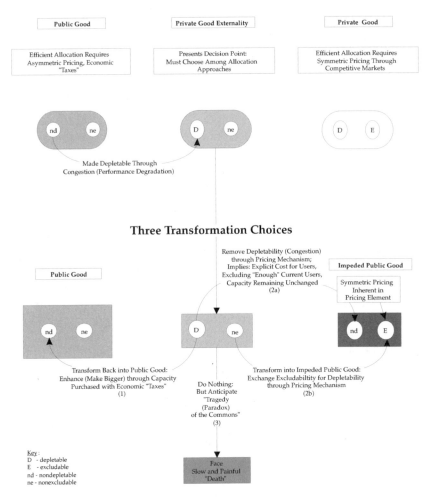

Figure 1
Economic Characteristics of the "Good" plus Outcomes from Transformation Choices for a Private Good Externality

introduces the impediment that results in the "impeded public good." Note that with this option the network (or other good) is not expanded or enhanced.

Transforming the private good externality (the congested network) back into a public good (an uncongested network) can be done by expanding the capacity of the constrained resource. For example, this can be done for a computer network by increasing the bandwidth of the network; for a physical highway, it can be done by increasing the number of its lanes. The attractiveness of this transformation is that a true public good has been reestablished, its capabilities have been enhanced, and it can again be efficiently priced to users at zero, through asymmetric pricing. Sufficient resources must be independently marshaled, however, to complete the asymmetric process.

In deciding whether it is preferable to transform the private good externality into an impeded public good or back into a public good, a number of factors must be considered. Perhaps the strongest negative for adopting the option of transforming the resource into an impeded public good is that the capacity will remain constrained at its preexisting level; the resource will remain scarce in relation to demand, and society will be saddled with the financial and economic costs of that scarcity. Users of the constrained resource will have to pay economic rents for the entry they achieve, while others will experience the costs of being foreclosed from any use of the resource.

The major negative in the choice of transforming the resource back into a public good is that it becomes necessary to somehow aggregate funds sufficient to remove the capacity constraint. The society is back at the fundamental conundrum for such resources (as Cornell was for GateD), the need for asymmetric pricing: sufficient funds must be raised to provide the resource at the necessary level, while the zero-price "charged" to users generates zero revenue. We have just discussed Cornell's approach to doing this, the GateD Consortium. In a section below we generalize this approach and identify the institutional form—an entire industry—through which economies worldwide have for centuries responded to such conundrums. It is called "The University." But first we look at an important illustration of what happens if the choice is made to do nothing.

A Retrospective on ARPANET

The Internet of today could face the same fate as did the ARPANET of old. The problem with the ARPANET was that once congestion occurred, neither of the above two choices was made. The Advanced Research Projects Administration (ARPA) could have upgraded the ARPANET to remove congestion, or it could have completed the transition exchanging excludability for depletability through pricing. The choice that was made was to do nothing. The ARPANET was permitted to become increasingly congested. As a packet-switching network, it became less and less useful. It was almost continuously overloaded, with increasing numbers of packets being lost with each ratcheting-up of the congestion. It became virtually impossible to get anything beyond a short message through, and often impossible to know whether or not even a short message had gotten through. The performance of the ARPANET became increasingly degraded (its service was depleted more and more) while access became more and more widespread (it remained nonexcludable).

This proved to be worst of all worlds. It is a fate—a tragedy—that could befall the Internet, as it befell the commons of old (Hardin 1968).

Implications

In a market of very rapid technological change subject to very significant economies of scale plus huge positive externalities (most of which have public goods characteristics), the choice among these options is indeed obvious: enhancing the network through increasing capacity and transforming it back into a public good is clearly preferable. By definition, the presence of very significant scale economies for a factor implies increases in capacity at much-less-than-proportional increases in cost. Given the history of the Internet, a creature of universities operating under the University Model (discussed below), it has been well demonstrated that unconstrained capacity in computer networks can be, has been, and is being, put to very good use.

The University Model and the Worldwide Knowledge Industry

The University Model (McAdams 1996) operates under an incentive structure appropriate to creation of public goods, such as knowledge and information. The shorthand statement of the incentive structure is "publish or perish"—give your best idea (or breakthrough) away before someone else comes up with it! This is because universities are "in business" to create knowledge. Knowledge is neither depletable nor excludable. Because one party understands the Internet, for example, does not somehow exclude you from understanding the Internet—in fact, quite the opposite is true: the better others understand it, the more readily they can help you to understand it and allow you to make use of it. Knowledge of the Internet is not depletable, nor is it excludable: knowledge enriching one party's understanding does not in any way interfere with the similar enrichment of others.

Internet users with good ideas continue to give them away. Among the innovative results are: the Internet itself; CU-SeeMe, innovative, free software from Cornell that enables desktop video-conferencing among multiple sites; and many of the tools used to access the Internet today, including Mosaic and Netscape (still available free, despite the public offering of the stock of its founding organization).

The publish-or-perish incentive structure that functions throughout this worldwide "industry" of the universities has demonstrated for centuries its ability to result in innovative new products and services. These did, and are likely to continue to, blindside even our richest and most admired private sector industrialists (as has been the case with the Internet as reported by Andy Grove, CEO of Intel).

An insight of even greater significance is that private sector firms operating through markets could not have produced the Internet! The Internet has grown up in response to incentives that fit the University Model, not the private sector market model of patents, trade secrets, high prices, destructive rivalry, etc.

Removing Depletability from a Congested Network

If a price or other form of institutional change is introduced to a
congested network either as a rent-seeking activity or as a means of
removing depletability, the result is an impeded public good (it has
been made excludable, but nondepletable), a transformation from
the private good externality (that is depletable, but not excludable).
Remember also, an externality is an unintended result. In the context of rent-seeking and in the situations depicted in Figure 1, pricing or other forms of excludability are intentional acts. The
characteristics of the public good and its optimal pricing are vio-
lated. The result is an impeded public good, rather than a plain-old
public good.

Society pays the cost of this violation in more ways than one. A
measurable number of users who would have benefited from access
if basic principles had been followed are excluded from access by
the price or other impediment imposed. Those who achieve access
must all pay the explicit price—a rent—while network capacity remains unchanged. It should be noted, however, that if the price is a
flat rate, this is a less virulent way to violate the characteristics of
optimal pricing for public goods than usage-sensitive pricing, for
example. The user's marginal cost of each use is unaffected: it is still
zero.

There is another possible set of characteristics that might emerge:
those of a private good. This could occur if the attempt to remove
the depletability was unsuccessful.[2] Then the introduction of the
attribute of excludability would have "bought" much less than intended: both depletability and excludability would be present—
where the preferable solution would be for neither to be present.

Freeways, Rush Hours and Other Oxymorons

Perhaps an intuitive example from a related network—the physical
highway or freeway—can help clarify the key parameters of the
above discussion. Freeways belie their name at rush hour when they

2. Thanks go to Research Assistant Matthew Wagner for this insight.

become congested; at that point, their use is no longer free. The arrival of an additional user imposes real costs on all users. Together, all pay the costs of delay, frustration, pollution, etc., associated with the congestion. This provides both meaning and contradiction to the term "rush hour"; at rush hour, traffic is stalled bumper to bumper. This represents the quintessential private good externality. The resource of high-speed highway travel is woefully depleted; drivers are not excluded; congestion worsens.

Incorporating an institutional change that introduces the other attribute of a private good, excludability, in exchange for removal of congestion, transforms the characteristics of a private good externality into those of an impeded public good: depletability has been removed, excludability has been introduced. The benefit of this exchange is that the usefulness of the resource as originally conceived has been reestablished—performance is no longer degraded along the freeway (or over the computer network). The original capacity of the resource has been reestablished. But it remains scarce in relation to unconstrained demand, and with pricing, all those who achieve access to the resource must pay this explicit monetary rent for the transformation.

In the case of a freeway, a system of tollbooths could be incorporated as the means of pricing to limit access (providing excludability) to the freeway. If the toll is a price sufficient to foreclose enough potential users so that the carrying capacity of the road is fully reestablished, then in this idealized condition, the above-stated objectives would have been achieved.

An alternative (also idealized) one-step institutional procedure to achieve excludability would be for potential users to bid for access to the freeway, with access provided to all those whose bids exceeded the price necessary to limit access to the carrying capacity of the freeway. Through this mechanism, persons valuing access most highly would achieve access. Those not willing to pay the market-clearing fee by definition value access less than do those willing to pay that fee or more. Congestion would no longer exist, traffic would flow up to speeds equal to the speed limit, and the resource would be optimally allocated (given the existing highway capacities and the existing distribution of income and wealth.)

It is important to emphasize that the costs of providing highway carrying capacity that is less than the unconstrained demand for such capacity will persist whether or not congestion is manifest or has been obviated. As noted, with a freeway that is free (i.e., nonexcluding) the costs are found in congestion delays, the opportunity costs of those delays, the frustration, the pollution, etc. With the introduction of even the optimal institutional pricing adaptation, the costs of unconstrained demand in relation to existing carrying capacity are no longer manifest in the physical ways just identified; rather, they exist in three other ways.

The most obvious cost is the explicit monetary price (rent) paid by users (at peak time) for access to that freeway. All actual users of the freeway pay this market-clearing price. Then there is the additional identifiable, measurable cost: the value placed on use of this highway by those potential users who were excluded from access to the no-longer-free freeway. The economic value lost is equal to the bid price each was willing to pay; it is the value foregone by those excluded from access by the market price placed on access. These costs are experienced while the capacity of the freeway remains at its preexisting level.

There still is a measurable consumer surplus for those achieving access, however. It is measurable through the administrative mechanism as the difference between the price each successful bidder was willing to pay and the market-clearing price.

Transaction Costs and Investments

Our model is an idealized one, assuming virtually instantaneous information flows and access authorizations. It abstracts from the costs of the technologies required to permit these phenomena to go forward. For example, major resource commitments are required to transform a freeway into a toll road, a crude mechanism for rationing access to the carrying capacity of the road. Three foreseeable but often ignored phenomena accompany this crude approach. The first is the cost of creating tollbooths and expanding the number of lanes to provide access to the tollbooths. The second is the requirement that traffic stop at the tollbooth in order to pay the toll, thus slowing throughput for the highway. The third is the congestion that usually builds up in the immediate vicinity of the tollbooths despite the expansion of the roadway to provide for multiple tollbooths. In other words, this crude mechanism for reducing congestion often causes congestion, lowers the carrying capacity of the road, while greatly increasing the costs of its construction as a direct result of the tollbooths themselves.

Similar costs accompany attempts to price access to networks. The hardware, software, and administrative paraphernalia can exceed the cost of the original network—and may even be economically or technologically impractical. Decision-makers must bear these facts in mind when making their choices.

Clarification of the Model and Summary

We started this discussion by stating that in a complex economy, public goods exist side by side with private goods, and that externalities are pervasive. No "one-size-fits-all" approach to allocation of goods of such diversity makes sense. Efficient allocation of a good must be driven by the characteristics of the good. When the characteristics of two goods are different, then for efficiency, the approaches to their allocation must be different.

We have presented extensive discussion of two Internet "goods," GateDaemon and service on uncongested networks, each of which is nonexcludable and nondepletable. By definition, they are public goods; and the marginal cost of supplying these goods is zero. Appropriate allocation for public goods, following the basic economic principle of price equal to marginal cost, is a price to the consumer of zero. In turn, this implies the need for asymmetric pricing: a way must be found to provide resources to the producer of the good sufficient to keep him or her producing the good. Economic taxes (whether from public or private sources) are used to achieve the latter.

If a public good experiences sufficient performance degradation, its characteristics are transformed into those of an economic private good externality. It has become depletable, but remains nonexcludable. There are three possible approaches to resolving the private good externality. One option is to do nothing; the good can continue to degrade until it is no longer usable and is finally shut down. The second option is to reinvest in the good to increase its capacity enough so that a price of zero is again efficient, using the resources (economic taxes) acquired through asymmetric pricing to fund the reinvestment. The third option is to impose some form of institutional constraint and transform the good into an impeded public good that is now excludable, but no longer depletable. Under the conditions of option three, the user pays a price (rent) for access to the good that is equal to the cost to society of removing the depletability (the congestion). That price is arrived at through a market mechanism with a market-clearing price (rent) that is symmetrical: what the user pays is what the institutional authority receives. This feature explains why the private sector so readily adopts this economic form (for movie theaters, cable television, commercially provided software, and myriad other activities)—they receive the rents.

Asymmetric pricing for unimpeded public goods is most effective when the agent that must deal with the asymmetry has the power to impose taxes (as "Ma Bell" did in its monopoly days). If the agent does not have this power, then in part it must "beg" or it must create an incentive program—consortium benefits—and invest considerable effort to generate the funds, even to the point of creating a good with mixed characteristics of both private and public goods.

The GateD Consortium represents a successful implementation of asymmetric pricing through a strategic alliance of organizations that value GateD. More important than proving that (somewhat modified) asymmetric pricing can work, GateD, as it has been implemented, has proven to be invaluable to the growth of the Internet and the Internet economy through its spillover benefits, especially those of enhanced interoperability of the Internet.

Since the decisions on the appropriate allocation mechanism for public goods, or for private good externalities, are at the heart of the debate over the commercialization of the Internet, it is extremely important to note why there is a "best" option in each case: that of asymmetric pricing for the public good, for the former; and for the latter, that of returning the characteristics of the good to those of a public good. In each case we have advanced the multiple reasons above. If the growth of the economy—and the growth of the Internet business—is a desirable goal, then it is to everyone's advantage to recognize that the appropriate allocation decisions will avoid the negatives and achieve the positives we have identified.

Conclusions

The competitive market is not the only approach to resource allocation currently being employed in the U.S. economy or in any other economy. It should not be considered a panacea—especially in the presence of instances in which there is an approach that is obviously superior for all. The Internet economy has blossomed because a market-pricing strategy was not imposed on its development.

There are clear guidelines for appropriate resource allocation approaches in the presence of public goods and in the presence of private good externalities. There are powerful reasons for following them.

The GateD Consortium is a foundation and a model. GateD provides a clear example of how a little cooperation can result in great benefits for all. It is consistent with a current incentive structure—the University Model—that has proven its worth, literally over centuries, in relation to economic public goods. It demonstrates that through the consortium mechanism, the university and not-for-profit sectors of our society can implement today, rational, efficient, resource allocation approaches on their own for the Internet.

We do not need to wait for, or rely on, government to do this for us. But we do need to exercise some internal leadership. What institution(s) will step up to fund Internet public goods?

References

Baumol and Oates. 1975. *The theory of environmental policy.* New York: Prentice-Hall.

Crawford, D.W. 1996. Pricing network usage: A market for bandwidth or market for communication? *Internet economics,* ed. Lee McKnight and Joseph Bailey. Cambridge, Mass.: MIT Press.

Fuller, V., T. Li, J. Yu, K. Varadhan. 1993. Classless Inter-Domain Routing (CIDR): An address assignment and aggregation strategy. RFC1519. http://www.ietf.org

Gibbons, R. 1992. Game theory for applied economists. Princeton University Press.

Hallgren, M. 1994. Funding an Internet public good: Definition and example. *Computer Networks and ISDN Systems* 27: 403–409; INET '94, Prague.

Hallgren, M., J. Honig. 1993. GateD and the GateD Consortium. *Connexions,* 7 (9).

Hardin. 1968. Tragedy of the Commons. *Science,* 162, 13, December, 1243–1248.

Katz, M.L., and C. Shapiro. 1986. Technology adoption in the presence of network externalities. *Journal of Political Economy,* 94: 822–841.

Katz, M.L., and C. Shapiro. 1985. Network externalities, competition, and compatibility. *American Economic Review,* 75.

Kelly, F.P. 1996. Charging and accounting for bursty connections. In *Internet economics,* ed. Lee McKnight and Joseph Bailey. Cambridge, Mass.: MIT Press.

McAdams, K. 1996. Different strokes (efficient pricing) for different strokes (different economic goods): The 'University Model' and the 'Market Model,', respectively. Draft in progress. Available at http://www.gsm.cornell.edu/mcadams/blast.html.

Rekhter, Y., and T. Li. 1994. A Border Gateway Protocol 4 (BGP-4). RFC1654. http://www.ietf.org

Rekhter, Y., and T. Li. 1993. An architecture for IP address allocation with CIDR. RFC1518. http://www.ietf.org

Smith, A. 1910. *Wealth of Nations.* New York: Dutton.

Internet Pricing: A Regulatory Imperative

Mitrabarun Sarkar

Introduction

While the notion of regulation may be regarded as taboo in the Internet community, this chapter argues that there are compelling reasons to consider an alternative to the pure free-market system. In fact, evidence suggests that regulation of the Internet may be very close to reality. While the U.S. Telecommunications Act of 1996 considers content regulation, the Federal Trade Commission (FTC) is considering a policy that would regulate direct marketing on the Internet. Meanwhile, Saudi Arabia, China, and Germany have all adopted policies that limit content.

As rapid commercialization moves the Internet toward usage-sensitive pricing, appropriate regulatory structures need to be designed and put in place. Various factors, namely new bandwidth-hungry applications; growth of the Internet; concerted entry by telephone, cable, and software companies; and the increasing appeal of electronic commerce all imply exponential growth rates in Internet traffic. However, the imminence of a potentially big problem, namely that of bandwidth scarcity, makes it imperative to develop a pricing system that would serve to effectively ration bandwidth.

Accordingly, it has been suggested that some form of usage-sensitive pricing may be inevitable. The Smart Market mechanism, proposed by MacKie-Mason and Varian (1995), and the Precedence model of Bohn et al. (1994) present innovative solutions to this problem. Since it is important to consider appropriate safeguards against potential system abuse in advance of any implementation, it is in good order to examine these models and assess their conceptual vulnerabilities. This chapter addresses this specific issue, examines the Precedence and Smart Market models of usage-sensitive Internet pricing with respect to their vulnerability to abuse, and concludes in favor of some form of regulatory oversight.

I argue that a potential pitfall of the prevalent models of usage-sensitive pricing is that they are vulnerable to abuse by firms that have market power emanating from control of the systemic bottleneck facilities. These firms could create artificially high network loads to inflate user prices, and thereby their revenues. Thus, it is argued that a usage-sensitive, free-market pricing system needs to be combined with some form of regulatory oversight to prevent anticompetitive actions by firms that control bottleneck facilities, to ensure consumer welfare, and to provide nondiscriminatory access to emerging service providers.

The Different Dimensions of Growth

The Internet, which has hitherto been restricted as a resource for high-level researchers and academics, is "expanding to encompass an untold number of users from the business, lower-level government, education, and residential sectors" (Bemier 1994, p. 40). The exponential growth rates of the Internet have been well documented.[1] Studies conducted by Merit Network, Inc., indicate that the Internet grew from 217 networks in July 1988 to 50,766 in April 1995, and the number of hosts from slightly more than 28,000 in December 1987 to around 9.5 million in January 1996, with around 1.8 million being educational sites, 2.43 million at commercial sites, 312,330 at government sites. Traffic over the NSFNET backbone increased almost 15 times in 45 months, from 1,268 billion bytes in March 1991 to 17,781 billion bytes in November 1994.[2] The traffic history of packets sent over the NSFNET shows similar exponential

1. See Merit's FTP site (ftp:/nic.merit.edu/statistics/).

2. After December 1994, traffic migrated to the new National Science Foundation architecture, for which no comparable statistics are available.

Internet Pricing: A Regulatory Imperative

growth trends. As against 85 million packets in January 1988, 86,372 million packets of information were sent over the system in November 1994—a thousandfold increase. The growth of the World Wide Web is estimated to be even faster, currently doubling every six months (Gray 1996).

These stunning growth figures are just a precursor to the boom in Internet traffic expected in the near future. As this chapter will establish, a set of factors are threatening to dwarf even these exponential growth rates.

The Causal Model of Internet Congestion

As illustrated in Figure 1, a set of forces working in tandem are threatening to create unprecedented levels of congestion on the Internet. It is argued that three main factors—incompatibility of the demands of new applications with the Internet's architecture;

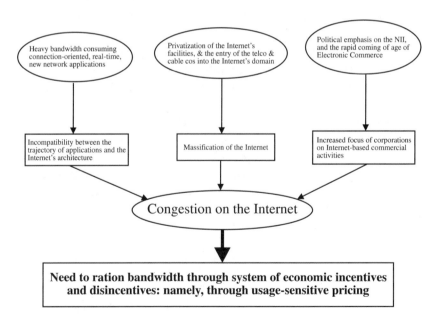

Figure 1
The Causal Model of Internet Congestion

growth of consumer demand; and the Internet's privatization and commercialization—are together responsible for structural changes of such magnitude that they mandate a reexamination of the economic system within which the Internet is embedded.

Incompatibility

New network applications, which typically require heavy bandwidth in near-real time, are fundamentally at odds with the Internet's design. As Bohn et al. (1994) note, "one may argue that the impact of the new, specifically real-time, applications will be disastrous: their high bandwidth-duration requirements are so fundamentally at odds with the Internet architecture, that attempting to adapt the Internet service model to their needs may be a sure way to doom the infrastructure" (p. 3).

The technical characteristics of the real-time applications, and consequently their demand on the network, are fundamentally different from the conventional electronic communication and data transfer applications for which the Internet was traditionally designed.[3] While conventional electronic communication is typically spread across a large number of users, each with only small network resource requirements, new real-time video and audio applications require data transfers of continuous bit streams for extended periods of time, along with a guarantee of end-to-end network reliability. Even though the data-carrying capacity of the networks is constantly being enhanced through upgrades in transmission capacity and switching technology, the current developments in communication software, especially multimedia, are creating network applications that can consume as much bandwidth as network providers can supply (Bohn et al. 1994).

---

3. For example, real-time video is closer to a Connection-Oriented Network Service (CONS) than it is to packet-switched connectionless network services. It does not exhibit the same stochastic burstiness that is characteristic of more conventional applications such as electronic mail. Russell (1993) notes that one way of distinguishing the kind of applications is to think of them as being either "conversational" or "distributive" (p. 190). Conversational applications are interactive where delays are critical to the natural flow of communication, and where a few hundred milliseconds can make a difference. Against this, in distributive applications, delays are not so critical. The newer applications are more skewed toward conversational than distributive.

Internet Pricing: A Regulatory Imperative

Multimedia applications, Internet fax, radio, and telephony are large users of network resources (Love 1994). Russell (1993) reports that while only 2.4 kilobits per second of bandwidth are required for communication of compressed sound, 3.840 megabits per second are required for compact disk-quality stereo sound. Real-time compressed video requires bandwidth ranging from 288 kilobits per second to 2 megabits per second, while studio-quality non-real-time video could require up to 4 megabits per second.[4] Bohn et al. (1994) report that many video-conferencing applications require 125 kilobits per second to 1 megabits per second. Although compression techniques are being developed, the requirements are still substantial. CUSeeMe, developed at Cornell University, uses compression, yet its requirements are approximately 100 kilobits per second.

In essence, the trend is clearly toward applications that require heavy bandwidth *and* near-real-time transmission, requirements that are essentially incompatible with the Internet's present architecture and protocols.

Privatization, Commercialization, and Growth

We are presently witnessing the simultaneous privatization of the Internet's facilities, its increasing commercialization, and a political agenda promoting the rapid deployment of the National Information Infrastructure (NII). All these are resulting in the Internet's growth as both the means and the incentive to get "wired" escalate. The bottom-line implication is that the demand for bandwidth is possibly rising beyond current levels of supply.

Prior to 1991, the Internet's physical backbone was government-funded. On December 23, 1992, the National Science Foundation (NSF) announced that it would soon cease funding the ANS T3 backbone. The Clinton administration's thrust on private sector investment in the NII has resulted in the privatization of the Internet's facilities. In 1994, the NSF announced that the new archi-

4. For a detailed overview of bandwidth requirements of different emerging applications, see James D. Russell, "Multimedia Networking Performance Requirements" in *Asynchronous Transfer Mode Networks*, edited by Y. Viniotis & Raif O. Onvural (New York: Plenum Press, 1993).

tecture of the Internet would utilize four new Network Access Points (NAPs), the contracts for which were awarded to Ameritech, PacBell, MFS, and Sprint, with MCI being selected to operate the Internet's new very-high-speed Backbone Network Service (vBNS).

Traditional telecommunications companies, operating in a nearly saturated and increasingly competitive domestic market, are turning their attention toward advanced data services, a market where the "number of data relationships is growing at more than four times the number of voice relationships" (Campbell 1994, p. 28). Spurred by the promise of the NII, a variety of communications companies are getting into the act. "[T]elephone companies, cable companies, information service companies, television networks, film studios, and major software vendors are all maneuvering to ensure that they are well positioned to profit from the NII in general and the Internet in particular" (Business Editors 1994).

Of all these players, the telephone, software, and cable companies are in a position to strongly affect one critical aspect of the market: user accessibility. User-friendly software and enhanced services, combined with aggressive marketing, are likely to have a dual effect. First, they will enable computer-literate users, till now outside the periphery of the Internet, the opportunity to connect cost-effectively; and second, they will drive the development of user-friendly tools of navigation. The second factor will have a multiplier effect on both the extent of network usage and the number of effective Internet navigators.

Bernier (1994) reports that the telephone and cable companies have already rolled out their plans for the Internet. In March 1994, AT&T introduced a national InterSpan Frame Relay Service and Internet Connectivity options, both dial-up methods for accessing the Internet. MCI offers access over its Frame Relay Services. Sprint, which offers a nationwide Internet access service along with providing international Internet connections, is now offering Asynchronous Transfer Mode (ATM) access to the Internet. Several regional Bell companies are also getting into the act. US West offers end-users access to two Internet providers via its Frame Relay Services. Pacific Bell, in collaboration with InterNex Information Services, now offers Internet connections, while Ameritech has won a contract to be one of the four National Science Foundation-funded Network Access Providers. Network access providers offer Internet Protocol (IP) connections over their Frame Relay, switched multi-megabit data service. Many cable operators are also offering access. Continental Cablevision and Jones Intercable are using cable modems hooked onto their coaxial lines to bring broadband Internet connections to businesses and homes. Continental, a Boston-based cable company, launched a service in March 1994 in collaboration with Performance Systems International, a national Internet access provider, to bring high-bandwidth service to residences and businesses in Cambridge, Massachusetts.[5]

The salient implication of these trends is that the number of Internet users is going to increase manifold as opportunities to interconnect become ubiquitous and affordable through the efforts of the telephone, software, and cable companies, and as user-friendliness and application utilities further develop.

Implications & Key Issues

The development of incompatible, bandwidth-hungry applications, the infusion of new users, and the privatized and commercialized nature of the Internet mean that the demand for network resources is likely to increase exponentially, possibly at a rate that far exceeds the supply of bandwidth, thus creating the specter of congestion on the NII. Thus, as network resources become scarce and as the system moves toward a free-market model, it is argued that a change in the pricing system is required for effective rationing of bandwidth. The key consideration, however, is that the pricing mechanism should be able to preserve the inherent discursive nature of the Internet, send the right signals to the marketplace, and be flexible and adaptive to changes brought about through technology, political initiatives, and software development.

5. For a more detailed discussion of the telephone and cable companies' involvement in the Internet, see Paula Bernier, "Opportunities Abound on the Internet," *Telephony*, Vol. 226, No. 13 (March 28, 1994).

Pricing Alternatives

Concern has been expressed that the Internet should continue to function as a vast, on-line public library from which virtually any kind of information can be retrieved at minimal cost, and that, should the present system of flat-rate, predictable pricing for a fixed-bandwidth connection be replaced by some form of vendor-preferred, usage-sensitive metered pricing, the current discursive nature of the Internet will be destroyed. A transition to metered-usage would make the NII "like a Tokyo taxi, so that for every passenger who takes a ride on the national data superhighway, the first click of the meter will induce severe economic pain and the pain will increase with each passing minute" (Rosall 1994).

Some consumer advocacy groups oppose a purely supplier-determined metered pricing of the Internet[6] and argue that the NSF should create a consumer advisory board to help set pricing and other policies to preserve and enhance the free flow of information and democratic discourse through Internet listserver and fileserver sites. In addition to the concern that a popular discussion site would have to pay enormous amounts to send messages to its members, it is feared that usage-sensitive pricing would introduce a wide range of problems for FTP, Gopher, and Web servers since the providers of "free" information would be liable to pay, at a metered rate, the costs of sending data to those who request it. This would have a negative effect on information sites, and would eliminate many such sources of free information.

In essence, the argument is that usage-sensitive pricing implies severe economic disincentives to both users and providers of "free" information, which would destroy the essentially democratic nature of the Internet.

---

6. TAP-INFO is an Internet Distribution List supported by the Washington-based Taxpayers Assets Projects, an organization founded by Ralph Nader. This letter, which was posted on various conferences across the Internet, requested a signature campaign addressed to Steve Wolff, Director of Networking and Communications for the NSF.

Arguments against Flat-Rate Pricing

This chapter argues that flat-rate pricing, in the current context of the Internet, is likely to run into severe problems, which, paradoxical as it may sound, are likely to severely impair the current discursive nature of the Internet.[7]

The basic role of a pricing mechanism is to lead to an optimal allocation of scarce resources, and to give proper signals for future investments. The mechanism in place should lead to the optimization of social benefits by ensuring that scarce resources are utilized such that productivity is maximized in ways society thinks fit. As Mitchell (1989) notes, "in a market economy, prices are the primary instrument for allocating scarce resources to their highest valued uses and promoting efficient production of goods and services" (p. 195). One critical issue, however, is the basis on which an appropriate pricing scheme is designed.

Given that the short-run marginal cost of sending an additional packet of information over the network is virtually zero, once the transmission and switching infrastructures are in place, marginal-cost pricing in its simplistic form is inapplicable. Cost-based return on investment (ROI) pricing is both infeasible, given the multiplicity of providers who would have to collaborate to bring about seamless, end-to-end service, and also inefficient, given the chronic problem of allocating joint costs in a telecommunications network.[8] A free-market policy may have unforeseen and undesirable implications, especially if the markets are not competitive in each and every segment of the network.

The principle most likely to be effective in the current scenario is a modified version of the marginal-cost approach, in which the social costs imposed by the scarcity of bandwidth—the bottleneck resource—are taken into consideration, and sought to be minimized

7. See chapter by Brownlee in this volume for more detail on implementing usage-sensitive pricing to solve the flat-rate pricing problems.

8. For a detailed and well-argued thesis on the difficulty of allocating joint costs in the telephone industry, see John T. Wenders, "Deregulating the Local Exchange," in *Perspectives on the Telephone Industry: The Challenge of the Future*, edited by James H. Alleman & Richard D. Emmerson (New York: Harper & Row, 1989).

through the pricing system. The scarcity of bandwidth, which is the speed at which data is transmitted through the network, implies delays due to network congestion. Congestion cost, therefore, is the social cost that needs to be incorporated into any efficient pricing scheme.

The Costs of Congestion

The packet-switching technology of the TCP/IP protocol embedded in the Internet has an essential vulnerability to congestion, since a single user, using a subregional line that connects to the regional-level network, can overload several nodes and trunks and cause delays or even data loss for other users through the discarding of cells or frames. The specific manner in which the problem is manifested, i.e., whether the network simply delays or actually discards the information (Campbell 1994), is protocol-dependent. However, the point remains that due to the the first-come, first-served principle of backbone resource allocation, users now pay the costs of congestion through delays and lost packets (MacKie-Mason and Varian 1994).[9] This problem of congestion is likely to exacerbate, since a Power PC such as a $2,000 Macintosh AV, combined with a $500 camcorder, would enable an undergraduate to send real-time video to friends on another continent by pumping up to 1 megabit per second of data onto the Internet, thus tying up a Tl line (Bohn et al. 1994; Love 1994).

The costs of congestion on the Internet are therefore a tangible problem, and not merely the pessimistic outpourings of a band of dystopians. Although it has been argued that the manner in which a user fills a leased line does not matter (Tenney 1994), the Internet

9. They also report that the Internet experienced severe congestion in 1987, and during the weeks of November 9 and 16, 1992, when some packet audiovisual broadcasts caused major delay problems, especially at heavily used gateways to the NSFNET backbone and in several mid-level networks. A posting by William Manning on the telecomreg list on May 4, 1994, at 20:50:46 reports that Rice University had to shut down the campus feed because some students were playing around and feeding live video signals into the Internet, thus saturating the link and making it unusable for other users on the ring. MacKie-Mason and Varian (1994) also report that delays varied widely across times of day, but followed no obvious pattern.

is not designed to allow most users to fill their lines at the same time. As new applications such as desktop video-conferencing and new transport services such as virtual circuit resource reservation emerge, it will become important for the network to provide dedicated and guaranteed resources for these applications to operate effectively (England 1994). For the Internet, whose architecture is designed for connectionless network services, reservation of bandwidth implies accomodating an incompatible class of service, which in turn implies additional costs in developing enhanced edge-functionality in the network (Pecker 1990), which decreases its overall efficiency.

In essence, the changing nature of network traffic implies a social cost imposed by users making unlimited use of the new bandwidth-hungry, incompatible applications. This cost is reflected in delays and data dropouts of those making use of traditional and asynchronous applications such as E-mail, FTP, and Gopher.[10] The flat-rate pricing mechanism may therefore be inefficient in transmitting correct market signals that would minimize social costs and allocate resources efficiently and effectively, especially since it is difficult to argue that the social benefits of democratic discourse are less beneficial to society than an undergraduate sending out real-time video of a birthday party to friends.[11]

There is a potential danger here. Should the present pricing system continue, it may result in a situation in which new applications drive out traditional uses. The inherent bias of flat-rate pricing, whereby light users subsidize heavy users, is a threat to traditional Internet usage. It is therefore clear that a new pricing scheme needs to be implemented, one that will ensure efficient allocation of bandwidth and enable the Internet to retain part of its original discursive character as it evolves into a more potent and futuristic medium of communication.

10. One is tempted to include the Web as a traditional application. However, the new multimedia applications over the Web are at loggerheads with the Internet environment.

11. It can also be argued that the real-time transmission of a heart surgery is more beneficial than an academic browser, and this is where the essential difficulty in assigning social values based on application software rather than specific uses comes in. This point will be elaborated later.

The Pricing Options

The polarity that lies on the other end of the pricing spectrum is pure usage-sensitive pricing. Given the shortcomings of flat-rate pricing, it seems certain that there will eventually be "prices for Internet usage, and the only real uncertainty will be which pricing system is used" (Love 1994).

The Telephone Pricing Model

One form of usage-sensitive pricing that may be adopted is telephony's system of posted prices. If the telephone model is adopted, the cost of Internet usage would be based on the distance between the sender and the receiver, and on the number of nodes through which data need to travel before they reach their destination, much like the computation of inter-LATA (Local Access Transport Area) calling. This, however, would be difficult to implement. The inherent nature of the connectionless Internet technology is based on redundancy and reliability, with packets routed dynamically through an algorithm that balances load on the network while routing each packet through alternative paths should some links fail (MacKie-Mason and Varian 1995). In addition, the associated accounting problems are enormous. While senders would prefer cost-minimization, because the Internet's routing algorithm is based on redundancy and reliability, it is not necessarily determined by the fewest links and lowest costs.

The telephone model of pricing is unlikely to work for another reason. Posted prices are not flexible enough to dynamically reflect network congestion at each point in time (MacKie-Mason and Varian 1995). Network congestion can peak from an average load very quickly depending on the application used. Also, time-of-day pricing is rigid. Under this pricing scheme, unused bandwidth cannot be made available at lower prices whereby it would benefit a price-sensitive category of users. Conversely, at moments of congestion, the network also stands to lose revenue because users who are willing to pay more than posted rates are crowded out of the network through the randomized first in, first out process of network resource allocation.

The system of posted and fixed prices thus implies multiple problems: it does not allow for revenue maximization under the free-market philosophy, it is inadequate in optimizing capacity utilization, and it fails to address congestion issues because it cannot allow for prioritization of packets. It is thus clear that the answer to the Internet's pricing problem does not lie in either flat-rate pricing, or in the telephony model of usage-based, posted pricing. Rather, the answer perhaps lies in an innovative approach.

Innovative Pricing Models

This chapter analyzes two innovative pricing schemes, the Precedence model of Bohn et al. (1994) and MacKie-Mason and Varian's (1995) Smart Market mechanism; identifies their shortcomings; and develops a case for regulation.[12]

The Precedence Model

The Precedence model proposes "a strategy for the existing Internet, not to support new real-time multi-media applications, but rather to shield . . . the existing environment from applications and users whose behavior conflicts with the nature of resource sharing" (Bohn et al. 1994, p. 4). The authors propose that criteria be set to determine the priority of different applications. Data packets would receive network priority based on these precedence numbers, which would be reflected in the IP precedence field of the data packets. In the event of congestion, rather than rely on current first in, first out queuing, the Precedence model presents a systemic and logical basis for deciding which packets to send first and which to hold up or drop. While noting that their proposed system may be vulnerable to users tinkering with precedence fields, the authors believe that this approach would "gear the community toward the use of multiple service levels, which . . . [is] the essential architectural objective" (p. 10).

---

12. Some other models have been suggested in this book, namely Clark's expected-capacity model based on sender profile, and Gupta, Stahl and Whinston's priority-pricing model. However, this chapter limits itself to the Precedence and the Smart Market models.

However, the Precedence model has some additional weaknesses. Since it rests on priority allocation of packets, the central concern revolves around the twin questions of how these priorities will be set, and who or which body will set them. *Prima facie,* the model relies on an increased governmental role in regulating content, and, as MacKie-Mason and Varian (1995) point out, "Soviet experience shows that allowing bureaucrats to decide whether work shoes or designer jeans are more valuable is a deeply flawed mechanism" (p. 16).

The Precedence model would also require continuous updating of priority schemes as new products and applications emerged. Setting priorities on the basis of applications might well be misleading. Real-time video might be assigned a lower priority than FTP, but it might possible that the video transfer of data was concerned with an emergent medical situation. Application-based priority would thus be limiting since it might not be possible to define each and every usage situation in a dynamic environment. The Precedence model relies heavily on the altruism of Internet users, and correct self-reporting and nonmanipulation of precedence fields by computer-savvy netters. The continuing survival of such a system is questionable due to its potential for being abused by opportunistic behavior.

The Smart Market Mechanism

Proposing the Smart Market mechanism as a possible model to price Internet usage, MacKie-Mason and Varian (1995) suggest a dynamic bidding system whereby the price of sending a packet would vary almost instantaneously to reflect changes in network congestion. Each packet would have a "bid" field in its header wherein users would indicate how much they were willing to pay. Packets with higher bids would gain access to the network sooner than those with lower bids. The authors acknowledge that this mechanism is preliminary and tentative, and is a theoretical model of implementing efficient congestion control that would only ensure relative priority without being an absolute promise of service.[13]

13. Both Crawford and Gupta et al. point out the incentive incompatibility problem in their chapters in this volume.

The Smart Market mechanism has great theoretical potential as a basis for implementing usage-sensitive pricing. By charging for priority routing during times of congestion, traffic that did not claim priority status, such as a large Internet mailing list of a listserv conference, would travel for free when the network was not congested. During congestion, users would bid for access and routers would give priority to packets with the highest bids.

A great deal of consensus would be required along the network for smooth functioning and to ensure that priority packets would not be held up. Users would be billed the lowest price acceptable under the routing "auction" and not necessarily their bid price. Users would thus pay the lower amount between their bid and the marginal user's bid. Thus the payout would necessarily be lower than that of all admitted packets. As a result, the Smart Market model would ensure that all users would have the incentive to reveal their true willingness to pay, and that there would be systemic incentives to conserve scarce bandwidth while allowing effectively free services to continue.

Building a Case for Regulation

Although dynamic bidding is theoretically very attractive, it renders the system wide open to potential abuse by those who control the system bottlenecks, thus establishing a case for implementing some form of regulatory oversight that would prevent anticompetitive activities and market-power abuse. This is the essential argument of this chapter: that a usage-sensitive pricing scheme needs to be combined with some form of regulatory oversight aimed at making the access of emerging networks to the Internet open and nondiscriminatory, and to prevent firms that control bottleneck facilities from indulging in anticompetitive behavior.[14]

14. In the emerging architecture, the Network Access Providers will play a crucial role. The four NAPs, as mentioned earlier, are all telephone companies, with the exception of MFS, which is a Competitive Access Provider (CAP). Historically, the telephone industry is replete with stories of monopoly abuse through the control of bottleneck facilities. It would be wise to realize that this legacy of decades-old management styles cannot be shed very easily.

The idea of using dynamic rates to price network services to balance loads, limit congestion, and avoid the high costs of adding capacity has been advanced earlier (Mitchell 1989). Vickrey (1981) has proposed that telephone networks could manage their congestion during peak-load times by alerting subscribers through a higher-pitched dialing tone, and charging premium rates for calls made at those times. According to Mitchell (1989), as local networks of telephone systems evolve into broadband systems and become even more capital-intensive, the gains from allocating capacity dynamically on demand would be large. Dynamic pricing would enable higher overall utilization of network capacity while allowing price-sensitive users to access telephone services at lower prices on a dynamic and daily basis.

The Weakness of the Dynamic Bidding Model

The weakness of the Smart Market proposal as a stand-alone, unmonitored, free-market pricing system lies in its assumptions.

Perceived Homogeneity The Smart Market model proposes to price scarce network resources based on network load. Because the Internet is not a single, homogeneous network, the load factor and the resultant level of congestion are likely to be very different along each hop on the Internet. The model accounts for the Internet's heterogeneity by suggesting that at each hop, a Vickrey auction would determine the service each packet gets from a router experiencing congestion. Thus, a user needs to make multiple payment commitments at multiple auctions to avoid congestion at each hop.

This poses a set of problems that may be difficult to resolve. Coordination among different service providers and network owners becomes mandatory to facilitate end-to-end service and settlement. If one hop does not conform to the same pricing model, a packet may be dropped or experience intolerable delay. Given the diversity of the Internet and the multiplicity of players, consensus sounds farfetched and difficult to achieve without any neutral oversight agency to coordinate and monitor the different players.

Network Load Manipulation Second, and more important, a pricing system based on network load renders itself vulnerable to potential abuse by those who control the bottleneck facilities. It may be argued that any system would be vulnerable to some abuse, but the anonymity of data carried by the Internet would make this system especially vulnerable. Unscrupulous firms controlling various nodes would have both the incentive and the ability to manipulate the network load to keep it artificially high so as to create upward pressure on the price of network usage. Given that marginal costs are at a theoretical minimum, firms would have incentives to maximize revenue, which they can do by tracking network usage, monitoring demand elasticity, and artificially keeping the network load at a point where overall revenue is maximized (Gupta et al. 1996; Crawford 1996).

The Smart Market system is therefore open to abuse by firm controlling the bottlenecks who would be able to peg network loads at artificially high levels in order to maximize revenue, and thereby manipulate the price of network usage upwards. For the system to operate fairly and efficiently, either the motivation for exploitation of market power needs to be eliminated, or a scrupulous control system needs to be implemented.

Internet Pricing: A Case for Regulation

These two issues, namely the ubiquity of implementation and incentive incompatibilities that may lead to manipulation of network loads, are the fundamental reasons why the Smart Market mechanism, or any variation of a dynamic-pricing model, needs to be associated with a regulatory institution responsible for consensus-building and preventing manipulation, anticompetitive behavior, and abuse of market power. Given the experience of the telecommunications industries, the essential contradiction in American free-market operations should be abundantly clear. The greater the degree of freedom for any industry, the greater becomes the role for regulation.[15] On the basis of the example of the telephone industry, it should be clear that potential bottlenecks and potential abuse

---

15. The form and focus of regulation may change, however.

need to be identified well in advance so that necessary safeguards can be put in place.

It is thus important to address control of bottlenecks, and their role in influencing the pricing mechanism. Although an oversight agency hypothetically could ensure that the consumer surplus[16] generated is not collected as excess profits by firms but is returned to consumers (MacKie-Mason 1994), it is more desirable to design a system whereby the transfer of excess funds would not be required in the first place. While it may be true that competition is the best form of regulation, the privatization of the Internet's facilities and the emergence of the NAPs indicate that the owners of the underlying trunks and access paths (the regional Bell operating companies, the inter exchange carriers, and the CAPs) are likely to have more market power than any private organization has had over the Internet to date. Accordingly, we need to guard against the eventuality of abuse.

Whether one envisions Internet carriage to emerge as a competitive industry or one that is effectively oligopolistic, there seems to be a role for regulatory agencies. There is a need to regulate pricing and control anticompetitive behavior in the event that the industry is less than competitive. However, even if the system is highly competitive, the dynamics of network pricing need to be implemented by some form of nonprofit consortium or by a public agency that will work toward consumer protection and coordination and consensus among various service providers. In the absence of such consensus-building activities, and given imperfect markets, dynamic pricing is likely to have a chaotic effect and the cost of accounting and regulatory oversight is likely to be prohibitively high. This might have undesirable consequences for the implementation of such a scheme in the first place.

It can be argued that, should a purely competitive situation emerge, then the form of pricing scheme becomes inconsequential (Bohn 1994[17]). However, this overlooks the fact that every pricing scheme has its own inherent bias and different associated social costs and benefits.

16. Consumer surplus in this case would be the excess bottleneck facilities.

17. Argued in response to my posting on telecomreg, wherein I invited assessments of pricing mechanisms in the context of systemic bottlenecks that are likely to emerge.

An added factor that needs to be assessed is how technology is expected to develop over time. Like pricing schemes, every technology has its own bias. Since technological development is likely to be unbalanced, and breakthroughs can be expected to be sporadic both in time and space, the pricing schemes that will be implemented need to reflect or obviate the effects of technological imbalances.

For example, transmission technology that is fiber-optic-dependent is presumed to develop at a faster pace than switching technology, which is currently electronic-based. If we expect switching technology to develop quickly and fiber-optic technology to be ubiquitously implemented, the fear of congestion at the nodes may no longer be valid. The bottleneck will then revert to the transmission lines, not in terms of the physical capacity of the fiber-optic trunk lines, but in the costs associated with overlaying all user lines, especially the last loop that connects customers' premises to the nearest switch.

Conclusion

The Internet market may transform incrementally. Initially, some form of usage-sensitive pricing, possibly dynamic pricing, may be combined with flat-rate pricing. For applications that need committed and reserved network resources, usage-sensitive pricing would be necessary to control their proliferation and to ensure optimal network performance. For more traditional forms of Internet usage such as email, flat-rate access may continue to be the norm. In other words, the pricing system that is likely to evolve would move the industry toward multiple levels of service. However, while it may be difficult to predict the exact form of pricing that is likely to be implemented in the future, it seems amply clear that as the Internet evolves there will be a definite role for oversight agencies and regulators.

References

Bernier, P. 1994. Opportunities abound on the Internet. *Telephony*, 226 (13): 40–48.

Bohn, R. 1994. Future Internet pricing. Posted on telecomreg @relay.adp.wisc.edu at 20:35:25, June 2, 1994.

Bohn, R., H.-W., Braun, K.C., Claffy, and S. Wolff. 1994. Mitigating the coming Internet crunch: Multiple service levels via Precedence. Technical report, University of California at San Diego, San Diego Supercomputer Center, and the National Science Foundation. [ftp://ftp.sdsc.edu/pub/sdsc/anr/papers/precedence.ps.Z]

Business Editors. 1994. Competition, controversy ahead in era of Internet commercialization. *Business Wire* (March 11, 1994).

Clark, D. 1996. A model for cost allocation and pricing in the Internet. In *Internet economics*, ed. Lee W. McKnight and Joseph P. Bailey. Cambridge, Mass.: MIT Press.

Cocchi, R., S., Shenker, D., Estrin, and L. Zhang. 1993. Pricing in computer networks: Motivation, formulation, and example. Technical report, University of Southern California Department of Computer Science, Hughes Airport Company, and Palo Alto Research Center. Available via Web from [http://gopher.econ.lsa.umich.edu].

Campbell, A. 1994. Distributed testing: Avoiding the Domino effect. *Telephony*, 226(14).

England, K. 1994. Future Internet pricing. Posting on telecomreg@relay.adp.wisc.edu at 08:04:26, May 7, 1994.

Gupta, A., D.O., Stahl, and A.B. Whinston. 1996. A priority pricing approach to manage multi-service class networks in real time. In *Internet economics*, ed. Lee W. McKnight and Joseph P. Bailey. Cambridge, Mass.: MIT Press.

Love, J. 1994. Notes on Professor Hal Varian's April 21 talk on Internet economics. Posted on telecomreg@relay.adp.wisc.edu at 00:02:55, May 4, 1994.

MacKie-Mason, J.K. 1994. Future Internet pricing. Posted on telecomreg@relay.adp.wisc.edu at 13:37:03, June 2, 1994.

Mitchell, B.M. 1989. Pricing local exchange services: A futuristic view. In *Perspectives on the telephone industry: The challenge of the future*, ed. James H. Alleman and Richard D. Emerson. New York: Harper & Row.

Mitchell, B.M., and I. Vogelsang. 1992. *Telecom pricing: Theory and practice*. New York: Cambridge University Press.

Pecker, C.A. 1990. To connect or not to connect: Local exchange carriers consider connection oriented or connectionless network services. *Telephony*, 218(24).

Russell, J.D. 1993. Multimedia networking requirements. In *Asynchronous Transfer Mode*, ed. Yannis Viniotis and Raif O. Onvural. New York: Plenum.

Rosall, Judith. 1994. International Data Corporation's Research Director quoted in Business Editors (1994).

Tenney, G. 1994. Future Internet pricing. Posted on telecomreg@relay.adp.wisc.edu at 18:42:09, May 4, 1994.

Varian, H.R., and J.K. MacKie-Mason. 1992. Economics of the Internet. Technical report, University of Michigan, Department of Economics.

MacKie-Mason, J.K., and H.R. Varian. 1995. Pricing the Internet. In *Public access to the Internet*, ed. Brian Kahin and James Keller. Cambridge, Mass.: MIT Press. 269–314.

Wenders, J.T. 1989. Deregulating the local exchange. In *Perspectives on the telephone industry: The challenge of the future*, ed. James H. Alleman and Richard D. Emmerson. New York: Harper & Row.

Vickrey, W. 1981. Local telephone costs and the design of rate structures: An innovative view. Mimeo.

Acronyms

ABR	Available Bit Rate
ADU	Application Data Unit
API	Application Programming Interface
ARPA	Advanced Research Projects Administration
ARPANET	Advanced Research Projects Administration Network
AS	Autonomous System
ATM	Asynchronous Transfer Mode
BECN	Backward Explicit Congestion Notification
BGP4	Border Gateway Protocol 4
B-ISDN	Broadband Integrated Services Digital Network
bps	bits per second
CAP	Competitive Access Provider
CBR	Constant Bit Rate
CBT	Core Based Trees
CERN	Conseil Europeen pour la Recherche Nucleaire
CIDR	Classless Inter-Domain Routing
CIR	Committed Information Rate
CIX	Commercial Internet Exchange
CLP	Cell Loss Preference
CONS	Connection-Oriented Network Service
CPE	Customer Premises Equipment
CPU	Computer Processing Unit
CSU	Channel Service Unit
DARPA	Defense Advanced Research Projects Agency

DBS	Direct Broadcast Satellite
DDS	Digital Data Service
DNS	Domain Name Service
DSU	Data Service Unit
DS3	Digital Signal Service over a T3 line (44.7 Mbps)
ECI	Expenditure Controller Interface
EDI	Electronic Data Interchange
EGP	Exterior Gateway Protocol
ELSD	Equal Link Split Downstream
ENHS	Equal Next-Hop Split
EPIC	Electronic Privacy Information Center
ETS	Equal Tree Split
FBI	Federal Bureau of Investigation
FCC	Federal Communications Commission
FDIC	Federal Deposit Insurance Corporation
FECN	Forward Explicit Congestion Notification
FIXen	Federal Internet eXchanges
FNC	Federal Networking Council
FNC-SWG	Federal Networking Council—Security Working Group
FR	Frame Relay
FTC	Federal Trade Commission
FTP	File Transfer Protocol
GGP	Gateway-to-Gateway Protocol
Gbps	Gigabits per second
HDTV	High Definition Television
HPCC	High Performance Computing and Communications
HTML	HyperText Markup Language
HTTP	HyperText Transfer Protocol
IP	Internet Protocol
IPv4	Internet Protocol version 4
IPv6	Internet Protocol version 6
IRC	Internet Relay Chat
ISDN	Integrated Services Digital Network
ISP	Internet Service Provider
ITU	International Telecommunication Union
IXC	Interexchange Carrier
JPEG	Joint Pictures Expert Group

Kbps	Kilobits per second
LAN	Local Area Network
LEC	Local Exchange Carrier
MAN	Metropolitan Area Network
Mbps	Megabits per second
MCR	Minimum Cell Rate
MLOC	Major Local Operating Company
MPEG	Moving Picture Experts Group
NAP	Network Access Point
NASA	National Aeronautics and Space Administration
NCSA	National Center for Supercomputing Applications
NII	National Information Infrastructure
N-ISDN	Narrowband Integrated Services Digital Network
NOC	Network Operations Center
NRC	National Research Council
NSF	National Science Foundation
NSFnet	National Science Foundation Network
NSTC	National Science and Technology Council
NTP	Network Time Protocol
OCI	Open Communications Infrastructure
ODN	Open Data Network
OMB	Office of Management and Budget
ONA	Open Network Architecture
PBX	Private Branch Exchange
PC	Personal Computer
PGP	Pretty Good Privacy
POP	Point of Presence
POTS	Plain Old Telephone Service
PPP	Point-to-Point Protocol
PSTN	Public Switched Telephone Network
PVC	Permanent Virtual Circuit
QOR	Quality of Route
QOS	Quality of Service
ROI	Return on Investment
RPCP	Research Program on Communications Policy
RTP	Real Time Protocol
RSVP	Resource Reservation Protocol

SLIP	Serial Line Internet Protocol
SMDS	Switched Multimegabit Data Services
SP	Shortest Path
SPC	Stored Program Control
SSL	Secure Sockets Layer
TASI	Time Assigned Speech Interpolation
TCP/IP	Transmission Control Protocol/Internet Protocol
TDM	Time Division Multiplexing
TOS	Type of Service
UDP	User Datagram Protocol
URL	Uniform Resource Locator
vBNS	Very-high-speed Backbone Network Service
VCI	Virtual Circuit Indicator
WAN	Wide Area Network

Contributors

Loretta Anania (lan@postman.dg13.cec.be) is with the European Commission, Brussels, Belgium. For the ACTS program, she is responsible for the Network Interconnection Accounting chain. Since June '96 she has served as Chairman of the Board of the ITS.

Joseph P. Bailey (bailey@rpcp.mit.edu) is a doctoral candidate in the MIT Technology, Management and Policy Program and a research assistant with the MIT Research Program on Communications Policy, Center for Technology, Policy, and Industrial Development.

Nevil Brownlee (n.brownlee@auckland.ac.nz) is responsible for The University of Auckland's campus network, which has about 4,500 connected hosts. He is manager of Kawaihiko and chairman of Tuia's Technical Working Group. He has been active in the IETF since 1992, and is currently co-chair of the Realtime Traffic Flow Measurement Working Group.

David Carver (dcc@rpcp.mit.edu) is an Associate Director of the MIT Research Program on Communications Policy.

David D. Clark (ddc@lcs.mit.edu) is a Senior Research Scientist at the M.I.T. Laboratory for Computer Science.

David W. Crawford (david@arizona.edu, dc@panix.com) is a doctoral student in the Department of Economics at the University of Arizona, and a software industry consultant living in Los Gatos, California.

Ketil Danielsen (ketil.danielsen@himolde.no) is with the Department of Informatics, Molde College, Norway.

Deborah Estrin (estrin@usc.edu) is an Associate Professor at the Computer Science Department, University of Southern California.

Branko J. Gerovac (bjg@rpcp.mit.edu) is an Associate Director of the MIT Research Program on Communications Policy.

David Gingold (dgingold@lancity.com) is a Senior Software Engineer with Bay Networks.

Jiong Gong (jgong@bellcore.com) is a Member of Technical Staff at Bell Communications Research.

Alok Gupta (alok@cism.bus.utexas.edu) is Assistant Professor of Information Systems at University of Connecticut

Martyne M. Hallgren (mh16@cornell.edu) is with Cornell Information Technologies, Cornell University, Ithaca, NY.

Shai Herzog (herzog@watson.ibm.com) has recently received his Ph.D. from the University of Southern California. He is currently a research staff member at IBM T. J. Watson Research Center, Hawthorne, NY.

Clark Johnson (clark@rpcp.mit.edu) is a consultant in data storage technologies in Minneapolis, MN.

Frank P. Kelly (f.p.kelly@statslab.cam.ac.uk) is Professor of the Mathematics of Systems in the Statistical Laboratory of the University of Cambridge, England.

Charlie Lai (charlie.lai@eng.sun.com) is with the Network Security Group at SUN Microsystems.

Jeff MacKie-Mason (jmm@umich.edu) is an Associate Professor of Economics, Information and Public Policy at the University of Michigan, Ann Arbor.

Alan K. McAdams (akm3@cornell.edu) is with the Johnson Graduate School of Management, Cornell University, Ithaca, NY.

Lee W. McKnight (mcknight@rpcp.mit.edu) is Lecturer in the Massachusetts Institute of Technology's Technology and Policy Program, Adjunct Assistant Professor of International Communication at the Fletcher School of Law and Diplomacy, Tufts University, Principal Investigator of the Internet Telephony Interoperability Consortium and Principal Research Associate at the MIT Center for Technology, Policy and Industrial Development.

Gennady Medvinsky (arim@cybersafe.com) earned his doctorate in computer science from the University of Southern California and is currently a senior engineer at the CyberSafe corporation.

John Murphy (murphyj@eeng.dcu.ie) is a Lecturer in Electronic Engineering at Dublin City University, Ireland. He is also a Member of Technical Staff (on call) at the Jet Propulsion Laboratory, Pasadena, CA.

Liam Murphy (lmurphy@eng.auburn.edu) is an Assistant Professor in the Department of Computer Science and Engineering, Auburn University, AL.

Clifford Neuman (bcn@isi.edu) a scientist and faculty member at the Information Sciences Institute of the University of Southern California, is one of the principal designers of the Kerberos authentication system. Recent work includes development of the security infrastructure supporting authorization and accounting. Dr. Neuman leads the design of the NetCheque and NetCash electronic payment systems.

Jon M. Peha (peha@ece.cmu.edu) is an Assistant Professor at Carnegie Mellon University, jointly in the Department of Electrical & Computer Engineering and the Department of Engineering & Public Policy.

Joseph Reagle (reagle@w3.org) is a Policy Analyst with the World Wide Web Consortium.

Mitrabarun Sarkar (sarkarmi@pilot.msu.edu) is currently a doctoral candidate in Marketing and International Business at The Eli Broad Graduate School of Management, Michigan State University, East Lansing, MI.

Scott Shenker (shenker@parc.xerox.com) is a Principal Scientist at Xerox PARC, Palo Alto, CA.

Marvin A. Sirbu (sirbu@cmu.edu) is a Professor of Engineering and Public Policy, Industrial Administration and Electrical and Computer Engineering. Department of Engineering and Public Policy, Carnegie Mellon University, Pittsburgh, PA

Richard Jay Solomon (rjs@rpcp.mit.edu) is an Associate Director of the MIT Research Program on Communications Policy.

Padmanabhan Srinagesh (pxs@crai.com) is a Principal with Charles River Associates.

Dale O. Stahl (stahl@mundo.eco.utexas.edu) is a Professor with the Economics Department at The University of Texas at Austin.

Hal Varian (hal@sims.berkeley.edu) is the Dean of the School of Information Management and Science, University of California, Berkeley. He is also a professor in the Haas School of Business and the Department of Economics.

Qiong Wang (qw22@andrew.cmu.edu) is a Doctoral Candidate, Department of Engineering and Public Policy, Carnegie Mellon University, Pittsburgh, PA.

Martin Weiss (mbw@pitt.edu) is with the School of the Information Sciences, Telecommunications Program, University of Pittsburgh, Pittsburgh, PA.

Contributors

Andrew B. Whinston (abw@uts.cc.utexas.edu) is the Hugh Cullen Chair Professor of Information Systems, Economics and Computer Science, Graduate School of Business, University of Texas, Austin, TX.

Index

Note: *Italicized* page number indicates figure; *t* indicates table; *n* indicates note

511

Index